Millennium 2000

The Decorator

For Louise Neese

Carleton Varney

*from Dan
&
from Carleton*

Carleton

Shannongrove Press
New York, NY

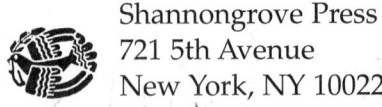
Shannongrove Press
721 5th Avenue
New York, NY 10022

Copyright © 1999 by Carleton Varney

All rights reserved. No part of this book may be reproduced in any form, except by a newspaper or magazine reviewer who wishes to quote brief passages in connection with a review.

Queries regarding rights and permission should be addressed to:
Shannongrove Press, 721 Fifth Avenue, New York, NY 10022

Library of Congress Catalog Card Number: 99-95115
ISBN 0-9664444-1-8

Designed by Reeser Advertising Associates

Manufactured in the United States

10 9 8 7 6 5 4 3 2 1

First Edition

THE DECORATOR

is a work of fiction. It is not historical reporting and is a product solely of the author's imagination. Any resemblance to any person, living or dead, is purely coincidental.

Other books by Carleton Varney

Decorating With Color
You and Your Apartment
The Family Decorates a Home
Decorating for Fun
Carleton Varney Decorates Windows
Carleton Varney Decorates From A to Z
Color Magic
Carleton Varney's Book of Decorating Ideas
There's No Place Like Home
Down Home
Carleton Varney's ABC's of Decorating
Staying in Shape: An Insiders Guide to Great Spas
Be Your Own Decorator
Room By Room Decorating
The Draper Touch
Kiss the Hibiscus Good Night

For my sons, Nicholas, Sebastian and Seamus,
	with fatherly love
and to the memory of my parents, Julia and Carleton,
who never would have understood the social changes
of the 60's and 70's, nor the professional world into
which their son had entered.

> Carleton Varney
> New York, NY 1999

Characters from the Novel

Pamela Raven	movie star
Julian Irons	CEO of Cosmetique (deceased husband of Pamela Raven)
Holly Raven	Miss Raven's niece
Miss Riley	Miss Raven's secretary
Mama	Miss Raven's maid
Deirdre Dawn	Dowager Queen of Decorating
Paul Hedges	president, Deirdre Dawn & Co.
Clark Calloway	designer/director, Deirdre & Co.
Thom Pearson	television executive, head of a network
Regina Stowkowski	aspiring TV news commentator/journalist, friend of Clark Calloway
Maria Pucci	aspiring actress
Luciano Navarrone	airline pilot
Doreen Flower	syndicated gossip columnist
Allen Friedberg	head honcho, Metropolis Studios
Bambi Friedberg	wife of Allen Friedberg
Adela Morgan	musical comedy star/film personality
Gabe Taylor	macho film star/matinee idol
Roland Lee	hotelier
Dannee Lou Baker	friend of Clark Calloway, White House Social Secretary
John Downing	Dannee Lou Baker's brother, CBS Washington News correspondent
Salvatore Caneletto	ex (disgruntled) decorating assistant to Deirdre Dawn
Steve Solinsky	Holly Raven's ex-husband, a film producer
Eric Von Halst	young Hollywood film director

1
CHAPTER

The morning traffic was quieting down as the cab turned on to Fifth Avenue. Most of the autumn leaves had been swept away by November's winds and Central Park was a grey haze of branches and dark tree trunks dripping with chilly rain. As the cab sped past the museum, the passenger unfolded a five-dollar bill and told the driver to stop at the next corner, which the driver did quite suddenly. Like most New Yorkers, the passenger knew the ways of cabbies and instinctively braced himself on the back of the driver's seat as the cab jerked to a stop.

The young man paid the fare absentmindedly, already gazing up at the penthouse windows of the sheer white tower on the corner. Her building. He had thought of little else since her secretary, Miss Riley, had called that morning. In fact, the memory of his meeting with Pamela Raven three weeks ago had been seldom far from his mind, infusing his most ordinary activities with a thrill.

It was a fascination he didn't quite understand. She was much too old for him, and such a couple was not imaginable in New York Society in 1965. Clark had no idea if Pamela Raven, movie star, chairwoman of Cosmetique Inc., and his most important client to date, had any such feelings for him. She had been nothing but warm and friendly, but with an intensity and acceptance he had never known, and he had responded electrically to her.

In a way he had not anticipated, he had felt safe with Pamela Raven, when they had been sitting in that tête-à-tête chair sipping Cokes, as the massive crowds at the Coliseum swirled around them and the photographers' flash bulbs popped. In that oddly public setting, Clark Calloway had felt mothered by Pamela Raven, and he had secretly welcomed it, not realizing until that moment how much he missed his own mother, who had passed away in June.

Pamela Raven had actually been his mother's favorite film star, while Clark had preferred the more lighthearted and voluptuous actresses like Betty Grable, June Haver and Ginger Rogers. As a teenager, he had enjoyed the tap-dancing comedies of Twentieth Century Fox. Pamela Raven had sailed through dark and stormy dramas with her fierce face and shoulder-padded silhouette, much like an imposing clipper ship.

For this reason, Clark had expected her to be taller. He had been nervous that day, anyway. Presenting his company's furnishing designs for the National Hotel and Motel's One Hundredth Anniversary Expo at the New York Coliseum was heady enough for a twenty-five-year-old interior decorator from Maine. The added pressure of presenting the important sponsors' products and the anticipation of working with Miss Pamela Raven, leading lady and spokeswoman for her late husband's cosmetic company, had been almost too much for Clark to contemplate. A crowd of several thousand people had gathered to see the magnetic star, and Clark's nervousness had been compounded by her reputation for unpredictability. At other events, he had heard, if the smallest detail was awry, or if she suddenly didn't feel like it, Miss Raven simply didn't show up.

Clark had been pleased with his hotel bedroom and bath designs, from elegant French Provincial to rustic Mexican Hacienda and masculine English Rugby to Debutante's fanciful resort setting — styled in white wicker with flowery chintz. The Debutante's Delight display was sponsored by Cosmetique Inc., and they had paid the production and building costs for the "Mod" bedroom and bath featuring the make-up so popular with the younger set. The dressing table in the bedroom had been accessorized by Clark with products available in the Cosmetique ads and brochures. It seemed Cosmetique was making a play for the hotel industry's business. After all, every hotel was now promoting a cosmetics package for the bathroom: shower gel, shampoos, face cream—and Cosmetique made it all.

Clark couldn't help but wonder how Pamela Raven, famous for her glistening dark ruby lips and deeply shadowed eyes, felt about the candy-colored make-up of Cosmetique. He

The Decorator

thought she would have preferred to represent the hard, vivid colors that worked well on the big screen, colors with the glamour and drama needed to balance her legendary glowering brows and angular cheekbones. But he knew the look was pure marketing genius, as the swarms of pinkly Cosmetiqued young girls squeezed against the velvet ropes testified.

The designer had been arranging peonies in the French Provincial bedroom model when the room suddenly became quiet. He watched the crowds part for a tight little cotillion of tailored escorts, with Pamela Raven, attired in pink Shantung silk from head to toe, as the center. Pamela's hat was pillbox in style, with a simple tailored button on one side, and her short-sleeved dress and jacket were definitely of the Chanel cut. The shoes in her tiny size five were covered in the same fabric as the dress. Pamela wore strands of pink pearls.

Clark's first reaction had been "She's so tiny! And so pink!" In his shock, he had dropped a peony and had to quickly scoop the creamy petals into the vase. He looked up and noticed Pamela, her large doe eyes fixed on him, had left her group behind and was marching straight towards him. He could feel his heart pounding, but Pamela had taken Clark's hand so warmly, and displayed a charming interest in his presentation. The young designer and the movie queen walked through the displays, posing for photographers and television news cameras in front of jeweled faucets, Southwestern pottery lamps, and, of course, Cosmetique products.

She had given him her full attention, insisting that they sit in the velvet tête-à-tête chairs he had designed for the Cosmetique display. A Coliseum guide assigned to Pamela had brought them water, and they half-heartedly ignored the cameras as Pamela asked Clark to tell her about himself. She was impressed that the young designer had become a director of Deirdre Dawn & Company at such a young age. Pamela told him that she recalled Deirdre Dawn for her big hats, and of course, her decor at the Arrowhead Springs Hotel, an important weekend watering hole during Pamela Raven's climb to stardom in the 1930's.

Clark, of course, had been completely starstruck, yet comfortably at home with Pamela Raven during those extra minutes she spent with him seated face to face in the tête-à-tête chair. While he drank in her knowing eyes and enormous, shining lips, the older woman had treated him as an equal, and he had felt she respected his talent and related to his ambition. It was love at first sight, the kind of instant friendship that develops between two people who recognize a comrade in their lonely campaigns to manage successful careers.

Twenty thousand people had attended the Expo that morning, and some thousand hotel people, display people, and participants later gathered in the ballroom of the nearby Ritz Plaza to hear Pamela Raven's keynote speech. She was to talk about the importance of new style for the Seventies—style in dress, style in accommodations, and style in fragrances and cosmetics. Everyone was anxiously awaiting the speech by the movie queen, and everyone wanted to get a good look at the star as well.

The room buzzed with whispers: Was she as beautiful as she was ten years ago in *Bewitched*? Was she really small? Was she in good physical shape?

Pamela and Clark had been seated together during lunch and the audience had waited an extra fifteen minutes for Pamela to finish her conversation with Clark. The waiters were clearing the dessert dishes when she arrived at the podium to thunderous applause.

Clark sat at a table with Cosmetique executives in attendance and had been enjoying Pamela Raven's speech when she abruptly stopped speaking and an uncomfortable silence fell over the room. She glared down the aisle like an angry schoolteacher, towards the buffet in the rear where the waiters were filling the bus trays with plates.

"I shall not continue until the noise of the dishes has stopped."

Her tone was cold, and the waiters shrank back from their work and stood nervously at attention. Clark saw many powerful and well-heeled executives squirm, as if their school days were suddenly not that far behind them. Pamela Raven had smiled at Clark and resumed her speech as if nothing had happened. It had seemed to Clark that she looked only at him while she spoke and that she spoke to him alone.

When Miss Reiley had called Clark's office that morning, both he and his senior partner, Paul Hedges, had assumed that

The Decorator

Pamela Raven wanted them to design an office at Cosmetique, which was in a building nearby, on Fifty-Fifth Street and Sixth Avenue. They were surprised when Miss Riley asked if Clark could come to "Mrs. Irons" Upper East Side apartment at nine. Everyone knew that the wife of the late Lucien Irons had a luxurious office, with a panoramic river view, in the Cosmetique Building.

And now Clark was about to see Pamela Raven's famous apartment. The door on the twenty-ninth floor was opened by a small, frail woman holding a struggling shih-tzu with a plastic lotus blossom tied in its hair. Two more shih-tzus barked around her ankles. The dogs had surprisingly low, quiet barks for such small animals, and their long black and white hair was silky and clean. The woman smiled and held the door open for Clark, and he thought he had never seen such a wrinkled, yet pleasant face. She waved him in and her bun of grey hair bobbed as she scurried lightly ahead down the foyer. Clark noticed that the woman, obviously a maid, was wearing noiseless slippers.

A familiar commanding voice called from within the apartment, "Come in, Clark dearest! Bring him in, Mama!"

"Oh, dear!" Mama whispered in a breathless panic, "Take off your shoes! Mrs Irons will have my head if you come in with your shoes on!"

Clark knelt to untie his oxfords and handed them to the housekeeper, who scooped them up and stored them in a hall closet before she led Clark through the living room. Clark felt unsteady in his stockinged feet on the highly polished wood floors. In a corner of the living room, a middle-aged man in grey flannel pants and a yellow cardigan was buffing the floor with a chamois cloth. He didn't look like a maintenance man.

As if Mama could read his thoughts, she whispered, "He's a fan. Mrs. Irons always hires her fans."

Clark could see why Pamela Raven insisted that her guests remove their shoes. The rugs in the apartment were polar bear white, and the floors shone like mirrors. The apartment was chilly. An all-glass wall let in a sweeping view of Central Park, from the Ritz Plaza Hotel to the Metropolitan Art Museum, and the expanse of grey winter sky seemed to float into the room. Clark glanced appreciatively at the Jeffrey Williams decor. It was California Modern: long sleek couches and chairs upholstered in white biscuit-quilted silk. Clear plastic coverings wrapped all the furnishings, keeping them showroom-clean and as shiny as new cars. The stark feeling was broken somewhat by the whimsical angles of the wide chair legs and triangular black marble coffee tables, but Clark felt that the lemon-yellow and beige pillow accents did not soften the austerity of the room. He hoped Pamela Raven would allow him to introduce some color into her decor.

Mama led Clark into the dining room door entrance, where Pamela Raven was seated at the head of a massive marble floating dining table that was bolted into the floor. A bevy of soberly-dressed businesswomen surrounded the table, which was covered with an array of colorful hats. Pamela Raven, in contrast to her business associates, wore a simple pink flowered muu-muu housedress and had her carrot-red hair pulled back in a rubber band. She wore no makeup, and it was obvious that her roots were in need of a touchup.

Clark recognized Miss Riley, reliable Miss Riley, who was taking notes and running back and forth between the table and the rows of discreet rosewood-doored cabinets that lined the walls of the room. The cabinets closed soundlessly as she returned with cups and saucers.

Clark was surprised to see his friend Genevieve Paige there. She was a public relations woman he often met socially. Genevieve quickly re-introduced him to Laura Parker, public relations woman for Milliners of America, and, as Clark was aware, Genevieve's live-in companion. Miss Parker and Genevieve had a similar look and style: they were both blonde, middle-aged, clean-cut and corporate, not a hair out of place. Miss Parker adorned herself only with gold button earrings and the popular gold circle pin from Tiffany's. Both women were handsome, still youthful, and Clark saw that they moved in concert, communicating with brief nods and subtle eye contact.

Miss Parker nodded a brusque hello and continued reading from a list. She had to lean across the table and nearly shout to be heard by Pamela Raven at the other end.

"After Philadelphia, you must catch a six a.m. flight to be at the Convention Center in Baltimore by nine. A representative of the Ladies'—"

"Miss Riley, you handle this!" Pamela interrupted. "These people don't seem to understand that it's my body that has to do this — not theirs!" She rose, leaving the group at sixes and sevens, and motioned to Clark. "My dear, I'm so glad you're here! Ladies, this is my new decorator, Clark Calloway, of Deirdre Dawn & Company. Mama, take that away! And bring me a Bloody Mary!" She flicked her hand at the tiny plate Mama had set before her. The plate held a single graham cracker.

Mama looked flustered. "But Mrs. Irons, you haven't eaten a thing all day — you must —"

"Mama, I *don't care!*" Pamela turned from her to break into Miss Riley's conversation with Miss Parker, "No, no, no! Tell them I need *six* pillows in my hotel room and *four* boxes of Kleenex! Or I won't do it! Come, Clark, let's get out of here! I'll give you a little tour!" She snatched a clear barrel-ribbed glass with a fishing fly embedded in the plastic from Mama and led Clark by the arm. On their way out she turned back to shout, "And *no wire coat hangers* in the closet, either! They ruin my silk dresses!"

Pamela Raven offered Clark a drink, but he declined. His stomach rebelled at the idea of vodka so early in the morning.

"Oh, but you mustn't let me drink alone! Miss Riley will never have a Bloody Mary with me either, that rude girl! I find them so healthful for clearing the cobwebs away!" She guided Clark through an expanse of imposing rooms, all furnished in impeccable Hollywood Modern.

"My Lucien built this for me. Such a dear man. We ripped everything out, of course, so we could start clean. I like things to be clean, immaculately clean."

Clark could see that she meant it when he saw her kitchen, which was a marvel of industrial efficiency. All white tile with stainless steel fixtures and cabinets, it would not have looked out of place in a hospital. Princess Lotus Blossom, the tiny shih-tzu, was trailing them, and Pamela stopped occasionally to feed her a mini-pretzel from a small bag in her housedress pocket.

"You know that Cosmetique has acquired Sunny Snacks, so I'm loaded with these — OH, Mama! Mama! Princess did poo-

poo!"

Mama came scuffling in with a box of Kleenex and swooped down to remove the offending dog poop. She used another tissue to wipe Princess Lotus Blossom's bottom.

Pamela continued, "Mr. Kirkeby sends me these pretzels, and corn chips, and popcorn. It's the least he could do, and he can barely do that."

Roger Kirkeby was the new chairman of Cosmetique. He had been promoted to a position equal to Pamela's when Lucien Irons died, and they shared the chairman's duties. But Pamela was not happy sharing that power, and she knew she had lost all support when Lucien died. If one read between the lines in the business section of the *New York Times*, it was clear that the executives at Cosmetique were squeezing Pamela Raven out of the corporate structure, though they couldn't get rid of her entirely. Her movie-star image was important for the promotion of the product. She had such an enormous group of fans, all over the world.

Pamela ushered Clark dramatically through her custom-built penthouse, the library and home office, her pink and white bedroom with its pink marble floor and beds with matching canopies for the dogs. They toured her exercise and massage room, and her fully-equipped hairdressing salon. The last room they saw was Lucien's bedroom. Clark struggled to hide his shock. After seeing the palatial grandeur of Pamela's bedroom, he could hardly believe he was looking at the bedroom of the chief executive of Cosmetique, the man Pamela had publicly claimed to love more than any other in her life — even more than her earliest co-star, the magnetic movie hero Gabe Taylor.

The room was small, which wasn't in itself shocking, as Clark imagined Lucien had often slept with Pamela in her big bed. What surprised him about the bedroom was its lack of character, its lack of any expression of the personality of its owner. It looked like a Hollywood motel room of the Forties, containing only two studio beds with studio headboards, both covered with fitted aquamarine spreads. There were gold lurex threads running through the upholstery fabric, and the headboards were protected with clear plastic slipcovers. Besides the studio beds, the room was outfitted with built-in cabinets, stained 1940's blonde, a small blonde-finished modern desk, a blonde night table, and two club chairs covered in the aquamarine and gold lurex fabric, and then slipcovered with clear plastic. There was also a blonde modern desk chair in the room, its seat upholstered in acid-green patent leather. The room did not have a masculine aura, or any feeling at all, for that matter. Clark would have felt exiled if he had been invited to sleep there.

Pamela was speaking to him. He followed her into her room, where they sat in quilted white silk armchairs. The chairs were slipcovered in the same clear plastic as those in the living areas downstairs and in Lucien's room. Clark did not sink into them quite comfortably, and there was a self-conscious creaking to the clear plastic that betrayed his smallest movement.

Pamela told Clark that she wanted him to help her move. She had taken a new apartment that needed decorating. Pamela explained that she could no longer afford the maintenance on her Fifth Avenue duplex, six thousand dollars a month, and her lawyer had insisted that she could no longer maintain a thirteen-room apartment, what with Lucien gone and her monthly income from Cosmetique reduced. A potential buyer had been found, Zelda Wilson, of the copper-mining Wilsons, whose socialite and philanthropic sister, Bernice, was married to a famous publisher of gardening magazines and coffee-table books. Pamela was preparing to move to a nine-room apartment barely three blocks away, but it wasn't on Fifth Avenue, and her beloved Lucien had not built it for her.

She told Clark all this in a matter-of-fact way, with little emotion in her voice. There was a lot to be done immediately. Pamela knew that all her furniture would never fit in the new apartment. She would need Clark's help deciding what to keep and how to decorate the smaller space. She showed him her closets, which were in themselves large rooms, actually, larger than most studio apartments his young friends lived in. There was a room for dresses, one for hats, a room each for shoes and handbags, and a vault of furs. All the shelves and racks were color-coordinated, and each item was tagged and numbered. The dominant colors were turquoise and pink. All of this clothing would have to be sorted through and moved, and cabinets and storage areas would have to be built in the new apartment to house the star's wardrobe.

As Pamela and Clark were discussing space problems, Clark thought about how far Pamela Raven had come. Here was this girl from Lincoln, Nebraska, who had grown up in the poor part of town, who had practiced her dancing in the cellar of her house, which early news reports indicated was somewhat of a shack. She had never known her father, and had grown up helping her mother earn money as a day domestic, cleaning houses. There was no money for dance lessons, nor for college, so Pamela had been waitressing in coffee shops to pay her own costs and tuition. There had been talk that she had once been a topless dancer — and a Hollywood call-girl as well — but this sort of gossip always surrounded the actresses who rose from obscure origins to fame as femmes fatales. Perhaps she had, indeed, done those things; it was not possible to separate rumor from fact once a star became a contract player.

Pamela, like the other stars of Hollywood's golden years, was recreated in the image chosen for her by Metropolis Pictures. She was given a new name and a new past. Her clothing, lifestyle, and even romances were subject to studio approval. Not being of the popular blonde bombshell model for leading ladies, Pamela had to work twice as hard to make a name for herself as a Hollywood legend.

And she had. She had pioneered roles of strong glamorous women who were not nice, yet got what they wanted. Her first three marriages had suffered and failed, many said because her husbands either couldn't abide her consuming ambition, or maybe because their stardom was not as enduring as Pamela Raven's and they were jealous of her success. She had won an Oscar for her portrayal of an entrepreneur, the first such leading role for a woman in film history. Her favorite part to play had always been the tycoon, and when she married Lucien, a man secure in his own power, she all but stopped making movies to devote herself to her real-life role as Mrs. Cosmetique.

Together, Lucien and Pamela had changed Cosmetique's image from one of bargain-basement cosmetics to the glamorous paint of the new "mod" art scene, and the signature look of the lean and leggy "Pepsi Generation" models who craved

The Decorator

Pamela's Golden Hollywood cachet. Lucien's slogan, "You're Everything That's Now," and Pamela's sultry appearances in the new ads had skyrocketed Cosmetique sales and positioned them as a competitor for the number one cosmetic company in the world.

The Fifth Avenue penthouse, the furs, the cars and jewels, the corner office, the television talk shows and the crowds of photographers that surrounded her whenever she went to dinner at 21 were all a part of the life she had created, the life a girl with an unknown name had dreamed of as she danced in a Nebraska cellar.

Clark wondered just how much of the pain she was not showing. He knew that changing apartments represented a loss, a step down that would create ripples in the Perrier of the Upper East Side. They both heard the doorbell ring faintly below.

"Oh, no," muttered Pamela. "It's that woman."

Pamela Raven was the model of hospitality when she greeted the Wilsons. Mrs. Wilson had brought her decorator, to show him the apartment she would soon own. Clark recognized the decorator, Fred Huntington, and Fred smiled as they shook hands. Fred was the prototypical society decorator, tall, blonde, handsome and gay, with a small moustache. He was impeccably dressed in a dark navy suit and wore a blue striped shirt with a white collar and white tie. He carried the requisite black briefcase in his manicured hand.

Clark had his own style, and though he took some ribbing for it, he wasn't about to conform to the standard mold. His sandy hair was a little longer than was conventional, and, like some daring artists among the younger set, he was beginning to let his sideburns grow. Greenwich Village, rather than Park Avenue, had been the neighborhood that attracted him to New York, and he was eager to expand beyond his staid, New England drawing room background. His dress, like his decorating, was more relaxed than most, and he was willing to incorporate unusual touches in his dress — including as his signature extra-wide, flowing silk scarves in vivid colors that he wore instead of ties.

Zelda Wilson was gazing around the foyer with a look of triumph. She was one of those sparrow-type older women, in a neat white Chanel suit, but her face was rough and mannish, and she had a deep voice to match. Her husband was a tall, heavy bald man in a grey suit. He would not have attracted any attention at all if it hadn't been for the sweet cologne he wore. Clark didn't like it when men wore heavy cologne during the day; something about it sickened him.

Mama took their coats and shoes and provided the Wilsons with white cotton slippers before disappearing into the dining room with a huge stack of mail. The Wilsons had taken off their shoes without comment, as they were overwhelmed by the element of surprise, but when it came to putting on the slippers, Mrs. Wilson glanced around awkwardly, as if looking for a hidden camera.

"Er — it must be a joke," he muttered, but when Fred Huntington put on his slippers without a comment, Mr. Wilson did the same, though it was evident from his red face that he had a difficult time bending over to pull up the heels.

Mrs. Wilson was less cooperative. She held up the slippers in her palms and glared at them. "What is this, a hospital? I'm operated on here?"

"Put them on, Zelda, the floor is cold," grunted her husband.

"Well, somebody help me, then, you know what happens when I bend."

Fred Huntington took her slippers and knelt solicitously on one knee, holding a slipper at the proper angle. Zelda leaned a hand on his shoulder and shoved her pointy little foot into the slipper. They switched sides and she was slippered.

She stared at her feet. "*Vogue* it's not."

Mama appeared in the entranceway and Pamela ordered, "Mama, tell Miss Riley to open that fan mail as soon as the meeting is over. We must answer it right away! Tell those Milliners I'll be right in!" Pamela flashed her famous wraparound smile at her visitors.

"Please pardon the interruption. There's a meeting going on, but it can wait."

Mr. Wilson had been staring, transfixed, at Pamela's face. His wife glared at him and said, "Well, if this isn't a good time, we can come back."

"Nonsense," said Pamela. "There's plenty of time. Come

right in." She addressed this, in her sweetest voice, to Mr. Wilson.

He had been looking sheepish since his wife's glare, but under Pamela's gaze, his face regained a boyish wonder. As the group followed Pamela down the hall, he said, "I just saw you in *Surrender,* Miss Raven. If you don't mind me saying so, you were marvelous. You should have won the Award."

"Why, thank you, Lionel," purred Pamela. "You know, that was my favorite role, too. I liked it much better than the role for which I did get the Oscar!" Pamela's English and diction were perfect at that moment.

Clark could tell that Mr. Wilson wanted to say something more, but they had come to the wide and open-treaded minimal Frank Lloyd Wright staircase that led to the upper floor.

"This has got to go!" said Mrs. Wilson. "Fred, I want this ripped out. I can't abide modern things. I want a marble staircase with a bronze handrail. I want angels on my newel posts, marble angels! And I want a big crystal chandelier to hang above the staircase! Call Charles Winston or Nesle and see if either of them has a Maria Theresa chandelier with mixed colored crystal ... maybe clear with ruby and emerald beads. This stairway needs something exciting, don't you agree, Fred?"

Fred nodded, not looking at Clark as he dutifully noted his client's requests on a pad, and he continued to write busily throughout the tour. Zelda Wilson was thrilled to be buying a movie star's apartment, but she hated everything about it. As she gave Fred more orders to make the apartment "livable" by redecorating it with French antiques, Clark watched Pamela's face freeze into a mask of haughty disdain. By the time they got to Lucien's bedroom, Pamela was as tense as an angry cat. The group of visitors stared into the tiny room. "What is this?" snarled Zelda. "Fred, what can be done with this? I don't want my maid's room up here. DO something!"

"Oh, this room has great possibility for a —"

Zelda interrupted her decorator, "What could it have possibility for? Possibility for what? I don't care. You'll take out this wall." She sneezed. "Why is it so cold in here? A person could freeze to death. Lionel, do you hear me, I'm getting pneumonia in this apartment! What this apartment needs is fireplaces and maybe we should install a fireplace in every room ... oh ... I so love French mantelpieces, Fred. Make a note to call Christie's or Sotheby's and see if there are any mantels coming up for auction."

Pamela cleared her throat, a low, dangerous sound. Clark wondered if Mrs. Wilson knew that the chill she felt was emanating from Mrs. Irons.

But when Pamela Raven spoke, her voice was bright and brittle. "Come. I have something that will keep you warm."

She took Mrs. Wilson's arm and led her to the wide doors of her fur closet. Pamela swept the doors open, and they crashed against the walls. The miles of soft furs, in every length and color, swung heavily.

"Choose!" commanded Pamela. "I'm sure you'll find something here to keep you warm."

There was no possibility of refusal. Tentatively, Mrs. Wilson touched a fur sleeve with the long, red-polished nail of her index finger. Pamela snatched the coat off the hanger and wrapped Mrs. Wilson in silver fox. For the rest of their visit, Mrs. Wilson kept silent, except for murmurs of "Very nice, very nice," as she absently stroked the sleeve of her new fur.

When the tour was over, Mr. Wilson made arrangements with Pamela to close the deal with her lawyer, and Mama saw them to the door. She handed them back their shoes and carried away the white slippers to be washed again.

As for the silver fox, Mrs. Wilson handed that back, smiling as she did so. "Lionel will get me one similar to yours, except mine will be Russian fox and I prefer the pelts to be sewn horizontally — much newer styling, and not so passé. But I guess you've had your coat for years. Designer styles have so changed."

As they left, Fred Huntington said, in a clenched-teeth whisper close to Clark's ear, "I wish I had your client instead of mine."

"Clark, now that we are rid of these people, we'll go see the new apartment. No, let's have tea first. Mama, tell the Plaza to expect me and have my table ready at three." Pamela sipped rapidly from the fresh drink Mama had handed her. There was no tomato juice in it this time. "My niece, Holly, will be here any minute. I'm giving her that vanity stool and some of these chairs. I want you to meet Holly. I think you'll like her."

The Decorator

Clark followed Pamela into the meeting room, where the Millinery women were scooping up their papers and hats into briefcases and hat boxes. Amiable chatter echoed throughout the room as they made lunch plans.

"Let me see that schedule," said Pamela. All conversation stopped. Miss Riley gave Pamela the sheet of paper filled with tiny handwriting. Pamela squinted at it, her thick brows drawn together in an ominous line. As she read, her face froze into the hard mask Clark had seen when she was showing the house to Mrs. Wilson. She looked up and fixed her burning gaze on Laura Parker.

"Goddamn it!" Pamela's voice was a siren in the room. "How do you expect me to do this! No one could do this schedule! Up at five, here by six, there by seven, across the goddamn country by nine — what do you mean by this?"

Clark felt his face turning red, even though she wasn't speaking to him. Everyone in the room was looking everywhere but at Pamela. Except for poor Laura Parker, who struggled to keep her dignity.

"But it's what we agreed —"

"Who agreed? YOU agreed? This is MY BODY we're talking about and I can't do it! I can't do it! I can't do it!"

Pamela tore the schedule in half, glaring at Laura Parker as if she would tear herself apart in half a minute.

"I don't want this job! I don't want this fucking hat tour!" Pamela's words fell heavily into the silence. "I quit this job! Get OUT of my house. Get all these goddamned papers and schedules out of my sight! Get out!! Out! Out!"

As the hat council women scrambled to leave and papers flew in many directions, Clark saw Pamela pull Miss Riley into a corner with a grip on the secretary's elbow that looked like it hurt. Pamela's fierce whispers poured like steam into Miss Riley's placid face.

"How does Miss Riley take it?" wondered Clark. "How does anyone survive working for Pamela Raven?" At the same time, he was impressed by Pamela's fire, intrigued by the Movie Queen — and thrilled to be working with the glamorous and powerful woman. He knew that he faced a challenge, but he was certain he and the lady would work well together. He knew he would survive.

As the Millinery people hurriedly left, Clark sensed a different presence in the room, and he turned to see a young woman his age, with dry, flossy, blonde hair and a horsy face, standing in the doorway. There was something nondescript and almost furtive about her as she stood stock-still against the door frame in an unflattering brown and tan glen plaid suit. She had a nice body, he noticed; she was willowy like Pamela, with great legs, but she had an awkward posture, as if she was prepared to duck. She didn't seem to see Clark at all, so engrossed was she in Pamela's angry words to Miss Riley. She stared at the two of them with a mixture of horror and fascination; Clark couldn't tell which expression was stronger.

He turned and offered his hand. "I'm Clark Calloway," he said. "I'm with Deirdre Dawn & Company. I'll be helping Mrs. Irons with the decorating of her new apartment."

The girl looked startled, then self-conscious. She shook Clark's hand and introduced herself gravely, "Hello, I'm Holly, her niece."

"You're also an actress, aren't you? And quite a good one, I've heard." Clark knew that Holly Raven had a part in a television comedy series.

"Why, thank you. Yes, I am." Holly seemed gratefully surprised to be recognized. "An actress, I mean, yes, I'm an actress." she stammered, "*Good,* I don't know ..."

"I see you two have met!" Pamela Raven swooped over to them, all smiles. "Clark this is my precious darling, my brother Bill's daughter. I raised her myself, and she's doing so well in life. I'm so proud of her. Holly, Clark is the president of Deirdre Dawn & Company — you remember Deirdre Dawn, don't you? Mama, bring Clark and Holly some drinks! What would you like?"

Holly ordered Pepsi, and Clark, a ginger ale. Pamela refilled her barrel-ribbed glass and nibbled on a graham cracker while she showed Holly the furniture she could take. Holly was also apartment shopping, and from her bleak references to "him" and the furniture "he" had taken, Clark got the idea that Holly had been recently divorced.

Holly excused herself to call her agent and Pamela marched to her dressing room, pulling Clark by his elbow.

"Come and sit while I put on my face. I can't go out looking like this — I must look like Pamela Raven, though it's getting harder and harder these days. Let me tell you a little story and I think you'll understand." While Pamela talked, she opened her jars and bottles and began applying layers of makeup to her face and neck in deft, upward strokes. Clark watched, fascinated, as the tiny, fragile, aging woman transformed herself into a creature of dramatic beauty.

"I always do my own makeup. Always did. Of course, on the set, I let the makeup people help! Makeup people can be a girl's best friend and many of them are dear, dear friends of mine.

"A long time ago, when I was working for Metropolis every waking minute, when I was in my twenties, Abie asked me to go to an exposition. You know, to splash some stardust around, bullshit like that. Well, I went, of course, though I hated public appearances; it was what you did. If Abie said 'Jump,' we jumped, and if he said 'Crawl,' you bet we crawled. But, you know, he was a lot better than the other studio heads. I won't name names, unless you twist my arm, but girls at other studios had to do a lot of auditioning on their backs. One of those guys even had his thing cast in bronze. Can you believe he showed it to me in his office when Abie traded me off to do a few pictures? That's how he used to punish us, by renting us out to other studios if we pissed him off."

Pamela surveyed her new flawless, glowing skin under the cold light of her dressing table. She patted herself under her chin.

"I can fix it all except my chin. That's a job for the light man. When I played Delia in that murder mystery last year, I told the light man, 'George, I feel a little hot under here,' and he gave me the shadow I needed. It helps to be friends with everyone, Clark. I hope you treat all the Little People well."

Liquid liner was stroked on without a blotch and thick mascara was brushed on over false lashes to create "The Eyes."

"What was I saying? I was telling you about Abie. I wore a pants suit to that exposition. Mind you, it was a green silk pants suit, from Paris, and I wore matching shoes, but Abie took one look at me — remember, Clark, Abie was short! He was about eye-level to my tits, but he was terrifying when he yelled. Boy did he let me have it! I thought he was going to slug me. I'll never forget what he said. He said, 'Girlie, what do you think this is, a labor union picnic? You get out of here, right now, and don't come back until you look like Pamela Raven!"

"I did. I was crying my eyes out, but I broke the speed limit getting home and I was back in twenty minutes! I poured myself into a satin gown and I wore a mink stole, heels and an egret feather hat. I never forgot it."

With that, Pamela rose and wiggled out of her muu-muu right in front of Clark. She kept talking as she stripped off her panties and changed into a white outfit that Mama had hung on a rack by her makeup table. Clark did not know where to look, so he looked at Pamela.

He tried to keep a neutral expression on his face by repeating to himself, "She's a piece of furniture. She's only a piece of furniture."

Though, in his mind's eye, Clark superimposed an imaginary Hepplewhite table, the firm ivory flesh of Pamela Raven was impossible to ignore. She had a lovely body with the slim ripeness of a well-maintained forty-year-old, though she had to be in her late fifties. Her legs could compete with those of any young chorus girl on Broadway. Her pubic hair was thick and black and trimmed into a demure oval. A faint shadow told Clark Pamela's bush would spread almost to her navel if it wasn't waxed.

"I keep in shape," said Pamela, out of one side of her mouth. "Have to maintain the equipment."

She chose a wavy auburn wig from among a large collection and adjusted it on her head. She swiftly pinned it up in a ruby clasp. A swoosh of red lipstick and a pair of dark glasses went on and she was ready.

Holly was waiting in the entrance hall with her coat on. She wore a plain navy pea coat with gold buttons. As Pamela swung herself into a raccoon coat, Clark thought she was taking the moving preparations very well, even glamorously, in true movie star-on-set manner. Pamela was even singing a tune from one of her early musicals as she slid a jeweled flask filled with one-hundred proof vodka into her coat pocket.

Holly frowned at the flask, and Pamela sang, "Come on, Holly, you know the words! Sing it with me!"

"I can't remember the words." Holly held herself back,

almost cringing.

"Oh, you're no fun, never were. Clark, you must get my niece to lighten up. She's no fun at all."

Clark did not look at Holly, certain she was embarrassed enough. He first helped Pamela, and then Holly into the elevator. A long black limo took them to the Plaza, Pamela's favorite place for tea.

After they had ordered, Pamela said, "Holly, how would you like to attend the Salzberg Awards in my place? They'll need you to present the award for the children's charity."

"Certainly, Auntie. When is it?"

"Next Tuesday, at eight. I'll send your dress over from Sara Fredericks."

"Yes, Auntie, thank you. I have a play reading that night, but I'll see if they can—"

"And I'll need you to fly to that cosmetic conference in Delaware for Cosmetique, as I'll be out of town. Try to put your lipstick on straight this time, dear. Remember the cameras are always watching, even if it's only for the trade papers."

As if on cue, two breathless middle-aged women in black and pearls huffed up to Pamela's table and asked for autographs. They were accompanied by a photographer, with flashbulb popping, and then a crush of tourists from Utah swarmed over to see what the attraction was. Pamela welcomed each fan with good grace and answered each avid question at length. She signed a stack of glossy photographs pulled from her purse with a personal message for each fan. Throughout the mêlée, Clark noticed that Holly maintained a frozen professional smile. Clark, himself, was only recently experienced with paparazzi, but he knew his left profile was his better side, so he turned to smile at Holly, knowing that the gossip columns would all be speculating as to his relationship with her in tomorrow's papers. The publicity would only help Deirdre Dawn & Company and, at all times, new business was what was needed.

When the crowd was gone, Pamela continued her address to Holly as if she had never been interrupted. "Also, I can get you on the "Larry Diamond Show" tomorrow if you'd like to go. Larry's a friend of mine from the early Hollywood days," she informed Clark.

Clark watched as the aunt and niece, who were, for all purposes, mother and daughter, pulled out their appointment books and coordinated a complex series of appearances, fittings and parties. He thought they made a good team. Pamela seemed genuinely eager to help Holly get as much exposure as possible, and Holly unquestioningly rearranged her schedule to help her aunt with this business, though she did look a little tense. Perhaps she's nervous, thought Clark. It mustn't be easy to appear in the place of Pamela Raven. And the next "Larry Diamond Show" was about children of celebrities. He wondered if Holly minded the inevitable comparisons.

"Wasn't Larry Diamond a star in his own right at one time?" asked Clark.

"Yes, of course, dear," said Pamela. "He appeared with Jeffrey and me in those college comedies. We did the first talkies together and left all those silent stars behind."

"Jeffrey Williams?" asked Clark. Jeffrey Williams was the actor who had designed Pamela's apartment during his second career as a decorator. The waiter brought their tea sandwiches and cakes and replaced the empty teapot with a full one. He ceremonially poured their Earl Grey tea, but Pamela did not touch her cup, nor did she eat more than a nibble of a watercress sandwich. She drank her own vodka, which she poured from its silver flask.

"Darling Jeffrey," mused Pamela, "I shall never forget him. He's the one who showed me the ropes, you know, when I was a fresh young thing. He was *the* man about town in those days. He had the Face that made all the magazines. He was everywhere, and so charming. You could never meet a better person. Jeffrey Williams was a gentleman, my dear, such as will never be seen again, I'm afraid."

"I'll never forget that terrible day I had to do my first scene in a picture, ever, with that old hag, Madge McGuire."

"The star of the silent films?" asked Clark, vaguely remembering an old movie featuring a heavily rouged and feathered actress whose acting display consisted of a heaving chest, rolling eyes, and a tendency to swoon into the velvet curtains.

"Madge McGuire could not act to save her life, and I was furious because she insisted I deliver my lines with my *back* to the camera!" And what Madge McGuire wanted, she

The Decorator

got! The director and even the studio heads fell all over themselves to please the Queen of Hollywood. Even Allen Friedberg caved in to her. He was the one who originally hired me, though he was barely a child himself, you know."

"Was he the head of Metropolis then?" asked Clark.

"Oh, no. Abie was still alive then. And he wasn't fooled by McGuire one bit. He respected the box office, but I think he knew, even then, that he could make cheaper pictures that would be just as successful. And the main obstacle to that were stars like Madge McGuire! Do you know she made a million a year in 1926!" Pamela's dramatic eyebrows were raised fiercely over her startling dark eyes.

Clark looked at Holly, to attempt to draw her into the conversation, but she was concentrating on her plate as she picked at a jam tart. During Pamela's monologue, she had not once looked up.

"No one made a million in '26," continued Pamela, "not even Abie. And here was Madge arriving on the set late every day, in her silver Phaeton with the yellow silk upholstery and her dress with miles and miles of satin and lace — you know they had to take the studio doors off the hinges to let her in — and we all *waited* for her. Dollars sliding away like sand in an hourglass.

"I was terrified of her. I was only nineteen, remember. Younger than you, Holly. If I so much as looked at Madge, she had the director cut another of my lines. But Jeffrey, dear Jeffrey, I'll never forget what he said to me. He said, 'Sister, her day is over. Our day has come. Lose twenty pounds, and with that face of yours and the right dress, you'll take Hollywood by storm.'

"And I did. I had friends in Costume, and Jeffrey helped me pick out the best tea gowns, even though we had to safety-pin them to fit me and return them by dawn. He also made me move out of my apartment to a place I couldn't have afforded if he didn't help me. You see, the secret is, and he knew it: you have to let them know who you *are*. The more luxurious your home is, the more confidence your fans have in you. A star must be glamorous to inspire her fans. We *owe* it to them.

"Jeffrey would dress me — honey he was the best girl-friend a girl could have — and we'd go to those tea dances at

Coconut Grove, and the press and cameras were all over us like a fog. And soon Jeff and I were an item! Can you believe that? We had a good laugh, that's for sure."

Clark nodded. "Jeff was a homosexual?"

"Oh, it was well known. His lover still calls me — José. Dear José. I'm afraid he doesn't have much to live for, now. You know, they were together for twenty-five years! Poor Jeffrey, he passed away in 'fifty-seven, and I miss him terribly. My friends are after me to change my furniture, but I just won't do it. Jeffrey was such a love to decorate my home, and it would be disloyal of me to change it. You do understand, don't you, Clark?"

"Of course," said Clark. "Besides, the Williams look is classic Forties Hollywood. So clean. It suits you."

Holly started to say something, but Pamela's famous silvery voice rolled over her.

"It was after Jeff and I were photographed dancing at the Coconut Grove that Abie cast me in *The Jazz Baby* and he bought me my roadster. The other flappers were sick with envy, and the monster Madge threw a tantrum that made Abie reconsider her contract. She died a nobody, you know."

Clark tried to imagine Pamela as a flapper, and he just couldn't. She seemed as if she had always been polished and tailored, with a cultured voice and regal gestures. But she did still carry a flask.

"It's terrible what happened to Jeffrey," said Holly.

"What happened?" asked Clark.

"Holly, why must you be so grim?" snapped Pamela. "That was ages ago." She signaled for the check and a waiter rushed over. "Jeffrey and José and their dog Monsieur Marcel were assaulted by a gang of white-sheeted cretins at their beach house in Malibu ... that was in 'thirty-two, I believe. The house was burned and Jeff and José were bruised up, but poor Monsieur Marcel had to be hospitalized. He was near death, but he was a survivor, just like Jeff. That's the important thing, Holly, to survive."

Pamela paid the check. "Jeff may have been blackballed from pictures for being a fag, but he became a marvelous decorator. There's no use feeling sorry for yourself, Holly, ever! The important thing is to survive!" Pamela raised her flask and

The Decorator

drained it of its last drops. "Come! Let us inspect my new home."

There was no arguing with her. Pamela seemed a bit unsteady on her feet as Clark helped her with her fur. Holly was shooting him miserable looks, but he didn't know what to do.

As they slid into the limousine, Holly whispered to Clark, "We've got to get Auntie home. She's too drunk." Holly gave the driver Pamela's address and got a furry elbow in her stomach for her trouble.

"NO! Fourteen East Seventy-Third," decreed Pamela.

"Hold on to her," whispered Holly when they got out of the car.

Clark did his best to guide Pamela safely across the polished marble lobby floor. Nonetheless, she slid a bit in her heels and he barely caught her.

Furious, Pamela snatched her arm away and strode over to the doorman. She was shorter than the doorman, but she seemed to tower over him as she screamed, "This floor is wet! There's a wet spot on this floor! I am moving in here and you will see to it that this NEVER happens again!"

"Yes, ma'am," said the doorman. "I apologize, ma'am."

He accompanied Pamela to inspect the "spot." Pamela was still raging. "I can't trust anyone anymore. What do I have to do, mop the lobby MYSELF?"

The doorman placated Pamela by saying he would tell the manager first thing in the morning, which seemed to cheer her up. She produced a second flask from her coat pocket and took Clark's arm.

"Let's go see the dump. Come on, Holly, stop dragging!"

Clark thought Holly looked like she was trying to disappear. He shrugged and smiled at her, and she returned him a pale, grateful smile.

On the way up in the elevator, Pamela talked excitedly about how good it would be to have a new, clean apartment to fix exactly her way. She would have no more bathtubs.

"I want those tubs ripped out, Clark, and stalls put in. I refuse to soak in my own dirt! And I want the walls covered with vinyl. That will be so much cleaner, don't you think!"

Clark agreed, and he used the key Pamela had given him

to open the door. They stood in the doorway while he found the lights. Pamela had an odd expression on her face as she looked around the empty rooms. The vivacious look was gone, as if she had only been play-acting. Perhaps she was, thought Clark. He had an intuition that she was seeing herself in this empty, smaller apartment for the first time, an apartment with no comforting memories of her beloved Lucien. Her eyes widened like a frightened child's.

"Pamela?" Clark began, but she was already falling back into Holly. He had to dive to catch her around the waist before she hit the floor.

"Catch her!" said Clark. "She's fainted."

CHAPTER 2

The old fashioned fat toaster had been a gift from Clark's grandmother. It was one of her presents to him when he left home to go to college. He had just popped an English muffin in the toaster when the phone rang. He knew it was Reggie because she called every weekend morning, or whenever she woke up, so they could have breakfast together on the phone. He never called her because she was a notorious sleeper. Reggie could sleep for fourteen hours or longer, especially on weekends. Because of this habit, Clark called her the Lioness.

He answered on the third ring. "Hello, Lioness, must have been a big kill. It's one-thirty."

She Yawned. "Is it? Oh, yeah. You could say it was."

"What was it? The football player?"

"Who?" She giggled. "Nahh. A pilot. An Italian pilot, with these aqua blue eyes! I'm black and blue, but I loved it!" Her buzzer rang dully in the background. "Hold on a minute."

Clark put down the phone while she received her usual breakfast from the delivery boy from the restaurant on the first floor of her apartment hotel on East Forty-Seventh Street. She would have a toasted bran muffin, no raisins, a coffee with milk, no sugar. He picked up his paintbrush again and dipped it into a coffee can of Pratt and Lambert Almond Creme house paint. Several dripping cans of colored paint surrounded a six-by eight-foot canvas on the floor of his living room, which was covered with a plastic tarp to catch the drips. He let some of the paint fall back into the can, eased the brush up, tensed his knees and arced the beige paint onto the canvas. The paint swirled around a vaguely nipple-like shape that spanned half the canvas. The voice on the other end of the line buzzed. Clark wiped the brush on a rag and picked up the phone.

"Hey!" said Clark.

"I got my muffin."

"And your coffee."

"And my coffee. Ahh! What are you doing?"

"I'm painting. I started something new last night. I was up till three, I think, or four."

"I just heard your muffin pop up," said Reggie, with her mouth full.

"Hold on." Clark went into his barely-a-kitchen, more like a recessed Formica work-station, and plucked the two muffin halves — lightly toasted, the way he liked it — from the toaster. He buttered them lavishly and as the butter melted into all the little holes, he spread the muffin halves with raspberry jam. He slid the muffin onto a plate, poured a fresh cup of coffee from the percolator, and wiped his fingers on the ochre linen hand towel that hung from a bar on the sink. The towel was also a gift from his grandmother, who believed in practical presents. He always drank his coffee black, and he always started with the smaller, fat side of the muffin because the large flatter side held the butter better and it could wait.

Clark placed the cup and plate on top of a hi-fi speaker. He propped his feet on the window sill where he could look out on to East Eighty-Eighth Street, four stories below. He reached behind him for the phone.

"Looks nasty out, all foggy and mushy," he said.

"It always looks foggy and mushy to me," said Reggie. "I've got to get a better view." Her bedroom window faced an airshaft.

"Why don't you eat in the kitchen, then?"

"Come on, silly, you know I have to eat in bed where the television is." Reggie always watched her new color TV, with the sound off, while she had breakfast with Clark. "Besides, when Feinberg promotes me, I'm leaving this dump." Reggie worked as a secretary and pollster for CBS, but she was almost ready to graduate from the Columbia School of Journalism, whenever she could finish those two nagging incompletes for the Social Studies requirement. Reggie wanted to be a television anchor woman.

"How was Miami?" she asked. "When did you get back?"

"Yesterday. The sunshine was nice, but Mr. Taggart certainly wasn't."

"Who's Mr. Taggart?"

The Decorator

"Didn't I tell you about Mrs. Taggart? We're decorating their house on Captiva."

"Oh, the one whose husband beats her?"

"Right. We've had that account for two years. This is the second house I've done for these people. And we're almost finished — the furniture's all in, the paintings and prints are hung and the accessories, including jardinieres and plants, arrived last week, and at this point in the game, *we've lost the clients.*"

"What do you mean?"

"Remember Salvatore? Salvatore Caneletto?"

"Mr. Hedges' assistant? The Junior Designer?" said Reggie. "How could I forget such a wolf? And that cologne! My eyes are stinging just thinking about it."

"Well, Salvatore Caneletto has stolen the client. He quit us without notice and started his own firm. His first order of business was to call the Taggarts, and heaven knows who else, and tell them that Deirdre Dawn & Company is taking them for all they're worth in very evil ways. He told the Taggarts that our charges aren't honest and the antiques we sold her are frauds. Suddenly, Mr. Taggart is on the phone to me, and I've never had to deal with *him* before. You know, I've always dealt with the lady of the house, if you can call Mrs. Taggart a lady."

"Right, you always dealt with Mrs. Taggart, and I remember you telling me about some of the bruises on her arms!" said Reggie.

"I know. So Mr. Taggart tells me I'm treating his wife in the worst kind of way. He told me I was betraying her, and that she was desperate because she had such confidence in us. Can you imagine?" Clark lowered his voice to a growl: 'You are taking advantage of us!' He says he's working with Salvatore now. He wants us to take back all the things in the house and give back all the money — fee money as well as merchandise money."

"Oh, how awful! What did Mr. Hedges say?"

"We've decided to buy back all the furnishings. We can use them on another project. But to return the money that was paid for design time charges is really wrong. Paul minds that a lot, and what bothers both of us a lot is the deceit, the abusiveness of that Salvatore. He's caused us a lot of grief, but we'll ride this out, too. Paul was so good to Salvatore. He lent him money; he helped him buy his New York apartment. And I even introduced him to the job where he met his wife just when he was about to be deported! He married the girl just to stay in the country. I can't believe the evilness with which he has treated our office after we were so good to him!"

"What a creep! I knew he was creepy. Didn't I tell you he was a creep! And not just because he came on to me, he had deep creepiness all over his skin. And he's going to fat, which makes him even greasier."

"That's not the worst of it. The worst was what Mr. Taggart said to me. I had to go down to Florida just to meet with him. I checked into the hotel and the next thing I knew: Boom! Boom! Boom! on my door. I let Taggart in and it was really ugly. He was yelling, 'If you don't give me and my wife our money back, I have connections with the Mob, a police captain,' and so on. It had my head reeling. Mr. Taggart was actually threatening my life. Then he said he would destroy my reputation and our design company with some of our clients."

"*Mon Dieu.* As if being killed wasn't bad enough. Can you get an appraiser to prove Salvatore wrong?"

"It doesn't matter. In this business, you can get an appraiser to say anything, and Mr. Taggart plans to get his appraiser to say our appraiser is wrong. So we're going to give the Richard Taggarts back their money. What evilness." Clark sighed. "And so unfair. I've given that subject all the time it's worth. What about this pilot of yours? Is this the same Italian pilot you snared last month, Antonio, or —"

"Very good! Only it's Luciano, and I think I'm pregnant."

"Already?" Clark was stunned. "How could you be pregnant, and *know* it, in what — six hours?"

"Easily, and anyway, it was from before, the pregnancy, I mean."

Clark groaned. "When?"

"Don't worry, baby, it's not yours. You're always so careful. You're so sweet. No, Luciano won't use any protection, and he wouldn't let me wear my flying saucer, either. He wants *bambini* to prove he's a man, or something."

Clark's stomach tightened. He pushed the cold second half of his muffin away.

"What do you mean, he wouldn't let you wear your diaphragm? I've never heard of anyone not letting you do something!"

"He pulled it right out of my hand. And threw it in the trash. He said he could feel it the last time, and it chafed him."

"What a load of bullshit," said Clark. Secretly, he wondered how Luciano could feel the diaphragm to such a bothersome extent. Either Luciano was very well endowed, or he was lying. Clark felt a pang of jealousy. He decided Luciano was lying.

"And I suppose he said he would pull out."

Reggie laughed. "You got it! Only of course he didn't. I know this sounds sick, but it was terribly romantic at the time. Then again, we were *really* stoned. You know how it is. Love, grooviness." She kept laughing her rollicking, royal laugh that usually made Clark join in, whether he wanted to or not, but this time he wouldn't.

"When will you know for certain?"

"Well, my period is a week — no, eleven days — late, and when it's two weeks late, I can get a test. Wow, I'm still hungry!"

"Oh, no," said Clark.

"Not that kind of hungry, not pregnant-hungry, though maybe I am because I've never been pregnant before. You know my period is never late."

"I know," said Clark. "Has the swine offered to marry you?"

"Yes, and he's not a swine. But I won't marry him."

Reggie did not believe in marriage. She said it was a "Bad Trip." She did not believe in being tied down in any way, not even to an opinion or a preference, except for bran muffins without the raisins and television in the morning. And Clark. They had been best friends ever since the night they met at the Saranac Bar. Not being terribly committal himself, he liked her agreeable way of seeing two sides to every issue. But he knew in a situation like this her inability to make a decision could be disastrous.

"What are you going to do?" he asked.

"Have an abortion, I guess. Maybe I'll marry him, I don't know. It would be a beautiful baby. And just think — I could fly anywhere I wanted to, for free! Oh, sugar! It's so late! Don't you hate these new digital clocks? They're so impersonal. It's brutal. I have to meet Maria at Bloomingdale's. We're buying bras. Wouldn't miss *that* for the world."

Clark admitted to himself that the vision of Maria modeling bras was fascinating. Maria was another of Reggie's "swinging" friends, a dark-eyed Italian blonde who swung both ways. He knew better than to try to get Reggie to return to an unpleasant topic. She hated messy things, but, like her housecleaning methods, if a mess was out of sight, it was out of mind. The memory of Reggie helping him spring-clean flashed into his mind. She had only washed the windows to her eye-level. Beyond that, she had left the grime intact.

"What are you doing today?" asked Reggie.

"Oh. I have to go over to the gallery to see the dealers. They're hanging my show this week. Frankly, I'd rather paint today. HEY! You'll never guess who my new client is!"

"Johnny Carson?"

"No."

"Joan Crawford?"

"No."

"Who, you nasty boy?"

"Pamela Raven."

"No!"

"Yes, and she's not only as beautiful as she ever was, she's nice, too! She's changing apartments."

"Far out! She must be a hundred and two! You'll have to tell me about it. Want to meet at Figaro at ten? I'm bringing Luciano. And Maria."

"That ought to be amusing."

"Not really. Maria *introduced* me to Luciano." Maria was a stewardess for Monte Napolitano.

"Oh, does he fly for Napolitano?"

"That's right. Figaro at ten?"

"See you then."

"Ciao."

Clark shook his head at the Italian affectation as he hung up the phone. Reggie was Czechoslovakian — via Brooklyn — but she wanted more than anything to be international. Luckily, these days, it wasn't hard. In the cafes and coffeehouses that were springing up like mushrooms on the Village streets, one could meet an intriguing In Crowd that didn't ask to see one's pedigree. Clark found the downtown melting pot of bohemian students, musicians, and self-styled revolutionaries the perfect antidote to his proper New England upbringing and the staid Uptown establishments where Deirdre Dawn's clientele flocked. Still, he was happy to return to his quiet uptown East Side apartment in a taxi when he had had enough adventure for the night.

Clark painted for a few more hours, until he finished the new piece, inspired by Reggie's tits. A new name for his work had come to him the previous night in a dream: "Sexpressionism." In his dream he had answered the usual critic who said he was imitating Jackson Pollock by saying, "I'm a Sexpressionist." It was true: sex always inspired new images for him and sex gave him the energy to paint them.

When he was finished, Clark shifted the painting to a less-trafficked corner of the room by pulling it by the tarp. He decided to confirm his early dinner date with Holly before he showered. Feeling pleasantly excited, he dialed her number. He had learned not to tell Reggie about his own extra-curricular activities until they were underway. For all her candor and freedom, Reggie could be subtly possessive, and she could find cleverly innocent ways to undermine Clark's plans with other women. Unless the date was her idea, of course. Though Clark did feel a tiny thrill about saying he was going to the gallery when he wasn't, it wasn't because he was devious, but due to an old habit of protecting his privacy. He justified the lie by telling himself he wasn't very attracted to Holly, anyway, so why incite Reggie unnecessarily?

The switchboard at Holly's hotel was busy, so Clark showered, shaved and exchanged his painting chinos and T-shirt for a pale yellow Oxford shirt, grey flannel slacks, and a grey jacket that wasn't meant to go with the slacks, but was of the same shade and fabric. Clark usually wore separates because he was so tall he had a hard time buying suits. He preferred his jackets loose, with plenty of room for movement in the arms and shoulders, and lots of pockets. He jazzed up his outfit with a wide, flowing striped silk scarf in blue, orange and green.

He reached Holly at the Fillmore Hotel on Central Park West, and agreed to meet her at the Jamaica Arms Restaurant at five. She simply had to catch a cab across the park at Sixty-

Fifth Street and the restaurant was right on the corner of Sixty-Fifth and Lexington. Clark had a few minutes to spare, so he brushed the black corduroy slipcovers on his studio couches, and ran the smaller vacuum cleaner attachment along his yellow felt draperies. When he had straightened the two Queen Anne chairs and hidden the paint pots in the kitchen broom closet, he dusted his pair of onyx ornaments, the twin Buddhas, his two jade vases, and the pair of brass candlesticks which had belonged to his mother. Clark liked simple accessories, in pairs.

When he was finished, the effect was neat, but not fussy; there was a lived-in clutter to the piles of magazine clippings he had yet to file, the gold watch he had begun to repair, and the pile of albums he was going to alphabetize once the record shelves were painted. Clark had a great ability to work on many projects at once, but new pressures at work had put these projects on hold.

Holly was perfectly prompt, and Clark saw her looking nervously up and down the block, clutching a white leather handbag. Clark's taxi had gotten snared in Lexington Avenue traffic, making him ten minutes late. He greeted Holly warmly and apologized for her wait. The maitre d' led them to a good table and Holly removed her thick brown wool coat to reveal a dark blue linen shift of classic but boxy cut. The dress seemed to be a size too large for her. She wore gold and pearl shell earrings and a gold pin at her throat. The monotony of the dress was further relieved by a sparkling white collar and white cap sleeves. As she removed her white kid gloves, Clark noted that they were spotless. Holly's hair had been "done," in a lightly bouffant style on top, gathered by a navy-blue headband. The ends of her hair were flipped outward and held in place with stiff hair spray. Her small green eyes were shadowed in pastel blue, and she had unsuccessfully covered an acne problem with foundation cream, but even though she had a large mouth and horsy teeth, or maybe because of that, her smile was pretty, even sexy.

Clark complimented Holly on her hairdo, and she shrugged and said it was done by the television stylist; she really had no say in it. The waiter took their drink orders and they studied the menu.

"Oh, dear," said Holly. "Everything I want is fattening."

"You don't have to watch your weight," said Clark. "You're so slender."

"Oh, no, I'm not," said Holly. "Not without a lot of effort. And, in case you haven't noticed, my legs are too short for my body. I have a long back and that's why I wear loose dresses. I'd better stay slim, or it looks like I'm hiding something."

Clark hadn't noticed. He wondered why some women were so critical of themselves, but he didn't comment on it. "I've heard that television cameras add ten pounds," he said.

"Yes," said Holly, "they do. And my aunt adds another ten pounds every time she sees me. She's always after me to lose weight."

"Well, she must know. She's had a lot of experience in the business. How was the show?"

"Larry Diamond? Terrible. All he did was ask me about her. It was a big mistake to go on that show, and I'm never doing it again. But I want to hear about *you*. Where are you from? And what's it like to be President of Deirdre Dawn & Company?"

"Well, I'm not exactly President, because Paul Hedges owns the company, and though I did buy a third of the stock, Deirdre Dawn is still around. She blows in now and then as a design consultant, but she doesn't have much to do with the business any more, and Paul is planning to retire soon, so he's let most of the day to day operations slide into my lap. I suppose you could say that I run the company at this point, because I do." He laughed. "But they call me the Director, so as not to offend Mrs. Dawn."

"That's so interesting," said Holly. "And where are you from?"

Clark told Holly about his small home town in Maine, and once he began talking, he found it relaxing and helpful to tell his story. He realized that no one but his psychiatrist ever really asked him about himself. Holly was an avid listener, even though she kept straightening the silverware, lining up the salt and pepper, and folding and refolding her napkin. She even sent the bread basket back because the rolls weren't hot enough.

Clark told Holly about his paternal grandparents, who

were descended from the Mayflower colonists, and related to the Miles Standishes. Clark's Grandfather Calloway had founded a textile mill for woolens, and Clark's father had been a supervisor at the mill. Clark's Uncle Ralph was President for Marketing, and his Uncle Harold was the sheriff of Berwick County, which included the town of Berwick, Maine and the surrounding farming community.

"Did you work at the mill?" asked Holly.

"No, I was closer to my Uncle Harold. I used to ride around in his sheriff's car when he went on patrols, and until high school, I thought I'd be a sheriff, too, when I grew up. I always liked to hang out at the sheriff's office with my Uncle Harold and his deputy, Red. Red was a big fellow with a crop of red hair and lots of freckles. Big Red was a pal, and he liked me a lot. I went home for his retirement party last summer."

The waiter took their orders and brought a second round of drinks. Clark told Holly how his maternal grandmother, a great Lithuanian beauty, had escaped from Soviet Georgia with her husband, a shoe staker who established a very successful factory in Berwick, Maine. Clark's parents had met at a Maine resort, the Poland Spring house, where Clark's mother, Julia, had worked as a waitress when she was a teenager.

"I don't suppose the Calloways approved of the marriage," said Holly.

"No, they didn't," said Clark. "But they didn't approve of much. They were pretty close-minded and Genalavitch — that was my other grandfather's name — didn't have the Social Register ring to it. But my father did marry Julia Genalavitch, and there really wasn't anything they could do about it."

Their plates were presented, sizzling platters piled high with sliced tenderloin of beef, baked potato and grilled tomato. Between bites, Clark told Holly about his older sister, Vera, and their hard-driven childhood, packed with elocution lessons, dancing, acrobatics, horsemanship and team sports, in addition to a conservative regional education and strict attendance at the Central Congregational Church. He told her of his fear of his Grandfather Genalavitch, who was a severe tyrant, and of his grandfather's effect on Julia Calloway, who was a nervous type and tended to drink a lot of sherry. When drunk, her rages were as violent as her father's, and Clark and Vera had tried to stay out of her way.

"What about your father?" asked Holly. "Didn't he try to help her?"

"He was afraid of her, I think. When he got married, he drifted away from the fabric mill. The woolen bedspread business was falling off and there wasn't much work for him. I frankly think he preferred to stay away from it. He liked to lock himself in his study and read. Most of our household's income came from Grandfather Genalavitch, so he was more of an influence in the family, and my father kind of withdrew. Grandfather always paid the prep school and college tuitions for me and my sister, and when Mother was sent to the sanitarium to recover from her drinking, he paid for that.

"I'm told Mother had an affair with a doctor at the sanitarium, Dr. Tierney, and everyone in town knew about that. I'm pretty sure the affair continued until her death."

"Oh, I'm sorry," said Holly. "When did she die?"

"Last summer, in late June. She fell down a flight of stairs in our house, and that was it. She had been drinking, of course, and the medical report showed she suffered contusions of the scalp and a concussion of the brain. My father died in August. Heart attack. I believe his death can be attributed to a broken heart. My father was ready to die after Mother died. Things do happen that way."

"I'm so sorry, Clark," Holly look pained. "We don't have to talk about it. My mother died when I was a baby and my father had been institutionalized since I was three, so I never knew them, but I can imagine how you must feel…"

"It's okay, really," said Clark. He didn't know why he was talking about his parents; he never did, but he felt comfortable with this girl he barely knew, and he wasn't surprised to find out that she, too, was an orphan of sorts. The wine was relaxing him as well, and vino somehow always made talking easier. He ordered another glass and told Holly how he had come to New York to study Art History and Architecture at NYU. Upon graduation, his uncertainty about his future was solved when he met Paul Hedges at a De Kooning opening and Paul asked him if he had ever thought about interior decorating as a career. Clark had taken drafting at St. George's School in Newport, Rhode Island, and he had been exposed to fine furnishings and design history by a friend of his mother's, Miss Beale, who owned an antique shop near Boston Gardens when he was growing up. He knew he had the necessary skills to be an Assistant Designer.

"What I didn't know was that I was coming to work for the Grande Dame of decorating, in the most prestigious decorating company in New York City, and some say the entire United States."

"Deirdre Dawn. I remember the lobby she did for the Palm Aire Mansion in Hollywood, where Auntie used to take me to lunch when I was a little girl. What is she like?"

"Formidable. Very much a presence. I learned a lot from her at first. She taught me how to combine unexpected colors and make it work. You know, Deirdre does a hotel room in greens and blues, and makes lipstick red the accent color. Most folk know that a Deirdre Dawn room features the unexpected. I like a bit of the unexpected colors too!"

"Unexpected colors," said Holly. "Like your scarf." She gave it a critical look.

"Yes, don't you like it?"

"It's a little much for me," said Holly.

Clark ignored the remark and continued the story of Deirdre Dawn, how she did every job with flair and unquestioned swashbuckling style, how she singlehandedly chased the postwar greyness out of lobbies and living rooms across America by introducing bold color and flamboyant patterns in a manner that spurred imitation and actually created the field of interior decorating.

Unfortunately, Deirdre, coming from an extremely wealthy family, had no understanding of finances, and when her costs overran the company's budget, as they always did, she called her brother on Wall Street for more money. This arrangement was beginning to falter. Deirdre was also becoming senile and rather paranoid, and while she sometimes forgot who her clients were and what she had done for them, alienating clients considerably in the process, she had also begun to turn on Clark and Paul, accusing them of undermining her and conspiring against her. They never knew when her venomous moods would strike, and it had been a long time since Clark had found her eccentric ways charming.

The Decorator

Clark had also noticed, as the years went by, that Deirdre's high-handed manner with clients had turned from royal astuteness to pure rudeness, and Clark, as the only member of her staff who would confront her, had become, in her mind, her enemy, and she made his life hell.

"How awful for you! And you have to work for this woman? How do you stand it?" asked Holly.

"It's not that bad," said Clark. "True, there are moments, like last Christmas, when she pointedly gave presents to everyone in the office except me. Since then, I haven't expected her to be nice, or fair, and she isn't, so I'm not disappointed." He laughed, pleased with himself. He hadn't really appreciated his own strategy until he explained it to Holly, and he felt suddenly mature.

"Besides, Lady Deirdre is too busy having lunch with the Duchess of Windsor and Hope Hampton to bother with the boring old business. Most of the time, anyway. That means more work for me. You know, most people in the industry don't give me a chance in hell of surviving after D.D. and Paul retire, but I will. Even if I have to work around the clock, which I do."

"You poor fellow," said Holly. "No wonder you look so tired. If I were you, I wouldn't socialize at all."

Clark did not like the idea that he looked tired, and he was beginning to wonder if Holly had a critical streak. When she called the waiter over to complain that her steak was underdone, Clark was not surprised. The steaks at the Jamaica Arms were always excellent, but the waiter took Holly's sliced steak back for another turn on the grill.

Clark decided he had talked enough about himself. "So, what was it like growing up in a movie star mansion in Hollywood? It must have been exciting?"

"Oh, it was, when I was really young. You know, birthday parties with tents and clowns and ponies. More presents than a kid would know what to do with. But when I got older, when I turned five, Auntie was always too busy for me, and I was raised by maids. Also, I always wanted a father, and none of Auntie's men stayed around long enough to be my Daddy. It was really lonely."

"Didn't Pamela have a long love affair with — what was

his name? The big male actor ..."

"Gabe Taylor. Yes, he was a big star all right, probably the biggest, and he and Auntie had a blazing affair for years, but he was married, and it was a huge scandal."

"I think I remember something about that," said Clark, vaguely wishing he hadn't brought it up.

"Uh-huh," said Holly miserably, cutting into her newly scorched steak. "They used to fight. Viciously. Auntie likes her men to get rough with her, but I didn't know that. I was only fourteen years old. How could I understand that? Actually, I still don't.

"One night they were really going at it in her bedroom. It was awful. Furniture was flying and glass was breaking and they were screaming. It sounded like he was throwing her against the wall. I heard him say, 'I'll kill you, you bitch!' and it sounded like he meant it. So I called the police. I made a mistake. I was scared. I was only trying to protect my aunt."

Clark remembered all to well what had happened. The police and the publicity that followed the incident had created a scandal that almost ruined both Pamela Raven and Gabe Taylor. In those days, adultery, not to mention violent scenes, was enough to end a star's career. The studios were closely monitored by government censors and stars were expected to uphold family morality.

"Auntie told the court that I was unstable, that she and Gabe were merely rehearsing a scene, and that I had overreacted. I almost got locked away in a home for disturbed children, but it saved her career. That's all she cares about. To this day, she believes *her* version of the story. And they believed her, the court, the press, everyone! That day in court was the greatest acting she ever did. She destroyed me to protect herself and I'll never forget it. And I was just trying to protect *her*. I loved her! I never wanted anyone to hurt her!"

Holly pushed her uneaten steak away.

"Excuse me." She practically ran to the ladies' room, causing quite a stir in the restaurant.

Clark was uncomfortable. He hated scenes, and he didn't know if he was supposed to go after Holly or not. He wished he hadn't talked about his parents. He worried that he had set her off, although he had kept his emotions in check. Their date

The Decorator

had turned into a grueling therapy session, and he couldn't wait for it to be over.

When Holly returned, she looked more composed, if a little green. Clark wondered if she had thrown up.

She sat down weakly and drank her glass of water. "I'm sorry," she said. "This isn't proper dinner conversation. You must think I'm a drag. The wine must have gone to my head."

"Who needs proper dinner conversation?" asked Clark. "That would be boring. What matters is if you're all right. Are you all right?"

Holly smirked.

"It's certainly not boring." She sighed. "I'm all right. In fact, I'd like to finish the story. It has a happy ending, sort of. You see, I did end up with a father for a while. You know, Auntie had my real father committed. Her own brother! I'm still not sure why, but I heard that it was because he was going around saying she had slept her way into stardom, that she was a prostitute when she arrived in Hollywood."

Clark nodded. He had heard those stories too. And he thought, so what?

"Funny how history repeats itself. She had my father locked away, and then she tried to do it to me when I was only fourteen! Anyway, Lucien Irons was very kind to me. I felt he really understood me. Auntie wouldn't let him spend too much time alone with me — she's crazy, you know that? She would get drunk and think we were up to something. But we were just talking. All I wanted was a father. I felt sorry for him. I don't think Auntie loved him."

"Really?" asked Clark. He was getting fidgety, thinking he was watching Holly act in a Grade B soap opera.

"She only used him to become Mrs. Cosmetique. He was a nice man. Funny, too. He told great jokes. And he wasn't bossy like Auntie. Everybody didn't have to be perfect around him. He gave me presents, and a car, for no reason, for the first time in my life. Auntie didn't like that; she said he was spoiling me, but I loved him and I hope he loved me."

"Of course he did," said Clark. "Who wouldn't? You must have been a sweet girl."

"Auntie, for one, though if she did love me, I'd wonder. You know, she's a lesbian."

"Come on," said Clark. "Pamela Raven?"

"That's right," said Holly. "What do you think goes on between her and Miss Riley? Hopscotch?"

"Hardly," said Clark, laughing at the idea of Pamela Raven and her secretary playing lesbian hopscotch. He changed the subject to Holly's comedy television series and she told him about her character and the joke writers, and by the time the waiter had cleared their plates and brought their coffee, she was laughing, too.

When Clark's taxi escorted Holly and dropped her off at her Central Park West hotel, he watched the awkward, vulnerable girl walk stiffly to her door, and he felt an admiration for her that was close to attraction. As his cab sped downtown on Broadway, he wondered why. She was too fussy, almost prudish in her dress, she wasn't very pretty, and he wondered if she wasn't frigid. And she was so critical about her aunt. Clark didn't believe in holding grudges or complaining about other people. There was always something more interesting to do. But he was glad Holly would be coming to his art opening, and for some strange reason, he was looking forward to seeing her again.

CHAPTER 3

Clark had never met a girl like Regina Stowkowski. All of the girls he had known, all of his life had focused on one thing: getting married. It was their drive, their highest purpose, instilled in them at a young age. Marriage was considered the ultimate achievement for a woman and motherhood was the expected finale. Clark was aware that if he dated anyone for any length of time, she would expect an engagement ring. No one in Berwick, Maine had ever questioned marriage and parenthood as important goals in life, and though Clark desperately wished to surpass the aspirations of the people of Berwick — after all, that was why he had left home — he hadn't doubted that he, too, would someday be married. Until he met Reggie.

Reggie liked men, loved them, in fact, though she wasn't terribly promiscuous and she never flung herself at anyone. The men came to her, and she believed in having fun. Reggie enjoyed sex; she used her diaphragm, and it just didn't concern her what people might think. The world was changing, and even if some people hadn't noticed, Reggie Stowkowski was determined to change with it.

When Reggie was a teenager, as she loved to tell Clark, she had been fascinated with Sputnik and the idea of space travel, and she had often fantasized about life on other planets. She gladly threw away her hula hoop to gaze at model rockets and pictures of the Earth taken from satellites. Television also fascinated her, and expanded her world, and she wanted more than anything to be on television, maybe as an upbeat Nancy Dickerson or somebody like that. She had saved her money from her secretarial job at CBS to buy the first Motorola color TV model, and she watched every show she could. Reggie knew she was no actress, and she didn't even like most of the silly comedies and melodramas that were televised, but the idea that they could be seen all over the country thrilled her.

She loved to walk down the city streets at night and see the electric blue boxes that filled mysterious apartment windows with flickering light, especially during the News Hour.

"They're all watching the same show. It doesn't matter if you live on Park Avenue, or on Delancey Street — you can see the same show as everyone else!" she once said breathlessly, as she grabbed Clark's arm so they could stop and look up at all the blue windows. "Imagine if it was *you* they were watching! Imagine if you walked by a store selling televisions and you saw your face on all the screens!"

Clark had found the idea of so much exposure a little uncomfortable, but he understood her attraction. Being a television personality would not be as glamorous as being a movie star, but it was so much more modern, and he liked modern ideas. Television brought people together, all over the world, and "Togetherness" was a value Clark and Reggie had grown up with. The backyard barbecues, large picture windows, and casual visits from neighbors were a part of life, both in his hometown and in her Brooklyn neighborhood. It was somehow un-American to be a loner, or an outsider, or to be troubled with secrets. The ultimate misfit, James Dean, had been a movie hero Clark had admired, but never emulated. Clark liked taking showers, and judging from what he heard from movie buffs, Dean wasn't much in the soap and water department.

"Why doesn't he think of someone besides himself?" Clark wondered.

Like Reggie, Clark was amazed by the way television brought distant places close, places that flashed by under John Glenn's orbit, places the astronauts had described on television to the millions anxiously listening below. Some of the new pictures were not so pleasant, yet even the televised violence in Mississippi and the murder of the President, and later of his accused assassin, shocking as they were, filled Clark with the hope that once such terrible things were seen by all, they would have to be changed, and prevented. Television could blow the lids off some dark canisters in the American mind, and Clark couldn't wait to see what was inside, from the safety of Reggie's bedroom.

He knew Reggie's dream was to be a television news

anchorwoman, and Clark believed she could do it. Every day, women were doing more jobs that had traditionally been performed by men, and he worked for some of these women. Deirdre Dawn was a good example, and one of the most well-known. In fact, a recent *New Yorker* cover cartoon spoofed a male decorator showing swatches to a busy female executive. The decorator had looked suspiciously like Clark, and he was amused, and flattered. He believed Reggie could one day be the one to give the world information that would make history. She watched David and Chet avidly, and practiced their sure delivery, their knowing chuckles and their sincere unwavering eye contact with the camera to entertain Clark.

She didn't have much spare time to practice. Between Journalism classes at Columbia, her job at CBS, and her very active social life, Reggie rarely returned to her single-girl apartment with the bathroom in the hall.

The other career girls in the all-female building always welcomed her return, eager as they were to watch her color television set and gossip about men they had met and men they hoped to meet. Reggie always rolled her eyes and groaned when she complained to Clark about their one-track minds. These girls had come from all over the country, following their dreams of glamorous careers in the Big City, careers which were only, hopefully, opportunities to meet and marry men more exciting than the boy next door. Of course they all assumed that they, and Reggie too, would quit their jobs when they hooked the right men. It was only a matter of time.

On the surface, Reggie agreed with them and listened sympathetically to their singles' soap operas, but she felt separated from her neighbors by her secret. Deep down, Reggie knew that if she could ever become a television anchorwoman, she wouldn't care if it was for a station in Nome, Alaska. At least she hoped she wouldn't mind, but she doubted that a husband would come along like a piece of luggage. She knew the girls would consider her unfeminine if she admitted that she might sacrifice marriage, or even wait a while, and she was wary of them. She didn't want them magnifying her tiny doubts about the price of her dream, and weakening her resolve.

"It's a man's world," she often heard, and she also heard that most women only had power when they were young, but she wasn't too worried about it. Her father had always encouraged her to be whatever she wanted, and the nuns who taught at her schools had praised her exceptional abilities. Anyway, she couldn't imagine ever not being young, and there were always men paying attention to her. She often told Clark that he was her favorite because he was her friend as well as her lover. To get where she was going, Reggie needed to understand men, in more than a sexual sense, and Clark helped her do that.

The girls in her building were always nosily asking when Clark would propose to Reggie. Had he dropped any hints? Was he showing any signs of wanting to make the relationship permanent? They glanced at her ring finger with ill-concealed sympathy when it remained bare of diamonds and gold. They thought friendship with men was a waste of precious time, and they were convinced that premarital sex would doom Reggie's chances with Mr. Right.

"If he can have free slices, why should he buy the loaf?" warned Shirley, a chubby legal secretary from Queens who lived down the hall from Reggie and shared the same bath.

To avoid prying eyes and a million questions, Reggie tried to stay at Clark's when they were together. Though her rent was cheap and her neighborhood respectable and convenient to CBS, Reggie was considering letting her new friend Maria convince her to look for a Greenwich Village apartment to share.

She had met Maria Pucci at the African Pavilion at the World's Fair. Reggie had gone to the Meadowlands Fair to cover it for a news article assignment for class, and she had been amazed to meet a pretty stewardess wandering around by herself. When she found out Maria was from Italy, she decided to interview her about her reaction to the Fair for part of the article and they got to know each other over a safari-style lunch.

Maria had confided that she had married an older man, a Chicago nightclub owner named Lou Rolff, at the ripe old age of eighteen, and she confessed to Reggie that she had done it for the US citizenship, and that she had gotten a Mexican divorce after the two-year grace period because the club had failed and the glamour of her former husband had faded with its demise.

"He was sooo ugly," said Maria. "But Lou had that animal vigor from head to toe. His chest was so beefy and hairy! He had a heart tattoo on his arm that said I LOVE MOTHER. He was a sweet, sweet little man right down to his stumpy, uncircumcised cock. He sure knew how to use that muscle! I'd say he was a champion in bed. He made me come a thousand times, but that was not enough reason to stay with him. He bought a butcher shop when the club closed down, and do I look like a butcher's wife to you? All that blood — aagh. I could have that in Roma."

Maria did not look like a butcher's wife to Reggie. Maria's exotic accent, open attitude towards sex, and freedom-loving femininity affected Reggie immediately. They were the same age, twenty-three, but Maria was miles ahead of the girls Reggie knew, and she felt she could talk openly with her new friend without being judged. Maria had a floaty, almost sleepy way of moving, as if she were above any effort, and she wore a diaphanous, gauzy, blue-green patterned blouse that floated with her lazy gestures. Her apple-green wool knit miniskirt was a shorter, bolder mini than Reggie had ever seen, and Reggie resolved to shorten her own skirts another inch when she got home.

There was something else, something about Maria's direct gaze as she wrapped her full pink-frosted lips around her soda straw. She knew what she was doing. As a busty, leggy blonde with hair like a heavy silk curtain and long false eyelashes emphasizing her deep-brown slanted eyes, Maria attracted plenty of male stares, but she was not coy.

"Look at the balls on that one," Maria said, staring down a sailor. "Wouldn't you like to just *grab* them, suck them up, and get him ready for a go?"

Reggie laughed, not shocked at all, though she knew many girls, and even men, who would have blushed. Her new friend took her arm as they explored the fair, and Reggie liked the way that felt. Maria was very physical; she smoothed Reggie's collar, often squeezed her shoulder, and once even slapped her behind.

"No candy for you," growled Maria, when Reggie had paused at a cotton candy stand. Reggie glanced around to see if anyone had noticed the slap, but it didn't seem that anyone had.

"You got nice cheeks," Maria whispered.

Reggie decided that Italians were just very friendly, as she had heard, and Maria's easy attitude was a refreshing difference from the aloof, virginal career girls Reggie often met. Reggie came from an affectionate family herself, and she didn't mind being touched, but she wondered why her eyes kept wandering to Maria's hard nipples, which were visible through the thin blouse. Maria was wearing the kind of bra called "Funderwear," a bright lime-green number that barely contained her lush breasts. Deep, snowy cleavage convinced Reggie that the breasts were real, and the gauze shirt did not conceal much of the action. Still, she hoped Maria would not catch her looking. God, don't let me be abnormal after all, Reggie prayed silently, just like she had in her Catholic school locker-room days. She had been taught that lesbos were a sin.

When the day was over, Maria promised to call Reggie the next time she had a long layover in New York, and they planned to go shopping. After meeting Maria, Reggie decided that her own wardrobe needed an update.

Two weeks later, Maria had come over with a pair of lovely Italian leather shoes for Reggie. She said to think nothing of it, they cost nothing because Maria's father owned a shoe store in Rome. Reggie gasped with pleasure as she slid her feet into the soft, camel-colored flats. Then Maria presented her with a matching handbag, and Reggie squealed with delight as she hugged her friend.

Reggie had the day off from CBS, and they spent their time in and out of the luxury department stores along Fifth Avenue near the park, stores like Bendels and Bergdorf Goodman, and then they darted over to Bloomingdale's because Reggie suddenly remembered that she needed some sheets. She planned to meet Clark afterwards for a drink, and she had convinced Maria to come along. Reggie called Clark from a phone booth on Fifty-Ninth and Lex, and Clark said he could easily scare up a date for Maria with a few phone calls before he left the office.

It was after five o'clock by the time Reggie found the right sheets, soft cotton ones with bold, oversized blue and white daisies. Reggie was pleased, as she was not too fond of those swirls and designs created by the other Pucci — no relation to Maria — that seemed to be everywhere.

"Look how Mod these daisies are!" cried Reggie.

"They are — how do you say it — Pop," said Maria, nodding her approval.

They were in line at the cashier when the lights in the store went out. A murmur went up from the floor and Maria grabbed Reggie's elbow. They waited. The store remained completely dark. The voices got louder and several crashes were heard as people walked into cases and racks they couldn't see.

"What the hell is going on?" asked Maria.

"Must be a power failure. Keep calm," said Reggie. "The lights will be on in a minute. Stand by me and we'll be just fine. I've got my Pop sheets, haven't I?"

Reggie and Maria waited for the lights to go on but they didn't. Surprisingly, no auxiliary or emergency lights came on, either. By the time the floorwalkers had found flashlights and candles and escorted the customers down the unmoving escalators, people were speculating wildly.

"It's the Chinese, I know it," gasped an elderly woman.

"It's those damn anti-war protesters," grumbled a man.

"No, it's space aliens!" Reggie joked, trying to relax Maria, and herself.

From the banks of darkened elevators came the cries and shouts of trapped customers.

"Those poor people!" said Maria

Reggie shuddered at the thought of being trapped in a crowded elevator in the pitch dark, with no fans blowing.

"I have to pee," she whispered.

At the main doors, the crowd discovered that there was no escape. The doors had been sealed in the closed position when the electricity went off. The crowd began to panic and people pounded on the doors. Reggie was afraid she would be crushed to death as the crowd swarmed towards the other exits. She was swept along faster than she wanted to go, but she never let go of Maria's hand. They soon found out that all the doors were locked.

"Oh, NO!"

"Damn it!"

People worried aloud about children waiting to be picked up, dinners unmade, and guests unmet.

"I have to walk my dog! I have to walk my dog!" complained a man with a high-pitched, effeminate voice.

"I still have to pee," said Reggie. "Let's find a bathroom."

They did, after following people with flashlights and candles, and they giggled in the dark as they tried to find the stalls and bumped around in the bathroom, unable to see much of anything.

Reggie and Maria managed to follow customers around the store for about an hour, as management had assembled lots of candles from the Giftware Candle Department and placed them around the store in attractive holders, giving a party-like atmosphere to all the floors. To make matters more festive for the captured audience, sandwiches and drinks, including cold coffee and pastry delicacies, were served in the Birdcage Restaurant.

Candles turned the strange gathering into a happy crowd, particularly for the crowd who discovered the Wine Cellar. By this time, most of the people were caught up in the novelty of their situation and began to chat amongst themselves. A radio someone had borrowed from the Electronics Department was on, broadcasting the news of a massive power failure. Everyone wondered how far the blackout extended and how long it would last. No one knew that the entire Northeastern seaboard was in darkness, even into Canada, and that it would be nearly twelve hours before power would be restored.

The telephones still worked, and Reggie stood in line until she could call her parents, and then Clark. Her parents were fine, though her mother said that her father had panicked and run into their basement bomb shelter.

"I did not!" he protested in the background. "I was just checking the fuse box!"

"Sure he was," said her mother. "You know how nervous he gets. He's lucky I'm here to calm him down."

Clark was also home, and he was relieved to hear from Reggie. He was astounded to hear that she was trapped in Bloomingdale's.

"It's okay, we're having fun," said Reggie. "We're going to try on makeup by candlelight and sleep in the bed department.

I might even try to use the designer sheets I've been carrying around, but not yet paid for." She was determined to have the sheets as a remembrance of her night in Bloomingdale's.

Clark told her the extent of the blackout, that they still didn't know what caused it, and that President Johnson had declared the East Coast an emergency zone, summoned his emergency planning board, and alerted the National Guard. Clark's transistor radio was working and he was listening to every bulletin, but he didn't tell Reggie that the newscaster had announced that sabotage and massive looting were feared, so as not to worry her.

"It's odd to look out my window and see no lights on in Manhattan," he said. "Wait there until the power comes back on. You're safer in Bloomingdale's than in the dark streets. I'll come and get you in the morning."

After Reggie and Maria had played with all of the suddenly available makeup, and smelled all of the perfume, they collected more decorative candles from the Housewares Department and followed a floorwalker's flashlight to the display beds. They chose the most glorious bed, a round bed eight feet across with a mirrored canopy. They threw themselves on the soft mattress, sank into the deep quilts, and bounced a few times. Reggie carefully placed the Pop sheets under the bed for safekeeping.

Maria set the candelabras around the bed and lit the long tapers with her matches. She pulled two slinky pink French slips from her purse.

"Maria!" whispered Reggie.

"It's not stealing if we can't leave the store," said Maria.

They changed into the silk lingerie. Reggie blew the candles out when she saw that the other beds were also being taken. The darkness gave them privacy, and Reggie was glad of it because she was as surprised as any of the other shoppers would have been when Maria snuggled up to her and clung tightly. Maria's body set Reggie on fire and her heart beat madly. *Those* breasts were pressed against her back, and one of *those* legs draped over her hip, and the softest lips she had ever felt pressed against her neck. She lay there, paralyzed for an endless time, too aware of her breathing, as she waited for Maria to do something else.

"Shhh," Maria's breath tickled Reggie's ear. "Just relax."

Reggie softened against Maria and she soon found her hands wandering across the satiny skin and smooth silk, as if her hands had a life of their own. Maria encouraged Reggie with little sighs, and Reggie finally slid her fingers into Maria's panties to explore. She discovered, to her pleasure, that she knew exactly what to do. It was hard for Reggie to keep silent, and the secrecy added to her own excitement as Maria responded to her hand by sliding her mouth over one of Reggie's breasts. Reggie decided that nothing that felt this good could be a sin. After all, hadn't God made Maria? She couldn't imagine that God had wanted Maria to be unenjoyed. When nothing struck her from the sky, Reggie decided this "sin," like so many others, was a rumor. When their passion was spent, only the glow of Maria's cigarette lit the Bed Department.

Clark had heard this story of course, in all its detail, as soon as the power was restored. At seven a.m. the next morning, Reggie had run over to his apartment to fill him in over breakfast. Maria had to be on a ten a.m. flight to London that day, so he didn't meet her. He told Reggie the cause of the blackout: an outdated relay box in a Canadian power plant had overloaded, causing a "cascade effect" power surge which shut down all of the generators along the grid. Immediately, the eighty thousand square mines of the Northeast Power Grid were plunged into darkness. It had been the largest power failure in the world to date. Mysteriously, only two small neighborhoods in Brooklyn and Staten Island had been unaffected. Eight hundred thousand people had been trapped in the subways, and even Governor Rockefeller had to walk up fifteen flights to his apartment.

"It was kind of nice," said Reggie. "I remembered how wonderful candles are."

"Yeah, especially when you have an Italian bombshell in bed with you! And here I was, all alone in the dark," Clark teased.

"You'll meet her soon," said Reggie. "Don't worry, she likes men, too." With that, she had begun to unbutton Clark's shirt. "Now, let me make you late for work ..."

On Maria's next visits, Clark had been too busy to go out,

but he had heard about the International Set parties Reggie attended with Maria. It was at one such party that Reggie had met Luciano, and though Clark was not eager to meet him, he was certainly curious about Maria. After his dinner with Holly, he hurried downtown to Cafe Figaro, wishing, though it was too late, that he had changed into something less respectable for the Village scene. He predicted that Luciano would probably be wearing a form-fitting black turtleneck and tight Italian slacks.

Clark was right about the pants, but wrong about the shirt. The tall, dark Italian sitting with the two women in the Figaro wore a heavy white silk shirt, very open at the neck, revealing his gleaming, tanned chest. A jeweled leather belt and swashbuckling black boots completed the image. When he turned to acknowledge Clark, Clark had to admit that Luciano was handsome in an arrogant way, but he thought that Luciano's penetrating blue eyes were too close together and that his heavy eyebrows gave him an angry look.

Reggie was amazing, as usual, in a pink sleeveless wool jersey top and culottes that swept the floor in wide bell bottoms. Her smooth, seal-brown shoulder-length hair was perfectly curled at the ends in a sassy flip, and her fine skin glowed against pink button earrings. Clark was glad Reggie did not wear false eyelashes. She didn't have to. Her large, sparkling brown eyes were accentuated with her own, naturally long lashes. She looked simply incandescent that evening, Clark thought. Perhaps it was her contrast to the milky blonde beauty at her side. The girl in the little white knit minidress and high zippered boots could only be Maria. Clark thought Maria was striking, as she lounged in her seat blowing languid puffs of smoke over Luciano's head, and though she was probably a golden fantasy come to life for most men, she wasn't as beautiful to Clark as Reggie was. Even from a distance, as Clark left his observation post at the café's plateglass window and crossed the crowded room, he could see that Reggie was entertaining her own table, and that the two male student types at the next table were leaning in to catch her witticisms, and were laughing heartily. Reggie was a jewel in any setting, and Clark was eager to join her.

Reggie introduced Clark to her friends, and they made

room at the table. He sat across from Maria and next to Luciano, who faced Reggie. Luciano reluctantly turned his burning gaze from Maria and fixed Clark in his stare. Clark was relieved when Luciano smiled sharkishly at him and offered his hand. The hand was smooth and hard, with several heavy rings, but, surprisingly, it did not crush Clark's in its grip.

"At last we meet," said Luciano. "Waitress, some nice espress' for my *paisan*!"

The waitress took Clark's order, which he changed to Cafe Mocha and cheesecake, and she brought fresh cappucinos for the women, who were sharing a cannoli, one overstuffed with sweet ricotta and diced glazed pieces of orange and lime rind. Reggie informed Luciano and Maria that Clark was about to have a *vernissage* of his paintings at a Madison Avenue gallery soon, and though Luciano seemed more interested in stroking Reggie's hands, Maria asked Clark about his work. As he described them, Clark noticed that Maria's gaze wandered.

She rubbed her neck and sighed, "You are telling me all these things I don't understand. I want to know what they *feel* like." She was pouting as if he was deliberately trying to confuse her.

"I guess you'll have to see them for yourself. You can even feel them if you like," said Clark. He could tell that Maria was one of those sensitive types who make an issue out of everything, and he was relieved when Reggie waved an envelope at him, postmarked from Saigon.

"I got a letter from Charlie," she said.

"Oh, how is he?" asked Clark. Charlie was Reggie's nineteen-year-old brother, and Clark quite liked him.

"He's not having fun, but he likes the Beatles tapes I sent him. He says it's still raining and they're getting shot at sometimes, but they can never see the enemy. It sounds frustrating, emptying you rifle into the jungle and not hitting anything, but at least it doesn't sound too dangerous. My brother is in Vietnam," she added for Luciano's benefit.

Luciano snorted. "Ha. The Americans, they will never win. They should get out now. They will never beat the Viet Cong."

Reggie looked hurt. "Listen, I want my brother to come home more than anything, but I hate to think he's wasting his time."

"She's right," said Clark. "Vietnam is a tiny country; what can they do? It will be a short war. While I'm not sure the South Vietnamese government is terribly stable, we have to protect—"

"Protect, nothing!" Luciano cut Clark off with the air of someone who cannot stand to be contradicted. "You Americans have learned nothing — *niento* — from the French. You have no business there. And your President Johnson is as bad as Hitler, killing innocent children and babies with bombs, experimenting with new horrible weapons to torture civilians. I'm a pilot; I fly everywhere. I meet people. I know. You think 'body count' is counting only soldiers? They are counting civilians, too."

"Oh, no," said Reggie. "If that were true, it would be on TV!"

"Just like a woman to say that," said Luciano.

Clark thought that last remark would offend Reggie, but he saw the flash of anger in her eyes melt into a different kind of heat when her eyes locked with Luciano's intense stare. Clark saw the animal passion between them, the passion of opposites colliding, each struggling for mastery. He was relieved, knowing that this kind of affair always burned itself out for Reggie. It was hot at first, but she didn't like to argue for long. Reggie liked light reading and light television. Television! Clark had hit on a good subject-changing topic.

"Guess who I had dinner with tonight?"

Reggie abandoned her staring contest. "Who?"

"Holly Raven!"

"Holly Raven from 'The Skipper's Kids'?"

"One and the same."

"That's my favorite comedy show!" said Reggie. "I'd love to meet her! What is she like?"

"She's very bright," said Clark. "A bit serious, though, and she's not what you'd call pretty." He was deliberately playing Holly down. "And very picky. I bet she's hell on the set."

"Oh, why didn't you bring her here? Holly Raven is a television actress," she explained. "Her aunt is the movie star Pamela Raven, and Clark is helping Pamela Raven move to a smaller apartment."

"What?" said Maria, as if she was coming out of a fog.

Luciano told her in Italian, and seemed to be adding some comments of his own, judging from Maria's smirk.

"Oh, Holly wouldn't like this place," said Clark. "She's much too tidy, looks like a junior nun. And anyway, she had to go home and read her script and have a facial because she had a five a.m. call tomorrow. I guess she has to get a lot of sleep to play a seventeen-year-old on the show."

"What is Luciano saying?" Reggie nudged Maria.

"Ah, you don't want to know," said Maria. "It's very rude." Her flirtatious glance at Luciano told them what she thought of his rudeness.

"Come on, Luciano, what are you saying?" demanded Reggie.

"He says that Pamela Raven is just a businesswoman, not an artist like Anna Magnani or Giuletta Massina. He says she's washed out."

"Washed up," said Luciano. "That old has-been bitch, so what? Who cares if she has to move to a smaller luxury apartment? In Rome, people live five, six, seven to one room. And I hate those little dogs of the rich! What a waste! They eat better than my brothers and sisters at home. Who was she married to? Cosmetique! What bourgeois nonsense. Real women don't need makeup!"

Maria nodded hungrily at Luciano, despite her false eyelashes and heavy makeup.

"Oh, come on," said Reggie. "Pamela Raven worked hard for her money. She is *too* a star, a real star, and those old-time stars made twenty pictures a year! And besides, Pamela Raven is a good example for women. She's as rich and powerful as any man."

Now Maria agreed with Reggie, smiling at her and batting her eyes. Clark followed the conversation like a hot ping-pong match, knowing that Reggie could hold her own.

"Pamela Raven gives a lot of money to charity and hospitals," he couldn't resist adding.

"Bah!" Luciano spat smoke at Clark. "She is useless, a parasite. What is a star, anyway — just image, lies! Throw her to the dogs!" He drained his espresso and looked at Reggie. "What can a woman do with money, anyway? A woman does not need to work. If she is a *bella donna*, like you, a man will support her. I would never let my wife work. Her place is at home, with my children."

"That's okay, Luciano," said Reggie. "Maria and I don't need you anyway. Do we, Maria?" She turned to face her girlfriend and they kissed, a long lingering kiss.

Clark and Luciano watched in stunned fascination, as did everyone in the café. The two men exchanged meaningful looks. Luciano's baffled and Clark's delighted.

Clark took charge. "Let's go to my apartment for a drink, shall we?"

"Oh, let's!" said Reggie. She whispered, "Luciano has some pot!"

Maria looked at Reggie as if she would follow her anywhere, and they gathered their coats. Clark wasn't sure about the pot, but he heard it was an aphrodisiac and he had been planning to try it. Once they were outside, he let Luciano and Maria walk ahead, and he took Reggie's arm.

"Do you smoke pot these days?" he asked her.

"Only twice," said Reggie. "The first time nothing happened. But Luciano says it's like that for a lot of people — you don't get high the first time, I mean. Luciano is always raving about it, how great it is for sex, and boy, is he right! I told you what happened with us."

"Well, you must know what I think of *his* opinions. I hope we don't join the Communists and stop bathing. It would be bad for business. What do you see in him, anyway?"

"Luciano? He's a rat, but he's an honest rat. He has to say those things because he's a macho male. Actually, he worships me. And besides, he has a huge cock. Look at those shoulders, mmm…"

"I'm worried about you," said Clark, but he was smiling and he knew she didn't take him seriously.

The foursome squeezed into a taxi and rode uptown. Clark kept the conversation light, and didn't let Luciano get a controversial word in. Luciano seemed content to listen, hemmed in as he was by the two women's bodies. He let his hands fall casually over the shoulder of each woman, until his fingertips brushed their breasts. They didn't seem to mind, and they laughed merrily at Clark's story of Pamela Raven's encounter with the Wilsons. His telling made it funnier than it was, and when they arrived at his apartment, he poured them all several rounds of good champagne, and then glass after glass of neat Scotch, while he treated them to selections from his excellent jazz collection.

Maria warmed up to Clark's paintings, and after the lumpy little cigarette had gone around a few times, she tried to enhance the gathering with her discovery of the meaning of Clark's work, its deep relevance and the true feeling of the work, but Reggie started to giggle and Clark found himself laughing too, at what he didn't know, but maybe because Maria's speech was pure bullshit.

"Isn't she a gas?" hooted Reggie.

Clark liked the harsh sweetness of the weed, but he had to be careful not to inhale too deeply, or he would cough uncontrollably. Luciano smoked like an expert, even holding in the smoke while he talked and then exhaling it in a large puff. Maria suddenly became kittenish and curled up against Luciano, staring at him with sleepy adoration. Reggie kicked the rug aside and started dancing to the spicy saxophones. She pulled Clark up into her dance, and they undulated together, stroking each other slowly.

It just happened. Reggie's culottes came off somehow, and then Maria was naked, her beautiful breasts in full view. Clark had to touch them. Reggie read his mind and guided his hand to Maria's breasts. The next thing he knew, he was on his bed, kissing Maria, and they were both naked. Luciano was standing next to the bed, his neck arched back in ecstasy as Reggie knelt before him, working her magic. Clark had a strong feeling that he wanted to stop Luciano from pulling Reggie's hair, because he knew she didn't like it, but Maria thrust against him, and he lost himself in her.

Even though he was stoned, and the touch of a woman's skin was a revelation, Clark wished Maria would do more than just lie there like a sack of potatoes. He did his best to arouse her, and she accommodated him, but that was it. She just lay there passively, and Clark didn't mind when Luciano's hands groped at Maria's tits.

That meant Reggie was free. She pulled Clark over to her side of the bed, and they had a wonderful time. Sex was always exciting for them, and the pot and the extra people made it a marvel. It was one of those times when they stared at each other in disbelief that anything could feel so good. And then they started laughing and couldn't stop. Pot was certainly a silly thing.

Luciano was attacking Maria from behind, and at first that looked like a silly thing too, but it was a little unnerving how he was tearing into her. He was slapping her, too, hard, on her flanks, and pulling her hair. He ground his teeth in a snarl as he slammed Maria with vicious force. Rhythmically her head bumped the headboard of the bed, and she gasped and wailed with an abandon she had not shown with Clark.

"Hey," Clark whispered to Reggie, "do you think he's hurting her?"

"I don't know," said Reggie. "He was rough with me, but never that rough. He knows I don't like anal sex. Maybe she likes it."

As if to confirm this, Maria gasped, "More, more," and Luciano obliged, first slapping her hard. With every thrust he grunted an obscenity at Maria, calling her a bitch, a whore, a cow, and Clark started to seriously dislike Luciano. He was considering throwing him out when Luciano bellowed and collapsed against Maria's back, crushing her down into the bed. She was sobbing, but she was clearly enjoying herself, calling out Italian endearments as she reached back to caress his hair. Luciano was out cold.

Reggie pulled Maria out from under Luciano's bulk.

"Come here, honey, I'll fix you up."

She wiped away Maria's tears and rocked her in her arms, and soon they were kissing passionately. Blissfully stoned, and too tired to move, Clark watched contentedly as the women played into the night.

4
CHAPTER

*C*lark was not late for work the next morning. In fact, he arrived twenty minutes early. He unlocked the outer office doors and was greeted by the distinct smell of stale chicken grease. The odor was completely out of character for such a chic office, and the large oil portrait of Deirdre Dawn in the reception area seemed to be sneering down its nose at the aroma. Clark had encountered the smell before.

"Don't worry, D.D., I'll find out what it is," he told the portrait. He was rather fond of the image of Deirdre Dawn in the Edwardian-style dress of her youth. She looked like a Gibson Girl, a solid one with a Roman nose. Deirdre was now in her seventies, though you'd never know it, thanks to a lift here and a tuck there, and a makeup job only Elizabeth Arden could handle. She had even had her nose "done" and Clark thought the petite new nose looked a little lost on her broad face.

Clark followed the chicken smell to one of the secretary's desks and checked the waste basket. It was empty.

"Hmmm." He opened the middle desk drawer and there they were: chicken bones, from at least four pieces of fried chicken, piled on a greasy napkin. There was quite a bit of stale chicken left on the bones, and one piece, a wing, was uneaten.

"Aha," he said. He pulled several tissues from the box on Belle's desk and used them to pick up the chicken bones as if they were one of Princess Lotus Blossom's poo-poos. He carried the wad of paper to the little office kitchen where he threw it into the kitchen garbage pail, which was deeper than the little baskets under the desks.

Clark heard the outer office door open and he knew it was Belle. It was ten of nine, and she, too, always arrived at the office a little early to settle in and get an uninterrupted start on the day. Clark knew she would be in the kitchen in a moment to make the morning pot of coffee, and he decided not to mention the chicken bones. Instead, he planned to spray air freshener in the outer office as soon as he could.

Because it was so unlike dependable Belle to be sloppy in any way, he knew it must have something to do with Deirdre Dawn. D.D. was always "dieting," but if one of her staff members was eating something appetizing, like Belle's chicken lunch from Stouffer's, Deirdre felt entitled to it and would snatch it up, as if everyone could afford to buy a second lunch. It was as if the calories didn't count if the food was ordered by someone else.

She also did this in restaurants, on the rare occasions when she took her staff to lunch. Clark remembered one such time when he had ordered a cheeseburger and Deirdre had told the waiter, "I'm on a diet. I'll have the broiled scrod."

When the orders came, Clark's cheeseburger looked much more appealing to Deirdre than her fish, so she took the cheeseburger platter, insisting that the waiter had made a mistake. Clark had ended up eating scrod, which he disliked. He could understand how Belle would quickly push her meal into a drawer when Deirdre happened by, and he could see how Belle could forget about the rest of her lunch, because Deirdre always had several "urgent" matters for Belle to attend to immediately.

Belle arrived in the office kitchen as she had faithfully for nearly twenty-five years.

"Good morning, my dear," she said. "And how was your weekend?"

She filled the coffee maker as Clark told her the abridged version of his weekend, trying not to make it sound too interesting, as he knew Belle would tell him, which she did, that she had done errands, or visited her mother in the nursing home, and then worked on her knitting while she watched television. Belle, a heavy-set woman in her fifties with a cap of curly brown hair and nice blue eyes, lived for her weekdays at Deirdre Dawn & Company. She spent her days typing, answering phones, and pining a bit in her heart for Paul Hedges.

Belle often asked Paul to supper, hoping that he would see her as someone more than his secretary, but Paul never responded. Clark thought Paul was asexual, that he preferred not to get involved, because he had never known Paul to be involved with anyone. Paul certainly never confided an interest in anyone to Clark, not even of the casual nudge-and-wink variety.

Paul Hedges came into the reception area as Clark was walking down the hall to his office. Paul called out his good morning and said he'd be in to see Clark in a minute. Clark hurried towards his office, hoping to clear a few things off his desk before Paul came in with a new priority.

At Deirdre Dawn & Company, color was the thing, and Clark never tired of the simple black-and-white suites with emerald green carpeting. Deirdre preferred to show designs and plans against the white walls and on the white-topped desks with black bases.

"Every room needs a touch of black!" Deirdre would always exclaim. When Hedges moved into the head office across from Deirdre's suite, the decor was not changed, and Clark, while he preferred a more mellow setting for himself, in his outer office, directly adjacent to the conference room, also accepted the stylish decor.

Clark stepped into the conference room to retrieve the preliminary plans for Pamela Raven's apartment from the conference table where they had remained since Friday evening. The conference room was his favorite spot in the office, and it was true to the Deirdre theory: all the walls were black and the carpeting was emerald green. The conference table was snow-white laminate, accented by a drop chandelier of rich, shiny brass. For conference chairs, Deirdre had designed chairs that had been upholstered in black patent leather. For dramatic effect, the conference room housed a large gold-leaf French console table with a green malachite top, very much like those found at St. Petersburg in the Summer Palace. Above the console, a large Venetian mirror hung, framed in glass and trimmed in gold leaf. To Clark, the Deirdre Dawn office decor was exciting, but certainly not contemporary in any way, except for the office machinery, and even the typewriters were out of date.

The call from Pamela Raven's secretary came as Clark walked into his office.

"It's Miss Riley," said Belle, when Clark answered the intercom.

Miss Riley greeted Clark and said that Mrs. Irons was having her massage, but that she wished to invite Clark to a cocktail party at the Ritz Plaza that evening: "Just an informal gathering, for the younger set, and could you please bring the new designs and plans for Miss Raven's apartment with you?"

Clark wondered again what the reasoning could be for Miss Riley to refer to her boss sometimes as Mrs. Irons and sometimes as Miss Raven.

"Let me talk to him!" The familiar authoritative voice sounded in the background and soon Pamela Raven was on the line.

"Hello, darling," she said, as if through clenched teeth. "Ugh! This bull-dyke masseuse is pounding the life out of me! Will you knock it off!" The masseuse must have stopped pummeling her client because Pamela Raven's voice relaxed into a purr. "The Swedish girls give the best massages, but this one is as strong as an ox, and she's killing me! Listen, the real reason why I want you to come to the Ritz Plaza is because Allen Friedberg is giving the party. You do know who Allen Friedberg is, don't you?"

Clark quickly said that of course he did. Allen Friedberg had become president of Metropolis Pictures when Abraham "Abie" Schwartz, the company's legendary founder, had died. Everyone knew that while Abie chose and shaped the stars, using a combination of generosity and terror, Allen Friedberg had managed them, interceded for them, and generally had run the productions, keeping the filming on schedule and trying to keep everyone happy. Allen Friedberg had been working with Pamela Raven, and the other major Metropolis stars, from the very beginning, when they were young, and he was just barely out of his teens. He had been the Wonderboy of Hollywood's Golden Age, and though the stockholders had more control of movie empires these days, he was still one of the most powerful men in America.

"The thing is, sweetheart, Allen needs a decorator for his penthouse on top of the Ritz, and he owes me a favor, so I recommended you. His wife, Bambi, is a whining, spoiled little pest, but she'll love you. She's like a ferret. You know how those crazy old bags love to have handsome young men working for them, particularly when they get no attention from their husbands."

Clark knew. He agreed to come, and thanked Pamela Raven for inviting him.

"Of course you'll come," said Pamela. "And it won't be all boredom — I've invited some nice young people, Holly and some young actors and actresses, all ladies and gentlemen of course, no trash like you see at El Morocco these days. Be there at eight, at the Ritz Plaza, Penthouse A, and don't forget your designs for my new apartment!"

Before Pamela hung up, Clark reminded her that his opening was on Friday, four days away. Would she still come?

"Oh, Clark, I hate public appearances. They terrify me and it takes me forever to look presentable these days. I'm scared stiff already, but if you want me to do it, I'll do it. I'll do it for you, because you're such a dear. I know if I come to the opening it will help your show. I'll convince Allen and Bambi to come along, too. God knows Bambi has no taste, but dear Allen may buy a painting for his office! Particularly if I tell him to."

Clark added the Friedberg party information to his calendar with a note to have the cleaners deliver his tuxedo to his apartment when the cleaning lady would be there to receive it.

He was glancing at the Remington Typewriter catalog when Paul knocked on the door frame and entered, followed closely by Belle, who carried their coffee cups on a silver serving tray. Clark noted that Belle was with it, as the coffee cups on the tray were designed by Deirdre Dawn: white porcelain with painted roses and green leaves. Deirdre had decided to upgrade to new Remington typewriters, and Clark noticed Belle's quick grateful glance at the catalog in his hands as she set the coffee tray down in a clear patch on his desk.

Paul took his coffee and perched on the arm of a comfortable club chair. Clark noticed that Paul, a trim gentleman in his sixties, had a deeper tan on his face since last Friday, though the weather had certainly not been conducive to sunning in Paul's rooftop solarium, and Paul had not flown South for the weekend. His tan was enhanced by Man Tan, a Cosmetique product. Paul Hedges was a bachelor, and as far as Clark knew, he had never been married. Clark thought of him as an uncle, and he worried about Paul a little. He wondered why this cultured, amiable man kept so much to himself lately, preferring to return to his apartment in the East Sixties after work hours

The Decorator

to watch television or go to an Elvis Presley movie. He had become more withdrawn even in the few years since Clark had first met him at the De Kooning show. Clark sometimes thought Paul had a secret past that did not permit him to relate to other people, a past that somehow or other scarred him for life.

"Caneletto strikes again," said Paul.

"What happened?" asked Clark.

"He was in here sometime during the weekend. I know because his office is completely cleared out now, except for that dying Spathophyllum. And more of my files are missing!"

"No!" exclaimed Clark. "Of all the — which files did he take?"

"It's hard to tell," Paul sighed. "Looks like rain again ... Definitely the Brewer account and a few others. He may even have taken the Garden State Racetrack files. I'll have to ask Belle, or the new intern — what's her name?" Paul snapped his fingers. "Pat, that's right. She can go through the Rolodex and see what's missing from the files. When she comes up with a list, I want you to call those customers and straighten this out. Tell them Mr. Caneletto is no longer representing us. It's an inconvenience, I know, but you're the only one who can do it with some finesse. Is that all right?"

"Of course," said Clark. "That's not a problem for me. But shouldn't we also —"

"Change the locks," said Paul. "I know. I'll tell Belle to call the locksmith immediately. And I'll see if new locks can be installed on our file cabinets today, even though it's such a bother. And D.D. would never agree to replacing our file system with security cabinets."

"No, she wouldn't," agreed Clark, remembering the fuss over the new typewriters.

"On a brighter note, how goes the Pamela Raven account?" asked Paul. "Can we have a meeting at, say, two o'clock, with sketches? I'm eager to see what we have to work with. Oh, also, a Roland Lee left a message for me last week. He wants to know if we'd be interested in decorating the public spaces of the Ritz Plaza Hotel, as well as the guest room corridors. I've never worked with Roland Lee, though maybe Deirdre has. This job is tailor-made for us. Of course, she says she doesn't remember any Roland Lee. I spoke to her this morning and she told me to 'handle it,' in that matter-of-fact way of hers. I think it's better if you call him and we can fill Deirdre in on the details when we have them."

Clark grinned. "You're going to love this! It just so happens I'll be at the Ritz Plaza this evening."

He told Paul about Pamela's invitation to the Friedberg party, and Paul's eyes lit up at the possibility of adding the president of Metropolis Pictures to their client list.

"I've seen Roland Lee's name in the papers lately," said Clark. He recently purchased the Ritz Plaza, and he owns a few other hotels, I believe, in Chicago and Los Angeles.

"Oh, of course," said Paul. "Is he the one who's married to Raina Owens of Owens-Meadows department stores?"

Clark's intercom buzzed. "Mr. Winterspoon calling," said Belle's voice.

"Okay, ask him if he can hold for one moment," said Clark. "Roland Lee is not married to anyone. Raina Owens divorced him after eight weeks, after she discovered he was only interested in her social contacts. According to Doreen Flower, they never even consummated the marriage. I'll call Roland Lee and see if we can set up an appointment before the party tonight."

"Great," Paul finished his coffee. "And I'll get the kids in the art department moving on the Raven designs."

Clark took the Winterspoon call. Martin Winterspoon, the gallery owner, was calling to confirm Pamela Raven's appearance at Clark's opening. Martin, an excitable, pudgy gay man, called his elegant gay partner to listen in on the extension. They were thrilled beyond belief to have two stars attending their opening. Imagine Pamela Raven at the opening, along with Adela Morgan, the Broadway musical star! Another of Clark's celebrated clients, Miss Morgan was also planning to attend the show, which promised to be quite a draw.

Martin was only worried about one thing, that the two actresses would show up at the same time. "Dearie me!" he kept saying. He knew that show business royalty like Raven and Morgan would never, ever agree to share the limelight, and that two such luminaries in one room would be like having two suns in the sky. What excitement! There would be an explosion, he delightfully feared. Also, wasn't it common

The Decorator

knowledge that the two women strongly disliked one another?

Clark said he was sure Pamela and Adela would get along perfectly; you couldn't believe everything you read in the *Journal American* or *Daily Mirror*. And besides, Raven always arrived early and left early. She was in bed by ten o'clock. Morgan, on the other hand, was a notorious party girl, even in her robust middle age. She would arrive after her last bow at the Majestic Theater, with full entourage in tow and ready to party it up. Adela always enjoyed arriving when the party was in full swing, and the maximum number of people would be on hand to worship her. Adela Morgan and Pamela Raven would not even cross paths. Clark left a message for Roland Lee in the manager's office of the Ritz Plaza, and then he dialed the White House. He asked for Dannee Lou Baker, the First Lady's Social Secretary. He needed to find out if she had received her invitation to his opening. When she answered her phone, Dannee Lou's sultry Texas accent charmed Clark instantly, as it always did. She told Clark she could actually leave her office early on Friday and catch a plane to New York.

"After all, Clark," she drawled, "It's not an election year, now is it? Of course, when Mr. Kennedy was here, I could never have gotten away at all! He did keep us busy. I swear, I grew another set of arms!"

Clark remembered Dannee Lou in her frantic octopus days. On his first White House visit, he had watched Dannee Lou handle two phone conversations at once, while typing a letter and communicating in rapid facial sign language with the Attorney General's assistant.

"How is life with LBJ?" asked Clark.

"Shhh! I'm lucky I'm still here after so many of the staff have been replaced. If I wasn't from Texas, I'd probably be history too."

Clark knew that President Johnson had fired and replaced most of his predecessor's staff, and that Dannee Lou, like many people, himself included, still mourned Jack Kennedy. Dannee Lou was a careerist, and she wanted to keep her job. Lyndon Johnson was also from Texas, and Clark was sure Dannee Lou banked on that connection, as well as her excellent administrative skills and famous social graces to keep her in the Johnsons' favor.

"There must be a lot of ten-gallon hats in the lobby of the Mayflower Hotel these days," Clark commented.

"Yes," she said. "And cowboy boots with business suits — makes me feel right at home."

Clark asked about Dannee Lou's husband, the FCC executive who was in a coma in Capitol Hill Hospital. Clark had met Steven Baker when Deirdre Dawn decorated the Baker's Georgetown manor. Steven Baker had been knocked unconscious in a boating accident in July.

"He's the same," signed Dannee Lou. "No change in him, though the doctors still have hope that he'll wake up. I feel real guilty coming to New York, but I think it would be good for me to get away. I can fly back on Sunday. I'm not doing Steve any good moping by his hospital bed. Shoot, this phone never stops ringing! I have to pinch myself sometimes to remember where I'm sitting. And everyone in America is entitled to call me! After all, it's the taxpayers who keep me in champagne and orange juice these days. 'Bye, sugar, I have to go! I'll see you on Friday!"

Belle brought in the mail and placed it in a neat pile on Clark's desk. She told Clark that Mr. Lee had returned his call and that the rolls of wall-covering samples had arrived from the mill, but wherever was she to put them? She also said that Reggie had called, but not to call her back until after one, because she was out of the office until then.

Clark got a warm thrill when he thought of Reggie and the night before, and while he wished he could call her to recap the previous evening's merriment, and tell her about the Friedberg party, he was also glad, in a contradictory way, that he could not call Reggie back. He wondered about these mixed emotions in himself every time he feared that he was getting too close to a woman. He was afraid of being needed too much; the responsibility bothered him. He was already thinking about the starlets he would meet at the party. Sometimes he wondered if there was such a thing as a male whore, and if he was one. These feelings flew through him quickly as he dialed Roland Lee's number.

Roland Lee was the fastest talker Clark had ever heard. By the time they had agreed to meet at five-thirty and confirmed that Roland Lee would also be at the Friedberg party, Clark felt that he had been sold the hotel rather than won a new client. Roland Lee had also dropped about forty names in five minutes, and he sounded like a real estate advertisement as he touted the hotel. He managed to make it sound as if he was doing Clark a favor by letting him decorate the property. After all, everyone knew that the Ritz Plaza was the top hotel in New York.

Clark's head was spinning from Roland Lee's flood of descriptions and ideas. Clark wasn't sure if Lee wanted an Irish Hunt Club or a Beaux-Arts atmosphere for the bar, but he could tell that Lee had good taste. Clark was excited to meet a hotel owner who had enthusiasm for fine decor, and the ambition to decorate a hotel with the genuine articles.

What Clark found most interesting was that Roland Lee had not asked for Deirdre Dawn's personal touch, and had not even asked about her. Lee told Clark that he had seen the Clark Calloway treatment of the Barbizon Hotel lobby in Washington, D.C. when he was negotiating its purchase. Clark supposed that his name as the actual designer, rather than Deirdre's, had filtered to Roland Lee through the Washington social grapevine, and that Dannee Lou was behind it, somehow. He would have to find a way to thank her.

The rest of Clark's day went smoothly, but he did not have a spare moment to call Reggie, especially with the last-minute changes in the Raven floor plans. Clark worked with the drafting department to get the sketches completed on time, and to add a few personal refinements of his own. As his hand danced over the tracing paper and boards, he hoped that D.D. would not make one of her unannounced visits and order the entire project scrapped and redone. His wish was granted, and by five o'clock, Clark flew out of the office to meet Roland Lee in the Ritz Plaza Restaurant.

Roland Lee had the sloped shoulders and slight build of an unathletic man, and he had the pale complexion of a true redhead. His hair was his best feature, as it was thick and shiny with an elegant wave.

He was not a handsome man, due to his small, pouchy blue eyes, long bumpy nose, and tiny mouth with thin, dry-looking lips, but he gave the impression of elegance in a deep grey shirt, pastel and emerald green striped tie, and pastel green cashmere sweater, worn under a grey flannel suit. Even his socks and suede shoes were deep grey. Clark guessed Roland Lee was in his mid-forties. Lee's movements were graceful as he savored his Earl Grey tea, and his eyes were quick, darting constantly around the restaurant.

"You gotta watch these people all the time, or they'll rob you blind," he said amiably.

Clark got the impression that there was little that happened in the hotel that Roland didn't notice, and the wait staff hovered solicitously, but not overly so, around the owner's table.

Roland, as he insisted he be called, treated Clark to amusing ghost stories over tea, and he was only too happy to discuss business, as well as stories about all kinds of people who stayed in the hotel. According to the chambermaids, there were at least two ghosts haunting the Ritz Plaza. The maids refused to go into rooms 508 or 913 alone. Roland said he had been in these rooms and had seen nothing out of the ordinary, but that those two rooms were the ones that guests most often asked to switch out of, for reasons most vague.

Clark asked Roland how his new tenants, the Friedbergs, were doing.

Roland clucked, sucking his teeth. "Allen Friedberg is all right; he's no trouble at all. A reasonable man, a reasonable man. You wouldn't think the president of Metropolis Pictures would have time on his hands, would you? Busy man, right? And why not, he's pulling in several million a year, nothing to sneeze at. But do you know, he enjoys chess, and he even comes down to my suite once every few days to play a game with me? Now, chess is my game, and he's not a bad player, and I enjoy a good game. Friedberg always compliments me on my game — I was chess champion when I was a youngster, you know, tournaments, world tours, the whole bit. There's no money in it, though. Frankly, I think Allen Friedberg plays chess with me so often just to get away from Bambi."

"His wife?" asked Clark.

"She's a difficult woman. Not much to look at either. I hate fat women. Actually, I hate fat men, too." Roland laughed. "Listen to me! You must think I'm a case!"

Clark found Roland charming in a rather deliberate, talkative way, and he liked Roland's sense of humor. Roland went on to tell him that he thought Bambi Friedberg was loony, that she didn't make sense when she talked, but worse, she had no taste and she was cheap.

"She's having a party tonight, right? And it's no ordinary bash. This is a black-tie extravaganza for Who's Who in show biz. And you know Allen Friedberg knows how to put on a show. He knows how to impress people. So they're having a party in the best hotel in New York City. So far, so good, right? This hotel also has three of the best restaurants in New York, all five-star restaurants, which is one of the reasons, besides the fabulous views, that people want to live here."

Clark felt as if he was being sold the hotel again.

Roland continued, "But does Bambi Friedberg want the Ritz Plaza Restaurant to handle her catering? NO! She doesn't even want to use our waiters. She's having a self-service bar! Is that chintzy, or what? I'm telling you, Bambi Friedberg could have caviar, lobster salad, and prime rib from the Ritz Plaza, and she's serving whitefish and crackers from the deli on Sixth Avenue!"

When they had finished their tea, Roland gave Clark the hotel tour, keeping up his energetic patter the whole while. Every now and then, Roland would look searchingly at Clark for encouragement, but he really didn't need a partner to have a conversation.

Apparently, Roland Lee's last decorator, at the Bel Vista, his Los Angeles hotel, had taken terrible advantage of Roland. Roland had paid for quality goods and received cheap imitations. The job had been completed well over budget and behind schedule, and even the painters the decorator had recommended had done a sloppy job, using inferior paint.

Clark felt that Roland was fishing for complete reassurance that Deirdre Dawn & Company would not take advantage of him. Clark knew that D.D.'s reputation stood for itself. Instead, he questioned Roland about how his affairs with the decorator had gotten so out of hand, and Roland showered him with the details of a complicated legal battle which was still underway. Roland complained that the dark paint colors used on the walls were smudgy. The decorator had apparently specified waterbased paints instead of oil.

Clark made copious notes as he looked about at the hotel's

public space decor. The Palm Garden definitely needed an uplifting and Clark thought how nice Victorian wicker settees and oval-back chairs would look in the setting to replace the rather English-y restaurant chairs now being used. Clark liked fanciful things, and he hoped Roland would like them, too. For upholstery on the settees, Clark envisioned a soft apple-green, cream, and rose stripe, and on the oval-back chairs, maybe a chintz of pink roses entwined with green leaves and sky-blue ribbons on a palm-green background. Light backgrounds were never practical for hotel decor.

Also, Clark planned to suggest that the Palm Garden ceiling be returned to its former palace splendor. The Palace Hotel in San Francisco had always intrigued Clark, and bringing that look to the Ritz Plaza would constantly bring in oohs and ahhs. But would Roland Lee want to spend the money? Clark kept silent, not wishing to frighten away a prospective client when the contract wasn't signed.

As Clark and Roland walked about the property, Clark noted that the hotel boutique needed work, particularly on the facade, and the elevators needed a regilding of the bronzework. No modern Formica panels for the Ritz Plaza, never, despite that name hotels were going for everything plastic. The plastic look was definitely not a Deirdre Dawn recommendation. Deirdre hated plastic flowers, those that Pamela Raven liked. Clark thought about Pamela as he walked around, hoping one day he could convince her, too, that plastic flowers would never do.

Clark told Roland that he would talk to Paul Hedges and Deirdre Dawn about the Ritz Plaza, and that they would get back to Roland within the week with a letter of agreement and a preliminary budget. Roland let Clark know that he was talking with other design firms and that he was taking bids from the competition. He wanted the best deal. Clark found this annoying, not because the practice was unusual, but because of the extra pressure Roland was applying. Clark did not like to be rushed when there was no need. And in fact, if Deirdre Dawn had anything to say about it, and she would, Deirdre Dawn & Company would probably change the Ritz Plaza very little. Except for the Palm Garden ceiling dome, no architectural changes would be suggested, and the corridor lighting needed upgrading. Perhaps new crystal baskets would do the trick.

After all, Deirdre Dawn herself had designed the original Ritz Plaza in 1932. Another designer had been hired in the fifties, and she had added a few incongruous glitzy touches, which would have to go, but on the whole what the Ritz Plaza needed was a face-lift: fresh paint, new punched-up color in the upholstery, new window treatments, and a few new good pieces. Deirdre would probably want to change the carpeting in the bedroom corridors as well. The room Clark was really excited about redoing was the bar. He fancied a Hunt Bar, which he knew would appeal to Roland Lee's taste

CHAPTER 5

The rain was pouring down in sheets out of a black sky when Clark stepped out of the Ritz Plaza doorway. There was a long line of hotel guests waiting for cabs, which the doormen were hailing with their whistles, so Clark decided to dash across Central Park West and try his luck on the northeast side of Columbus Circle. As soon as he left the safety of the Ritz Plaza awning, he was drenched to the skin. He could not even see through the buckets of rain, and he was so suddenly and comically wet that it felt good and he almost laughed. Then the chill shuddered through his body and he ran across the street to grab the first available taxi.

Once he was home, Clark had only a few minutes to change into his tuxedo and comb his hair. He hoped the rain would lighten before he tried to get another cab because it was the kind of torrential rain that umbrellas are useless against, and he did not wish to arrive at the Friedbergs' house looking like a wet penguin. Fortunately, that sort of downpour does not usually last very long, and it had slowed to a manageable shower by the time Clark emerged, waterproof plastic design plan case in hand, ready for the party.

The music of a live jazz band filled the little foyer as the Ritz Plaza elevator door opened on the Penthouse floor. The tune created a fantasy in Clark's mind that on the other side of the door marked "Penthouse A" was a Hollywood party of the nineteen-twenties, perhaps in an imported Chinese Den full of Vaseline-haired zoot-suiters and kohl-eyed Jazz Babies doing the shimmy and defying the Eighteenth Amendment.

A butler opened the door to Clark's ring, took his raincoat, and led him through a foyer to a place where the floor dropped dramatically away. A long marble balcony hung above a sweeping ballroom, giving Clark a magnificent view of a sea of heads bobbing through acres of crystal and gilt under an arched, all-glass ceiling. Towering potted palms completed the

The Decorator

Babylonian spectacle. A roar of voices rose up and enfolded Clark as he descended a marble staircase from the balcony to the floor below. Several different voices were distinguishable above the din, drawing Clark's attention to their owners: the self-amused meowings of chorus boys, the clipped, finishing-school consonants of silver-haired women in black and pearls, the hoarse, throaty voices of badger-faced men in black tie, and the high-pitched giggle of a new starlet whom Clark recognized immediately, but above them all rose Pamela Raven's silvery alto.

"Clark, darling! You've arrived at last!"

With her face upturned toward Clark, Pamela Raven looked like a Greek muse, so clear and sculptural was her beauty: there was the broad patrician brow, haughty arched eyebrows, sensitive painted mouth, and luminous, glowing eyes. Before Clark stepped into her embrace, he admired Pamela's black satin cocktail suit and diamond earrings. A small diamond pin lit her reddish hair, which was swept into a woven chignon.

"Clark, meet my favorite ogre, Allen Friedberg! Allen, this is Clark Calloway," Pamela wrapped her arm around a tall, redhaired gentleman's waist, and squeezed. She stage-whispered to Clark, "In the old days, you had to stand in line just to hate him, and just think, here he is, Allen Friedberg, waiting only for you! Oh, Allen! You naughty boy!"

Apparently Allen Friedberg had pinched Pamela Raven with his left hand while he offered Clark his right.

"Welcome to the land of the Heavenly Bodies, Mr. Calloway! Help yourself to a drink at the bar, and I'll introduce you to some of these other old fogies."

"Oh, you will not!" cried Pamela Raven. "How *dare* you steal my date, Allen? As if stealing my decorator isn't bad enough! Allen, Clark has been good enough to bring his decorating plans for my new apartment with him. We must all sneak away from this brawl and admire them!"

"Yes, we must, indeed," agreed Allen. "And my wife will give you a tour of this mess, Clark, if I can ever find her. But don't listen to a word she says about keeping all the old junk that she has cluttering up the place. I want you to talk her into getting rid of it!"

Allen was right. Up close, the ballroom that had seemed so spacious from above looked like a warehouse of art and antiques, good and bad, all jumbled together. Cheap lucite-covered family photograph collages vied for space with grotesquely ornate gilt-framed paintings of various periods and in a dizzying variety of styles. There was too much drapery; none of it matched, and there wasn't a square corner or bare patch of wall visible anywhere. Even the furniture was draped; the room was lined with the kind of low couches and chairs that were so soft and deep that once one sat in them, it was nearly impossible to get up again.

"Allen, you'll have to excuse us," said Pamela. "But there's Lenny."

She dragged Clark along, whispering in his ear, "I have to talk to Lenny Mills so he doesn't feel left out. He's my agent, and he never gets me anything interesting to do in pictures any more, but he and his boys have been wonderful to me, and I don't want to hurt his feelings. You know, I told Lenny not to call me unless he has a script that will really challenge me, and I think he's been afraid to call me ever since!"

Clark could not believe he was about to meet Lenny Mills. Mills was the president of TMI, Talent Management Incorporated, the largest and most powerful talent agency in the country. In fact, TMI had recently purchased Metropolis Pictures, so, in effect, Allen Friedberg worked for Lenny Mills.

Lenny Mills looked like a typical theatrical agent, and in fact he had defined the style: dark suit, thin tie, white Sulka shirt, and an air of somber dignity. He was a little, balding man, with thin, dry lips, and he was deep in discussion with a tall, lanky gentleman who could only be Thom Pearson, the network president. Clark would have recognized the handsome man with the mane of silver hair anywhere, and as he and Pamela drew closer, Clark heard Thom Pearson's distinct Princeton accent.

"Yes, it is too bad, about Tiffany's, a dreadful flop as a film, as so often happens with good books, and I doubt they'll do much better with it as a play," said Pearson.

"Well, Thom, you know I never read books," said Mills. "My idea of relaxation is a night reviewing corporate tax structures — hey, if it isn't my favorite Goddess!"

"Are you guys making enough money off me yet?" teased Pamela. "Clark, I want you to meet these two old flesh peddlers! TMI just bought the Metropolis film library and now Lenny's selling my old movies to Thom for TV! What a racket! And I'm not getting residuals!"

Pamela Raven made the introductions and Clark's intimidation evaporated a little at Pearson's warm reception. It was hard for Clark not to be slightly in awe of the man who owned the biggest television network in the world. Pearson was unchallengeable, even by Washington regulation, as he had hired former FCC men, including Clark's friend Dannee Lou's husband, Steve Baker, as consultants. Pearson, a man of impeccable taste, represented the invisible Madison Avenue force that had swallowed local television stations by completely conceding to sponsors. This cultured, sophisticated man, a proper New England fellow who probably wore linen underwear, was responsible for the low level of taste in television programming. It was also hard for Clark to ignore the impulse to put in a good word for Reggie, though he knew it would be socially suspect, and he doubted that Thom Pearson would remember one person out of the thousands of entry-level employees in his offices.

Thom Pearson rescued Clark with his legendary charm.

"So, you're the Clark Calloway I've heard so much about! You know, you oughtn't to let it get to you when people comment on your age. Or, I should say, your youth! Let me tell you something: I bought my first radio station when I was twenty-one years old. When I tried to go to my office, the first day, the office boy wouldn't let me in! He didn't believe I was old enough to be president of the company!"

"Mr. Mills! Hey, Mr. Mills!"

Thom Pearson and Pamela Raven looked over in annoyance at a redheaded man who was pulling on Lenny Mills' coat sleeve. It was Roland Lee, and he had a chorus girl on one arm. He was nearly yanking the young woman off her high heels in his desperation to speak with Lenny Mills.

"What is it?" asked Mills gruffly. "Make it quick!"

Clark caught the gist of Lee's fast-paced patter as he continued his conversation with Pearson. It seemed Roland was having problems with the bands booked for his hotels through

TMI, and he was demanding replacements.

"How rude," said Pamela, loudly. "Poor Lenny shouldn't have to listen to this at a party. Why can't little pissants like that learn some manners? And look at that hooker with him! Who let these people in?"

"I'm afraid he owns this hotel," said Clark, and Thom Pearson had a good laugh.

Clark listened with interest as Pamela and Pearson discussed the popularity of Pearson's new quiz shows. Pearson said that one show in particular was so popular that the Las Vegas casinos emptied out on the nights it was broadcast, and he asked Pamela Raven if Cosmetique would be interested in sponsoring the show.

"Well, you know I would love to say yes, Thom," said Pamela. "Only it's Cosmeco now, and with the name change, which they didn't consult me about — you know I can't abide that Roger Kirkeby, and he feels the same way about me! — and with the move of the corporate headquarters to Pennsylvania, there have been all these changes, and Kirkeby's always screaming that I have to go through 'channels'!"

She paused, thinking. One satin-gloved finger tapped her lip.

"You know what? Fuck him! I'd love to sponsor your show! Let Kirkeby be pissed off in Pittsburgh! But make sure the show is clean, Thom! You know I won't back a fixed show."

Pamela was referring to the recent quiz show scandals in which it had been revealed that celebrity guests, and the more appealing contestants, had been given the correct answers in advance, and had even been coached on which wrong answers to give, to make the game appear realistic.

"Oh, no, heavens no, Miss Raven," said Pearson. "The people responsible for that little mix-up are no longer working for my network. And we certainly won't misuse our advertising dollars. Those days are, thankfully, over."

"Glad to hear it, Thom," said Pamela. "And you know I'll break my ass for you. I just want you to do me one small favor. Have my girl Holly on the show as a celebrity contestant! You will, won't you! She's such a bright girl, and she looks so beautiful on television!"

"That she does. Her show is doing wonderfully on Tuesday

nights," said Pearson. "Consider it done."

There was a small commotion as a bulky, blonde-rinsed woman in blue satin escorted Roland Lee away from Lenny Mills by the elbow. She hissed a stream of expletives into his ear that made even Pamela blush.

"Who is that?" asked Clark.

"Mrs. Mills," chuckled Pearson. "Wife and bodyguard. Come on, Lenny, let's get a fresh one! So nice to make your acquaintance, Clark. And my dear lady!"

With a little bow, Thom Pearson was off into the crowd.

"Let's do tell Holly the good news!" said Pamela. "Where is she? Oh, no, it's the Happy Couple," Pamela groaned. "Here they come!"

It was the Friedbergs, Allen and Bambi.

"Ooooh, Pamela! Hi!" squealed Bambi.

"I got good news for you, Pam!" said Allen. "I got a part for you!"

"In what picture?" asked Pamela, ignoring Bambi's hello.

"Low budget. Horror. No, no, before you get mad — it's a great little picture. Starring you and Adela Morgan! You'll love this part: you get to be blind, a blind murderess!"

"Do I get to murder Adela?" asked Pamela.

"No, no nothing like that. Isn't she a kidder? I love this kid!"

"What did she say?" whined Bambi. "I didn't hear her!"

"Who's directing?" asked Pamela.

"Barney," said Allen.

At last, Pamela's face relaxed. "Costumes?" she asked.

"Whoever you want — Edith Head, Adrian — anyone you want, baby, just say you'll do it!"

"I don't know," said Pamela. "I can't believe Adela agreed to this. I'll have to think about it."

"I'll send the script over tomorrow, Pammy. You'll love it, that's a promise!"

A willowy blonde with a very short pixie haircut interrupted Allen Friedberg. "Pamela Raven? Doreen Flower. I'm sure you've read my column, 'Starlite.' And I hear you're going to be my new neighbor. I'd like to officially welcome you to the building." She stuck out her hand. "So, how does it feel to be the Last Movie Queen?"

Pamela Raven waved away the hand. "I'm no queen," she snapped. "I started in the chorus line, and with hard work and a few good breaks, I became, I hope, an actress. Come get me a drink, Allen, this conversation is degenerating. Clark, I'm sure Bambi here has a few matters to discuss with you! Have fun!"

With a broad mocking grin, Pamela Raven disappeared, taking Allen Friedberg with her.

Clark looked down at his new companion. She was staring up at him expectantly.

"I'm Bambi. So pleased to meet you!"

Bambi had a strong Long Island accent, and when she squeezed Clark's hand he noticed that her hand was as plump and soft as a baby's. Bambi was about five feet tall as as fat as one of her overstuffed chairs. She was draped in shimmering mauve crepe layers of an indefinite shape, but the gown was not unflattering, and Clark could see that Bambi had once been cute, if not beautiful. Her voice was terrible, though, nasal and shrill.

"Oooh, Clark, let me show you my babies!"

Bambi dragged Clark by the hand out of the ballroom and down a hall to a large kitchen where two white Irish wolfhounds reclined on the floor. The dogs both had jeweled collars.

"This is Missy and this is Snowy! Aren't they beautiful?"

Clark admitted that the dogs were, indeed, beautiful, and he listened to Bambi's description of their personalities, likes and dislikes, and illnesses. By the time Bambi opened the refrigerator door to show Clark what Missy and Snowy liked best to eat, he was wondering when the evening would ever end. He noticed, with annoyance, that every item in the Friedberg refrigerator was labeled and dated.

As Bambi led Clark through the penthouse and its four master bedrooms with a sunken tub in each bath, Clark examined the arches, drapery, sconces, and crowded paintings without comment. he really had no time to comment, as Bambi told him the stories behind each sentimental object she stopped to fondle. She told him the names of all the people and animals in each family and pet portrait, and the places where she and Allen has purchased each displayed souvenir.

"I just love to travel, don't you?" Bambi stopped at a pic-

The Decorator

ture frame enclosing pressed flower petals. "These are the roses Allie gave me on our honeymoon in Paris. It was so romantic! We used to go places all the time, and we don't travel together so much any more, except we do go sailing. I adore sailing, don't you? What sign are you? I'm a Pisces and Allie is a Capricorn, wouldn't you know it?"

The chatter continued into their bedroom where Bambi threw open the closet doors and asked Clark if he couldn't design her some closets with more space. In the closet hung racks of Bambi's gauzy, unfinished-looking dresses, but the main crowding problem was caused by the shelves of shoes, hundreds of them, all in plastic boxes and labeled with prices and places and dates of purchase, just like the items in Bambi's refrigerator.

Another walk-in closet contained racks of Allen's heavy conservative-cut suits, all in shades of grey and black. His shoes were all of good English leather and lined up in neat rows. Clark thought the closets expressed the extremely different personalities of their owners perfectly.

As Clark looked over the apartment, it was easy to tell, at a glance, which items belonged to Allen Friedberg. The framed law degrees, army commendation medals, and motion picture and philanthropic awards, were, of course, Allen's, and Clark guessed that Allen was also the reader of the few history books and biographies in the bookcases, while the hundreds of romance, travel, and astrology books must belong to Bambi. There were also many photographs of the same two children, at various ages, covering the walls and every available surface.

"Sam and Julie, Sam and Julie," Bambi crooned every few minutes. She obviously loved her children very much, and was quite proud of them. She did not hesitate to tell Clark all about Sam and Julie's careers, spouses, children and pets. She told Clark that she had never had the heart to discipline her children, that she had always cried when they did, but that Allen was very strict; Allen had insisted that his children have the best educations, and that they did their homework. Bambi said she was no good at that kind of thing because she had never even graduated from high school, but she told Clark that she was a good mother because she was a good listener. Clark wondered when Bambi Friedberg ever had time to listen.

On their way back to the party, Bambi showed Clark the photographs of her parents, particularly her father, a diamond dealer. She told him that she and Allen had grown up together on Long Island, and that when Allen came back from the war, he had married his "little girl next door." Clark had to admit that in the Friedberg's wedding portrait Bambi did look dimpled and cute, if already a little chubby.

"Don't think I was so innocent!" Bambi winked at Clark. "I had my fun, and I still do. What Allen doesn't know won't hurt him!"

She linked her arm through Clark's elbow and squeezed him.

"I'm sure you do," said Clark, dreading the turn the conversation had taken. He was relieved when they returned to the party where Allen and Pamela intercepted them and summoned him to a small conference room a few doors from the ballroom to look at Clark's design plans for Pamela's apartment.

Afterwards, Allen invited Clark out on the balcony for a smoke. Clark declined the cigar Allen offered, but he enjoyed the nighttime view of Central Park with its twinkling lanterns. He was glad it had stopped raining, and the air was fresh.

Allen Friedberg was not a bad-looking man, and he had the relaxed, self-assurance of a rich man who is accustomed to getting what he wants. His curly, rust-colored hair was partly silver and his face was deeply lined from too many years in the California sun, but he was still slender, and his tuxedo fit him well.

Allen lit his cigar and stared out across the park.

"It's not Malibu, but it'll do. God, I hate this weather. This is why I left the East Coast in the first place. So, you got a star client, Sonny Boy. And she *is* a star, let me tell you. She's five foot four, but she looks six feet on the screen. In a two-shot with anyone, even Gabe Taylor, she's the only one you watch. She's got no great range as an actress, but within that range — whew! — no one can beat her. That's because the kid's got heart. And guts. She always said Gabe was good because he had balls, but, boy, she's got 'em, too."

"That's true," said Clark. "I wonder why she never married Gabe Taylor."

Allen glared at him. "Are you for real? You mean you don't know? Well, I guess a lot of people don't know. They believe what they read in the gossip columns. Everyone thought those two were in love, like in the movies. Love? It wasn't love, it was sex, but it was sex like you've never seen in your life. Or smelled. It was a volcano kind of thing, those two sneaking around behind the sets. It scared everybody out of their wits. Especially Abie. Because they were married to other people. We had *morality* affecting the box office in those days. HA! Those days are over!"

"They certainly are," said Clark.

"You bet your ass. There was none of that 'I Am Curious Green, Purple, Orange!' The way it worked was, Abie calls Gabe into his office one day. He shows Gabe a head shot of Pamela Raven. 'See this face?' he says. 'Well, forget it!' And Gabe did."

"Just like that?" asked Clark.

"I guess Gabe didn't want to go back to being a waiter. They were all replaceable, and he knew it. Abie used to call the actresses 'the meat' and the actors, he called them 'serfs.' What a character. Anyway, Pam got over it. She's not the romantic type. The only thing she melts for is the camera. Bet lover-boy never saw that side of her."

Clark wondered if Pamela had gotten over it. He thought Allen sounded a little bitter about, if not jealous of, Gabe Taylor. Clark hadn't missed Allen's dreamy expression whenever Pamela Raven touched him or spoke to him.

"Well, it's wonderful that you've found a picture of her," said Clark.

"Yeah, you don't know how hard it was. She's not exactly an ingenue, not that she ever was that type, but that kid's on fire. She's got a fire inside of her and it gets hotter the closer the camera gets. Now, the daughter, the niece, whatever, that's another story."

"You mean Holly?" asked Clark.

"Yeah, Holly," sighed Friedberg. "Holly, Holly, Holly. Pamela's always on my back to get Holly in pictures, but that kid ain't got it. She's too — nuthin'. You know what I mean? She's okay for TV, but … forget it."

Allen started to laugh, and choked on his cigar. He slapped

Clark on the back.

"Time for Round Two," he said. "The girls are waiting," and he led Clark back to the party.

The girls were waiting. They flocked to Allen as soon as he re-entered the room, and Clark saw Bambi scowl as she watched the young women play with Allen's hair, finger his lapel, and whisper in his ear. Bambi soon rushed over to show Allen the housewarming gift Pamela Raven has brought, six platinum picture frames, extra-large. The actresses fell back for a moment, with condescending, pasted-on smiles for Bambi on their faces, but they hovered, ready to close in again when her show-and-tell was over.

Clark noticed Holly sitting on the stairs with her arm around the shoulder of a buxom, big-lipped brunette actress whom he yearned for every time he watched one of her films.

Holly was surrounded by young people who seemed to know each other well. Clark joined the group and caught Holly's eye.

"Hi, Clark!" said Holly. "Hey, guys, this is Clark Calloway!"

She made introductions all around and when she got to the actress in the white-sequined dress, whom she was obviously comforting, she said, "Anne's kind of upset right now!"

"Kind of upset!" said Anne. "I'm very upset, and so would you be, if you came here with Lew Fine!"

"Who's Lew Fine?" asked Clark.

"He's my agent," said Holly. "And Anne's boyfriend."

"Not for long," said Anne, tossing back her shining hair and swallowing her drink. "He's been on the phone all night!"

Clark looked in the direction of Anne's glare, and saw a dapper little man who was, indeed, on the telephone.

"That's all he does!" Anne groaned. "We went up to his country place in New Hampshire last weekend — 'Just the two of us, honey! We'll spend some time together,'" she mocked. "Ha! What does he do but drive down to this dinky gas station every hour to call his office, just for the hell of it! Remind me never to go out with another agent."

Clark didn't care what Anne was saying; she was so beautiful, he could have listened to her recite catechism all night, and he hoped he might get the chance.

"I never talk on the phone," he said.

Anne snapped, "What do you use, carrier pigeon?" but she shot him an interested glance, and when Clark offered to get her a fresh drink, she smiled at him, a wicked smile that made his heart soar.

Laughter from the group made Clark remember where he was.

"They're making fun of me," Holly mock-pouted. One of the guys told Clark that they had all grown up with Holly at the studio, that they were all kids from picture families, sons and daughters of electricians and makeup people and so on, who had all played on the lot while their parents worked. Anne had been one of the kids who had tested well for the screen, and she was still working. He explained that they always joked around with Holly and her sister because Pamela Raven made them wear white gloves, even when they were playing.

"Your sister?" asked Clark.

Holly shook her head as if to say, "not now," and Anne thrust her empty glass at Clark.

"Champagne," she said slowly, "and anything else you got."

Jubilant, Clark accepted Anne's glass and was making his way to the bar when Pamela Raven grabbed him by the arm.

"I want you to escort Holly home," she whispered.

"But—" said Clark.

"All. The. Way. Home." Pamela gave Clark a very pointed look, leaving no doubt as to what she meant.

"Sure," said Clark. "I was just going to..." he gestured with Anne's glass.

"Now!" said Pamela.

At that moment, Doreen Flower accosted Pamela again. She stood too close to Pamela, and she leaned dangerously, as if she might topple over and crush the smaller woman. In an instinctively protective gesture, Clark put his arm around Pamela.

"Pamela, I need you to help me settle a wager. Is it true that Lucien Irons left you with nothing but his debts?" asked Doreen.

Pamela looked at Clark as if to say, "Who is this idiot?" but she smiled tightly and answered Doreen. "No, my dear. There's not a word of truth to that. Lucien was the greatest lover I ever had, and that's all I'm going to say about him."

"Tell me," said Doreen, "do you miss the old glamour girl days of Hollywood? You know, when you were still getting good parts?"

Clark could feel the angry heat rise from Pamela as she stared at Doreen. "First of all, I do not live in the past. Secondly, this is a private party." She raised her voice. "Who invited this woman? Allen did not inform me that he had invited the press, and if you cannot behave yourself, I will see to it that you are never invited here again!"

Pamela snatched Clark's arm and whirled around, away from Doreen. She strode quickly through the crowd, with Clark in tow.

"The young ones are so rude these days!" she snapped. "So badly brought up! And *that* one is digging her own grave with that dress. *No one* is interested in her knees, much less her thighs. It's revolting, really."

Pamela sighed. "Oh, well, I suppose she needs the publicity, and if she thinks she can get it by trashing me, I feel sorry for the wretched skinny thing!"

As they drew nearer to Holly and her friends, Pamela whispered in Clark's ear. "There's another one to stay away from — that Anne What's-her-name! She's unkempt! Spoiled! Always late on the set, I hear. And absolutely no morals. Who wants to see her ass on the screen? All that nudity is boring! Seen one ass, you've seen 'em all! All these young actors go to head-shrinkers these days, and what they really need is a kick in the pants."

Pamela slowed her pace and smiled sweetly as they approached Holly. "Holly, dear! Clark has offered to escort you home. Isn't that nice? I know you have an early call tomorrow and it's so sweet of Clark to offer!"

Holly looked surprised, but she shrugged and smiled at Clark. "Okay, I guess. Let's go. 'Bye, you guys!"

Anne was deep in conversation, and clearly amused by a young man who seemed to be doing a cruel impression of someone they knew, but she did give Clark an appraisingly raised eyebrow as she waved good-bye to him with her fingertips.

CHAPTER 6

The Friedbergs' butler presented Holly and Clark with their coats and umbrellas and Clark helped Holly into her brown Country Coat.

"Are you hungry?" asked Clark.

"No, I'm not, thank you," said Holly. "I could be convinced to have a drink somewhere! That is, if you'd like a nightcap, too."

"Marvelous idea," said Clark. "How about the Ritz Plaza bar?"

"No," said Holly, "I prefer to get far away from this place, if you don't mind."

"I've got it," said Clark. "I know a cozy little bistro in the Village. It's a great bar."

"Not that far out." Holly laughed nervously. "Would you mind terribly just stopping in at Trader Vic's? Of course, if you don't want to — it's just that it's so near by, and I really don't feel like seeing anyone I know tonight. Anyone else, I mean. I hope you don't think I'm a bore, but I've had quite enough of the 'Scene' for one evening. Besides, I don't want to hear any of those tatty folk singers."

She shuddered. "Joan Baez is not one of my favorites."

"What, no 'Shoofly, Baby' for you? C'mon, I know you're hiding a tambourine somewhere in that coat!"

When she didn't smile, he just said, "Trader Vic's it is," and gave Holly his brightest grin. He offered his arm protectively as they left the hotel lobby. Holly stumbled against Clark as she took his arm, and he realized that her stilted, overly polite manner of speech was an attempt to conceal how much she'd had to drink. Clark had the feeling that Holly, like Pamela, had to be in control, but that she wanted her escorts to appear to be in the traditional masculine lead. He was not fond of Trader Vic's, with its tacky giant tikis and batik prints used together. He thought of the bar as a place that served dried-up puu puu platters for tourists, but it was close by. Holly was admirably practical.

When they were settled in a booth, and had ordered stingers on the rocks, Holly lit a Parliament cigarette.

"Now, tell me about this mystery sister of yours," said Clark.

"Oh, it's no mystery, really," said Holly. "Actually, there are thousands of publicity shots of us with Auntie moldering away in some Hollywood historian's files, I suppose. Frieda and I always smiled and performed our best curtseys for the photographers, but away from the cameras, it wasn't so happy."

Holly stared at herself in the mirror over their table and started to rearrange her hair. She made a wry face and turned away from the mirror. "I give up. We were cute back then, I guess. Especially Frieda. But, yes, even I was cute," she said bitterly.

Clark studied Holly. She was attired in a formal gown, a glittery sheath of stretch material in pink and silver with large, pink-sequined daisies. The gown was loose-fitting and not revealing in any way. It must have taken her hairdresser hours to style Holly's hair, he observed. Shiny bangs and perfectly curling side pieces were shellacked in place beneath an enormous bubble of a bouffant. A blonde fall had been braided and twisted and sprayed to hold the flossy mountain of hair aloft, and pink and silver metallic ribbons dangled from the bouffant. No amount of makeup could hide Holly's almost albino coloring, bad skin, and bumpy nose. Clark deplored the current style of drawing women's eyebrows on in a single pencil line, and on Holly's bald brows, it looked particularly false. He noticed that she already had fine lines at the sides of her mouth. The mouth was okay, though, and he especially liked her lips.

"No, I wouldn't say you were cute," he teased, but her frown made him add, "Cute is for kids and bunnies. You're a glamorous sexy woman."

Holly fidgeted with her bar napkin, and ignored the compliment, but she stopped frowning. She continued her story, talking quickly.

"Frieda and I were Hollywood princesses. We had our own topiary maze, pet monkeys, ponies, and servants. We were pretty spoiled, I guess. You know, the clothes, trips, and presents that come along with being the children of a movie star. But what no one knew was that when Auntie was drunk, or between boyfriends, or both, she used to beat us for the littlest things — usually because our rooms weren't neat enough, or we had gotten stains on our clothing. It was impossible to please her. She was an irrational bitch. Frieda got the worst of it because she kept running away. She never got very far. You know, Auntie dressed us as twins, although Frieda was a year younger than I."

"So, Pamela Raven was pretty strict," said Clark lightly. "So was my mother. And my grandfather. I suppose a lot of folks were in those days before Doctor Spock. 'Spare the rod...' and all that. Still, it must have been better to have a sister to help you through it. My sister Vera and I —"

Holly interrupted him. "You don't get it, do you? That's all right, no one gets it — how bad it was. I'm used to that. No one wants to believe anything bad about *Pamela Raven*, their all-American movie star. Pamela Raven, who was so good and self-sacrificing to take in her brother's two little waifs after he was shipped off to the funny farm! Well, Saint Pamela Raven sent my sister Frieda away to a convent school, as a punishment for running away, when she was only twelve years old. Frieda ran away from the convent when she was sixteen and she died of a barbiturate overdose on Hollywood Boulevard three months later. Of course, Pamela had it all hushed up in the press. Or she tried to, anyway."

"I'm so sorry, Holly," said Clark. "That's a terrible thing to have happened."

"Yes," sighed Holly. "But, you know, the worst thing is, I never really knew my sister. We were always sent to separate schools, always kept apart, and we were not allowed to really know each other. There wasn't enough of Auntie's love to go around, and of course, we couldn't *both* be in her favor at the same time. I think she enjoyed making us compete for her attention. And there were all the times we tattled on each other, to avoid getting punished for whatever it was. And you know what?" Holly lowered her voice to a whisper. "I feel just awful about this, but as much as I was terrified of being next, I was secretly glad when Frieda was being spanked, because, at least *that* time, it wasn't me."

Holly's eyes filled with tears, and Clark took her hand.

"Hey," he said. "I know how you feel. I bet all kids feel that way at times. My psychiatrist says it's perfectly natural, sibling rivalry, you know. You shouldn't blame yourself for that."

Holly sniffed. She tossed her head back in a breezy manner Clark recognized.

"I'm only telling you this for your own good. After all, *you're* working for her. You should know what kind of person she is. You can't just think it's so easy to please her, you know. Don't think that just because I was raised by her that I have a grudge — she treats everyone the same way: unfairly. Believe me, I was alone with that drunk most of my life, and she's not normal. Do you know — and you had better not tell *anyone* this — she used to make me sleep with her on certain nights, and she sometimes slept...well, *sans negligee*! I slept as far away from her on that bed as I could! My aunt is a lesbian because only a certain kind of woman will let her be a man — that's what I think!

"I want you to remember that there isn't enough you can do for Pamela Raven! And she never forgives what she calls an insult! You are punished forever! Remember this about your precious Pamela, before you get in too deep!"

"I wonder why she adopted children," said Clark.

"Why did she adopt us? Because we were cute when we were little? For the publicity? I've often wondered. You know what's really crazy? I found out about my sister's death on the radio. And Auntie didn't even allow me to go to her funeral." Holly finished her drink and Clark signaled the waitress for refills.

"Oh, let's not talk about *her* any more," said Holly. "I feel I've spent my whole life talking and thinking about *her*."

"Good grief, Charlie Brown," said Clark, borrowing one of Reggie's favorite expressions. He changed the subject. "Your friends seem very nice," he said.

"Pooh, don't let's be naive," said Holly. "One does not really have friends in this business. That 'friendliness' you saw is all show biz. I mean, well, *some* of them were my friends, Jackie, Bill, even Anne, but you know how people change. They drift apart."

She blew a line of smoke at Clark. "And if you think it bothers me, it doesn't. I've been alone most of my life, and I can handle it."

She finished her drink. "Let's make the next ones doubles, shall we? Did you see Mary Tyler Moore? She was there. And what ridiculous hair she has now! She was with Dick Van Dyke! I know you noticed Anne Bates. I saw you noticing *her*. No one could have missed that!"

Clark loved Mary Tyler Moore's delicate pixie face; he thought she was one of the most beautiful women in television, and he knew Reggie planned to imitate Miss Moore's new hair style, which featured the bubble cut curling out and back, rather than straight up. Miss Moore had achieved daring, yet sophisticated, new dimensions in hair that night, which he could not wait to report to Reggie.

He thought Holly probably meant to tease him about Anne, but her raised chin and pressed lips were a challenge. He could see he would have to watch out for Holly's jealousy.

"Oh, Anne, yes, she seems like a sweet girl. She's a 'type,' though, and quite ordinary up close. And that spooky mole on her chin! Isn't it a shame how some actresses lose their appeal off-screen? Wasn't she with —"

"Lew Fine. My agent, and hers. No wonder she gets offered all the good film roles and the best I can do is 'To Tell the Truth.' You're not her type, anyway!"

Holly finished her drink and stabbed viciously at the cherry in her empty glass with her straw. "Anne only goes out with guys who can help her career. That's how she got where she is."

Clark signaled the waitress for another round. He realized it would be difficult to bring any romance into this evening without more one hundred-proof help. As the double stingers arrived, he had a momentary flash of guilt. Reggie will understand, he told himself. Holly means nothing to me, but it's not every day that you can get intimate with a star client, or even the relative of one. Only a fool would let such an opportunity pass him by. And it wasn't as if Reggie was at home waiting by the phone for his call. The Lioness does not wait for her prey — she hunts it. She was probably out having fun. More fun than I am, Clark thought, as he gulped his drink.

Holly had been explaining some legal maneuver her agent wanted her to make, either to sell her television show as a corporation and pay a smaller capital gains tax, or take a share of the profits as a shareholder. She said Lew Fine called it giving an actor "an estate," and that Pamela Raven disagreed with the plan, for some reason that Clark couldn't follow, mainly because he hadn't been paying attention.

"Anyway, that's what *Anne* does — she does anything Lew tells her to do, and it's working well for her, though, frankly, I think Lew treats her more like an investment than a girlfriend. She's crazy if she thinks he's going to marry her."

"Well, so many actresses get ahead that way," said Clark. "And there's no guarantee that they'll last. But some," he whispered, looking meaningfully into Holly's eyes, "some have talent."

Holly's face relaxed. She even looked a little smug as she lit another cigarette. "The word is, our show will be nominated for an Enemy — I mean *Emmy* Award. Enemy? Can you believe I said that?"

She laughed, and so did Clark, genuinely pleased at the accidental play on words. "I suppose you do win enemies when you get an Emmy," he said.

"I have enough of those," said Holly.

"Well, that's good," said Clark. He felt the vodka blur through him, making his tongue fuzzy. Everything seemed warmer and brighter, including Holly. "What did my last fortune cookie say? Oh, yes! 'Judge a leader by the quality of his friends — judge a ruler by his enemas.' Did I say enemas?"

"Yes, you did!" Holly was laughing helplessly, gripping the edge of the table to hold herself up. "If enemies are what it takes, call me Cleopatra. Everyone thinks the only reason I get any work is because of my aunt."

She stared at Clark and her expression suddenly softened. Her cheeks were appealingly flushed from the vodka. "You have such fair hair. So smooth-looking. May I?"

Clark had not been expecting his date to become affectionate so soon, but Holly ran her fingers through his hair with a surprising intimacy and persistence.

"I'm so glad you don't wear it long, like so many men do these days," she said in an uncharacteristic whispery baby

The Decorator

voice. Clark wondered if she was doing a bad Marilyn Monroe imitation.

"I so much prefer a clean-cut look to those awful mop tops. You can't tell the boys from the girls. Why, just the other day, I saw a man with a pony tail, walking along Fifth Avenue! Can you imagine! I don't know *what* kind of girl would find that attractive."

Holly's eyes swam a bit, and her voice was beginning to slur.

"I hope you don't mind that I'm touching your hair. It's just that it's so soft ... Soft?" She giggled, and then looked embarrassed, and somewhat sad. She gazed wistfully at Clark. "It's been so long since ... oh, Steve, my ex-husband, was practically bald on top, and he was only twenty-six. Can you take me home now?"

Although Holly's hotel was only a few blocks away, Clark thought it a good idea to take a taxi, due to Holly's unsteady walk. He asked the driver to take them "once around the park," and Holly immediately cuddled up to Clark in the back seat. She put her head on his shoulder and leaned back to watch the bare treetops sail by, so it was an easy matter to kiss her. Clark loved kissing in cabs. It was one of the fantasies he had imagined he would experience when he came to New York. The cab driver helped things along by taking the turns on the curving park roads at a fantastic pace, which threw Clark and Holly into each other's laps. Clark took advantage of the violent ride, and managed to get one hand inside the bodice of Holly's gown, though she slapped his other hand when it crawled up her thigh.

She's still a little nervous, he thought, wondering whether to slow down or persist. He had learned that subtlety was the best approach with women, but not so much subtlety that they missed the pass. Clark liked the breast Holly let him feel, and when she crushed his lips with her open mouth, he knew she enjoyed him feeling it, too.

By the time the driver stopped at the Fillmore Hotel, Holly's bird cage of a hairdo had fallen over and was squashed onto one side of her head, and one of her false eyelashes was stuck to her cheek. She insisted on paying the driver, and when she caught a look at herself in the rear-view mirror, she shrieked and ran into the hotel lobby.

Clark followed cautiously. He found Holly by the elevator; she was peering into a hall mirror, trying to stick the eyelash back on.

"Oh, the hell with it," she said, and tossed the gummy black fringes into a cuspidor. "And these too!"

She pulled off the other half-moon of false lashes and threw them away, too. Clark hated the way false eyelash removal stretched women's eyelids grotesquely, and he hated the little crumbs of eyelash glue that remained on their lids. He couldn't wait until this particular fad went the way of the hula hoop.

"All right, I'll admit it, I'm square." Holly clearly misinterpreted Clark's look of shock when he saw her suite. After all, he hadn't expected pot posters and a revolving waterbed covered in purple fake fur: this *was* a suite at the Fillmore Hotel, and a rather dowdy suite at that, with decor straight out of a 1950's Howard Johnson's. What he wasn't prepared for was the mess. Nothing in Holly's straightlaced behavior could have led him to expect her to live in a room covered in discarded clothing and empty take-out containers.

The couch, covered in a scratchy-looking brown and orange woven upholstery, was strewn with crumpled dresses, skirts, sweaters, stockings, and panties, all of expensive materials, and mostly in browns, brown being a "Thing" that fall. Stacks of heavy fine art books and piles of plays were pushed against the walls and in a corner by the television was a sewing machine on a desk draped with tissue-paper patterns and fabric. More fabric and envelopes of patterns covered the floor and spilled out of boxes by the desk. There were no pictures and no personal ornaments, unless overflowing ashtrays could be counted as accessories. From what Clark could see through the open bathroom door, Holly treated her cosmetics in much the same manner, leaving all of them out in plain view.

"I know, I know, you're probably thinking of ways I should re-decorate," said Holly, talking around her cigarette. She was digging for something in her purse. "Don't worry about it — I won't be here long. Sit down, anywhere! I have some champagne in the fridge."

Clark looked for a place to sit and found none.

Holly laughed, "Look at you! You should see your face!

You look like a poor little lost prep school boy! You are so cute! Let me just move this stuff…" She grunted under an armload of clothing which she carried into the bedroom and dumped on the floor.

"You probably think I'm a slob, but I'm not! I'm really very neat, when I have time to be. It's just such a relief not to have to live with Auntie and her white glove treatment any more. Finally, I can relax!

"Aha!" said Clark, as he sat down on the couch. He grinned, thinking about what his analyst would say about "unconscious hostile behavior."

Holly kicked off her shoes and padded into her room. "I'll just be a minute!"

She came out with her hair down, wearing a voluminous white terrycloth hotel robe, belted securely across her waist. She handed Clark a dripping bottle of champagne from a tiny refrigerator behind a miniature bar, and plopped down on the couch next to him.

"Oh, there they are!" Holly found what she was looking for in her purse, a fat prescription bottle.

Clark popped the cork. "What are those, vitamins?" He poured the champagne. "Vitamins? They're more like rocket pills. I use them for extra pep when I'm working, but they come in handy whenever I'm feeling a bit tired.

Holly was sitting up rigidly, very far away from Clark on the couch, and he didn't have the desire to move any closer to her, so he turned on the television.

"Mind if I see if there's anything on?"

Holly said nothing, so Clark switched off the most glaring overhead lights, hoping the dim glow from the television and a small side lamp would make Holly, and himself, more comfortable. It certainly was a rocky night, he thought. He wondered if Holly would ever relax for more than a moment. She was much more attractive when she was relaxed, though the bulky terrycloth robe was doing nothing for him.

It was a black and white television set, and as he switched channels, they both noticed a familiar face flash by on the screen.

Holly gasped, "It's *her*! Go back!"

Clark turned back to the Late Movie on Channel Seven,

and it was an old Pamela Raven picture. They watched a young, smokily angry Pamela Raven throw a full cocktail glass at a young, dapper Gabe Taylor, just missing his head.

"Oh, turn it off, turn it off!" cried Holly. "It's a horror movie!"

"No, this is a love story," said Clark as he watched Gabe Taylor grab Pamela's arm to twist it behind her back. Taylor's hand was raised to strike the defiant Raven across her upturned face, but she whispered, "Darling," and they kissed, passionately.

"Change it," demanded Holly. "All her pictures are horror movies. She's not acting at all when she plays a bitch. That's how she really is! Oh, it gives me the chills! See, I'm all goose bumps. The only good thing about this picture is that she gets killed in the end. It's a great relief!"

Clark switched to another channel. It was a commercial for Libby's spin-cooked canned vegetables. "Dig our dizzy corn and peas!" sang the announcer. On the next channel was a map of Vietnam with red line graphics spreading out across the Pacific towards California. The anchorman was intoning "—Stop the spread of Communism—". Clark turned it off.

"Good," said Holly. "I don't want to watch the news. I was told if I voted for Goldwater, we'd be at war in six months. I did, and we are!"

Clark had heard the line before, but he laughed anyway. He turned on the radio, and spun the dial until he found a rock station. Gary Lewis was singing "I'm Down."

"Wanna dance?" asked Clark.

Holly tossed back some champagne straight from the bottle. "Fraid not. I'm no Shindigger."

"You mean you can't do the Hully Gully?" Clark demonstrated.

"No. Nor the Watusi, or the Frug either. I'm strictly a rhumba gal. Told you, I'm a square."

"Well, I'm sure we can find a cha-cha station!" Clark squatted down by the radio. Holly shook her head, so Clark left the dial on the rock station, which was playing Beatles songs.

When Holly suddenly jumped and started whisking clothes and garbage out of sight, Clark realized that her pep pills must have begun to work. She was also talking a mile a minute.

"Oh, that's where it went!" Holly blew the dust from a framed photograph she had found behind an end table. She handed it to Clark.

"That's my husband — my ex-husband — my, how soon we forget. With me, of course, and Auntie!" Pamela Raven was in the photo, squeezed between Holly and Steve. She had her arms around both of them, and her trademark flashing smile looked genuine. Holly and Steve were smiling as well. He couldn't tell where the picture was taken, but it was outdoors, perhaps in Central Park, and they all wore fur coats.

"She seduced my husband, like she did all of my other boyfriends — I don't mean she slept with him, or the others, of course, but she seduced him with her charm, and she took all of his attention whenever we went out. Oh, how she wined and dined Steve, and introduced him to all of her famous friends. It was a big deal to him, because he was just a way-off-Broadway stage manager, just out of college. I met him when we did this little play together, and now he's a big producer. That's what Auntie made him, and he wanted it. More than he wanted to be married to me, I guess." She finished the bottle of champagne, and lit another cigarette, though she already had one burning in an ashtray. She ran a carpet sweeper furiously across the rug.

"We got a divorce in Vegas. I lost fifteen pounds after that. You know, I keep losing weight. And I'm sick a lot, too, more than I used to be. I don't know why. Do I look thin to you?"

Clark said, no, she didn't look too thin at all. And of course it was hard to tell with the bathrobe on. He smiled slyly, which she ignored. He watched in awe as she vacuumed the inside of several paper shopping bags. When she dumped her checks out of their box and vacuumed the box, his mouth fell open.

"Loose hairs get in here, you know, and hairs make me sick. I'm worried that being sick so much is making the producers of my show nervous. I'm afraid I'll be replaced. You can't miss days in television. But I can't help it if I'm sick. They just have to change the script on those days, and I can tell the writers don't like it. The director told me it can't happen again. That's what I'm worried about. Of course, I get no sympathy. God forbid I get any sympathy from Aunt Pamela, who danced her way through an entire musical with a broken ankle in 1936! Oh, she never lets me forget that!"

"She's one tough lady," said Clark. He was amused at the lightning speed with which Holly cleaned, and amazed that the suite was actually starting to look better. The room seemed to be getting larger as Holly cleared away the debris.

"Let's not talk about her! I want to show you something!" Holly dashed into her bedroom with an armful of clothes. Clark watched as the clothes flew onto hangers and disappeared into an enormous closet. "I never want to talk about Aunt Pamela, though half the time I feel like I am her! See these clothes? Not *these*, the ones in the other closet."

Holly opened a second closet to reveal racks of designer suits, gowns, and furs, all swathed in plastic. Rows of sleek, European-made shoes nestled in shoe racks below.

"These are the clothes she gives me. I have to *become* her to attend all those awards shows and benefits and Cosmetique exhibitions. Do you think anybody notices?" She imitated Pamela Raven's haughty expression fairly well: chin up, shoulders back, and eyebrows raised. She collapsed in giggles on the bed.

"Is there any more champagne? Of course there is! Do be a sport and get the other bottle."

Clark did, and he filled a paper cup for Holly. He sat down on the bed next to her, but she jumped up.

"Do you notice anything different about *my* clothes? Here, I'll show you!"

She thrust a wool skirt into his hand and turned it inside out to show him the seams. "I sewed it myself. I learned to sew when I was a little girl. I had to. At first it was just mending, so I wouldn't get in trouble with Auntie if I tore my dress. Then I learned to make my own dresses when she sent me away to boarding school with hardly any clothes. She didn't want me to appear 'spoiled,' you see. I can sew anything, do tailoring, you name it."

Clark had an idea. He was losing hope that he could sweep Holly off her feet, unless he could get her to sit still.

"I've been admiring that sewing machine all night. I so admire people who can handle mechanical things. Never have the patience for it, myself. Do you think you can show me how

The Decorator

it works?

He watched, fascinated, as Holly explained the mysterious hooks and levers on her Singer. He especially loved the little trap door that slid back to reveal the bobbin. As Holly showed him how to thread the bobbin, he leaned forward and gently kissed her ear.

She froze, electrified by his touch, but at a loss as to how to respond. She stared stiffly ahead, clutching the bobbin.

"Per-perhaps I could make something for you," she stammered, "a shirt, or something. I could make you a shirt. I used to make all of Steve's..." She bit her lip, embarrassed.

"That would be nice," Clark whispered in her ear, making sure his lips brushed her ear, and that his hot breath warmed her neck. He leaned against the back of her chair and let his hands lightly stroke her shoulders.

"Why don't you measure me?" he suggested.

"Yes, I'll measure you." Holly scrambled to her feet and grabbed a tape measure from the desk top. Clark stood still and closed his eyes as Holly held the tape across his shoulders in back and then down his arms, muttering numbers. When she wrapped the tape across his chest, he pulled her close and kissed her. She dropped the tape and melted against his chest. He kissed her thoroughly, delighted by her pliant body in his arms. She let him pick her up and carry her into the bedroom.

Clark laid her on the newly-made bed, and slid her out of her robe. He knelt by the side of the bed and began kissing her stomach.

"Wait," she whispered.

"Do you need me to use something?" he asked.

"No, I'm on the Pill, but if we're going to do this, I have to take a shower."

"No, you don't," murmured Clark, kissing her neck. "I like the way you smell."

He moved his mouth down to her small breasts with their large, rosy nipples, but she wriggled away. Holly looked appalled.

"Of course I do. I'll only be a minute." She marched into the bathroom.

Clark groaned. This evening was torture, body and soul. While he waited, he took off his clothes and folded them in a neat pile on a chair. He was just adding his folded socks to the top of the pile when he heard Holly make a teeth-sucking sound of annoyance.

She stood in the bedroom doorway, wrapped in a towel, emanating a strong smell of lemon shampoo.

"What's wrong?" he asked.

She snorted. "Mr. Passion folds his socks! I didn't know you were a Boy Scout."

Clark growled and lifted Holly off her feet. He threw her on the bed and fell on top of her. "You little brat!" He slapped her tits playfully. "I'll show you something they don't teach in the Boy Scouts!"

He began to bite and scratch his way down her body, not roughly, but hard enough to show he meant business. When he got down to her waist, Holly's hands stopped his head.

"No," she said. "Don't do that. I never let anyone do that. I'll do … it for you, if that's what you want. And we have to turn out the light."

Clark declined Holly's offer by attempting to thrust himself into her, and finding her too dry, as he expected, he stumbled into the bathroom to find some Vaseline or lotion. When he got to the bathroom, the floor shifted and rose towards him, and he realized for the first time how drunk he was. He braced himself on a wall and the sink until the room stopped reeling. Clark caught a glimpse of himself in the bathroom mirror, and he looked positively demented, with a shock of hair fallen over one eye. He liked that. He liked the idea of being set up by a movie star to bang her little niece. So what if Holly didn't like oral sex and wanted to have sex in the dark? She probably tolerated only the missionary position, too. It didn't matter. In the dark, she could be anyone, Anne Bates, Sophia Loren, even Pamela Raven herself.

Clark climbed onto the woman in the dark and found her softly yielding. It wasn't enough to turn him on, so he focused on his own performance. He watched himself and tried to beat his own records, thinking, how fast can I fuck? How hard? His frustration with Holly made him ruthless, wilder than he'd ever been, and he was inspired to whisper to Holly what a bad girl she was, knowing she couldn't enjoy it unless she was "forced" to. She did yell and scratch his back, and he liked that,

The Decorator

but he worried that Reggie might see the marks, and he let himself come before Holly's nails could do any more damage.

Clark collapsed at Holly's side, breathing heavily, and she turned the light on so she could smoke and stroke his hair.

Was it really worthwhile? Clark wondered to himself. He heard Holly wash down some more speed with champagne, and he groaned, hoping he wouldn't have to perform again.

"What's wrong, wasn't I any good?" Holly meant to tease him, but her voice had an edge to it that set off his danger sensors. He knew he couldn't sleep here.

He kissed Holly, nuzzled her neck and sighed, "You were great, babe, but I have to go home. Gotta work tomorrow. I'll call you—"

Holly jumped up and flew out of the bed. She was trembling all over.

"Oh, so that's how it is! I should have known!" She threw a pillow at him and he winced. Holly grabbed her robe and wrapped herself quickly. She tied the sash with an angry snap. "Well, let me tell you something, Mister! You think you're so great that you can just fuck me and leave me here! Well, you're not so great. Your sexual technique is primitive, and immature, and — and *immoral*!"

"Sorry," said Clark. "I didn't know you were such a connoisseur. I'd love to stay, and I wish you wouldn't take it so personally, but I really must—"

"GO! Go, then!" Holly shouted. She threw his clothes at him and rushed out of the room. From the next room, Clark heard the sounds of ferocious cleaning. Papers were rattled and then torn and the toilet flushed again and again. Clark got dressed quickly, eager to get away from Holly Raven as fast as possible. As he stepped into the living room, he saw Holly shredding the boxes and papers that had littered her apartment and feeding them into the toilet.

"You can't be too careful," she snapped. "Stars can't throw anything in the trash, or the press will get ahold of it and use it to write their poison."

She grabbed a can of Zud from under the sink and dashed mounds of white powder onto her bathroom floor. She glared up at Clark. "You know all about those reporters! Don't think I don't know what you are. You're a nobody, a star fucker! I've seen your trashy type before! You're just using me to get to *her*!"

Clark just shook his head, a low whistle of disbelief escaping his lips. He let himself out.

The Decorator

CHAPTER 7

By seven o'clock, it was difficult to see the paintings through the crowd. The Winterspoon Gallery was full to capacity. Bartender and waiters were kept busy pouring champagne and serving the special hors d'oeuvres delivered by the Westbury Hotel. Clark had decorated the Westbury lobby a year before, and the manager, as a favor to Clark, had provided him with trays of crusty honeyed bacon, fresh shrimp, and lump crabmeat canapés. Reggie had enlisted CBS guides and pages as waiters for the opening, as these young aspiring actors were invariably good-looking and charming. Clark found them to be a bit too affected, but he knew they were crowd pleasers, especially popular with the older women.

The gallery assistants had their hands full taking coats and answering questions about the work. They were also engaged in sticking red dots on the labels of the paintings which had been sold, and Martin Winterspoon was pleased to witness each new red dot. The gallery owner hovered close to Clark from the start of the opening, especially when the photographers' bulbs were flashing. Martin had nothing but praise for Clark's appearance. He adored Clark's strawberry pink shirt with the gold bar collar pin and gold coin cuff links. And he thought Clark's English double-breasted suit was perfectly cut and very Savile Row on Clark's slim figure. Martin even dragged his morose partner over to show him the very narrow pin-stripe of Clark's suit.

"It's so elegant, so fab! Doesn't he look just like Prince Phillip? And look at his nails! He had his nails done!"

Winterspoon's partner, a lean, dapper man with chalk-white skin and a pencil-thin mustache, was always in a bad mood. "Really, Martin," he sneered, and walked away.

"Clark, I can't tell you how many of these artists show up for their openings with grubby nails and paint on their hands!"

Martin flashed a dirty look in the direction of two well-known painters who were examining Clark's 'Pink Lady Cocktail' painting with flattering amusement. As usual, they had scorned formal attire, though they did sport highly unusual ties, one an Op Art pattern, and the other looking as if it had been handpainted by Mondrian. The two artists were flanked by a bevy of celebrities so international that columnists often said they constituted their own country, though they did maintain substantial residences on the East Side. They had arrived with Deirdre Dawn.

Deirdre Dawn had come and gone as quickly as a summer storm on the Cape, and with as much drama and bluster. She swirled into the gallery at six in her black cashmere cloak, magenta satin hat, white gloves, and famous nine-millimeter pearls. She had blinked foggily at Pamela Raven and looked at each painting with her characteristic lack of focus, as if she wasn't quite sure where she was.

She had paused by a work featuring phallic imagery and Clark overheard her murmur to Lady Van de Whosis, "And what is that large thing that looks like a tower?" On her way out the door, she told Clark, "I love your paintings. They're so lovely aren't they? But what are they? And who is that creature who is eating all of the crabmeat hors d'oeuvres?"

Clark informed Deirdre that the creature was Bambi Friedberg, but before he could introduce the women, Deirdre was gone, leaving several important collectors to consult the clear plastic-coated price list of paintings conveniently placed on an altar-like front desk by a large Chinese porcelain vase of rare bronze mums. From all appearances, Deirdre's associates were, once again, investing in art. Deirdre had taken Clark completely by surprise by supporting him in this way, and he knew he would never figure her out.

Bambi Friedberg rushed over, giving Clark no time to contemplate the mystery of Deirdre Dawn. She was wearing another of her indistinct, layered gauze creations, in black with heavy gold jewelry. She had a crab canapé in each hand, and one in her mouth.

"Oh, Clark, these waiters are so cute! The blond one with the gorgeous heinie —" She squeezed a passing waiter's. He whipped around, but smiled when he saw who had groped him.

"I just love aggressive women!" He flounced, and gave a little growl in Bambi's ear.

"Bobby, you better remember to save those crab ones for me," said Bambi, as she grabbed two more hors d'oeuvres from his tray.

"Honey, I wouldn't dream of giving them to anyone else!" With his free hand, the waiter pointed to his own toned behind. "And if you want *these* cakes, see me after the show! And I do private parties, too — here's my card. Ta!"

Bambi took the card and watched the waiter disappear into the crowd. "Isn't he adorable? I said I'll make Allen give him an audition, but I can't get my husband away from that *meshugganeh* Pamela Raven. She keeps putting her hands all over him! And I'm used to that! I'm used to Allen and his ways! Don't you think I let him get away with it! I get him back good! Wanna know what I did to him today?"

Clark had to bend over to hear Bambi's whisper as she told him that she had fed the dogs baloney, because Allen doesn't allow it, but it was the maid's day off, so he'd never find out. She had also turned the thermostat way up and walked around the apartment naked.

"I like it when he's gone because I can pee with the door open. He's a mean son of a bitch. I use his razor when he's out because he hates it. Oh, speak of the devil!"

"And he shall appear," said Allen Friedberg.

Pamela pushed Bambi out of the way to show Allen Clark's largest work, 'Taco, Enchilada, and Egg Roll.'

"Now, Allen, wouldn't this painting be divine in your dining room? I think it's just beautiful."

"Forget it, Allen," said Bambi. "We're getting French paintings in there, aren't we, Clark? These paintings are fine in a gallery, but not in my house. I wouldn't know if they were hung upside down!"

"Allen, if Bambi were hung upside down, would you notice?" breathed Pamela as she squeezed Allen Friedberg's thigh. "Oh, look, here comes another tray of crab hors d'oeuvres!" She nudged Bambi.

"Well, anything is possible. That gallery in Manchester did hang a Rauschenberg upside down last summer!"

Clark turned to see who had spoken and found Roland Lee at his side. Lee wore a Damon of Italy soft-shouldered suit in a style called "the egg" which Clark hated. A leggy black chorus girl held tightly to Roland's arm, perhaps to remain steady in her very high heels. Even barefoot, she would have towered above Ronald Lee, and a clinging, backless red chiffon dress emphasized her height. She had the juciest red lips and the most beautiful smile Clark had ever seen, and Clark wondered what it would be like to spend the night with her.

"Remember that, Clark?" Martin Winterspoon took Clark's attention away from the chorus girl. "It was a scandal. Of course, it's almost forgivable that a nothing gallery would be confused by a Rauschenberg, but right before that disaster the National Gallery of London hung Van Gogh's 'Grass and Butterflies' upside down!"

"Why did they do that?" asked Roland Lee's date, whom he had failed to introduce.

"You really wouldn't understand it anyway, babe," Roland said as he followed Martin Winterspoon through the crowd, leaving the chorus girl to struggle after him in her high heels.

Bambi Friedberg was still looking for the invisible crab hors d'oeuvres Pamela had seen. "Where are they?" Bambi spun around. "I don't see them. Oh, never mind, I have to pee! Where's the bathroom?"

Holly stood on the edge of the group, trying to get Clark's attention. "Clark —" she began, but Bambi grabbed her arm.

"Holly, you know where the bathroom is! I want you to take me." She took Holly's hand and led her away.

Pamela Raven was engulfed by two reporters and four photographers, and Allen Friedberg stepped casually away from the mêlée.

He patted Clark on the back. "Good show, kid. Good turnout. I like the klieg light effect out front. You sure you never designed a Hollywood premier party? I should hire you for my next one."

"Thank you," said Clark. "I'd be honored."

"I don't know about this Modern Art stuff, though," said Allen. "Some of these shows look like someone crashed a car into the gallery. It's just junkyard stuff, you know what I mean? And some of these guys think they can put their name on an enema bag and call it art! I don't know. But the women, whew! I should come to these openings more often."

Clark followed Allen's eye to where Maria, Reggie, and Luciano stood by the bar. Reggie's shining dark hair was cut in a new style with bangs and she wore a little black dress of stiff black satin with only a little bra bow across the low-cut back. The dress was short and showed Reggie's legs to advantage, but it was Maria who had the attention of half the room, including Allen Friedberg. Four-inch clogs gave her extra height and she wore the tightest, lowest-slung hip-huggers Clark had ever seen. The gold suede pants were laced with gold leather thongs in front and they exposed Maria's sleek, milky-white midriff almost to her ribs, where a ruffled silk blouse of Pucci swirls in deep green-blues and magenta hugged her curves. Clark thought she had a bit too much makeup on, but he liked the lipstick she wore, in a shade called "Sneaky Pink" that went well with her pastel blonde looks.

"What's New, Pussycat!" Allen Friedberg whistled.

Luciano, looking bored, lounged against the bar. He waved to Clark and when Clark waved back, both Maria and Reggie spotted him and smiled.

"Get her over here," said Allen. "Now. What's her name? Can she act?"

"Of course not," hissed a familiar voice. Pamela Raven had dismissed the reporters and rejoined Clark and Allen. "Except maybe in porno. That's Maria Tucci, or something, and she can barely speak English."

"Pucci," said Clark, "Maria Pucci." He heard an odd, muffled banging coming from somewhere in the back of the room and wondered what it was. "I don't know if she can act, or even wants to, but her English isn't that bad."

"Well, darling, we all know there's a lot more to acting than that, don't we?" said Pamela, in her "no arguments" tone. Her honeyed smile reappeared. "Oh, here come the cameras again. And that nasty fat Winterspoon," she said through the smile.

Pamela had arrived promptly at six and was on hand to greet each guest at Clark's opening. She, of course, had not come alone. Flanked by Holly and the Friedbergs and followed by her loyal staff of five, with her makeup man carrying Princess Lotus Blossom, she had made quite an entrance.

Martin Winterspoon was positively bursting with self-importance and reflected glory, and he commanded the photographers to take many shots of himself with "La Raven." He loved Pamela Raven's marabou hat and stole; he loved her turquoise satin gown and matching shoes; he loved her eyes; and he loved every picture she had ever made.

Clark waited for Martin Winterspoon to draw breath in his stream of gushing compliments while the photographers posed the group, and then Clark muttered, "Do you hear that? Do you hear a banging noise?"

Martin listened for a moment and shook his head. "No, my dear, all I hear is champagne corks a-poppin' and the lovely sound of money! Unless it's your future you hear knocking, which is very possible!"

"Mr. Calloway!"

Clark tried to take a step back as Doreen Flower, the tiny, blonde, pixie-haired gossip columnist, shoved a microphone in his face. There was no room to step back.

"Mr. Calloway, you're an interior decorator. What do you mean by calling yourself a 'Sexpressionist'? These paintings are very sexual, but are they art? Or are you just going for shock value?" she demanded.

"I am influenced by life," Clark said. "I treat a subject and that subject is sex. Whether it's art or not, I'll leave that up to the individual."

"Of course it's art, look how it's selling!" snapped Martin Winterspoon.

Doreen Flower ignored him and turned her microphone on Pamela Raven. "Rumor has it you'll be starring in Allen Friedberg's next film with your old rival, Adela Morgan. Have you two patched things up?"

"Well, we never were rivals, Doreen," said Pamela. "You write enough gossip to know not to listen to it. Allen is producing a marvelous picture for us, a murder mystery about two sisters, set in the deep South, and that's all I'm going to say!"

"What about your finances, Miss Raven? What about the rumors that you're flat broke?" Doreen asked.

"No truth to them," said Pamela. "Get out of my way. I see the perfect picture for Allen. Oh, Allen! You absolutely must

The Decorator

have this wonderful painting!" She nearly knocked Doreen Flower to the floor in her insistence that Allen look at a painting hanging on the opposite wall of the gallery.

"Martin, get me the show catalogue!" Pamela commanded. "I simply must purchase that painting over there for Holly, the butterfly one. Where is that girl? Wasn't she with that Bambi monster?"

Clark saw Holly waiting in a line to use the rest room. She was leaning against the wall and Luciano was leaning over her, talking intently.

"There she is," said Clark.

"Clark, would you be a love and fetch her?" asked Pamela.

"Get Maria over here, too," Allen Friedberg whispered in Clark's ear.

As Clark approached the rest room, he wondered why there was a line. The banging he heard got louder as he neared the rest room door. At first, Holly and Luciano did not notice him, and he overheard a bit of their conversation.

"Diet pills?" asked Luciano. "Forget diet pills. They only make you think small and do a lot of cleaning. I've got something for you much better than that. I've got something for your chemistry. Do you believe in chemistry? Like between a man and a woman?"

Holly laughed nervously as Luciano leaned close enough to look down the décolletage of her blue Empire dress. "I don't know about that, but you're right about the cleaning. Last night I cleaned the bottles in my medicine cabinet."

She looked up and saw Clark. "Oh, hi, Clark."

"Hi," said Clark. "What's going on? Why the line?"

A fresh barrage of banging on the door answered his question before Holly did.

"Someone's locked in there," she said. "Two of the gallery assistants went to find a screwdriver or something to open the door. I think it's Mrs. Friedberg in there."

"Oh, it figures," said Clark. "What a hassle. You might as well come see what your aunt wants, and Mr. Friedberg wants to meet Maria." Maria was talking with Reggie at the bar and Clark reached out to tap Maria's arm.

"What does that old guy want with her?" asked Luciano.

"Now, now," said Clark. "That old guy is Allen Friedberg

of Metropolis Pictures."

Clark led the women into the crowd. Luciano, looking suspicious, followed them.

Holly walked ahead of Maria and Reggie and spoke in a low voice to Clark. "Clark, I'd like to apologize for last night. I wasn't myself. You know, I usually don't drink that much."

"Don't worry about it," said Clark. "It happens to the best of us."

"Look," Holly lowered her voice to a whisper, "I know Regina is your girl friend. She told me, and I don't want to cause any trouble between you. I just hope we can be friends."

As their group neared Pamela and Allen, Allen grabbed Pamela's arm and bulged his eyes in mock terror. "I tell you, I feel them!" he cried. "They're all around us! Young people! Getting closer and closer!"

"Of course we can be friends," Clark told Holly. He gave her hand a quick squeeze, just as a flash bulb popped and Doreen Flower came rushing over.

"Smile for the cameras, kiddies!" Pamela Raven pushed Clark and Holly closer together for the photographers. "Get out of the picture," she snapped at Reggie.

Doreen thrust her microphone at Holly. "Fess up, Holly, it's all over town that you and Clark Calloway are an item. Any wedding bells?"

Clark saw Reggie gasp and turn red with rage. He was so flustered he didn't hear what Holly told Doreen. Before he could say anything, Bambi Friedberg was carried over, swooning in the arms of one of the waiters.

"Allen, Allen," she croaked. "Where's my Allie?"

"Here I am, dolling. Excuse me, Maria." Allen rushed over to collect his wife from the waiter. "What happened? Are you all right? Can you stand up?"

"It was terrible," said Bambi. "I was locked in there for hours! I don't know what I did to the lock."

"It's all right, dolling. We're going home now," said Allen. "Somebody bring us our coats!"

Martin Winterspoon dispatched one gallery assistant to bring the coats, and another to alert the Friedberg's driver. He brought a glass of water to Bambi and the show catalogue to Pamela.

The Decorator

Pamela opened the catalogue to the page featuring the painting she had convinced Allen to buy. She held the book up to Bambi's face. "Now, look. Doesn't that look lovely? While you were lost, your husband bought this treasure for you, and I'll leave it to you to stick on the little red dot."

"You did?" Bambi gazed up at Allen, lovestruck. "Allie, you bought that for me?"

"Yes, I did, honey. Let's go home," said Allen.

"It is getting late," said Pamela. "Whyever is Holly talking to that swarthy Italian? And now Doreen is interviewing Maria. As if it were a slow night for news."

Pamela dashed over to Maria and thrust herself between Maria and Doreen's microphone. "Maria, darling! You do look divine in those pants!" she cooed. "And those shoes! I must know where you bought them! They're splendid."

"Oh, thank you," said Maria. "But I didn't buy them. My father is a shoemaker. In Italy."

"Of course!" said Pamela. "How lucky you are. Well, you simply must come over and bring me a pair of those clogs in every color. Size four and a half! And tell your father I love the heel, but that Pamela Raven wants him to cover the soles with black rubber. Those wooden heels are far too noisy for me."

Pamela invited Reggie into the conversation by giving Reggie's shoulder a fond squeeze. "And you must come over with your friend, my dear. We'll have a nice lunch."

Reggie could do nothing more than look stunned and murmur something that passed for "yes."

A young couple rushed over to interrupt them. "Miss Raven, may we please have your autograph? Oh, hi, Clark. Congratulations! Great show!"

Clark thanked the girl who held a program catalogue out for Pamela Raven to sign, and he greeted the young man with her. Marie Rose Connelly and Tony DeMarco had been classmates of Clark's at Pratt. Reggie had told Clark earlier in the evening that Tony was hissing Clark's work to anyone who would listen. Reggie had overheard Tony saying that Clark's show would make more sense if hot air could come out of the paintings.

"The work looks good. Guess you're the next Jackson Pollock," said Tony.

"Thanks," said Clark. He never knew where to look when he was talking to Tony, because Tony had a walleye.

"You know, these paintings would look good as a background for some of my nudes," said Tony, as he took another vodka from a waiter's tray.

It wasn't a compliment, because Clark knew that though Tony called himself an art director, he worked for Muscles magazine. Marie Rose hadn't exactly made it with her art, either. She got her autograph and told Clark she was now in the fashion business, designing for a top furrier. Marie Rose was a pretty little redhead, but she had been hitting the wine heavily and her face was bloated and flushed.

"Are you still with Reggie?" she asked.

Clark was beginning to wonder himself. "Excuse me, there she is now," he said.

He worked his way across the room toward where Reggie stood talking to her parents. On his way, he passed Paul Hedges, Belle, and some junior designers from the office. He accepted their congratulations and listened with astonishment when Paul told him that Salvatore Caneletto had been seen skulking amidst the crowd.

"I think he came to gloat and he was disappointed," said Paul.

"He'll be more than disappointed if I get my hands on him," said Clark. "Excuse me."

Clark pretended not to notice the two art critics from competing magazines who had come to review the show. He knew that artists often did more harm than good if they attempted to influence the critics or, even worse, explain their work.

He saw that Reggie was making her way towards him with her little parents in tow. Clark embraced Reggie's mother and then her father. They were the nicest people he knew, and he had never heard a critical word from either of them. Of course, they were very proud of Clark. Reggie's father said the work was bold and exciting. Reggie's mother said it was fun, and that Clark should come over for breakfast again soon. It had been too long since Clark had been to their aluminum-sided house on Java Street for Mrs. Stowkowski's homemade kielbasa.

Seeing the Stowkowskis made Clark miss his own parents,

and he wished they were alive to share in his success. He told Reggie, for her parents' benefit, that his sister, Vera, had called from Maine, but that she couldn't come to the show as she was due to have her second baby in two weeks. Reggie made him promise that he would take her up to see his new niece as soon as possible, and Clark promised. He secretly marveled at Reggie's ability to be bubbly when he knew she was furious at him.

As soon as she politely could, Reggie said, "Hey, Mom, Pop, there are Maria and Luciano! I want you to meet them."

As they walked away, she turned back to Clark and whispered fiercely, "How could you? I could understand if you fucked Pamela Raven, but how could you with that pimply, pasty-faced thing?"

It was not a question that could be answered.

Reggie smiled meanly and said, "By the way, I'm pregnant."

"You know I'll take care of that," Clark said as she walked away.

"I bet you will," Reggie snapped without looking back.

"Gal trouble?" Roland Lee had floated up unnoticed.

"What? Oh, no," said Clark. "She's fine."

"She's more than fine," said Roland as he watched Reggie's departing ass. "But I'll tell you, there's one I really want you to introduce me to."

"Who's that?" asked Clark. "And what about the girl you came with?"

"Oh, that broad? She's just a show girl. But this blonde! I'm in love."

Clark saw that Roland meant Dannee Lou Baker. She was admiring the paintings with her brother, Johnny Downing, an ex-football player turned Washington reporter. She did look marvelous in a Galanos strapless wonder of red, pink, and plum chiffon that was all spirals and knotting in the front.

"Sorry, Roland. That one's married."

"Look, man," said Roland impatiently. "I know who she is. I know her story. Her husband's a vegetable. He is never returning to the land of the living. Face facts, pal. She's no fool. She's gotta be shopping around for a new model. And I'm perfect for her. Whadd'ya say?"

Clark was appalled. "I don't know, Roland."

"Listen, you get me a date with her, you've got the Ritz Plaza job. It's yours. *Carte blanche*. And if you redo my apartment for free. I'll throw in the Bel Vista contract."

"The Bel Vista Hotel in Hollywood?"

"You got it," said Roland. "How about giving me one of these paintings, too?"

"I'm afraid they're all spoken for," said Clark. "Unless you care to speak to Mr. Winterspoon."

"No, no forget it! But Dannee Lou?"

"Well, I did invite her and Johnny out for drinks with Adela Morgan and me after the opening, if you'd care to join us."

"Swell, swell," said Roland. "Let me just ditch the tomata over there." He slapped Clark on the back and trotted off to convince his date that she was terribly tired. Clark hoped Dannee Lou would forgive him.

Holly and Luciano came over to say goodnight.

"Thank you for introducing us," said Holly, even though Clark hadn't. "Did you know that Luciano's brother-in-law is Bacalao Gatto, the famous director? We're going to talk about auditioning for this part which sounds perfect!"

Luciano winked at Clark. "*Ciao*." He helped Holly on with her coat and buttoned it for her, slowly. "Don't wait up for us," he said.

With a great flurry of coats and scarves, Pamela Raven and company prepared to leave.

"How was I?" asked Pamela. "Was I good?"

"You were splendid." Clark kissed her hand. "I can't thank you enough."

"Yes, you can," said Pamela. "You can come over tomorrow at six and help me plan my move. I simply must go now. I'm never up this late."

A great commotion at the top of the stairs leading down into the gallery heralded the entrance of Adela Morgan.

"Come on, kids, quit draggin'! This is the joint!"

Miss Morgan's foghorn voice was unmistakable, and the extra-wide black pumps and solid legs of the great lady herself soon appeared, followed by a mountain of peach organza swathed in an imitation mink coat, and finally all of Adela

Morgan descended. Her rounded cheeks were heavily rouged; her bouffant hairstyle was too young for her face; and her mascara was dripping, but she plowed proudly into the fawning crowd with her massive bosom held high. A glittering assortment of chorus boys in makeup frolicked around her and they soon had the squealing attention of all the waiters.

"Oh, my God! I can't believe it!" Marie Rose Connelly shrieked and flung herself at Adela Morgan. "It's Adela Morgan!" Though Marie Rose was quite unsteady on her feet, she held her wine glass carefully.

"That's right, honey, you can see," snapped Adela Morgan.

"I don't get it," wailed Marie Rose. "You're Adela Morgan and you're wearing a fake fur coat! You gotta be able to afford the real thing!"

"You don't get out much, do you, kid?" Adela gave Marie Rose an expert elbow in the ribs and red wine spilled all over the bodice of Marie Rose's dress. "Oops, you better go clean yourself up. Everybody knows Adela Morgan doesn't believe in killing poor little animals for their coats."

"Come on, Marie Rose," said Tony DeMarco. "It's time to go home." He pushed the still-protesting Marie Rose ahead of himself and out of the gallery.

"I see it's the riffraff hour," said Pamela, as she pushed past Adela's throng.

Doreen Flower was already in place, microphone extended.

"We are blessed with two starlight ladies at one opening this evening! What an occasion! Miss Morgan, would you care to comment on your new film?"

Adela was happy to oblige. She slapped Pamela Raven heartily on the back as she hollered, "Yeah, we're doin' a flick with Allen! Who'd think they'd pay to see two old broads like us!"

"Speak for yourself," said Pamela.

"Oh, the Widow Irons, I beg your pardon!" Adela honked. "She's hard as steel and just as cold. Leaving so soon, Your Highness? Won't you stay and have a drink? That is, unless you've emptied every bottle in the house already!"

"The bar," said Pamela, "is over there. And unlike some people, I can hold my tongue as well as my liquor."

"That Raven, ya gotta love her!" Adela winked at Doreen.

"She's an ice maiden, but, you know, she tells me things I bet she doesn't even tell her kid, and two weeks later she's goddamning me all over the place. She likes me very much."

As Doreen Flower watched Pamela Raven's departure, the gossip columnist's eyes shone like stars.

The Decorator

8
CHAPTER

There was a buzz in the gallery. Guests stared at one another. A moment of silence prevailed and everyone, without saying so, seemed to agree that since no one could top Pamela Raven's exit, it was time to go home. Most people did, except for the usual hangers-on at such events, the ones who stay until the bar is dry and their eyes are bloodshot. Martin Winterspoon never wanted a party to end, particularly his own, and he was in heaven dishing with the young waiters. Because he was known for being a bit eccentric and always having *avant-garde* shows of work with sexual content, the party banter was more risqué than usual, even for such art world events, especially at the end of the night when the participants were well-oiled.

The phalluses in Clark's paintings reminded each waiter of what *he* would or wouldn't do with such equipment and just who the models must have been, or could be, from the selection at Fire Island last season.

"No, no, Miss Thing, don't even try it! No way Randy is hung like that one! She may be thick, but she's stubby, honey, short and stubby!"

"Maybe she was stubby for *you*, Mary, but I have ways to get her going!"

"Lies! Don't listen to her, girls!"

Martin Winterspoon and Bobby the waiter were well into a spirited discussion of the virtues and "drawbacks, ha ha," as Bobby quipped, of circumcision, when Martin's partner Ralph started screaming.

"Marty! When and how are we going to get these people out of here! Or are you planning to stay here all night! Tell these dizzy queens to start cleaning up! That's what they're paid for!"

"Don't mind him," murmured Martin. "He hasn't taken his medication today. Why don't you just toddle along home,

Ralph, and I'll help the boys clean up?"

"I bet you will," cried Ralph. "And don't be surprised if I do just that!"

"Now, now," said Martin. "Bobby here was just telling me he's a painter too, as well as an actor! How talented can we be? We may have just discovered the next Andy Warhol."

"That's right," said Bobby, and they giggled.

"Oh, Marty," groaned Ralph. "Will you never stop? That's it for me. I'll see you in the morning, if you're lucky!"

Clark turned to Reggie. "Let's get out of here," he said. "I've had enough. I guess we've taken in enough! I'll buy you a nightcap and maybe a special present. I know how much you like those three-band gold roll rings."

Clark gathered his crew, and as they put their coats on, Roland called to Martin Winterspoon:

"Hey, Mr. Gallery Owner! Stick a big red dot on the choicest painting for me! Make sure I buy the most expensive picture." He winked at Dannee Lou. "How much is it?"

Martin Winterspoon waved a catalog at Roland. "Look for yourself, precious. I'll never tell. You can leave your check with my assistant."

"No, no," said Roland, winding a beige cashmere scarf around his neck. "Just send the bill to the Ritz Plaza. Make sure it's marked for my personal attention! That way, it'll get priority treatment."

"Whatever you say," said Martin. "And Clark, thanks for being so popular and bringing all these fabulous people!"

The group repaired to the Polo Bar in the Westbury Hotel, a Madison Avenue room Clark had decorated with bright red naugahyde lambrequins around the wide windows, with red banquettes to match. But what fascinated Clark about the Polo Bar were the walls, which were painted with murals of polo ponies in an Arabic-style design with Arab riders on a light green playing field. The scene had a mystical gentility he never tired of. The Polo Bar was an in spot, more like a club than a restaurant. It was rumored that Elizabeth Taylor and Mike Todd had frequented the bar when they were in town. Gene Tierney had been courted there by Ali Kahn, as well as by the Texan Howard Lee. Doreen Flower was usually at her table just before midnight. In fact, it was The Place for the last drink of the evening because the Polo Bar served a two-ounce drink, by decree issued by the hotel's owner, a good-looking, hard-drinking sportsman millionaire. Clark had seen businessman sock away four or five double martinis in the Polo Bar *before* lunch. He knew Dannee Lou was a hard-drinkin' gal too, and he wanted to show her a good time before she returned to her White House office.

"What do you think?" he asked her, as they settled around the special table selected for them by the Polo's maitre d', Mr. Kay Apollo, whom everyone called "Mr. Kay."

"It's charming," said Dannee Lou. "But do let's talk about Pamela Raven! What an amazing-looking woman she is! I mean, I always knew she was glamorous, but it is surely something else to see her in person. In all those feathers, too! My, my. Now, Clark, you know I'm not a 'fan' type — I've always been a *serious* career girl," she told Roland. "But let me tell you, I almost swooned when I saw her coming across the floor toward me. That smile of hers could power Austin and maybe the whole state of Texas!"

Roland Lee added that Pamela Raven most convincingly demonstrated the old show business cliché that movie stars are "larger than life" on screen and appear shockingly small in person.

"It's her face," he said. "Like all the great ones, she may be tiny, but her face appears huge. Did you notice that her features are enormous? Those eyes and those eyebrows!"

Reggie asked who all of the people with Pamela Raven were and if she always traveled that way. Clark told her that he didn't really know, but that he got the impression from Pamela Raven's housekeeper, Mama, that the star hired her fans. She somehow found jobs for them, which they gladly accepted, though he wasn't sure if they were paid. People just fell in love with her, and Clark got the idea Pamela Raven was shy of public appearances. She needed the protective coating of her entourage.

Clark noticed that Reggie was barely listening. Her attention was with Johnny Downing, Dannee Lou's brother, and as soon as she could, Reggie returned to her conversation with Johnny about journalism in the Capital. It was only natural, Clark supposed, that Reggie would grab the opportunity to chat with someone so successful in her chosen field, and it was only natural that she would be hypnotized by Johnny's football player physique and Texas charm. Johnny also had the face of a movie cowboy, with penetrating green eyes and black hair, which Clark knew was Reggie's favorite combination. It annoyed him slightly that Reggie was oh, so enthralled with Johnny. He wondered if she was getting even for his night with Holly.

"Well, I hope Pamela Raven isn't planning to bring her entourage to the State Dinner," said Dannee Lou. "Lady Bird has invited Miss Raven to a dinner for the Supreme Court Justices next month," Dannee Lou explained to Roland. "And was it a surprise for Miss Raven to meet me at the opening? She talked to me about what she should wear to the dinner, and she even asked me who she could expect to find at her dinner table. I got the idea she wants to be seated next to Lyndon! She thinks she's a bigger star than he is!"

"Just how does one get invited to a State Dinner?" asked Roland. "I certainly have my connections in the White House, of course, and I'm sure I could attend if I really wanted to and had the time," he added hastily. "But I've always been curious — just how do you seat a State Dinner. How do you decide who sits next to whom?"

Dannee Lou threw back her head and laughed, and Clark joined in.

"I don't see what's so funny," said Roland Lee.

"Popsicle sticks!" cried Dannee Lou, laughing some more.

"Popsicle sticks?" asked Roland.

"Popsicle sticks," said Clark, wondering why Reggie didn't break off her intense conversation with Johnny even to find out what they were laughing at.

Roland Lee looked very annoyed.

"I'm sorry," said Dannee Lou, wiping her eyes on her napkin. "But I just had to laugh when you asked me that. It's our little personal joke. You tell him, Clark. Tell Mr. Lee about the last State Dinner we designed. I just can't."

Clark told Roland about the time Jackie Kennedy had him help decorate a State Dinner in the Gold Room. Deirdre Dawn did not wish to associate with people so *nouveau* as the Kennedys. After all, Jacqueline had not even debuted in Bal-

The Decorator

timore, which marked her as hopelessly *arriviste* in Deirdre's book. That was when Clark had first met Dannee Lou. He described the chaos they encountered as Dannee Lou tried to coordinate the seating of 160 people around sixteen tables, using paper wheels for the tables and wooden popsicle sticks for the guests. The names of the guests were written on the popsicle sticks and divided into "men" and "women," but the seating kept changing as people in the State Department, the Executive Department, and the East Wing kept calling Dannee Lou with their requests. Each of the 160 people had something to say about who they wanted to be seated with and who they wanted to avoid. And some of them kept changing their minds.

It was the most unbelievable task to seat them because, as Dannee Lou added, protocol demands certain seating arrangements for foreign dignitaries in relation to each other, their families and ambassadors, to say nothing of the friends of the First Family.

"It's quite complicated," she explained. "And it didn't help that Clark and I started drinking champagne. Everyone kept calling and screwing everything up, and finally we just threw all the sticks up in the air and let them fall where they may."

"And Dannee, remember what you said?" asked Clark.

"No, what did I say?"

"She said, 'Let them all go and fall where they may and have a good time!' And they did, didn't they?"

"That's right," said Dannee Lou. "Everybody was talking about it for months. Fortunately, or rather unfortunately, in another sense, it was near the end of the administration and it didn't matter too much in the end, did it?"

Clark and Dannee Lou both fell silent as they remembered JFK, but the spell was quickly broken by a commotion at the entrance of the bar as the one and only Adela Morgan flew in with Paul Hedges. Her vocal cords were at full volume: she wanted the best table and the hotel manager, Kevin O'Toole, instructed Mr. Kay to accommodate her.

O'Toole came over to Clark's table, mopping his bald head with a napkin. He had been at Clark's opening and he told Clark how much he had enjoyed the paintings. He said he hoped Clark had been happy with the hors d'oeuvres. Clark assured him they were great and thanked him for the favor.

"Oh, it was my pleasure," said Mr. O'Toole. "Now, if you'll excuse me, Mr. Hedges has invited me to sit with him and Miss Morgan."

No sooner had Mr. O'Toole reached that table when the bar was again treated to Adela Morgan's voice at full throttle:

"Oh, for Christ's sake, Paul, I'm not sitting next to that fag! Don't invite that fag over here!"

"Someone's getting sloppy," hummed Dannee Lou, and even Reggie and Johnny took their eyes off each other to stare at Adela.

Kevin O'Toole made a hasty exit.

"Oh, you can't say that," said Paul Hedges.

"Can too!" said Adela. "And tell me something — why don't you come up to my apartment and take care of me instead of sending that silly boy over there? You know, that silly one who does all those paintings that look like tits and cocks and everything!"

Everyone in the bar turned to stare at Clark and Reggie giggled nervously.

But all eyes were back on Adela and Paul as she continued her tirade at Broadway volume: "Get rid of him, Paul. You come to see me! 'Cause I'm your kind of gal! You're gonna sit with me! Don't invite any other fags over here."

The bartender announced last call, which enraged Adela Morgan. "I'll tell ya when it's final call! I'm the last one to take a curtain call in this place. Not you!"

Reggie nudged Clark, "Clark, why don't we ask Adela to sing? The little pianist is over there. Let's have her sing!"

"Are you crazy?" asked Clark, but Reggie was already on her way to Adela's table.

"She's got spunk," said Dannee Lou.

"That she has," said Clark.

Reggie walked up to the Broadway star and said, "Miss Morgan? You know, I've always loved your singing and my favorite song has always been 'I Get No Kick From Champagne" — I mean "I Get A Kick Out Of You," that's right. Do you think you could —"

Adela Morgan glared at Reggie. "Whaddya mean you want me to sing? For this freaky crowd? Bring me another drink, bartender!"

The Decorator

Paul Hedges said, "Oh, Adela, I'd love to hear you sing."

"I'll sing it for you, honey, if you get rid of that cat who comes over and tries to decorate for me. He's a fairy, too. 'Cause I only want you doin' it! So strike up the band, Kay! Strike up the band!"

"Oh, Miss Morgan," said Mr. Kay, "we don't have a band, but we do have a piano player. He'll play anything you want."

"Well, have him play "I Get A Kick Out Of You,'" said Adela as she hefted herself out of her seat, nearly knocking the table over. Paul Hedges dove to save her drink.

"That's good, babe, save it for me," Adela purred as she sat on the end of the piano and hiked her skirt up to show her garter, which was rolled and had slid down from her thigh to above her knee.

There was an audible rip as the slit in Adela's dress widened past the breaking point, and there were a few chuckles, but no one laughed when Adela Morgan began to sing. A respectful silence fell as her luscious trademark notes swelled and echoed throughout the room. There was no doubt in anyone's mind that they were in the presence of greatness and that this was a moment that could never be compared.

Reggie stood transfixed by Adela's table, glowing with astonishment. She stood there still as Adela waddled back to her seat. Reggie gave her a look she had formerly reserved for living saints, if she ever met one.

"That was unbelievable!" she gasped. "What a great job!"

Adela pushed past Reggie and sank into her seat. "I don't need you to tell me I did a great job."

"Miss Morgan, I've always wanted to be an anchorwoman. I'm not really an actress, but I take acting lessons for elocution, and my coach says I'm pretty good —"

She's babbling, thought Clark. He covered his eyes. Couldn't Reggie see Adela's stony expression turning colder by the second? Sit down, he mentally commanded Reggie. Sit down. Shut up.

But Reggie chattered on: "I hope the acting lessons help! Of course, I never want to overact —"

Adela rumbled, "Honey! Ya don't have to worry about overacting until ya learn how to act!" But her expression was no longer unkind. "This kid's got guts! Bring 'er a drink! Now get lost! What did you say your name was?"

She slung a heavy arm around Reggie's neck, gave her a squeeze, and pushed her away. "Beat it! How old is she, twelve? Paul, these kids are too young. Take me home."

Reggie came back to her table, flushed and slightly shaking. "Geez. What made me do that? I think I better get out of here. I have to go home."

"I'd be pleased to see you home," said Johnny.

"Well, it's been super. Quite an experience," said Dannee Lou. "But we have to catch the shuttle back to D.C. in the morning. The *seven a.m.* shuttle!" She nudged her brother pointedly.

"Don't worry, Sis, I'll make it." Johnny grinned. "I just can't let this little lady go home all by herself. I can't think when I've had a nicer time."

"Me neither," said Reggie, smiling up at Johnny in a silly way that Clark tried to ignore, the same way he was trying to ignore Reggie's sudden Southern accent. He hated it when people "picked up" accents; he thought it was rude, and Reggie, of all people, should know better.

Roland Lee was also making a fool of himself, Clark thought, as he watched the hotelier try to solicit an invitation to a Senators' game from Dannee Lou, to be followed by drinks and dinner at his Washington hotel, of course.

But Dannee Lou was a model of Southern warmth and tactful dodging. Clark was struck by the stupidity and blind instinctual greed of some people and he suddenly felt very tired. He decided he didn't care who went home with Reggie. Weren't they supposed to be "friends," with no strings attached?

If that was so, he wondered why he found himself whispering to Reggie in the corner by the coat check: "You can come home with me, you know. And I think we need to talk."

"We can talk later," said Reggie sweetly.

"Come on," whispered Clark, "You don't need to sleep with this guy to help your career."

"Look who's talking," said Reggie, just as sweetly as before. "Goodnight, Clark."

The Decorator

CHAPTER 9

The night was clear and sparkling as Clark and Paul strode up Fifth Avenue, whistling "Joy to the World." Clark had helped Dannee Lou into her taxi and watched, amused, as Paul Hedges tried to ease Adela Morgan into her car without getting dragged in with her. Every time it seemed that all of Adela was squeezed into the back seat, some part of her would pop out and she would grab Paul, as she tried to coax him to climb in and come on over for a nightcap. She even gripped Paul by his necktie with both hands, certainly choking him, and Clark feared her driver would take off, dragging Paul Hedges alongside the car. Finally, Paul begged off and Adela released him, but only after he had promised several times to call her the instant he arrived at home.

"You call me! You will call me, won'tcha? As soon as you get home! You call me, honey, and we'll have a li'l pillow talk. I'll be waiting!"

Clark thought Adela sounded like a cow, a large and insistent cow, like the ones on his neighbors' farm in Maine, when they bellowed to be fed or milked or something — he never knew which. Clark wasn't very good with animals. He was just glad he wasn't the one Adela was mooing at, groping at, and staring at with her eyes wide and overly sincere in her champagne-reddened face.

Only when Adela heard Paul's multiple assurances that he would call her immediately when he got home did she finally let go of his tie. Blowing kisses, she slammed her car door closed on the hem of her dress. The car sped away with Adela's peach chiffon ruffles sticking out of the door.

"By the time I get home, Adela will be asleep," said Paul, "I hope! Did Regina leave already? And John, too? Nice young man — I never did get to say goodbye properly."

"Oh, they escaped during Adela's hullabaloo," said Clark. "They caught a taxi that was right behind the one Mr. Kay hailed for Dannee Lou. You were a bit preoccupied at the time."

"I'll say!" Paul brushed the front of his coat fastidiously with both hands, as if flicking off invisible dust. "That woman is strong-willed. Of course, one can't refuse her. That wouldn't do at all. So, I must bite my tongue."

He selected a menthol cigarette from his silver cloisonné case and lit it with a matching lighter. "Say, did Regina and John take the same taxi? I thought you would surely be seeing Regina home this evening."

Clark laughed. "Paul, couples haven't been 'seeing each other home' since the days of the church social! Goodness knows, I attended far too many of those for my liking back in Berwick. I can't think of anything more boring. Let's walk, shall we? It's such a nice night. It's refreshing after that smoky bar. Doesn't feel cold at all."

"Yes, let's," said Paul. "Only let's walk up Fifth Avenue, past the Christmas windows. I haven't seen them yet."

Fifth Avenue was illuminated as bright as day and decorated with all of the cheerful displays of Christmas.

"It gets better every year," said Paul and when Clark began whistling "Joy to the World" he joined in.

"My, that's high-pitched," Paul broke off. "Women have changed, haven't they?" he asked, suddenly serious. "I don't mean just that they are taking jobs that only men used to do, though Heaven knows that's a big change. And it's hard for an old man like me to get used to those short skirts. If they climb any higher, they might as well be wearing nothing at all. What I mean is, young ladies never used to sow their wild oats the way young men do, not if they wanted to keep their reputations. Why, my wife hadn't even kissed anyone but me before we were married."

"Reggie's a girl after my own heart," said Clark. "Far be it from me to stand in her way. It would be hypocritical, wouldn't it? And, besides, she does what she wants."

"You're quite a pair," said Paul. "In my day, we never discussed such things and if there was any hanky-panky, well, there were certain kinds of 'ladies' for that and it was all hush-hush. They were definitely not the kind of girls one married. It wasn't a very fair arrangement, when I think about it. Do you think you and Regina will get married?"

"I've thought about it," said Clark, wondering if he had, until that moment, thought about it. "It certainly wouldn't be a conventional marriage."

"No, it probably wouldn't," Paul agreed. "Though people do tend to settle down a bit when they get a little older."

"Reggie's a good sport; that's what I like about her," said Clark, thinking that now, if she had a fling with Johnny, she would have to let his little adventure with Holly drop, "but neither of us is ready for marriage."

"I enjoyed being married," said Paul. "Maybe Marguerite, God rest her soul, and I were too young when we married. Who knows? Everyone married young in those days."

"I'm sorry," said Clark. "I didn't know she had passed away."

"Oh, it's all right," said Paul. "It was a long, long time ago. Almost twenty years ago…Could it be? That's right, Richard will be nineteen in May and Marguerite died a year after he was born…"

Clark was shocked and it was an effort not to stop right there and stare at his boss in amazement. "Do you have a son? But you never mentioned—"

"Oh, I apologize, carrying on so. It must be the brandy talking. I hope you don't mind. Or maybe it's Adela, reminding me."

"Adela?" asked Clark.

"You may have noticed Adela's…*affection* for me tonight." Paul chuckled.

"It was hard to miss," said Clark. "Whew," he whistled.

"Yes, it's about as easy to miss as a battalion of tanks with you in their sights. But that's not what bothers me. When I was in Germany I saw things that make Adela look like a kitten. Adela has a good heart. She's quite a lady. Something about her touches me. She was a great beauty once, and she's still very beautiful to me. Oh, she's not petite like your little Reggie, but Adela's all woman, and I like a gal with comfortable curves. She's such a great talent, too, and like so many stars, she's had so much tragedy in her life."

"Right," said Clark. "Didn't her last husband commit suicide?"

"Yes, he took his own life in '59. He always did suffer terrible depressions, and they say when his business went under, so did he. Remember, Adela's teenage daughter also died horribly, when she took one of those lysergic acid tablets, the ones that make people hallucinate, or something. I don't know why anyone would purposely choose such an experience. Apparently, she got high on this pill at a party in Los Angeles last summer and she thought she could fly. She flew right out of a seventeenth-story window in one of those high-rises. I don't know if you can call it suicide, exactly, but Adela was already broken-hearted, and her daughter's death was another terrible blow for her. So, if any one can, I understand why Adela drinks so heavily, but I can't accept it, and I certainly can't bear to watch it. It reminds me too much of Marguerite."

"Did Marguerite have a drinking problem?" asked Clark.

"Well, not always, certainly. It's a long story," said Paul. "Oh, my goodness! Could that be the time? It's past two a.m.! I should really be getting home."

"Well, it *is* Friday night," said Clark. "And we don't have to meet Roland Lee until tomorrow afternoon. I know I have to see Pamela Raven earlier than that, but all I need is a few hours of sleep. We're close to that big coffee shop on Lexington Avenue that's open all night. We could get a bite to eat and I don't mind hearing your story. In fact, I'd like to hear it. I don't care how long it is."

"Oh, to be young again," said Paul. "I never stay up this late, but it's funny, I don't feel tired at all. It must be the excitement. Yes, let's get out of the cold for a while. I'm not hungry, but I'll have a cup of tea and keep you company."

They turned right on Sixtieth Street and continued east. "The nerve of that Roland Lee!" Paul fumed. "Imagine suggesting that we compete for this project with the Parkhurst and Kahane offices!"

Clark knew the work of William Parkhurst. He surely would use maroons and beiges in the styling, and the furniture would be slightly contemporary with maybe a glass and brass coffee table for shine. And Clark knew Parkhurst would be using overall geometric carpets, which Clark thought were inappropriate for the Ritz Plaza.

And as far as the Kahane office was concerned, Clark knew

Molly's work, and you could be certain lots of animal skins would abound in the settings. Why, Molly even used animal skins, tigers and leopards, to cover the seats and backs of good gilt French chairs.

"Never mind how juvenile the idea is," Paul continued. "Think of the *waste:* paying each of us to decorate three separate floors of the Ritz Plaza when it's all only going to have to be redone by whoever gets the job. I'll tell you what I think — the man is just publicity mad!"

"Maybe he's just plain mad," said Clark. "And why can't I help feeling that it's all a sham, that he's just sucking us all in?"

"Well, we are sucked in, Clark. It's a very important contract, and I have no doubt that it will be awarded to Deirdre Dawn, as it should be! I imagine this is just Mr. Lee's way of forcing us to come down on our price. Don't worry, we'll handle Mr. Lee. I've dealt with his type before. In fact, all I want you to do is come up with some ideas for that Ritz Plaza living-and-drawing-room suite that overlooks the park. I know you can dream up something fantastic, if you haven't already. I want you to call me tomorrow around noon, from Miss Raven's apartment, if it's an appropriate time to take a short break, of course. In fact, I will meet Mr. Lee by myself. I'd rather you gave Pamela Raven your full attention for as long as she needs you."

"Of course," said Clark. "This is the place."

They sat in a cushioned booth in the window, and Clark ate a turkey club sandwich with French fries, which he sprinkled with apple vinegar. He drank a vanilla malted and coffee while Paul sipped a cup of tea and told Clark his story.

"Let's see, where do I begin?" mused Paul. "At the beginning, I guess! I don't know if I ever told you that my mother is French Canadian. I grew up in upstate New York, but my mother's parents lived in Quebec all of my life, and our family spent summers with them when I was a boy. They had a lovely little lake cottage. Marguerite's family owned the cottage next to ours and we were summer friends until, you know, that time when I realized that the skinny little girl next door had somehow, overnight, become the girl of my dreams. I dated other girls in school, of course, and when I graduated from high school, I immediately enlisted in the army because that was always my plan. There were no draft dodgers in my town, then. No one, myself included, had any doubts that America should fight and win *that* war.

"I'm not going to bore you with my war stories. Suffice it to say that it was awful and terrible and wonderful in a way that I will never forget. Can't forget. And I was lonely, too, very lonely, and Marguerite was my faithful correspondent. She never doubted that I would come home, and her letters kept me going. There were days when I lived for those letters and the news from home, and whatever little surprises she could squeeze into a package. I realized that I loved Marguerite, and I don't know about you — you kids seem to have no trouble...ahem...*expressing* yourselves these days — but we were shy youngsters, brought up to be so polite that it's a wonder we could speak to each other at all."

"I beg to differ," said Clark. "Remember, I grew up in Berwick, Maine! Why do you think I left?"

"My apologies," said Paul. "I suppose you do know the frustrations of a strict upbringing. Anyway, I found that in letters, I could pour out my heart to Marguerite. Believe it or not, I even tried my hand at some poetry! Bad stuff, pure treacle really, but Marguerite loved it, and she sent me a photo of herself in her bathing suit that really rang my bells. I had to hide it from the other guys who weren't so lucky.

"In the meantime, we lost half our company in a terrible air raid, including our commanding officer. He bled to death before the medics arrived and it was just the worst thing I have ever witnessed. The remainder of our poor, raggedy unit was assigned to another group that had just helped achieve a great victory in France. The commanding officer was a fellow named David Dawn."

"Deirdre Dawn's husband?" asked Clark.

"That's right. Only he's her *former* husband now," said Paul. "He promised me a job with his Wall Street firm when we got out of that nightmare war. And we swore we would get out alive, and victorious. We swore on all that we believed in, and I promised, that night, with David Dawn as my witness, that when I returned home I would marry my sweetheart, Marguerite.

"Obviously, I did. And also, obviously, Wall Street didn't

The Decorator

work out too well for me. The stock market didn't hold my interest, and I felt I was just fading away there. It was discouraging to know that I wasn't doing a top-notch job, and I felt that I was letting David down, but that he was too much of a gentleman to say so. Marguerite and I socialized occasionally with the Dawns, and Deirdre fell in love with the little watercolors I often gave her as gifts. I had always liked sketching at the shore in summer, and I had quite a collection of my paintings. Deirdre was overcome with the idea that I should do watercolor sketches of her design plans, as her new interior design company was growing faster than she could manage.

"At first, I was afraid of offending David, but he managed to open the door for me in a way that offended neither of us, and we never said anything more about the matter. At first, Marguerite was shocked that I had given up my Wall Street position for what she thought was an insecure artistic career in a field that wasn't even recognized as a profession. She was afraid interior design was just a passing fancy of Deirdre's. Well, we know better now, but it *was* a gamble in those days. When Marguerite heard what my salary was to be and who some of our latest clients were, she was impressed.

"I don't blame her for worrying. We did have very high household expenses, as we lived in a neighborhood suitable for a broker for the illustrious David Dawn, Inc. Of course, she did not want to give up our comfortable lifestyle, and not only that, she informed me that she was 'expecting!' Our baby was due in May.

"I can't tell you how happy I was. I was walking on air. Not only was I enjoying my new occupation immensely, I was soon to be a proud father. I had no way of knowing what was about to happen. Sometimes I think if I had it to do over, I would have stayed in Germany or France, and Marguerite would still be alive..."

"Did she die in childbirth?" asked Clark.

"Oh, no," said Paul. "But she never dilated more than one centimeter, so the baby was born by Caesarean section. The waiting was awful. You don't know that, but I'm sure one day you'll have your chance to find out. It's hard because there's nothing one can do but wait. It was a trial in my mind. I remember all of the flowers in Marguerite's room and the amazing feeling of holding my newborn son for the first time. He looked perfect to me. Marguerite was fine, too, though she was weak from her operation. I was so happy when I finally went home that morning.

"The next evening, after work, I was in Marguerite's room, holding her hand. We had decided to name the baby Richard, after her grandfather, and the phone kept ringing with calls from family and friends calling from all over the country to congratulate us. Three doctors and two nurses came in, and their expressions were so serious that they frightened us. We both immediately suspected bad news. They said our child might be a Mongoloid, but they weren't sure. They had to run some more tests. The senior obstetrician said he had thought Richard's head was too wobbly, even for a newborn, and that preliminary tissue tests indicated Mongoloidism."

"Mongoloidism? Isn't that a level of mental retardation?" asked Clark.

"Yes, technically, though I don't think it's used any more. What Richard has is called Down's syndrome nowadays, and Down's syndrome people are moderately to severely retarded. They are easy to identify because they have slanted eyes and different degrees of shortening and flattening of the skull. these physical signs were not visible in our baby because it was too early, yet, for them to appear. No one says 'Mongoloidism' anymore. You can imagine how awful it sounded to us. When it was clear that the doctors couldn't answer our questions, or offer us any reassurance, and they had all left, Marguerite called for the nurse and asked her if she could call in a priest so she could pray for the baby. I wasn't ready for that. I'm not Catholic, you know, and I wasn't ready to give this over to any God. At that time, I wanted to believe the doctors had made a mistake.

"I went into a spell of disbelief. I had so much strain and anxiety that the doctors offered me a prescription for tranquilizers. Although I envied Marguerite's easy unconsciousness once the drugs they gave her took effect, I refused to take any tranquilizers. When the final test results were in, I had to face the reality that I had fathered a then-called Mongoloid child."

"Is Down's syndrome hereditary, then?" asked Clark.

"No, it isn't," said Paul. "There's no way they can tell

The Decorator

which parent is genetically responsible. A Down's syndrome child has only one chromosome less than a normal child. It may be caused by the fertilization of an egg which is not healthy."

"One bad egg, huh?" asked Clark.

"Yes, only I wouldn't call it a 'bad egg.' It is said that Down's syndrome children know no sin. They are the most perfect children because they remain innocent all of their lives. That's certainly true of my Richard. But I didn't know that, at first. You can imagine, I was in total shock. I remember having to grab onto lamp posts at red lights on my way home so I didn't walk into traffic. I had a sense of unreality because having a child with birth defects was the sort of thing that happened to *other people*, and if it was happening to me, who was I? Suddenly all of the details of my life seemed meaningless. This kind of shock lasts for a long time, and it's amazing what it does to your head.

"On the second day, Marguerite was in complete tears and desperation. Our relatives and friends gathered around her and there was a feeling of shame in it because we didn't breed something 'perfect.' I felt that her relatives were blaming me, and my wife seemed to take all of my mother's comments personally. The worst was the way we blamed each other, the accusations in the slightest speculation the other made, and soon we were arguing. I did the only thing I could think of: I researched the disease in the library. I pored over medical books and magazines until I decided to call one expert whose name kept appearing in the literature. He met with us, and his advice was that we should not take Richard home because we did not know how to care for and educate a Down's syndrome child. He told us about group homes where they have a system of teaching them. It's like foster care, rather than an institution. If Richard grew up in such an environment, he would have a chance to learn to his capacity, but if we took him home, we would spend the rest of our lives caring for him without knowing how to really structure or control the environment to fit his needs.

"Marguerite agreed, and so did I, to find a home for Richard, and after that she refused to nurse him. The expert said this was normal, and the hospital agreed that she should not create a bond because she would have to let him go. I was heartbroken. From the moment I held my son in my arms, I had felt a bond that would never leave me. Marguerite was not speaking. She refused to say a word about Richard, or anything. She just kept asking for more painkillers until she could fall asleep.

"I had the difficult job of taking apart the room I had designed for our baby. I didn't want Marguerite to see it when she got home because it was just so sad to see that bedroom and know that our child would never sleep there. Oh, it was a great room, a fantasy room! We didn't know the sex of the baby when I designed it, so I did it in yellow and white stripes with a great beautiful border of dancing gray elephants with flowers in their trunks. The white furniture and changing table were upholstered in the dancing elephant print, too. The yellow vinyl floor had an aqua blue border around it, and the pretty white organza curtains were tied back with yellow bows."

"It sounds beautiful," said Clark.

"It was," said Paul. "I had been planning for the arrival of the baby for a long time, and I can't even tell you how it felt to go home and look in that same room and see the empty bassinet. After I called the contractor to come and take everything away and paint the room white, I had to figure out where to take Richard. All of the experts seemed to agree that one particular home in Delaware County was the best, and I drove up there to see it myself. I liked the hilly, wooded environment, and the home was immaculate, attractive and well decorated. The couple in charge gave me a good feeling right away. They were warm and knowledgeable, and I could tell they really cared for the children. After a long talk, I enrolled Richard, and I offered to create rooms for Richard and the other children — there were five or six of them, I believe. And I did. I created a different environment for each one of them, each as nice as Richard's room had been at home.

"When Richard was ready to leave the hospital, I took him in the back of the car up to the home. I was accustomed to him not crying — Down's syndrome children don't cry — but during that ride it struck me just how silent he was. In the beginning, I visited Richard every weekend — Marguerite refused to

The Decorator

go with me — and now I see him every few weeks and on holidays. Richard is in really good shape. He's eighteen years old, and he has the thought process capability of a child of about seven. He knows who people are. He speaks and eats well at the table; his manners are perfection. He goes to bed like clockwork and gets up on time. He's a very sweet person. He has a good sense of humor, in fact, he's a bit of a clown — very good at getting attention, his teachers say. I'm proud of him, and I only wish Marguerite could have known him."

"Wouldn't you have wanted to have another child?" asked Clark.

"I was willing to try," said Paul. "The expert said that there was no reason we should worry about having another Down's syndrome child. Actually, because we had one, which was a fluke, we probably wouldn't have another. But Marguerite didn't see it that way. She never let it go, and she couldn't cope. She saw it as a failure on her part and she used drinking and pills until her mental condition deteriorated. And I had to live with that. I fought to keep her from the pills, but one day, a year after Richard's birth, I found her dead in our bedroom. She overdosed. Now do you see why I can't get involved with Adela Morgan? Her drinking frightens me. When she talks about that husband and daughter who died, and she blames herself, it's like she's got this huge ego, and this terrible guilt for things she didn't cause. I'm afraid she'll drink herself to death."

"That's understandable," said Clark. "I didn't realize Adela discussed these things with anyone. And now I also understand where you disappear to on so many weekends. I'm so sorry about your wife. I know how it is to lose people. I don't know if you ever really get over it."

"No, you don't," said Paul. "They say time heals all wounds, but you never really forget them." Paul looked at his watch. "My stars! Could it be 3:25? I must get to bed. I can't think when I've been up this late. And you! Don't you have to meet Miss Raven at eleven tomorrow morning?"

"Yes, I suppose all of the sane people are asleep, and perhaps I should go to bed too," said Clark. Their check had long been paid and all that remained was for them to tip the waiter, which Clark did.

"You're not going to walk all the way home, are you?" He was concerned that his frail and well-dressed boss would consider walking alone up Lexington Avenue so late at night.

"Goodness, no," said Paul. "The Polo Bar glow has worn off and it's chilly out here. I see a cab up there and I'll get him to turn and go up Park. Good night, Clark! Call me tomorrow!"

Clark watched the little man in his cashmere coat and neat gray felt hat climb into the taxi and he felt warmth for Paul Hedges. He decided he wouldn't mind looking like Paul Hedges one day, though he doubted he would ever wear a hat. No one wore hats any more. Where have all the hats gone? Clark pondered on his way home.

The phone was ringing as he unlocked his door. He dove for it, hoping it was Reggie. The voice on the other end was very soft, and at first he didn't recognize it.

"*Ciao, bello*. There you are. I have been calling all night. I come over now, okay?"

"Maria?" he guessed.

"I come now."

"What? Where —" he asked, but she had hung up.

"Great," Clark groaned, and sank to the couch, his head in his hands. He was suddenly very tired. The phone rang again and he picked it up.

"Maria? Can't it wait —" he began.

"Maria who?" boomed Adela Morgan. "One of your girls, I guess? One of your models for those sick paintings, I bet! HAW, HAW, HAW! Hey, Clark, how about having me model for you? I'm better than any of those broads you use."

"Hello, Adela. What can I do for you?"

"You can tell me why he hasn't called!" Adela demanded. "You were with him last. Where the hell is he? It's been two hours and I've been waiting up for him to call. He's gotta be home by now! He did go *home*, didn't he?"

"Of course he did, but he was very tired and I'm sure he thought you were asleep, too, and he didn't want to disturb you. We've had a long day, Adela. Why don't we all get some sleep?"

"Bullshit! Don't give me that! You're just a fresh kid! No fresh kid tells me when to go to bed. Wha'd he say? Wha'd Paul say about me?"

The Decorator

"He said you're a great talent and a great lady," Clark yawned loudly.

"He did? He did? What else did he say? Do you think he likes me? God, I got the hots for that man! I'm sweet on that man, you betcha! He'd better call me, Clark, or he don't know what he's missin'! Is he gonna call me?"

"He said he would call, didn't he?" Clark said, making his voice sound as tired as possible. His intercom rang, jarringly. "Adela, that's my door. I have to go."

"You just make sure he calls me. I mean it!" Adela hung up.

Clark opened the door for Maria. She stood rather shyly in the hallway, wavering from one foot to the other. She look ravishing in a white fur jacket, white ribbed tights, and high white fur-topped boots. Her doll-like face was framed in a puffy white fur hat. She was made up in flowery pastels and her eyelashes were as long as dandelion petals. Clark stared into the cool amber of her eyes.

"Hello, Maria."

"Hello, Clark."

He let her in and poured red wine for them both. Some classical music would fit the occasion, he thought, and he turned the volume down low so as not to disturb his neighbors. Maria took off her hat and slid out of her coat to reveal a slinky beige jersey dress with gold buttons and no sleeves. Clark realized he was still wearing his coat.

"How silly of me," he said, as he took it off. "Would you like an ashtray?" He found one in the sink for Maria, who had lit one of her strong-smelling French cigarettes. They sat at his kitchen table and drank while Maria smoked cigarette after cigarette. She didn't say much, but she sighed, often and dramatically, and each sigh made her bosom heave until Clark was panting. What could she want? He hoped he knew why she had come, but she wasn't talking.

After four glasses of wine and five cigarettes, Maria began talking about Italy. She told Clark about her mother's garden and the beautiful vines, flowers and tomatoes that grew there. She told a long, breathy story about when she was a little girl playing in the garden and how she had seen some sort of friendly spirits who said they made the beans grow. The story was charming, but it seemed to go nowhere and the wine made

Clark's head heavier and heavier until he had to prop his chin up with his hand. He fought to keep his eyes open. He felt like he was watching an incomprehensible foreign film.

"Damn Luciano!" Maria spat.

"Luciano?" Clark asked foggily.

Maria only released a stream of Italian curses. Her eyes were smoldering. Clark had a vague memory of Luciano leaving the opening with Holly Raven. Had Maria gotten involved with Luciano? He was afraid to ask.

"Tonight, he went home with that square chick, Holly! How could he prefer her over me?" Maria thrust her chest out for emphasis. "Luciano says he will marry me! He lies! He is already married! He has a fat wife in Italy, with a mustache! And two babies."

"Why aren't I surprised?" asked Clark. "Why do you want to marry Luciano? Do you love him?"

"I did," said Maria. "No more. I did everything for him. He got everything he wanted. Was it good enough? NO! I want to quit the stewardess shit! I thought it would be glamorous, but I am just a sky waitress and all of the bastards pinch my ass. I want to quit that shit and have babies and a garden like my mama. Soon I will be old and alone!" Tears flowed from Maria's eyes, smearing the black petals of mascara into inky rivers that ran down her cheeks.

"Hey. Oh," said Clark. "You'd better cut that out, or you'll have a mustache like Luciano's wife. Or maybe that's what he likes." He dipped his finger into his wine glass and playfully drew a red mustache above Maria's upper lip. She laughed and wiped away her black tears.

"That's better," said Clark. "Forget him. You're young. You have plenty of time. You'll find someone else in no time at all. Look at you. You're beautiful. He's a pig."

That made Maria cry again and she clung to Clark, sobbing into his chest. After a while, she sighed heavily and stopped crying. Her face was now bare of makeup and she looked all of fourteen years old.

"Do you think I am beautiful?" she asked.

"Yes," said Clark.

"Mr. Friedman says so too," she said, lighting a cigarette.

"Allen Friedberg?" asked Clark.

"Yes, Friedberg. He will put me in movies. He can make me a big star, he says. Believe me, I am not stupid." Maria poured wine and looked slyly at Clark. "I know what he wants. I know what is the price of his stardom. So what. He is the real thing, no? He is what he says he is?"

"He is," said Clark.

"Then I will do it," said Maria.

"Good," said Clark.

"I am a good actress, too," said Maria. "If I can pretend to like Mr. Friedberg, I can pretend anything."

Clark raised his glass in a toast. "Here's to you," he said. "And to no more tears!"

"No more tears," said Maria, touching her glass to his. They drank. "Let's go to bed," said Maria. "But, not to sleep. Not just yet. I want you to hold me."

"I thought you'd never ask," said Clark.

The ringing phone jolted Clark out of a deep sleep and his hangover kicked in with a painful roar. Maria didn't budge. He fumbled over her for the telephone and croaked a hello.

"Asleep? You? I don't believe it!" Reggie was all good humor and post-bran muffin energy.

"What time is it?" asked Clark.

"Ten-thirty. It *is* Saturday, but I thought you'd be up already, lazybones. What's wrong?"

"I don't know," said Clark. "I'll tell you after I've had a bottle of aspirin and maybe some hair of the miserable dog—Ouch!" It hurt to sit up.

"I can't believe you're hung over. I've never heard of such a thing. What did you do?"

"You know what champagne does to me, and I usually don't drink it, but I wanted to celebrate. And the Polo Bar on top of that! Oh, my head. I'm glad you called, because I have to get up."

"Good. I thought we could go out for brunch and maybe catch a movie."

"Sorry, hon, I have to meet Pamela Raven at eleven to work on her new apartment and then I have to call Paul about Roland Lee. Damn that Roland Lee!" a surge of anxiety shot Clark to his feet and into the kitchen to make coffee.

"Why are you damning him?" asked Reggie. "I mean, yeah, he's a terrible square, but you can handle those types."

"Well, he keeps going back and forth, jerking us around on the Ritz Plaza deal. At the show he told me we've got the contract. He thinks I can deliver Dannee Lou as if she's a sofa or something. That idiot. But as we were leaving the Polo he dumps this stupid competition idea in my lap. Maybe because Dannee Lou wasn't impressed. I told him she's married, and she has more taste than to fall for Lee, even if she were single! He's such an obvious social climber. Anyway, he wants to give each of the top New York decorating firms a suite at the Ritz to design, and whoever does the best job, according to him, 'wins' the contract."

"That stinks," said Reggie.

"You bet it stinks," said Clark. "I tried to tell Paul what I think about it last night, but that Morgan bitch had him buttonholed. Do you know she called me at four a.m. last night, demanding that I make Paul go out with her again? 'Do ya think he likes me? Do ya?'" Clark imitated Adela's brassy baritone perfectly. "What could I say? Especially after all the crap she was shoveling about me last night! I tell you, this job is hard sometimes. It's just not worth it."

"Poor Clark," said Reggie. "What did Paul say about Roland?"

"All he said was, 'Do something dramatic.' I was going to get up early today and try to come up with something, but right now I don't give a damn about Roland Lee and his big nose. I haven't seen a dime from that guy yet and he's taking over my life."

"Oh, come on. You'll think of something. You always do," said Reggie. "Drink your coffee. You'll be fine. Anyway, here's the deal: I want the dirt on Johnny. What do you know about him? Is he gay? Does he have a girl friend, or what?"

"Reg, I've never met him before last night. Dannee Lou is crazy about him, but he *is* her brother, and he has a good reputation as a reporter, as well he should, with all that football-player aggression of his. He was an all-star or something until he was injured. You know I don't follow football. Didn't you find out everything you wanted to know last night?" Clark hoped Johnny had been terrible in bed so that he could tell her his Holly horror story. He could use a laugh.

"Oh, not that I didn't want to, but we didn't do anything," said Reggie. "He just held me all night. And we *made out!* Clark, I haven't made out with anyone since I was fourteen! Remember when we used to say 'made out?' He said I'm too special to rush things with. Isn't that sweet? Can you believe it? Are they all like that in Texas? Does he have a girlfriend? Can you sort of subtly ask Dannee Lou for me?"

"I guess I could do that," said Clark. He poured his coffee and sat down on his living room couch. "Ahhh...Hey! I've got it! What about an all-white Ritz Plaza suite overlooking Central Park? Because this is a living room and drawing room that looks over the park, I can make it a fantasy room. What do you think?"

"I don't know. All white? Are you sure?" Reggie sounded doubtful. "It sounds too Jean Harlow."

"But that's perfect!" said Clark. "It ties in with the Jean Harlow craze that's everywhere. It'll ring all the right bells."

"Clark, it sounds nice, really, but just because they're showing Harlow films in all the revival houses this week and some bimbos are bleaching their hair until it falls out…isn't a white room a bit impractical?"

"Never mind that," said Clark. "Lee can rent it to corporations or on a yearly basis. No one else is going to do white. Can you imagine how sick and tired I am of dark hotel colors? Roland Lee will flip out. That contract is *mine,* sweetheart!"

"You amaze me," said Reggie. "Honey, the reason I called, besides to hear what goes on in your amazing head, is, I'm wondering if you can take me to the doctor today? He's going to tell me if I'm pregnant or not, and I'm terrified, and I don't know where Luciano is, and Maria's not answering her phone either. I'm kind of nervous about this. Please say you'll come."

"I wish I could, but I have to — wait a minute, didn't you tell me you were pregnant last night?"

"Well, I'm pretty sure I am. I feel gross every morning, but I don't know for *sure —*"

At that moment, Maria walked naked out of the bedroom and Clark almost dropped the phone. He tried to make a shushing gesture at her, but she grabbed the receiver and meowed into it on her way into the bathroom.

"What was that?" asked Reggie. "Clark?"

Clark quickly decided that, knowing these girls, a lie would get him in more trouble than the truth.

"I think I've found someone who'll go to the doctor with you. Hold on a second. Maria!" Clark called.

Maria came to the phone, and while they made excited plans for breakfast before Reggie's appointment and a movie after, Clark took a shower, shaved, and got dressed.

Maria called him over and said, "Reggie says you are a naughty boy, but if you will give a repeat performance tonight with both of us, she will forgive you. She's coming now over to get me."

"Tell her the curtain goes up at eight o'clock, at her place. I won't be late!"

Reggie agreed and she dashed over to Clark's apartment, stopping only to pick up some bagels and a newspaper at a deli. Clark buzzed her in and she rushed in the door, breathless and waving a New York *Post*.

"Look at this!" she said.

The headline read: "PAMELA RAVEN BANKRUPT."

The Decorator

CHAPTER 10

"I won't grow old! I won't grow old!" Pamela Raven did not see Clark standing behind her as she glared into her mirror. The cold fluorescent light outlined her stark features as she pushed back the skin on her cheekbones with both hands. Her special lighting was unforgiving; it shone glaringly on each tiny line and skin flaw and reflected mercilessly off her grey roots.

"Oh, I'm sorry, Miss Raven! I told Mr. Calloway to come right in! That's what you wanted, isn't it?"

Pamela Raven turned in her chair to regard Mama, who hovered behind Clark with a measuring tape and a sheaf of bristol boards in her hands.

"Oh, it's all right, Mama. Clark is welcome in my dressing room any time! Hello, Clark, darling! My, don't you look like a gentleman in that divine suit!" She tilted her head for Clark to kiss her cheek, which he did. Both sides. "Clark, remind me, I have the perfect cufflinks for you to go with that suit! Luckily today is jewelry day, when I have all my gems brought over from the vault! Mama, when you're through measuring that closet, come into my room and help me find those golden cufflinks I gave Lucien, the ones with the emeralds! But before you do that, fix Clark something to drink. What would you like, Clark? A cocktail? Some juice? Coffee or tea?"

"Coffee would be fine, thank you," said Clark.

"Mama, fix a tray for Clark and bring it into my room. Which boards are these?" She shuffled through the pages Mama had brought in. "You see, Clark, I have each of my ensembles sketched out in story boards and colored in. Here's my pink Chanel — Mama! These pages are out of order! How sloppy! And the hat page is missing! Where's my pink puff?"

"Oh, I'm sorry, Miss Raven, I must have left it on top of the other pink pile! I'll just go look!"

"Don't bother," said Pamela. "She's old. But she's the only

one I can trust with my things. Miss Riley is hopeless with color and Holly is a disaster. I suppose you've seen how she lives."

She noted Clark's expression and raised one eyebrow. "I'm ashamed to say I reared that child. That's not the kind of housekeeping I taught her. I never go over there, anywhere where she lives. It's unhealthy."

Pamela was applying makeup with high-speed motions as she talked. "There! That's the best we can do today, considering what I have to work with. Let's go upstairs and I'll telephone Miss Riley and ask her where she put the check my accountant wrote for you! It's not in the usual place, and I told him to have it delivered yesterday. We don't expect anyone to work for free, do we?"

Clark followed Pamela upstairs and into her bedroom, which was transformed into a scene from *Pirates of the Caribbean*. Enormous glowing jewels and precious gems of all colors sparkled on white terrycloth towels which covered every surface. Glistening ropes of gold chains and pearls draped Pamela's snowy covered bed and piles of diamonds on her bureau reflected thousands of tiny lights along the walls.

Clark sat in one of the two chairs that were unadorned and gazed at the splendor all around him. He was speechless.

"Oh, I see you are admiring my jewels," said Pamela, as she dialed a phone number. "Once in a while, I have them bring the jewels out so I can inventory them, but most of the time I keep them in the vault. Too much temptation for thieves to have them lying around. I've had them all copied in paste. Every piece of jewelry you see me wear is an imitation of one of the originals in my collection. No one ever guesses! Where is that girl? Five rings! Oh, hello, Riley! Where is that goddamn check for Deirdre Dawn? Mama and I have turned this place upside down and we can't find it! He what? What do you mean there's no money in the account? What about Cosmetique? That too? Why didn't someone tell me — You didn't get paid, either? That's outrageous! How dare he say I can't afford you! I'll tell him what I can afford! I can afford to hire a new accountant! What?"

There was a deadly silence as Pamela Raven listened to what Miss Riley had to say. Her face grew fearsome and there were ice crystals in her voice when she said, "Fuck the New York *Post!* And if they ask again, you can give them that as a direct quote from me!"

She slammed down the receiver, braced herself on the bedside table, and screamed, "MAMA!"

Mama was right outside the door, holding the coffee tray and Pamela's scream made her drop it. Cups shattered and hot coffee flew everywhere. Mama ran out of the room to get a mop and Pamela threw herself down on the floor by the edge of her bed. She clutched the corner of a towel and sobbed into it. Jewels slid off the bed and landed in her lap like hot sparks.

"How could he do this to me?" she sobbed. "My Lucien! NO! NO!"

Clark assumed Miss Riley had told Pamela Raven about the newspaper headlines that announced her bankruptcy. He stood awkwardly above the wailing movie star, uncertain about what to say or whether to touch her. He settled for patting her on the shoulder and mumbling, "There, there, it's all right," which sounded ineffectual and downright untrue to his own ears.

Meanwhile, Mama was sweeping up the broken china. The coffee made a swishing sound under her broom. "I didn't want her to see those papers," she said. "I knew it would only upset her!"

Pamela lifted her head. Her eyes looked even bigger when they were filled with tears. "Oh, Clark, you must think I'm terrible. However can I pay you now? It will be weeks before the Metropolis contract is signed, and I won't have a cent until then! How could Lucien do this to me? Miss Riley said Cosmetique emptied our account to recoup the advance salary he drew from them. It's that hideous Roger Kirkeby who's to blame. I'll bet he's at the bottom of all this! I'll get him for this!"

Pamela rose in a fury, rubies and pearls falling from her skirts. Mama squeaked and dove to retrieve the precious stones. She laid them carefully on the bed.

"I'm sure the office will understand," said Clark. "It's not a problem for us to wait a few weeks until you can iron this out. In the meantime, we might as well get you settled in your new place. The Wilsons won't wait forever."

Pamela made a disgusted face at the mention of the

Wilsons. "That shriveled little monkey of a woman. I can't abide the thought of her in my apartment. Well, thank heaven I have a job! If Allen hadn't offered me this picture, I don't know what I'd do! I'll have Miss Riley — Oh! I don't have Miss Riley any more! Damn it to hell! Never mind, I'll call Allen myself and ask him for an advance. We can't have people going unpaid. And I'll get Miss Riley back, too. How awful this is! From riches to rags, and surrounded by jewelry! Look at me — my hands are shaking. Mama! Vodka!"

"Right away, Miss Raven. And I'll get you some more coffee, Mr. Calloway!" Mama gathered her cleaning supplies and a dustpan full of china shards.

"And bring me your list of the final measurements!" said Pamela. "We'll need it over at my new apartment."

It was a bizarre request, but Clark made no comment as he masking-taped the floor to outline where the furniture would go. He watched as Pamela floated around the marked spaces as if she were on an empty stage practicing her blocking. She chattered continuously, in a stagy character voice, as if she were addressing Clark, but she seemed to require no answers, so he only watched her. He had never seen anything like it.

"Now, which sofa are we going to put in this place! What tables are we going to use? Have we measured everything from the old apartment? I'm sending the extra things to auction, you know. We're all very upset about that, but it can't be helped, can it?" She paced around the tape marks, mentally measuring: "One sofa, seven feet long, thirty-six inches deep. One end table, twenty-four inches wide."

Clark was amazed at her memory. All of her recited figures matched Mama's list, which he held in his hand. Then, even stranger, Pamela Raven began to talk to her invisible furniture.

"Now, my little table! We're going to have felt on you! Have we got the right lamp on this table? Of course we do. There you are, darling! Clark will cover all of you window sills in plastic laminate. You know we don't like paint that smudges and cracks!" she threw back her head and laughed, a young, tinkly little laugh, as if the window sill had just said something terribly funny. "And you new curtains will all be pre-washed. We'll have no shrinking, do you hear? Now let's walk into the bathroom."

Clark followed her in. It was time to call Paul Hedges, but he didn't want to interrupt Pamela Raven's performance.

"I'm sorry, tub, but you'll have to go. Clark is taking you out, and all of the other tubs are going too. So, it's nothing personal! We never soak in our own dirt. Never, never. Shower only!"

Clark hoped she wouldn't start talking to the dirt.

"Clark, we're in the bedroom now. Try to keep up!"

When he got there, Pamela Raven was all seriousness. She addressed him with her hands on her hips.

"Clark, where am I going to put my sheets? Because during the day I never have the bed exposed. Not the bed that *I* am going to sleep on! I always have it covered with extra sheets, especially over the pillows, so that no bad air and no bad dust will get on my white pillowcases."

Clark made a note of her request on his pad. "Won't they fit in one of these closets?" he asked.

"Oh, no," said Pamela. "Those closets are horrible old things — impossible to keep clean! We'll never get the smell out of them. Smell in here!"

Clark did. He smelled nothing but old wood. He looked at Pamela, waiting to hear about what he was smelling.

"Clark, what I smell in here is the musty, old-lady smell of someone's pathetic life. I want these closets removed. The maid's room will be converted into my wardrobe, in glass as we discussed, and Mama will be in the second bedroom. That maid's room is much too small for her."

She led Clark into the maid's room and they peered into the maid's bathroom, with its miniature tub.

"What did they hire, midgets?" Pamela cried. "This room is *out*. That way, there'll be more space for hats. Tape the maid's room wall. I want you to divide it into color groups for my dresses. Forty-nine inches of pinks, twenty-five inches of mauves, two feet of purples, a yard of blacks, thirty inches of yellows, and about a foot of greens, and I want them hung in color groups from avocado to jade." Pamela measured each space with her arms as Clark taped it.

"Reds," she said. "And turquoise. Beige here and white. Now, we'll do prints and stripes all the way to the window.

Remember to get the measurements of these closets accurate from the top; hats that match our suits, that match our gowns, that match our belts and gloves, all the way down to our shoes. We didn't have them dyed to match to have them end up all scrambled. That's why I invented the story boards! A good idea, isn't it?"

Clark had to agree.

"Now, we'll finish up with Mama's room and get all of the things in order in the old apartment. I want to see your sketches for my new closets, and then I'm taking you out to dinner. We're going to the Café Brazil."

"I'd love to go to dinner with you, Pamela," said Clark. "But I'm not exactly dressed for it. I'd have to go home and change."

"Nonsense," said Pamela. "That suit is perfectly fine for Café Brazil. And you will shower in Lucien's bathroom. I insist that all of my escorts shower at least twice a day. Why, I shower four times a day, myself. We'll put those new cufflinks on you, and I can take you anywhere. No arguments."

Clark had none.

When they arrived at the penthouse, Clark had phone calls to make. He called Paul Hedges and told him that his meeting with Pamela Raven was going along well. Pamela grabbed the receiver at that point to rave happily about Clark's talents. She told Paul she was very pleased that she had engaged the Deirdre Dawn office, she was recommending its services to her friends, and that Paul simply must come over for cocktails one evening. Laughing girlishly at his answer, she handed the receiver back to Clark and marched off upstairs.

Paul approved of Clark's ideas for the Ritz Plaza suite, and Paul added that Roland Lee wanted Clark to call him. In fact, Roland wanted to know if Clark was free this evening for drinks or a movie. Clark did not appreciate the last-minute, second-hand invitation, and he decided to ignore it. He had better things to do on a Saturday night.

"I'll pretend I didn't hear that," he said, laughing.

Paul was a little shocked at Clark's attitude: "Oh, my, oh dear. How awkward. You really should call him to say you are otherwise engaged."

Groaning at Paul's old-fashioned manners, Clark dialed

Roland Lee's Ritz Plaza suite and, as he had suspected, he had a difficult time extracting himself from the conversation once he had made his excuse. It turned out Roland Lee also had four tickets to "The Nutcracker Suite" for the weekend before Christmas and he, naturally, wanted Clark to bring a date and to invite Dannee Lou for the fourth. Clark said he couldn't promise anything, as he didn't know Dannee Lou's schedule, but he would certainly ask, and anyway, he was using someone else's private line and he would have to hang up.

"Yeah, baby, I know you're at some chick's pad, and you're about to get some action! Tell me, who is she? Does she have a friend?" Roland demanded.

Clark hated it when men called him 'baby,' and the pseudo-hipster lingo was especially distasteful coming from Roland Lee, who had grown up in a drab suburb of Chicago and was about as unhip as one could be. Besides, the "chick" was Pamela Raven and she had planted herself in Clark's view and was holding out a bathrobe and towel in a commanding way that could not be ignored.

Clark found Lucien's bathroom warm and comfortable and he liked the high, wide green marble ledges of the glassed-in shower stall. The hot water was soothing and it made him a little sleepy as it drummed on his head, reminding him of the excesses of the night before. Suddenly, the door opened and the cool air startled him.

"What!" he exclaimed.

He peered out through the steamy glass to see Pamela Raven, smiling like a sphinx as her gaze traveled up and down his body. Slowly, she dropped her pink silk bathrobe to the floor and presented herself with an air of serene glory. She slid the shower door open and stepped into the shower. Her arms wrapped around him and she pressed her body into his. She closed her eyes and turned her face up into the falling water as if it were a spotlight.

"I know you're gay, honey, but don't be afraid," she whispered. "Just pretend I'm Clark Gable."

Pamela's comment was as unreal to Clark as the scene she was playing, a seduction straight off the set of *Mogambo*. His head went as fizzy as a faulty television set as the water poured down and Pamela Raven climbed up on the marble shower ledges to straddle Clark and ride him vigorously. He didn't have to do anything but brace himself so that he could keep his balance, and he marveled at her strength. He just let the sensations fill him until she satisfied herself with all of the noisy passion she was famous for. She dismounted, gasping and rubbing her thighs.

"I knew all those exercises were good for something. That was rather good, if I do say so myself!" Her silvery laugh echoed in the shower stall.

"Now, out! Out, you!" she cried pleasantly. "I must wash again. Be a good boy and get dressed! I'll meet you downstairs in my office."

Clark stumbled out of the bathroom, grabbing a towel along the way. He felt dazed as he dried himself off. So, it's over for her, he mused. The scene is finished. Cut! Wardrobe! And there it was, his suit, a freshly ironed shirt, clean socks and underwear, and an unfamiliar tie, all laid out for him on Lucien's bed. On the dresser next to the bed lay a sparkling paid of emerald cufflinks and a little note from Pamela:

Merry Christmas, Clark Darling!
You are a love — Pamela Raven.

When Pamela came downstairs she was all business. "Mama has made reservations for us at Café Brazil for six-thirty! In the meantime I want you to help me rearrange the living-room furniture! I've got a new idea for a seating arrangement that will be much more practical for a small space! Let's try it!"

Clark was only too glad to help her. He was impressed with the way she avoided any awkward feelings that might arise since their relationship had taken such a sudden and intimate turn. Or perhaps there were no awkward feelings for her. She just seemed to have a boundless supply of energy that she needed to express. While he appreciated her idea to create conversational groupings of loveseats and chairs rather than line the walls with long couches, he would have been content to sketch in the new plans at his drawing board. He could imagine the final results, but Pamela had to see them. And dust. And vacuum the rugs so that the old marks from the furniture did not show. And then she had to vacuum the rugs again so that their naps all ran in her preferred diagonal direction.

Clark did not like meticulous maintenance work. It seemed

to him a waste of time better spent dreaming up a new exciting idea or meeting new clients. But he, of course, indulged Pamela Raven, as it was impossible not to, and in a strange way the exertion helped him avoid a feeling that was almost like hurt that Pamela did not at least want to talk about what had just happened in the shower. She was acting as if it hadn't happened at all, and Clark missed the friendly sort of discussions he and Reggie always had, during and after sex. He was glad Pamela was not a clingy, cuddly type like Maria, and he hoped Pamela would remain friendly and not expect regular "extras" from him.

At least she wasn't like Holly. He didn't think he could handle another scene like that, but he couldn't help wondering what Holly would say if she knew she had been right. Am I a star-fucker? He smiled to think how little his desires had to do with his encounter with Pamela Raven, Movie Star, and he thought, if this is what being used feels like, I could use more of it.

When Pamela was satisfied with the results, she called Mama in to look.

"Oh, it's very nice, Miss Raven! Very nice," said Mama. She gave a *TV Guide* to Pamela. "I thought you might like to know it's 'Pamela Raven Week' on the 'Eight O'Clock Movie'."

Pamela snatched the Guide and flipped it open. "Oh, that Thom Pearson! He did this intentionally, I'm sure! What an angel! You remember him, Clark, the gentleman you met at Allen's party! Thom knows I never miss my old films when they're on TV! You know, I won't get a color set because everything good that's been done is in black and white! What's on tonight! Let's see...Oh! Yes! Tonight I get the man away from that insipid little Mary Scott! Mama! Cancel our reservations at Café Brazil and order us something nice from Casserole Kitchen! You know, one of the hot dishes I like so much, and something for Clark! He's a meat-and-potatoes boy if I ever saw one! And more meat than potatoes!" she cracked.

Clark calculated anxiously in his head: dinner, a movie at eight ... he probably wouldn't get downtown until nearly eleven. Unless Pamela wanted him to stay the night, but he doubted it. He hoped Reggie and Maria wouldn't mind.

They ate their dinner on a stainless steel countertop in

Pamela's industrial-looking kitchen.

"You probably think being an actress, I never cook, but I never forgot my cooking skills. You have to come over for meatloaf sometime!" said Pamela. "Speaking of which, what are you doing for the holidays? Are you going to visit your family? Or have you made other plans?"

"My sister Vera is the only family I have left, and she lives in Maine. I'll be going up to visit her and her husband and my two little nephews for Christmas. She just had a new baby this week. I expect they'll be home from the hospital today."

"Oh, I apologize, Clark. I had forgotten that this is your first Christmas without your mother and father. How tactless of me. Do forgive me, it's just you're not at all the poor little orphan type."

"No, I'm not," said Clark. "And I'm glad you can see that. I don't like it when people pity me and behave as if I'm so fragile that they can't mention my parents being gone. Of course, I'm sad, and I do miss them, but I'm not paralyzed by it."

"Of course not," said Pamela. "You are a realist, just like me. In fact, I can't tolerate oversentimentality about family — or anything else! It's a lot of rubbish. One doesn't *choose* these people, and while I did love my mother, she absolutely ignored me when I was young; she was no help at all. Not that I expected her to be; the poor thing could barely manage! One must never blame one's parents, Clark! Self-pity is a most wretched sin!

"And my mother was a terrible burden to me in her old age. I took her in, you know, into my Bel Air house, and she was always running around demanding attention and scuffing my floors with her noisy slippers! She wouldn't wear the nice things I bought for her, so when the tour buses came by it was a terrible embarrassment unless I could get her to stay inside. And she was always trying to get money from me for my no-good brother Bill. He would just gamble it or drink it away. Bill was in and out of detox and casinos for most of his life; when he was sober the best he could do was pump gas. She always liked him best, though, and neither of them ever showed me a bit of gratitude. I didn't have to buy them houses in Los Angeles and finance my brother's ridiculous schemes, but I did it out of love. And not one word of thanks did I ever get

The Decorator

from any of them. But your family is so much nicer. Let's talk about them!"

"Well, Vera inherited our family home in Berwick, but she couldn't bear to live with the memories. She took the loss of our parents very hard and she's still very sad about it. So she sold the house and moved into a very nice old cracker saltbox house in Poland Spring, where her husband is a land developer."

"Well, that's a good business to be in. I've never been to Maine, but I hear it's very pretty and rustic up there. Gabe, Gabe Taylor that is, once tried to convince me to come with him to a cabin in Maine where he liked to fish, but I wouldn't go. Send me a picture, I said. I'm not a rough-it kind of gal. I guess I had enough of that when I was a kid."

"Oh, Maine is pretty. I didn't appreciate it either when I was a boy. Somehow I always knew the variety of a big city would suit me better. But Vera loves to take me by our old school, Deering High, so we can reminisce and have a few laughs, and we'll have some of our old teachers and neighbors over for wassail and tree trimming. Vera's not up to cooking this year, with the new baby and all, so we'll probably go to The Village, an Italian restaurant in Portland, for Christmas dinner. It's simple, but nice. And there's an old waitress there — she's been there for years — she's always been sort of a mother figure for us. And that will be it."

"Well, you must tell me all of the names and ages again, so I can send a few little things along with you —"

"Oh, no," said Clark. "You mustn't bother —"

"Don't worry about it, Clark! It's just something I do every year. My Christmas list is miles long and I adore sending every gift with a handwritten note to old friends and new! It's just the way I do things. Do you know I remember every Cosmetique employee on my Christmas card list? And their spouses and children? I do! Miss Riley and Mama have been working on that list since Thanksgiving."

She frowned and pushed away her barely-eaten dinner. "I just don't know what I'm going to do about Holly this year. Speaking of ungrateful people! I can hardly bring myself to tell you that after all of the trouble I went to to convince Lew Fine to represent her, she's running off to Italy like a little slut to make trashy films with that ill-bred monster, Mr. Mediterranean Muscles! If they make films at all! That girl is so naive, but do you think she listens to my voice of experience? I told her that neither Lew nor I can protect her over in that primitive country, but she is so stubborn! Not only is she ruining her career, but she *insulted* me! She had the nerve to tell me to get off her back! I'll get off her back permanently, if that's what she wants. Then she'll see. Of course, I sent her Christmas present right back to the store. She'll get nothing from me this year, and we'll see how she likes that!"

Pamela saw Clark's pained expression and said, "Oh, you must think I'm horrible, but that girl has to learn. I know, I'll not send her a button! No, I'll reconsider and send her a box of tea! That will get my point across, don't you think?"

"I'm sure it will," said Clark.

Mama rolled the television on its stand out from a recessed cabinet where it was kept, made a tray of iced vodka and Frito-Lays for Pamela, and retired to her room for the evening.

Once the movie began, Clark did not know whether to watch the television, or Pamela. It was as if she had never seen the film before and did not know what was going to happen to her character.

"Oh, no! Where is she going? Will she be all right? Will she?" she worried.

"Don't you remember the script?" asked Clark.

"Shhh!" Pamela glared at him.

"Sorry," said Clark.

During the commercials she smoked, knit furiously, and counted her stitches. Clark drank the vodka and ate the chips she didn't touch. Near the end of the movie, the phone rang. Pamela picked it up.

"Gabe! Gabe Taylor! Why, it's been some time… Of course I know *Surrender* is on; I'm watching it as we speak. Aren't you handsome, though? You will come back to me in the end, I just know you will…Why, thank you, you're such a devil!…You don't say! I must tell my friend; hold on a moment, Gabe."

She turned to Clark. "It's Gabe Taylor calling, my old friend. He says he wants to be the first to congratulate me on getting the part in *Tigress in the Dark*. And you'll never guess: he's been cast in it too, as the detective who becomes my lover and has to arrest me!

She shouted into the phone, "Gabe, darling, that's wonderful news! Oh?"

She listened for a long time without comment, except for an occasional "Oh, dear." She finished up by saying she would call him when she arrived in L.A. and they would catch up on old times. She said goodbye several times before she could hang up.

"Poor Gabe," she told Clark. "Divorced again. And is he drunk! He always did like his whiskey and I suppose he's lonely, poor guy. He never could marry the right type of girl after Miranda died in that terrible accident. He really did love her, you know. But the others!"

She made a twisted face while she lit another cigarette. "Studio fluff. Weak little blondes, too young for him. Gabe's a man's man, you know. He'd rather be out hunting and fishing in the wilderness than home playing some godawful card game. Of course, Miranda could always keep up. She could rough it and look elegant in a workshirt and jodhpurs. It was after she died that he came back to me the last time. For comfort, at first. But he and I just couldn't be alone together in the same room without something happening. You know how it is. And then we ended up in the *police* station, thanks to Holly! Well, she was hardly old enough to understand the crazy side of love. Isn't life funny?"

"Would you take him back if he asked you?" asked Clark.

"Oh, no," said Pamela. "Those days are over. I like my solitude and my freedom! I couldn't bear some smelly man about the house all the time. And Gabe Taylor is a very smelly person. Despite that romantic leading man image. Most of them are, I'm afraid. That's why I prefer clean young men of your type, Clark. At least you know how to present yourself."

"But I'm not—" Clark began. "I've never been —"

Pamela yawned loudly. "My, look at the time! It's past my bedtime, and I'm sure you have a nice young fellow waiting for you out there on the dance floor tonight!"

Clark followed Pamela Raven to the door, accepted his coat from her, and traded the white slippers for his shoes.

"You are sweet, but I never have people stay the night. I have to polish the floors every morning, and it's such an inconvenience for guests. So nice of you to come! And thank you again, Clark. I'll see you soon!" Pamela practically pushed Clark out the door.

When the elevator man opened the door on the first floor, Clark was surprised to see Miss Riley waiting there.

"Changing of the guard? Or are you here to do the floors?" Clark asked facetiously.

"Just checking on Pamela. She hasn't been feeling well at night," said Miss Riley, who had changed her conservative suit for stretch slacks, a sweater, and a leather car coat. She wore a red kerchief and sunglasses. She took her sunglasses off and grinned.

"Better you than Doreen Flower!" Miss Riley winked at Clark as the elevator door closed.

So, Holly's right and the papers are all wrong, thought Clark as he hailed a taxi on Fifth Avenue. Pamela Raven is no grieving widow living a lonely life as punishment for her selfish, bitchy character. Clark had come to New York to learn more about women, among other things, and Pamela Raven had just taught him a lesson he hadn't bargained for.

He couldn't believe Reggie wasn't home. But that was what the fat concierge lady said. She had never been nice to Clark, and he thought her little eyes gleamed maliciously when he told her to ring again. No answer. Having the strong sensation that he had blown it, Clark wrote Reggie a note:

Dear Lady Regina,

It is with much sorrow that I note your absence from the Tower. The guardian at your gate is most slavering. Perhaps I shall slay this beast as I have the many villains who have kept me from you tonight, dear heart. Do not despair, my love. I will seek you on the Boulevard of Dreams.

Lord Calloway

He promised himself to send her flowers in the morning before he remembered that tomorrow was Sunday. Ignoring the nosy stare of the concierge, he used the pay phone in Reggie's lobby to call Maria's hotel.

"Ahhh, Signor Clark!" Maria's voice was breathy. She lowered it to a whisper. "I cannot talk now, Clark, Allen Friedberg is here. Yes! He is in the *pissoir*, but he will be out soon. He says

I will be the next Marilyn Monroe!"

"Is Reggie there?"

"Oh, no. She's not here. You are a bad boy, Clark. She's very angry with you. You made her cry and I have never seen her cry. Me, I cry every day, but Reggie is very strong. You should not have left her alone tonight in her condition."

"Where is she?"

"She's in Brooklyn, at her Mama's house. She is going to fly to Puerto Rico very early tomorrow morning for you-know-what. How could you make her wait like that? Oh! I have to go now — Allen is back! *Ciao!*"

She hung up. It was too late to call over at the Stowkowskis, and Clark was dead tired. He could not wait to go home to bed. He left the note with the concierge and she took it greedily. He didn' t care if she read it or not.

CHAPTER 11

"Where's my painting?"

"Hello?" said Clark. He hadn't even heard the phone ring. He had merely picked it up the minute his eyes opened to call Reggie's mother, and there was this voice on the line.

"I said, where's my painting?"

"Oh, Roland. What time is it?" Clark fumbled for his alarm clock.

"It's time I got my painting!"

It was seven a.m. on a Sunday morning.

Roland continued, "Look, Clark, you know you've got the Ritz Plaza contract, just between you and me. What more can I give you?"

"But you haven't paid the gallery," said Clark.

"We're talking three hundred thousand in fees for your company, Clark, and you're gonna weasel me over a little painting? It's not even that good!"

"Excuse me?"

"Just kidding! Kidding! You artist types are so sensitive."

"Okay, Roland, you win," said Clark, hoping to get rid of him. "We'll send the painting down to you tomorrow. You don't have to pay me for it, but somehow down the line into the art project for the hotel, you've got to include the cost for this painting, because Winterspoon has to make a commission. I don't mind not collecting the money, provided Deidre Dawn gets the hotel job."

"Baby, you got a deal. You got a great deal — *two* hotel jobs for one painting. You're a lucky guy, and it's just 'cause I like you. Don't say I never did anything for you! Hey, I've got a great idea! I'm gonna commission a painting from you, and I want you to paint a portrait of Dannee Lou Baker! I want you to make it huge — ten feet long, a nude, okay? Real artistic-like, nothing low-class! And you can do your abstract thing, so

The Decorator

long as I know it's her, ya know what I mean? Think you can get her to pose?"

"I sincerely doubt it," said Clark. "Look, I have to take someone to the airport right now, I'll talk to you later." He hung up and dialed the Stowkowskis' number as fast as he could, hoping he wasn't too late. Mrs. Stowkowski answered the phone. "Oh, Clark, you're just in time! Reggie's leaving in five minutes. She's going on a vacation with her girl friends. Our little girl, can you believe it? Reggie! Telephone!"

When Reggie picked up the phone, her voice was decidedly cool. "Hi, Clark. I can't talk now, 'cause my taxi will be here in a minute."

"Tell him to go away," said Clark. "I'll take you."

"I can't," said Reggie. "I'll miss my flight." She lowered her voice to a whisper.

"Where were you last night? I can't believe you stood me up!"

"I'm sorry, Reg, I really am. I was working late at Pamela Raven's, and I had no idea you'd be leaving so soon. Where did you get the money?"

"I took care of it," said Reggie. "The taxi's outside honking. I'm staying at the Caribe Hilton, call me there."

"Take care of yourself. I care about you," said Clark.

"Oh, lighten up, kid! You sound like my father," Reggie dropped the phone and Clark heard Reggie's giggle and "Oops!" and her mother calling for her to hurry up, and then Reggie's distant "Goodbye, Clark!" fading off. Someone hung up the phone and Clark got an earful of dial tone.

"What did I just say?" Clark was annoyed with himself. But he was worried about Reggie. Women died from bad abortions all the time, and he wished she wasn't going by herself. He had wanted to tell Reggie how much he cared about her, but he hadn't wanted it to get 'heavy,' as she would say. He knew if he was really the romantic type, like in the movies, he would be on the first flight to Puerto Rico and he would propose to her in the airport or something:

"Don't do this, my darling! Marry me, Regina!" Down on one knee and everything, like Gabe Taylor in *Surrender*. The idea was ridiculous. Reggie would probably laugh in his face. And what would they do with a kid? Luciano's kid, no less.

No, it just wouldn't work. He hoped Reggie would be back to her old self after the abortion. As for Luciano, Clark would have liked to wring his neck. Clark hoped Reggie had learned her lesson about bullies like Luciano. And now Holly was getting the Luciano treatment! To think she had called Clark insensitive!

He wondered if Holly wasn't a little "off" and if Pamela Raven really had been the evil witch Holly described. Clark got goosebumps all over when he remembered his shower with Pamela Raven. He couldn't believe it had happened to him. He had been ravished by a goddess, and he would never be the same.

He knew just what he would do: the perfect way to spend this icy Sunday would be to catch an old Pamela Raven film on television. After all, it was "Pamela Raven Week," and he needed a day off. He wanted to watch the movie star's delicate young face and dark eyes in the glory of her silver screen passion. He wanted to see her look the way she had looked at him last night.

"My movie star. My little movie star." Clark went out to get the newspaper.

He was in the middle of a peaceful Sunday morning breakfast and New York *Times* ritual, listening to "La Traviata" on his hi-fi, when the call came from Allen Friedberg.

"Listen, Clark, you gotta get over here. Bambi's beside herself. Something about an armchair and some faucets or something. She's all worked up. Can you come over and straighten it out? I'm sure it's nothing: you know how women can be. My kids are here and the grandkids, and it's chaos, so why don't we go to the Sunday buffet at the Four Seasons, just the three of us, after you look at whatever Bambi's carrying on about. I need some peace and quiet, and she's driving me nuts!"

Clark said he would get right over. He had anticipated trouble from Bambi because the drapery people and the carpet layers had all complained to Paul Hedges about the way Mrs. Friedberg was treating them, and Bambi was already costing the office money. Sending the contractors back and forth each day to correct nonsense wasn't the most economical way of doing business. Bambi just wasn't satisfied with any of the workmanship, and was refusing to pay to have it redone.

The Decorator

Clark was treated to this unpleasant side of Bambi Friedberg before he could take off his coat.

"Clark, is that you? Come over here and look! I'm glad you're finally here, thank god — I want you to see something! Come look at this!" She was on her knees by the window, holding a drapery hem in her hand. She turned it over.

"See, this flower doesn't line up with that one! It's terrible!"

"But, Bambi, no one sees that side. It's the hem," Clark explained.

"I want them out!" Bambi started ripping the sewn hem apart. "I paid for quality draperies and I got these sloppy ones! How could you let this happen? You call yourself a decorator? You said these were the best draperies. Why, I'm more knowledgeable about draperies than you are. Remember, my mother made all her own clothes, and I'm good on a sewing machine myself. But *look* at this!"

Bambi stepped back to include all of the draperies in her wide-armed gesture of disbelief. "They hung them all wrong! The rods cover the sides of the windows so the housemen can't get outside to clean the fucking windows. It's your fault!"

While Bambi rasped on with profanities, a naked baby with soap bubbles on her head ran giggling into the room, followed by a little boy, also naked and yelling, and their harried-looking mother, obviously Allen's daughter.

Allen Friedberg appeared and began beating the drums loudly too, "Julie, get these kids out of here before they ruin the rugs!"

"I'm trying, Dad!" Julie staggered by with a wet child squirming under each arm. She gave Clark a wry look from under a shock of reddish hair that had fallen over one eye. "Hi, I'm Julie Friedberg-Walsh. I'd shake your hand, but I've got my hands full — Nanny's day off!"

Clark thought Allen Friedberg's daughter was attractive in a hard, almost mannish way, and she looked quite athletic in her tennis whites. He guessed she was in her late twenties.

Bambi continued on as if nothing had happened, and her voice rose to a shrieking whine, "It's your fault and I want these drapes taken down…and out! I don't want them this way and you can be sure Allen is not paying for them! Allen, remember what I said: No paying for the fucking draperies!"

"Shut up, Bambi, you do-do bird!" barked Allen.

"Oh, Allen, don't say that to me!" Bambi began to cry with loud, exaggerated sobs.

"You bitch!" said Allen cheerfully, annoying Bambi with a sweeping head motion. "Come on, Clark, I want you to meet my son!"

He led Clark into the kitchen where a tall, fattish young man with curly red hair, a younger version of Allen, in a rugby shirt and jeans, was watching golf on a little color television set while eating a bagel stuffed with cream cheese and lox.

"This is my son Sam, the big-shot entertainment lawyer, my *consigliere*, and his wife, Gloria."

Clark recognized the blonde, freckled woman from dozens of television commercials in which she played the same perky housewife. She looked up from her newspaper to smile a hello to Clark, but Sam only grunted, not looking away from his television. Under the table, two little boys were wrestling.

"Those are two of my grandsons, Eric and Mike. Say hello to Clark, fellas."

Two dirty faces popped out for a moment to stare at Clark. One of them said "Hi," in the most bored voice possible, and the other one showed Clark his skinny fist. "You want me to pop ya one?" he growled.

"Cute, cute kids," said Clark. "How old are they?"

"Four and five," said Allen. "They're really little devils."

"Six, dummy!" screamed Eric or Mike — Clark didn't know which — "I'm six! Don'tcha know *nothin'*?"

The two boys shrieked with laughter until their father said, "Shut up! Gloria, can't you take these kids outside? I'm try'nta watch something here!"

"You saw our Julie and her two," said Allen. "Her husband's a pro golfer. We're just nuts about golf around here."

"Where do they live?" asked Clark.

"Boca Raton," said Allen. "And Beverly Hills. Julie's at Metro too — she's a casting director and I know she'll be a great producer one day. She's got the balls for it. Let's get out of here; these kids are giving me a headache."

Allen Friedberg drew Clark into his wood-paneled home office and closed the door.

"That little thing with Bambi, you can fix it, right? She's so

The Decorator

emotional, but she doesn't mean any harm. I think she's going through what-do-you-call-it, change of life...This home is important to her, you know. She hates Los Angeles, always has. And believe me, she doesn't win any social points living here half the year: people are beginning to talk. They're calling her a recluse. Now that the kids are grown up and she can't play stage mother any more — now don't you ever tell her I said this, but neither Sam nor Julie can act their way out of a paper bag! Nor did they want to, but dragging them to auditions was her big thing in life, and she's very disappointed it didn't work out. This house is all she has — I mean, look at her. You wanna know the reason I stay with her?"

Clark did not. He wondered secretly if Julie hadn't gotten her revenge on her mother by becoming a casting director. What he did know was that he wasn't going to get any help from Allen and that Deidre Dawn & Company would probably have to eat the cost for new window treatments. So he smiled and nodded.

Allen was knotting his tie, so his words were directed to the ceiling.

"The only reason I stay with her is, I love my grandkids. If I unloaded Bambi, she'd make sure I never saw them again. She's got our kids wrapped around her finger. Big babies, they are. Bambi spoiled them rotten and she gets 'em to feel sorry for her and they take her side against me every time. Well, somebody's got to run the ship, right? And nobody ever said they'd like you for it. Remember that, when you're in my position one day, though you got a long way to go yet. If you don't mind me saying so, man to man, the first thing you gotta do is get your company away from that old lady, Deirdre Dawn. If you ask me, that high society fossil doesn't know what's going on, anyway. Probably won't even miss it."

He examined his tie in the mirror, evidently pleased with himself. "Yeah, Clark, old boy." Allen clapped his arm across Clark's shoulder and steered him to the door. "You'll get it right one day. But one thing I gotta give you, you sure can pick the babes! Maria is one hot number, whew! Had a hard time dragging myself out of there last night, 'cause she's still wanting more! What can I say — when you got it —"

"You got it," said Clark.

When Clark and Allen emerged from the office, they bumped right into Bambi. Clark wondered if she had been listening outside the door.

"Oh! Allen!" exclaimed Bambi, fluttering her hand to her heart in an overdone gesture. "You scared me! I didn't know you were in there. I was looking for you because Adela Morgan called and I want to show Clark the guest bathroom faucets, the gold ones in the bathtub. When you turn on the hot water, the amethyst piece — the 'H' for Hot — it turns a little and jiggles and it shouldn't do that! Julie saw it, too, she showed me, so I'm not making it up! Come and see, Clark."

She pulled on his arm. "And when you look at the faucet, look at the tissue holder, too. The holder has been installed too high on the wall."

"Bambi, let go of the man!" snapped Allen. "What did Adela want? Or did you forget already?"

"Oh! I almost forgot! Can you believe it — there's just so much going on in my mind! The last performance of Adela Morgan's show is this afternoon, the last one Adela's in, I mean, before she leaves the production and gets replaced by some other actress, whoever they're gonna get, and that person won't be as good as Adela, you know, but Clark, see, my Allen needs Adela to star in his *movie* —"

"Get to the point!" Allen pointed his two index fingers against his temples like guns. "I'm dying here! I could die right here — I could hemorrhage to death from her talking, and she wouldn't notice. She just goes on and on and on."

"What I was saying is Adela invited us and Sam and Julie and the kids and Gloria to see her show and when I told her Clark was here, she said 'Bring him too'. Isn't that nice! Clark, you're coming! Front row seats and Adela Morgan. I'm so excited!"

Allen groaned. "Fuck. I hate musicals worse than death. Is it really the finale already? I don't need those girls on the set for weeks. You know, I told Adela I'd go, and I'll never hear the end of it if I don't. I gotta work with that broad for the next six months! I shoulda been a lion tamer — it would have been easier."

"Allie, you have to go — I've already told Adela and the kids —"

The Decorator

"Shut up, Bambi, shut up already. I've told you over and over again, you whine too much! Go call the driver — and make sure the kids are going in a separate car. I don't want them in the car with us. Their whining and yours are all too much to take."

"But —"

"NO buts. Just tell Julie to take care of it. I don't want to hear those monkeys all through the show. I've got enough problems. And we're not dressing — it's freakin' Sunday, even the *goyyim* are resting, for Christ's sake!"

"I wanna wear my new blue silk with the pretty sequins!"

"It's a matinee, you moron — you'll go as you are. I'm not waiting for you to go through all that dressing again. Go call the car."

"Allen!" Bambi whined.

"Go…Call…The…Car."

Bambi scurried off, sniffling.

"Christ, what do I have to do to get things done around here?" Allen fumed. "Sorry, Clark, but you see what I have to put up with?"

"Well, I…" Clark fished for an excuse. "I did say I'd help Maria design a new closet system in her hotel suite."

"Now you're talkin'." Allen snapped his fingers. "We'll take Maria with us. She'll be good company and at least we'll have something to look at. Go call her, sport! I'll have Bambi call the theater and reserve another seat, the one right next to me, in case there are any photographers around. Bambi can sit with the kids. That way, I'll be certain not to have all that whining around me."

Clark kissed his quiet afternoon off goodbye.

Allen Friedberg's hunter-green Rolls Royce was completely lined in sable. Maria could not stop petting it. The chauffeur had collected her outside her hotel on the way to the theater, and she had not had time to change. She was still wearing her Sunday white knit tights and long white turtleneck sweater. She did not have time to do her makeup, but she looked gorgeous anyway. In fact, Clark thought Maria looked better without all of that heavy eye makeup and foundation. If the sweater was not meant to be a dress, it was now, and Maria had created a new level for the ever-shrinking miniskirt. Her high white boots added a dashing, glamorous look. Maria looked like a snow princess or an early version of Sonja Henie… on ice.

"Here she is, my sweater girl!" Allen had sung out, while Bambi gave Maria a dirty look as she climbed into the Rolls.

"I was sleeping," Maria murmured to Clark. "But I just can't miss seeing Adela in her show. I'm so excited!"

Bambi interrupted their conversation with her childish whine, "Clark, I'm not finished telling you about the furniture! There's something wrong with the new loveseats for the ballroom, too. They're pink! I didn't order pink."

She glared accusingly at Clark and blinked back — could those be *tears*? Clark could not believe her ability. *She* should have been an actress.

"But Bambi," he protested, "you were in the showroom with me when we picked the fabric. You insisted on the cerise pink moiré, and you even asked the showroom girl to give you a swatch of the current dye lot, to be certain that the pink was exactly as you wanted it to be."

"No, I didn't! I never chose that color!" Bambi cried.

"Did you do it, Bambi? Did you?" Allen roared. "If you did, admit it and stop harassing Clark."

"No, I didn't, Allen — he's not telling the truth!" Bambi was sobbing and shouting at Allen, a scene Clark was learning to expect in the Friedberg family.

While the Friedbergs argued, Maria spoke in a low voice to Clark. "Did I tell you I went to Pamela Raven's apartment this morning? She called me at nine o'clock. She wanted to see some shoes I brought from Italy in her size. I said, 'Can't we do it later?' You know it was so *early* and I was up all night with you know…"

Clark knew.

"But she wanted to see the shoes right away and it is a big sale for my father, so I took a taxi all the way uptown."

"Did she buy the shoes?" asked Clark.

"Oh, yes. She loved them and she ordered them in several colors. They are the kind with the open toe and ankle strap. Pamela Raven said 'These are my stand-me-up-and-fuck-me shoes!' I never knew she had such a mouth," said Maria.

The Decorator

"Ahhh, I could just go to sleep in this fur."

She closed her eyes and kept talking. "And she wanted me to look while she tried every pair on and she asked me 'Do you like this one? And this one?' She was very nice. And then you know what she did?" Maria's eyes flew open.

"No, what?"

"She lifted her dress! She just pulled it right over her head and I'm standing there in front of her boobs and her pussy right there in front of me, naked!"

Clark laughed, "Guess she's going after all of us."

Maria shrugged. "What do you mean, 'all of us'? She said she wanted me to see her body and what great shape she is in at her age. I said, 'Yes, you are in great shape,' and she smiled and pulled the dress back down."

"Maybe she wanted you to play 'I'll Show You Mine If You Show Me Yours,'" said Clark.

Maria laughed. "I played that game in school when I was a little girl, too, when we were hiding from the nuns, but I am too tired for games today. Trying to be an actress is hard work. And don't think the nights with Allen are fun, either!"

"How did your 'audition' go, by the way?" whispered Clark, although he didn't need to. The Friedberg shouting match would have drowned him out if he had screamed. The driver didn't even flinch, so this must be a regular routine. "How was the old fat cat?"

Maria sucked her teeth, making a little bird sound. "He is a lazy old bastard. He ordered the best bottle of Scotch and smoked his stinking cigar and he just lay there. He expects me to do everything, work my ass off on top. And, like, he pushes me to move faster. He takes fucking forever to come. I don't like that. I like the man to be on top — it's more natural, don't you think? But I think he gets what he wants. And he wants it on schedule, like room service. I never met a man like this before. And now here is his wife in the same car with me. I feel weird. Anyway, he'll make money off me, so I might as well make some money too, for once in my life, right?"

"Maybe you'll be famous, like Garbo, Crawford, Monroe," said Clark.

"Maybe," said Maria. "But I'm not going to be like Pamela Raven. She's too weird. Her house was so clean it was scary.

She even made me sit on a towel so I wouldn't get her upholstery dirty and the craziest thing was — she laid the towel *over* the plastic slipcover! What is her problem? She's afraid I'll get the *plastic* dirty!"

"I know," replied Clark.

They had arrived at the Majestic Theater.

"Oy, will you look at that!" Allen glared out the window at a circular parade of ragged hippies carrying signs that said REVOLUTION and PEACE NOW and chanting "We want pot!"

"What are they doing here?" Allen groaned.

"It's just another one of those demonstrations parading for something. I read that the mayor is in Times Square today. Seems that these folks have nothing better to do on a Sunday afternoon," said Clark.

"Well, they're never going to get anywhere smoking banana peels or whatever it is they do," said Allen.

Clark had to agree. He was sitting in a Rolls Royce that symbolized the most powerful media corporation in the country and he worked for Deirdre Dawn, who embodied American royalty so old that she considered the Allen Friedbergs of the world to be mere flyspecks of bad taste.

"Those hippies sure are naive," he said.

"I think they're cute," said Maria. "That one looks like Che Guevara."

"Chay who?" grunted Bambi.

"That monkey? You're nuts!" snorted Allen. "We gotta straighten you out, girlie." He rolled down the window.

"Take a bath! Wash your hair! Wash your underwear, if you're wearing any!" he yelled at the protesters.

Clark had a brainstorm while staring at a young woman who carried a sign reading THE MEDIUM IS THE MESSAGE. Well, the media is the power, he thought, and the puppet. These people want revolution, but there will never be one because culture and commerce are so intertwined. And the only way out of the machine is to own it. He wished Reggie were with him so he could tell her what he was thinking.

Allen asked the driver to bring the car around to the rear of the theater, so they could enter through the stage door and avoid the ragamuffin hippie group in front of the theater. Allen

The Decorator

had recently been profiled in Life magazine and he couldn't risk being recognized or drawn into the protesters' 'street theater.'

"Come on, honey bunch," he said to Bambi, as if they hadn't been arguing.

"We're not payin' for those chairs in the living room either." Bambi smiled sweetly at Clark, but she might as well have stuck her tongue out at him, or given him the finger.

Clark loved musicals. He had always been a Betty Grable fan, and he longed for the days when movie sets were dazzling, dramatic, and colorful. After all, Clark was a designer, and he thought of how well he could design sets for a Broadway musical, lots better than Oliver Messel or Jo Melziner. As the curtain went up on the dream-like set and the first characters entered, he felt that thrill of watching live actors work their magic.

"This show got lousy reviews." Allen leaned across Maria to grunt in Clark's ear, whisking him out of the fantasy. "It's all schmaltz. But Manny, the producer, he's a genius. He starts fights with the critics in Sardi's, makes it look like their beefs are personal, see? You know Manny Wood? Looks like an undertaker, but he's the best producer on Broadway. He's got four hit shows right now. He only puts on tested *British* shows. Pre-sold audience. American playwrights hate his guts. Oh, here's our Morgan."

Allen settled back, and Maria breathed a sigh of relief.

Adela Morgan marched on stage amid a fanfare of orchestra, spotlights, and applause. As usual, her performance was over the top; she delivered her lines in the obvious vaudeville comedy style she had first learned.

Allen's breath tickled Clark's ear again. "Manny hates actresses, but he knows how to handle 'em. You know what he said when Adela called in sick? 'As long as you can talk, you go on!' He sent her a bouquet of plastic roses and a lie detector test. What a riot!"

When Allen pulled back, Maria massaged her sore ribs.

"I hope he doesn't talk to me through the whole show," Clark whispered to Maria.

"You hope!" she shot back. "Every time he does that he crushes my breasts."

Clark got his wish when Morgan sang her first number. That shut everyone up, including Allen. The whole audience sighed with pleasure as they soaked up her thrilling, golden notes. The lyrics weren't that great, but Clark didn't care. He decided Adela could sing "Patty Cake" and make him melt. By the end of the show, he was on his feet, cheering and whistling for Adela.

Maria kept pulling on his jacket. "Sit down," she said. "You sound like a fag."

He ignored her and cheered Adela until she looked his way and blew him a kiss.

"Let's go backstage," said Allen. "I'm glad I saw that. If she performs like that in my picture, she'll steal every scene from Pamela Raven. That oughtta keep the Queen in line. I'll get my best work out of Raven yet!"

Allen Friedberg chuckled, a happy man.

The Decorator

CHAPTER 12

All was not well in the Deirdre Dawn office when Clark walked in on Monday afternoon after a morning of helping Pamela Raven unpack in her new apartment. The wicked task of organizing the wardrobe room to Pamela Raven's specifications was beyond anyone's possible comprehension.

Clark's head was filled with Pamela's commanding voice chanting color groups: "The lavender *dresses* go with the lavender *shoes*, the lavender *bags*, the lavender *hats*, the lavender *belts*! How many times do I have to say it? I'm not angry with *you*, Clark, I'm angry at the mess!"

Only Pamela Raven could insist that pinks followed fuschias and never reds. Clark figured Pamela, Miss Riley, and Mama would be organizing dresses and gowns — to say nothing of furs — for months.

Paul Hedges was in a vile state and Miss Belle was running around with stacks of files like a worker ant with too many bread crumbs. It looked as if the file cabinets had exploded.

"What's happened? Or what's happening?" Clark asked.

"Oh, Clark, there you are. It's Deirdre," said Paul. "It was terrible. She couldn't find one of her files and she accused *me* of hiding it. She tore the office apart and left us to clean it up."

"Did she find it? Where is she now?"

"No, and she's in her office, but I wouldn't go in there. Allen Friedberg has been sending nasty telegrams all morning, and she's ready to have your head. I wish she'd stay out of all the business. She really doesn't know anything about the jobs and she does more harm than good every time she talks with a client. And do you know when Friedberg called and she got on the phone, she even asked Allen Friedberg who he was! I think Deirdre is losing some of her marbles. She can't seem to remember anything. And I have the feeling that Caneletto has been ringing Mrs. Friedberg, inquiring if everything is all right with her job. Caneletto may even be offering his services. Could it be that Deirdre is talking to Caneletto, not realizing that he is no longer employed by the company? It is possible, you know!"

"But I saw Bambi and Allen yesterday, and he was fine. It's Bambi who..." Clark trailed off, remembering that Allen hadn't exactly defended Deirdre Dawn & Company against Bambi's attacks. Allen had a way of being understanding at one moment and a bastard at others. Obviously, dear little Bambi was getting to him, and insisting he get on to Deirdre Dawn.

"If you think she's bad, Allen is insane," said Paul. "What ever happened to all of our nice clients? He doesn't like anything we've done and I don't think he plans to pay for any of it. His wife has told him not to release any funds."

"But that's absurd!"

"You're telling me!" said Paul.

The buzzer on the office door sounded and a messenger came in. "Telegram!" he announced.

Belle received it and handed the envelope to Paul Hedges. "It's from Metropolis Pictures again," she said.

"You have to see this," said Paul, ripping the envelope open. "These aren't just telegrams — they're filibusters, all in the most pathetic tone. Poor Mr. Friedberg, anyone would think we're abusing him most terribly. Oh, read this!"

Clark read:

> DEAR DEIRDRE DAWN:
> MY WIFE BAMBI AND I ARE DISTRESSED TO THE POINT OF DESPERATION REGARDING THE WORK YOU AND YOUR ASSOCIATES HAVE PERFORMED IN OUR APARTMENT. STOP. RECENTLY WE HIRED YOU BECAUSE OF YOUR SUPPOSED EXPERTISE IN THE DECORATING WORLD. STOP. WE HAVE FOUND THAT WE CANNOT LIVE WITH THE QUALITY OF CRAFTSMANSHIP PERFORMED BY YOUR SUBCONTRACTOR, THE ROGERS COMPANY. STOP. THE CONTRACTOR HAS NOT INSTALLED THE AIR

The Decorator

CONDITIONING PROPERLY AND MY WIFE, BAMBI, CANNOT WORK THE CONTROLS PROPERLY. STOP. YOUR CONTRACTOR, THE FOSTER FIRM, WHO DID THE PLUMBING, DID A POOR JOB. STOP. MY WIFE, BAMBI, HEARS RUNNING SOUNDS IN THE TOILET ALL NIGHT LONG. STOP. PLEASE SEND BOTH THE ROGERS PEOPLE AND THE FOSTER PEOPLE BACK TO FIX THEIR WORK. STOP. YOU HAVE SENT ME BILLS TOTALING $29,600.00 FOR BALANCE DUE. STOP. I SHALL NOT PAY THEM UNTIL MRS. FRIEDBERG OKAYS THE WORK. STOP. AND FURTHERMORE — I WON'T PAY YOU FOR ANY DESIGN TIME CHARGES EITHER. STOP. AND TELL THAT CLARK CALLOWAY TO GET HIS ASS OVER HERE TO SUPERVISE THE WORK — EVEN IF HE HAS TO SLEEP NIGHT AND DAY IN OUR APARTMENT. STOP.

A.F.

"That's ridiculous," said Clark.

"What's even more ridiculous is that Roland Lee is in your office waiting for you."

"Oh, why? Why is HE here, Paul?"

"It's something about Miss Raven's suite at the Bel Vista in Los Angeles. I don't know what she wants, but he's *extremely* upset. Won't leave until you talk to him. He's like one of those sit-in kids protesting in the schools, I suppose." Paul laughed, in an unbalanced way, Clark thought.

"Belle?" called Clark. "Can you bring some tea into my office — Earl Grey for Mr. Lee."

"He's already had his tea, Mr. Calloway, but I'll bring yours in directly," said Belle.

"None for me, thank you," Clark sighed. "But bring him a refill and keep a shot of arsenic on the side, in case I need to put it into his cup in lieu of a lump of sugar."

Roland Lee bolted out of his seat when Clark entered the room. Lee was wearing sage-green gabardine slacks with a matching shirt and tie, and his jacket complemented the outfit — in kelly green glen plaid. Lee looked like a shorter version of the Jolly Green Giant. And all the greens made Roland's orange hair blaze in contrast. The hotelier shook his rolled-up umbrella at Clark and waved it at a letter he had placed on Clark's desk.

"Mr. Calloway," Roland squeaked. "Help me decide what to do with this letter! I'm being insulted!"

"What's the matter?" asked Clark, taking off his jacket and dodging the dangerously swishing umbrella.

"It's a memo from Pamela Raven's secretary, a Miss Riley. It was hand-delivered to my office today. Miss Raven's requests are outrageous and I don't think any hotelier would accommodate that movie star's demands."

"Let's see," said Clark, settling behind his desk. "I'm sure we can work out Miss Raven's requests, although I don't know why I should be involved in your business with her. Remember, I'm a decorator, yours and hers, but I'm not a hotel manager."

He read the note.

> DECEMBER 20, 1965
> TO: ROLAND LEE
>   THE RITZ PLAZA HOTEL
> RE: PAMELA RAVEN'S REQUIREMENTS FOR HER BEL VISTA HOTEL, LOS ANGELES, CALIFORNIA, BEGINNING ON JANUARY 15TH, 1966, AND IN EFFECT FOR THE DURATION OF MISS RAVEN'S STAY AT THE BEL VISTA WHILE SHE IS FILMING *TIGRESS IN THE DARK*:
> - Three (3) of the best bedrooms atop the Bel Vista Hotel, for Miss Raven, Mama, and the wardrobe.
> - A single room for Miss Riley;
> - A uniformed security man at Miss Raven's door. No city police or house detective.
>
> <u>IN HER SUITE PRIOR TO ARRIVAL</u>
> 1) Several buckets cracked ice

The Decorator

2) Lunch and dinner menus
3) Pens, pencils, and pads of paper
4) Professional-size hair dryer
5) Steam iron and board
6) One (1) carton Sano cigarettes
7) One (1) bowl Peppermint Lifesavers
8) Red and yellow roses
9) One (1) case of Pepsi and ginger ale
10) A maid on hand until dismissed
11) Two (2) fifths of Smirnoff's Vodka (100-proof only)
12) One (1) fifth of Old Forrester Bourbon
13) One (1) fifth Chivas Regal Scotch
14) One (1) fifth Beefeater Gin
15) Two (2) bottles Moët & Chandon/Dom Perignon Champagne.

In addition, all surfaces of the carpeting, seating areas, and bedding are to be covered in clean white sheets, to be changed twice a day. Miss Raven will bring her own towels and bedding, and all hotel bedding is to be removed. The hotel will provide ten (10) king-sized pillows, all down-filled and in their cellophane covers. Miss Raven wants to make sure the pillows have never been used by others and are the white down which she prefers.

Meet Miss Raven in an air conditioned, chauffeured, newly-cleaned Cadillac limousine. Drivers are not to smoke and not to drive over 40 MPH.

Meet Miss Raven with a closed van for her fifteen (15) pieces of luggage. Have a handler inventory the luggage off the plane and into the suite. There may be more than fifteen pieces.

MISS RAVEN IS A STAR IN EVERY SENSE OF THE WORD, AND EVERYONE KNOWS SHE

IS A STAR. AS A PARTNER IN THIS FILM, MISS RAVEN WILL NOT APPRECIATE YOUR THROWING AWAY MONEY ON EMPTY GESTURES. YOU DO NOT HAVE TO MAKE EMPTY GESTURES TO PROVE TO MISS RAVEN OR ANYONE ELSE THAT SHE IS A STAR OF THE FIRST MAGNITUDE.

"Who does she think she is?" blustered Roland.

"She doesn't *think* who she is — she knows who she is, and she's Pamela Raven, movie star," said Clark. "And there are other Los Angeles hotels she can stay in if you don't want to meet her standards. Just remember: you don't have to provide her with your body. Which of Pamela's requests do you find you can't provide?"

"What does this have to do with my body? Hell, this is all extra work for the staff! The Bel Vista is a top-flight hotel, and we have celebrity guests all the time. White sheets covering the floors is beyond the pale. What is she, germophobic? Whatever, we can do that. I'll call the housekeeper, Mrs. Hauser. She's a smart German lady, and I'll get her to look after Pamela's needs. It's Raven's tone I don't like. She's so rude. She's got to know that my staff and I are not her serfs. She doesn't have to get snotty with us."

"Don't take it personally," said Clark. "Pamela is demanding, and I know this all too well. She's meticulous about herself. She's even removing all the bathtubs in her new apartment. She told me she never soaks in her own dirt, and you know very well Pamela makes guests take off their shoes before entering the apartment. And she makes her guests sit on terrycloth towels, so the dye in their clothing doesn't come off on her upholstery. It's crazy, I know, but I'm working with her, right down to installing white plastic laminate on the window sills.

"Think of the publicity you and your hotel will be getting. The stars and producers of *Tigress in the Dark* are all staying at the Bel Vista Hotel — your hotel."

"I know all that. I've taken fewer reservations because Metropolis Pictures has reserved so many suites."

"Think of the parties, Roland. The people you'll be meeting. The women." Clark was laying it on thick — he knew what Roland liked. Roland was visibly relaxing and the umbrella had settled to the floor. The arsenic wouldn't be needed for the tea, after all.

"I see what you're saying. It's worth it to humor Pamela Raven. But what about Adela Morgan? Is she going to be a pain in the ass too?"

"Probably," said Clark. "I wouldn't leave any breakables in her suite. She has some wild parties. And she's allergic to roses, so don't let any flowers be delivered to her until all the roses are removed, or she'll have a fit. One thing to remember about Adela: just stock her kitchenette with cans of meatballs in gravy and she'll be content — and a case or two of vodka and white Almaden. Paul tells me Adela likes only jug wine…her background, you know. To wash down the canned meatballs around three in the morning…As for the Friedbergs, you know how they are."

"Yeah, thank God it's only Allen I'm dealing with. Bambi's staying in their Malibu house — you know their estate in Holmby Hills is on the market, though it may take a while to find a buyer ready to spend ten million! Allen booked a penthouse suite for meetings and those nights he works late on a shoot, if you know what I mean. The first menu he asks for is a list of the top call girls in L.A.

"Oh, and Doreen Flower will be there, too, so I'm sure I'll get some complaints from the guests. She's a damn pushy chick and she gets her nose into everything. Doreen even asked me to comp her room. She says she'll mention the Bel Vista in her column — if I'm real nice to her! You have to keep your eye on Doreen Flower: she's a real snoop. One time one of my maintenance guys caught her climbing out of a ventilator duct. She was spying on Aly Khan and Gene Tierney, or was it Governor Ronalds, since he was staying in the hotel? Can you believe that?"

"Speaking of the Bel Vista, what decorating plans have you and your office arranged? Are you going ahead with your designs for the pool deck and Jockey Club? I'd like to see all the cabana doors striped — some pink and white, others aqua and white, and some jonquil yellow and white. I want the pool deck to look like Eden Roc on the coast of France. Let's paint the interior of the individual cabanas to match the stripes — some pink, others aqua, and some white. I've got some great ideas for lounge chairs..."

Clark asked Roland to excuse the momentary interruption while he called the design department to bring in some of the working drawings of the Bel Vista. He and Roland settled into a long work-and-think session.

The day was over and Clark was glad. Pamela Raven's move was complete, somewhat (at least the furniture was in place) and a success, and Pamela was off on the train to Washington to the State Dinner. He knew Dannee Lou would look after her. Roland Lee had left the office satisfied, but the long telegrams from Allen and Bambi Friedberg kept arriving all day, one complaint after another, and Clark had to listen while Deirdre Dawn lectured him about "client relations." It was an exercise in absurdity, but Clark kept his mouth shut, though it drove him crazy. He knew it was useless to argue with Deirdre. She was talking about taking a long vacation in Spain and he dearly hoped she would go. Deirdre had once designed a collection of fabrics called the España Line, and she longed for another visit to the Escorial, plus she enjoyed dining at Horcher in Madrid.

His own Christmas travel plans had been resolved by the end of the day, thanks to Belle, and all he had to do was pick Reggie up at the airport at ten that night. Maybe she could help him shop for Christmas gifts for his family tomorrow. She was good at that.

Reggie had sounded wonderful on the phone when he had finally reached her at the Caribe Hilton on Sunday night. She had spent the afternoon on the beach and had quite a few banana daiquiris in a surfside bar, and she was very giggly and unconcerned about her abortion on Monday morning. Clark was relieved to hear Reggie sounding like her carefree old self; they had gossiped about Maria's rising star and fantasized about the Hollywood parties they would be invited to when their friend became famous. Reggie was completely over Luciano and didn't even register his name when Clark first mentioned him. When Clark told her Holly had gone to Rome with Luciano, Reggie just laughed.

The Decorator

"They deserve each other!" she said. "You can be sure I'll never speak to him again, nor do I even want to see him! And you know what else I'm gonna do?" Reggie's voice slurred a little. "I thought about this while I was on the beach: I'm going to ask for a new job at CBS. I'm going to march right into Thom Pearson's office and ask him to transfer me to the news division, in any part of the country. I'll take a cut in pay, I'll do an internship, I'll live at home; I'll do anything — I'll even finish school."

She laughed. "Because you know what? I plan to be the best anchorwoman in the world!"

"Of course you will be," said Clark. "I've always believed in you and your ability, and I know whatever Reggie sets her mind to doing will be done — and done well!"

There was a package waiting for Clark on the doorman's desk in his lobby. It was almost two feet long and half as wide, but only a handsbreadth deep. It was heavy. Clark recognized Pamela Raven's showy script immediately. He set the package down on his coffee table while he mixed himself a drink. He needed it. When he was relaxed, he tore off the meticulously taped brown paper box and peeled off the silver wrapping paper beneath. It was Lucien Irons' engraved mahogany cufflink box, and one pair of gold and oval diamond cufflinks sparkled in the center slot. An attached note from Pamela Raven read:

MERRY CHRISTMAS, CLARK DEAREST!
HERE'S TO A LONG FRIENDSHIP.
THIS IS ONLY THE BEGINNING!
LOVE,
PAMELA RAVEN

It was a wonderful present, but too generous. Clark turned a heavy cufflink in his hand to catch the light. He loved cufflinks, the only kind of jewelry he thought a man should wear. Men who wore gold chains and link bracelets, or even identification bracelets, were showy guys. Clark liked the simplicity of a cufflink that would appear only when the cuff emerged from the sleeve of the suit jacket. He thought about what he might give Pamela in return. Maybe Reggie would have an idea.

"What do you say to an angel?" is one question, but "What do you give to a movie star?" is another — especially to a movie star who has taken you for a shower ride.

Clark ordered Chinese food from Imperial East for dinner and ate it while he watched the news. President Lyndon Johnson was starting to look haggard and shifty on the subject of Vietnam. Shouldn't that war be over already? Clark wondered. He felt lucky that he had been just above the age of conscription during each new draft, and he worried about Reggie's younger brother and other boys fighting over there who were just teenagers. There were guys in his home town who had rushed to enlist, and Clark already knew of two who would not be coming home. He was not looking forward to seeing their mothers at Christmas.

Clark changed into jeans and a white polo shirt and at nine o'clock he caught a taxi to JFK. Anxiously, he watched for Reggie's dark hair amid the passengers streaming through the gate from the Puerto Rico flight. Most of them were Hispanic, he noticed, and met by large families, probably visiting for Christmas. There were a few tourists, flushed red from their brief winter vacations. When he saw Reggie, Clark rushed to take her bag.

"Hi, Clark, I'm so glad you came. It's been a rocky flight and I really don't feel so good," said Reggie. "Geez, I've got to sit down for a second. I'm so thirsty! Can you get me a cup of water?"

She looked very pale and her face was perspiring with a cold sweat. She leaned heavily on Clark as he guided her to a seat in the Arrival Lobby, just outside the Baggage Claim.

"What's the matter? Did you eat airplane food again? I told you never to do that," Clark joked.

"No, it's not that, I'll be all right. Maybe I do just need to eat something, though I have no appetite. I don't know what's wrong with me, but I feel real dizzy and I'm seeing little white dots everywhere. I know I shouldn't have spent the day in the pool splashing about after the…operation. I may have opened up a wound or something. The nurse said I'll be bleeding for a few days, and not to worry, but I'm bleeding an awful lot. And I'm so tired." She leaned her head on Clark's shoulder.

Warning bells were ringing in Clark's head. He knew

Reggie needed to go to a hospital fast. The situation was serious. "Reggie, rest here for one minute. I'll be right back! I'm going to get you a cup of water and call an ambulance."

"No, no ambulance. I'm really okay," Reggie said very weakly. "Just take me home. I'll get lots of rest in the apartment — I'll be okay, really."

She laid her head down on her pink and green canvas Caribe Hilton bag and collapsed. She couldn't even hold her head up. Clark arranged the bag as a pillow for Reggie and gently and carefully covered her up with his jacket. Her skin was so clammy cold and she looked very pale, despite the sunburn.

"I'll be right back," he said. "You're going to be fine. You're going to be okay. I'll take care of you this time, believe me."

Reggie smiled. "I know," she said sleepily. "You're sweet. Stay here."

Clark squeezed her hand and ran to call the ambulance.

Fortunately, there was an empty bed in the busy emergency room, but it was an hour before the doctor was able to see Reggie. She threw up a few times, and Clark held her and comforted her while she cried and a nurse cleaned her up and gave her a shot of sedative. Reggie was very shaky and not making much sense, but when the sedative took effect, she seemed to physically relax. Her mental condition was edgy and Clark did not know what she was talking about. She kept crying about a "Dr. Juan" and asking Clark if she might go to hell. Clark wondered why her Catholicism was harking in her head.

"Is it my fault?" she asked.

"No, it's not your fault," Clark answered.

"I tried to stop him," she said, and her eyes grew dreamy. "I really did try to stop him…Oh, that's nice," she said. "Fuzzy…"

She smiled like a child, and Clark wished the nurse would give him a shot of whatever she gave Reggie.

The doctor finally came and Clark had to leave the little white-curtained enclosure around Reggie's bed. He answered a lot of questions for the nurse, questions he answered truthfully and directly, for he feared Reggie's life was at stake.

Then there was nothing to do but wait. Clark drank cups of

hospital coffee, read an ancient copy of *Yachting* (which can always be found in waiting rooms, the pages fingered and bent), and tried not to take notice of the people with various wounds who were admitted to the Emergency Room, an impossible effort!

Finally a nurse called him over to the Triage Desk, where a Dr. Phillips, a doctor who looked about his own age, told him that Reggie would be all right. She had suffered an incomplete abortion and the remaining tissue in her uterus had been removed. The doctor commended Clark for bringing Reggie into the hospital immediately, for if they had waited it was likely that Reggie would have developed an infection which could have killed her. He had seen too many such cases already. The doctor was concerned that Reggie had undergone an illegal, unsterile abortion, but no report would be made to that effect. He said she was a very healthy and lucky lady.

"There's another thing, however, that I must tell you. Miss Stowkowski apparently was raped — according to what she told me, either by the doctor or by the anesthesiologist in San Juan; it's hard to tell by whom from her statements. We have examined her and taken some samples, but because of the bleeding I doubt we'll come to an absolute conclusion. The lab will notify us in a few days about their findings and we'll discuss the results with Miss Stowkowski. She has informed me, however, that she does not want police involvement, for reasons relating to her parents and the illegality of the abortion. That's her choice, but I suggest you have a talk with her. She asked to see you."

Reggie was groggy when Clark entered her hospital room, but he could see that her color was returning. When Reggie looked into Clark's face, her eyes were lucid. He sat at her bedside and held her hand. He knew she had been through a traumatic experience and he hoped he would say the right things to let her know she could trust him. He was furious with the doctor in Puerto Rico and he struggled to contain his rage.

"Dr. Phillips says you're going to be all right. He told me what happened in Puerto Rico. What did that doctor do to you in the abortion clinic?"

"Oh, Clark," said Reggie. "I was so scared and the second abortion hurt so much because they only gave me a local, but I

The Decorator

didn't want to go under again. The doctors are so nice here. They said I'm going to be here for a few days. Please explain to my parents that I've stayed on the islands for a few extra days. You haven't told my parents about anything, have you?"

"Of course not. No one's mad at you, Reggie."

"Did Dr. Phillips tell you what happened in the clinic?"

"I was told you were raped."

"He forced me," said Reggie. "Not my doctor, but the doctor's assistant, the younger one who gave me the anesthesia. He put the mask on my face so tight, too tight. I could feel him touching my breasts. He lifted my hospital robe and stuffed his fingers in me and he made sexual comments in Spanish. He got on top of me and he forced his way into me. It was so disgusting. It hurt, too. He kept telling me to relax, as if *that* was the problem! He told me I was no Madonna, and I should be ready for anyone and anything. He was so nasty to me, so cold. I tried to push him off me, but I was strapped down to the table and when I screamed the mask almost choked me. Then I passed out. Everything was spinning and it all went black.

"When I first woke up I thought I dreamed it, but I can't forget his sweaty face and that feeling of being crushed by him. I didn't dream it. And his horrible breath! I couldn't have dreamed that. It happened to *me*. How could a doctor do that? He raped me and then they performed the abortion! How could they let that happen to me?"

Reggie started crying and Clark held her. She cried for a long time and Clark waited for her to stop.

"I wish I'd never gone there," said Reggie. "I should have known better. It's all my fault. I'm a sinner and I know I sinned. God is punishing me."

"No, you haven't," said Clark. "You didn't sin. Get that idea out of your head. You've been abused and the sin was committed against you. In fact, a crime was committed against you. You would have stopped the crime if you could have. You were helpless. Listen to me, Reggie: you had a right to get that abortion. You know you're a good, religious, and wonderful person. If I could get my hands on that guy…I'd let him have it good. I think I could teach him a real lesson, if that's what you want. Do you remember his name? What is the hospital's address?"

"I never did know his name. It happened so fast and it wasn't in a hospital or even a regular doctor's office, I don't think. I was picked up at the hotel, as the clinic had arranged, by a private car service. The driver drove a new navy blue, a Buick, I think it was, without any markings on it, or cab company name, and he took me to a house in a private neighborhood. It was near El Convento, the mission-style hotel, and there were lots of small Spanish restaurants in the neighborhood. It was so residential I felt lucky to catch a taxi back to my hotel."

"I never should have let you go there," said Clark. "I could just destroy that Luciano. I could kill him. I know there is something in Luciano that is evil, something brewing in him that gives his eyes a frightening quality. I wouldn't be surprised to find that Luciano is actually a wanted man — wanted for some strange dealings or something, in one country or another. He seems to take lots of leaves from the airline. He calls all his leaves vacations, but think about it: how many airline pilots can do their thing — leavewise — as often as that bastard... And another thing about Luciano: he changes hotels every time he's in town... or does he really stay in a hotel, or with some of his underground cronies? I'm told he always has lots of money to spend, too. Does he make all that loot as a pilot, or is he into some other trade?"

"What could I do?" asked Reggie. "I couldn't have Luciano's baby. And it doesn't matter what the doctor's name is because I'm not going to the police, no way! What I did was illegal in New York and I doubt the Puerto Rican police would be much help to me or to you if you tried to find Dr. Juan. Abortions are performed all the time in Puerto Rico. I bet there were a few other girls on that flight headed right to doctors just like him. An abortion is expensive in San Juan, fifteen hundred dollars! I bet a lot of people benefit from that income. Though Dr. Juan probably takes the money and runs. I bet these guys move around a lot.

"And besides, I don't want a word of this out. It would kill my parents to know their daughter had an illegal abortion — they don't even know I have sex! Or they don't want to know. They want to believe I'll be a virgin until after I'm married, to you, of course. Dad is so Catholic — he just wouldn't understand about these things. I bet he and Mom were both virgins when they were married, and do you know, they always told my brother and me that the stork brought us to them?

"I also have my career to think about, a career I really want to see happen. I don't know what I'm going to do about my sex life now, but you can be sure I'm going to be really careful with birth control from now on and I'm not letting any man near me who doesn't respect that. I'm through with all those macho guys who won't use condoms and tell me they'll pull out before... It's over for me! Right now, I feel like never having sex again. That's where all the trouble started." Reggie stared out the window contemplating the bare, street-lit trees and thinking.

Clark was worried. He was worried about Reggie's head. He didn't want her to blame herself for having the abortion and he didn't want her to dwell on the rape, and that was what she was doing.

"Reg, why don't you talk to my psychiatrist, Dr. Stern, about this. This is a terrible thing that happened to you, a trauma, and you need someone to help you deal with it. If Dr. Stern can't help, maybe he'll suggest someone who can. I know he'll see you. Just talk with him for a session or two. It will really help you straighten out your brain. I just think you would feel better if you saw someone, and soon..."

Reggie took a sip of water from the glass on her bedside table. She blew her nose. "Maybe you're right — I've just got to think..."

Reggie closed her eyes and fell into a semi-state of sleep. Clark let her be. He didn't feel like going home just yet and soon he found himself dozing in his chair. A nurse woke him up when she came by at 1 a.m. to give Reggie a shot of painkiller. Reggie refused the shot and asked the middle-aged, heavy-set nurse if it was all right if Clark stayed in her room for the night. The nurse said she didn't see why not, especially since Dr. Phillips had already told her it was okay.

"That's why I didn't ask your husband to leave when the usual visitin' hours were over." The nurse winked and left with her tray.

Clark was so pleased to hear a real Irish brogue for the first time in years that he didn't correct the nurse. He noticed Reggie didn't correct her, either. Reggie asked Clark to get them some tea from the coffee machine in the lobby downstairs. She felt like talking, and when Clark returned with the steaming cups of machine-tasting tea, she told him all about her trip to Puerto Rico, how she had gotten the name of the abortionist from a pal at the network, and how she had lied to her parents about the reason for her trip. She had emptied her savings account to pay the doctor, who asked for his fee up front. In hindsight, she did think it was strange and annoying that the doctor and his assistant had eyed and ogled her body, but at the time she was too nervous to pay much attention to their behavior.

She remarked that the doctor had looked strangely like Luciano, with his dark hair, dark eyes, and neatly cut mustache. She wondered how many girls from wherever came to Puerto Rico to meet the abortionist with the manicured and lacquered nails, if they too wondered why he wore his pants so tight, if, like Reggie, they were reassured by the golden medal of the Mother and Christ Child revealed by the doctor's open-necked polo shirt, and if they too thought the medal made up for his hairy chest. At the time, Reggie had wondered if the Catholic doctor was married, if he had children, and if he liked women or not. Obviously he did not, since he had allowed Reggie, his helpless patient, to be raped by his anesthesiologist, who justified his offense by saying she was "no Madonna." Maybe the other doctor had raped her too; Reggie would never know. She wondered if the doctor's wife knew, and if she did, how she could remain married to such a man.

"I don't know if I can ever bear being examined by a male gynecologist again. Even though the doctor who actually did my pelvic exam in this hospital was female, I screamed so loud and struggled so much, it took three nurses to hold me down. I couldn't help it — I felt like I was being violated again. And I even felt ashamed when Dr. Phillips looked at me down there, even though he's so nice, because the rape keeps happening in my mind over and over. Clark, you know I was never ashamed of my body before, and I know in my head that I didn't do anything wrong, but I feel so dirty now, I want to take a hundred showers. Maybe I'll take four a day, like Pamela Raven, and cover my furniture in white terrycloth towels until I feel clean again!"

Clark was happy to hear the humor returning to Reggie's voice, but he felt very strongly that young girls needed to be protected from cruelty and men like Dr. Juan and his anesthesiologist. "Will the day ever come," he asked, "when a girl doesn't have to find some quack doctor to perform the cutting?"

"The suction," corrected Reggie. "Perhaps, yes, perhaps no. Some women try to do an abortion on themselves, which is really dangerous. I learned about that when I did the story on the women's clinic in the East Village. Remember that interview I did for class, the one where that film student guy, Jim McGee, put the wrong kind of film in the camera? I wonder if I should go there and ask the counselors at the women's clinic for advice. Or maybe I will call your Dr. Stern. Dr. Stern sounds so... I don't know, *stern*.

"Really, I just want to go home. And I'm not sure where that is. Not my parents' house, and my hotel room...well, I guess that's home to me. Anything is better than being in the hospital. I want to be in my own bed, such as it is, with my comforter and my own Pop sheets."

She studied Clark with an intensity that disturbed him.

"What is it?" asked Clark. "Why are you staring at me like that. Are you in pain? Should I call the nurse in to give you a shot of sedative?"

Reggie didn't say anything; she just shook her head and continued to regard Clark seriously, as if she were memorizing his face. Clark felt a bit like a lamp or a chair under Deirdre Dawn's critical inspection.

"I don't know," sighed Reggie. She looked out the window again. "I probably shouldn't say this, but I'm wondering if and when I can actually have a baby, a baby we both want, with someone who loves me. I feel so empty and I want to be filled up again. I know you love me, but I don't know if you're ever going to be serious. When I'm with other men, I always end up wishing they were you. The way we are... The way we have fun... I just want someone to love me."

She looked dangerously close to tears, but she just twisted her mouth and threw her empty paper cup at the wastebasket. She missed.

"Just my luck. I told you God is punishing me." She looked

at Clark out of the corner of her eye. "Oh, shit, now you're all uncomfortable. I knew I shouldn't have said that. Stop fixing your cufflink, you big ape. It must be the drugs talking. If anyone asks, you can tell them I was all doped up, speaking in tongues, whatever. I'm gonna be a big anchorwoman, remember?"

"That's the ticket, Reg," said Clark. He looked up from his diamond cufflink. "That's the super-powered girl I know."

"I'm gonna be like Dannee Lou, in and out of the White House all day: 'And how are you today, Mr. President? Oh, I'm just peachy! A press luncheon in the Green Room will be fine — hold the mustard!' And then we'll push through some legislation for women's rights and we'll protect ourselves against the evil Dr. Juans of the world!"

"It's got to be done, and there's no one more qualified to do it!" said Clark.

"That's right," said Reggie, as she started to doze off. "And you'd better be nice to me." She fell asleep and Clark could tell from her peaceful expression that she trusted him to be there when she awakened.

CHAPTER 13

When the concierge in Reggie's lobby bent her fat back over the cigarette machine to fumble for something behind it, Clark made his move. He breezed through the hotel lobby on tiptoe, an empty duffel bag in his hand. Chuckling silently, he sprinted up the stairs to Reggie's floor and let himself into her suite with his key. The air in the rooms was stale and overheated. He glanced around quickly, deciding what to pack and suppressing the urge to dust. A spider plant on the sitting room window sill badly needed water, and he took care of that. Out of habit, he opened the miniature refrigerator and scooped some rubbery carrots, a pint carton of sour skim milk, and a plastic bowl of something green and fuzzy into a garbage bag to toss into the hall garbage disposal.

The crystal prisms Reggie had mischievously stolen from a chandelier in the Ritz Plaza lobby cast little spots of colored light on the kitchenette wall and Clark admired the crazy little mobile Reggie had made from the prisms and a few wires. She'll want this, he thought. He pried the mobile loose from its little hook on the window frame, trying to keep it intact. The crystals tinkled as he wrapped the mobile in a dishtowel and packed it into the duffel bag. He found another towel to wrap Reggie's favorite coffee cup, a motley-glazed clay bowl made by a potter friend in Santa Fe.

Next to go into the duffel bag was Reggie's wooden-beaded curtain, which always annoyed Clark with its clakity sound every time he passed through the bedroom doorway. He took it anyway because he knew Reggie enjoyed the curtain and he wanted her to feel at home. Her windchimes, however, he left in place; he pretended not to see them. (They drove him crazy.) Her candles, he decided, would stay too, as their wax drippings had covered the Chianti bottles which held them; the wax had even dripped and pooled onto her mantlepiece where the candle-holding bottles sat. Clark was tempted to scrape the rainbow-colored mess away, but he restrained himself.

He packed a few of Reggie's favorite albums, Maria Callas, Charlie Parker, and the Beatles, and he rolled up her poster of Jean-Paul Belmondo for the journey. He had almost given up on the idea of bringing any of her books, as he did not know which ones she had read, but, with a surge of inspiration, he packed two journalism and sociology textbooks she had "been meaning to get to" to complete her coursework. He made a mental note to buy her a few magazines too, for light reading, and some new candles, which would *not* be allowed to drip on his furniture.

Before moving on to more practical items, such as clothing, toiletries, and makeup, Clark rummaged through Reggie's little spice rack until he found the jar that pretended to contain oregano. Reggie's ceramic pot pipe was under the sink, behind the cleanser. She was paranoid about getting busted by her landlady or one of the straight girls in the hotel if they were to see her stash. Clark also remembered to take a few sticks of the "Musk" incense Reggie favored. He disliked the heavy, sweet smell of incense, but he thought Reggie might be right about masking the smell of marijuana. He wanted her to be happy, so that she would recover quickly from her bad experience in Puerto Rico.

He stripped her bed of its Pop sheets and pillowcases, folded them, and stuffed them into the bag. On top of the sheets, he packed her pink satin comforter with the lurid red roses that he called "Whorehouse Red Roses." Reggie loved to nest under the comforter for days at a time in a haze of stoned euphoria, and she was very receptive to lovemaking on those days. Clark was no fool about creating the right atmosphere for good sex.

Before he left her dark bedroom, Clark filled his jacket pockets with Reggie's colorful glass bead necklaces, big fun rings, and a little Lucite-framed photograph of a teenage Reggie with her younger brother Charlie and their dog, Piglet, smiling by their parents' above-ground plastic swimming pool. Lastly, he strapped Reggie's new acoustic guitar over his shoulder, counterbalancing the duffel bag in his other hand.

The Decorator

Clark breezed through the lobby again, not caring if his obese nemesis saw him.

He laughed when she bellowed: "Git back heeah, Mista! No unannounced gennelmen allowed upstaihs!"

Clark slammed the old door behind him and took the four steps outside in one leap, loving the shock of frosty air on his cheeks. As a cab pulled up, spraying grey slush, he marveled at the fact that he would soon be in Los Angeles, where it wasn't even winter, at least compared to northeastern temperatures. As a matter of fact, they would be having Christmas in two weeks in Los Angeles, without snow! Back home in Maine, bone-chilling winter began in October. Clark wasn't looking forward to spending Christmas up north, but he imagined it would be thrilling to walk on a warm California beach in January. He had never seen the Pacific Ocean and he hoped he would have time to explore.

Clark decorated his bedroom with care, creating a cozy cave for Reggie. He arranged all of her things in his room so that she would be completely surprised by their impact. He just wasn't going to let her recuperate in a depressing midtown hotel. In his usually-empty refrigerator, Clark stocked all of Reggie's favorite bran muffins, cheeses, fruits, deli salads, and Sara Lee cakes; the Campbell's Soups and cream-style corn, which she loved, were in his cupboard. There would be no reason for her to leave. The last thing Clark did before leaving for the hospital was to pull his black-and-white television set into the bedroom.

Reggie loved the surprise, and she kept kissing Clark and squealing with delight. She lit the new candles and Clark poured them some wine. They drank the bottle of wine and smoked pot in bed until Reggie turned off the television and they made love, very carefully.

During the day, when Clark was at work, Reggie read her textbooks and composed a letter and resume to send to news agencies across the country. The office manager at CBS knew Reggie was recovering from a surgical procedure, but as it was also close to holiday vacation time, Reggie did not have to use her sick days. Instead, she would came back to work early, before the New Year, to allow other secretaries to take that time off. In the afternoon, Reggie ordered groceries to be delivered from Little India on lower Lexington Avenue, and she experimented with some recipes for Clark's entertainment when he arrived home from work. As Reggie ground cardamom and chopped fruit to stew for chutney, she was surprised and delighted by her new, temporary housewife role. She anticipated seeing Clark's expression when he came home to the aroma of curry, coconut, and tangy mango chutney.

They quickly fell into a comfortable evening routine of eating Reggie's feast of flavorful little dishes, drinking and smoking while they played records and talked until bed. Deirdre Dawn closed the office a week before Christmas Eve, and as Clark was not traveling until early on the morning of Christmas Day, he was happy to relax with Reggie at home. He was comfortable just to lounge with her in the living room without talking at all. Instead, he sketched while Reggie read or practiced the guitar.

Clark discovered that smoking grass gave him the ability to concentrate on a drawing for hours at a time, and he never felt the urge to add any Deirdre Dawn-approved decorative touches. The main reason he had enjoyed creating his large paintings was because they were done quickly, in contrast to the painstaking drafting methods he had learned as a designer. Now, he felt free even of the "unconventional" conventions of Modern Art: he used only colored inks on bristol board, drawing intricate optical patterns and cartoon figures, much as he had done so unselfconsciously as a child. He had never possessed such a long attention span before. Reggie said it was "zen."

Reggie and Clark became uncharacteristically reclusive. They blamed their hibernation on the bitter cold, but sometimes, when they had smoked particularly strong marijuana, they did not even answer the phone. Reggie giggled as Clark let it ring, so absorbed was he in his drawing. Neither Clark nor Reggie noticed when they stopped having sex, nor were they surprised that it bothered neither one of them. Clark was reminded of a comfortable, long-forgotten time in his childhood when he and his sister Vera would hide in the attic from their mother; they always became so absorbed in their games of imagination that they forgot they were hiding, or that there even was a world downstairs.

The Decorator

For once, there were no worries at Deirdre Dawn & Company. Pamela Raven was satisfied, Roland Lee was occupied with construction at the Bel Vista, and Paul Hedges had smoothed matters out with Allen Friedberg, exactly how Clark did not know. He greatly admired the older man for his diplomatic ability.

The Grande Dame herself, Deirdre Dawn, had danced off into the winter season socials. The New York Imperial Ball was on the fourth, followed by the opening of the Palm Beach Winter Season on the 17th and the Debutante Cotillion and the Christmas Ball on the 21st. After that Deirdre would just have to attend the Washington Debutante Ball on the 24th of December. Her seasonal fit of jollity had dissipated the tension at the office and the company holiday party was relaxed and even friendly — though Deirdre had somehow overlooked Clark's Christmas present again, he had received a large bonus, which was present enough.

After much consideration, Clark reluctantly canceled his trip to Maine, he explained to Vera that Reggie was recovering from an operation and could not travel, nor did he want to leave her alone. It was also true that he would have so much work to do preparing to decorate the Vista that he felt the Maine trip was ill-timed and would interfere with his work, though of course he could not say that to Vera. She would never understand if her brother used work as an excuse not to see his new nephew, especially at Christmas. How could Clark tell his motherly sister that babies just didn't excite him at all? He couldn't.

Reggie and Clark had a pre-Christmas snowbound evening with hot chocolate and "Amahl and the Night Visitors" on the hi-fi. Clark had come home with a tiny Christmas tree, which Reggie decorated with her jewelry, the Ritz Plaza crystals, and their little wrapped gifts. They got stoned and made love on the rug in front of the tree, which was nice, Clark thought, but his mind wasn't really with it.

Reggie noticed and teased him: "Don't look so interested, Clark!" It was their joke that he only looked interested when he was paying no attention and that he appeared to be bored when he cared the most.

So, he thought, I should try to look bored now, but the pot

wove such permutations in his mind that he didn't know what he was doing with his face, and he felt he was going crazy from self-consciousness. He had smoked too much. He wanted to go for a walk in the snow-covered park and clear his head.

When Reggie had satisfied herself, collapsed on top of him, and started breathing evenly, he felt smothered beneath her. Her breasts were too sweaty and heavy on his chest, and he had a sudden desire to be out somewhere where there were party lights, cold drinks, and crowds of people. He eased out from beneath Reggie and rolled her onto her side, where she made a grumbly little moan. Clark jumped into the shower, eager to go anywhere, even to Adela Morgan's Christmas party, which suddenly seemed magically enticing.

Reggie had promised her parents she would come home for Christmas and a large extended-family dinner and celebration. She dragged herself up to shower too, complaining about heavy Czech Christmas cooking, her weight, and not feeling like traveling to Brooklyn to lie to her relatives about what a fabulous time she had in Puerto Rico. As she put on her make-up, she kept shooting sideways looks at Clark and he could feel her irritation growing.

"You're not coming with me, are you?" she asked lightly, while glaring into the mirror with her eyebrows bunched together.

Uh-oh, thought Clark. Not this again. "I haven't decided..." he began.

"Oh, come on, honey — what do I have to do to get you to come with me?" Reggie was still using a light, flirtatious tone, though Clark could see the tension in her hand as she gripped her hairbrush.

"Aw, Reg," Clark pleaded. "Your parents aren't even expecting me, are they? So it's not like I'll be disappointing them. You did tell them I'm in Maine, didn't you?"

"Not exactly..." Reggie applied mascara, a bit shakily. "I said you were *going* to go to Maine, but that you *didn't* go, so Mama invited you for dinner tomorrow and she *is* expecting you, like I already told you ten times and you won't even answer me... Damn!" Reggie had accidentally poked herself in the eye with the mascara wand and the resulting tearing made her eyeliner run into a black smudge under her eye.

The Decorator

She gave up her cool act, and started snapping, her Brooklyn accent coming out toughly: "Clark, why the hell can't you do one thing fa me? I don't ask you fa too much, do I? Huh? Can't you just come to my parents' house with me and act like a boy friend fa once in ya life, so I don't have to heah about how I'm not so young any more and meanwhile they're all thinkin' I'm a whore?"

There goes her Columbia University "Standard Speech" training, Clark thought, but he wisely kept his mouth shut.

Reggie scrubbed at the makeup with a tissue dunked in cold cream and glared at Clark through the grey grease. With her wet hair and grey-smudged eyes, she looked like an angry rat to Clark and he back away, almost falling into the closet.

"Reggie," he mumbled, "I'm…"

"What? You're what?" Her look was cold.

"I made other plans," he lied.

"Fine!" she barked. "So much for counting on you." Then she looked sharply at him and demanded, "What plans?"

"Pamela Raven's coming back from Washington tonight and I…"

"Oh! I hate Pamela Raven! She thinks she owns you! But you don't hate her, do you? You're in *love* with her, admit it! You're in love with that old dyke movie queen! And you're letting her use you like she uses everyone else!"

"Come on, baby, let's not do this," Clark reached for Reggie's shoulder and she twitched away. "I should have told you before now that I don't want to go anywhere for Christmas. I apologize."

Reggie sighed. "All right. Apology accepted. But you *can* talk to me, you know."

"I know," said Clark. That was the problem, he thought. He didn't always feel like talking or telling people what his plans were. He waved away the smoking bowl of pot Reggie had filled as a peace offering. He finished dressing as she inhaled deeply and exhaled clouds of smoke that filled the air with their sweet scent as she redid her makeup and sang along with the radio in her pleasant low voice. Clark liked Reggie when she was cool like this, like a sister. When she became demanding he wanted to push her out the door. It happened with most women, and even some male friends, at one time or another, and even though he knew they weren't being unreasonable, Clark felt so *crowded*. He wondered if he would ever get used to the pushy, emotional way of New Yorkers. Where Clark was from, folks kept a civil distance and didn't reveal too much private feeling. It was unseemly and somehow weak. And they certainly didn't raise their voices. It seemed city people had forgotten their manners, if they ever had any. Or perhaps manners were going out of style, like men's hats.

The cold night air was a great relief to Clark; it snapped him awake as he walked east to Adela Morgan's apartment on Sutton Place. Adela's party had been his second choice for the evening's activity, but Pamela Raven's telephone had been answered by Mama, who politely informed Clark that Miss Raven was already out for the evening. Clark should have remembered that Pamela Raven liked to socialize early so that she could retire at a decent hour. At the moment, he craved her lean, strong legs around him, and he wished to retire with her, after a sparkling evening on the town and plenty of icy vodka.

However, Clark knew the evening would not be a disappointment when a tuxedoed butler opened the door to Adela Morgan's party, and light and swing music splashed out over Clark like a welcoming waterfall.

"Clark Calloway!" the butler announced in a Bronx accent. It was just like Adela to hire a boy from the old neighborhood for the night, probably the son of an old friend, and he hadn't shaved too closely, either. Clark didn't care. He thought the fellow had a sort of junior-gangstery sort of charm, and that the party already looked like a speakeasy. Clark gladly tossed the butler his coat.

Adela's apartment was packed to the rafters with chattering people, mostly middle-aged, in gowns and black tie. As Paul Hedges had described, it was also cluttered with every conceivable knick-knack, souvenir, tschotschke, and ornament Adela had gathered during her tours. The walls were crowded with a claustrophobic array of photos and show posters. Festoons of winking colored lights, glittery fringed banners, and an enormous wall-mounted electric Christmas tree created a carnival atmosphere. The furnishings, what Clark could see of them, were strictly granny-style, and comfortably overstuffed, like Adela herself.

The Decorator

The festive clutter and loud cheerful crowd were just what Clark needed, and he gratefully accepted a glass of champagne from a frilly-attired young maid. The champagne was pink and loathsome, but it was perfectly chilled. He drank it in one gulp and grabbed another plastic goblet.

"Thoisty, aint'cha?" Another Bronx accent.

"Yes, indeed," said Clark. The maid was pretty in a hard way.

"What, no date?" she spoke out of the side of her mouth. "Or you got gal trouble?"

"You must be reading my mail," replied Clark.

The maid laughed raucously and elbowed her way back into the crowd with her tray, braying, "Pahdon me, 'scuse me, champagne?"

A skinny arm shot past Clark; the pale hand just missed the champagne tray. "Oh!" the breathy sigh of disappointment was familiar and Clark turned to see Doreen Flower's pouting pixie face.

"For the love of Mike, I'm just try'nna get some bubbly!"

Clark gallantly fetched Doreen a glass from the bobbing tray. "Mike or no Mike, I have to tell you it's pure swill," he informed Doreen.

"Who's Mike?" Doreen took the glass. "Thanks, guy," she purred. "It's those long arms of yours. Say, what are you doing in this creep joint?"

She sipped the champagne and said, "Ugh, you're right about the swill."

"Just trying to entertain myself tonight. Is the party so bad?"

"Not any more. Don't take it so big if it is. It's my third soirée tonight, and I've got two more to hit. You can come along with me if you want."

"Sounds tempting, though I should pay my respects to the hostess."

"Oh, her. She's over there wagging her chins. Can you believe they cast her in a movie? What can Metropolis be thinking? She's way too old — who'd want to look at that big butt of hers? She's about to burst her black sequins. And Pamela Raven is starring with her? At her best, she was a cheap version of Elizabeth Taylor, and she's sure not at her best any more. You know, the word is that she's cracking up. Did you hear what she pulled in Washington last week? At a State Dinner?"

"No, I didn't," said clark. "Shouldn't you save it for the papers?"

Doreen fluttered her false eyelashes. "It's already in. Nobody scoops Doreen!"

Clark liked her shiny blonde bob and her little rosebud mouth, but he decided she would be more attractive if her eyes weren't so close together.

"Don't get me wrong, baby," said Doreen. "I wouldn't want to be a movie star. It's too hard, and too embarrassing. I think all those old starlets had guts, and I've got a feeling Maria Pucci might be in that category. She's a friend of yours, isn't she? What's her story? You can tell old Doreen."

When Clark did no more than nod, Doreen changed the subject.

"Oh, here's that champagne again! Grab me another, will you? I need to get blind if I'm gonna convince my date he's not funny-looking. But back to Pamela Raven! I have my ways of knowing what she's about. She lives in my building now, you know. All I have to do is sweet-talk the super, and he lets me see her garbage — we're talking six or seven quart bottles of vodka a week! She must walk around with a hangover out to *here*! Oh, here comes A.M. — I must escape the hag! Clark Calloway, you simply have to promise me an interview, and soon! We have so much to talk about!"

She squeezed Clark's arm and departed. Clark wondered how Doreen Flower ever got anyone to trust her or even talk to her. It must be her association with the late Lady Starlite, the original doyenne of bi-coastal gossip. Doreen Flower had been Lady Starlite's assistant until they parted ways over a difference of opinion, to hear Doreen tell it. Others said Doreen was simply fired, but it was too late to ask Lady Starlite.

Adela Morgan's voice cut through the room like a dinner bell: "Clark, ya big lug! Get over here! I've been waitin' for ya!"

She flung out her arms, knocking Doreen Flower nearly to the ground. Clark let himself be pulled down and enfolded against Adela's massive bosom as her huge feathered coiffure tickled his face.

The Decorator

Adela led him into the thick of the crowd, announcing, "I hate blondes!" for Doreen's benefit. "And frails. What'ya wanna talk to a bird brain like Flower for? Stick with me, Mon Petoot, and I'll introduce ya to real class!"

Clark made the rounds, shaking hands with Adela's Broadway friends and associates. He greeted Paul Hedges, who was sitting primly in a corner of the couch, and was swept into the circle surrounding Thom Pearson.

The subject was Vietnam. Pearson was speaking in his characteristically charming and low-key manner. "Well, my feeling is that the situation had changed since my old friend Henry Cabot Lodge was the ambassador to Vietnam and he was dealing with the late President Diem. Lodge's carrot-and-stick idea, while a very good idea, would work better in a country in which we were more certain of the leadership, of course. With the coups, I don't think the 'limited risk gamble' policy Jack Kennedy inherited — and he did inherit it, you know — the risk is not quite as limited as we once thought. I'm concerned about the economic angle. The deficit is growing and I don't see how we can keep it in check while President Johnson funds both the war and his Great Society programs."

"Great Society!" boomed Adela. "Great Snow Job! If they don't end this war soon, my son's gonna be a draft-dodger! You don't know what it's like to raise kids backstage, teach 'em every trick you know about singin' and dancin' and how ta make people laugh, only to have one of 'em end up there in Moose Jaw or something. There is no Broadway in Canada! I didn't raise my boy to be a Canadian!"

That got a laugh, which Adela wanted, and it gave Clark a chance to change the subject and start his own conversation with the network chieftain.

"Say, Thom, what's the word on the next big thing in television?" he asked.

"I'm glad you asked me that," Thom turned to face Clark as Adela buttonholed a bald man in a suit.

"Oh, here's my shingle!" Adela howled. "Eddie, did you get me Barry Weissman as my publicist for *Tigress* or what? Is he free? Is there a deal? I want conformation in writing!" She followed her lawyer and her booming voice followed her.

"Lawyers, what would the world be without them?"

mused Thom Pearson. "The money always comes in late and the lawsuits come in early. But on to a more interesting subject, Clark, television, as you so wisely brought up! My inventor is working on an interesting innovation, one that will change television as we know it, and..." he lowered his cultured voice, "seriously challenge the motion picture industry." He smiled a thin, proud smile.

"And what is that?" asked Clark.

"Video cassettes," said Thom.

"Are they similar to audio cassettes?" asked Clark.

"Similar, indeed. There are technical challenges at present, but we are working on them. I hope to have a marketable video cassette by 1967. That way people can bring quality programs such as ballet and opera, as well as movies, into their own homes, without the necessity for a projector. My competition has nowhere near the technology that we have and they don't have my inventor! There's no one like him in the world. I have found that there is no way to make decent programming profitable on network television, though that was my goal in the beginning."

Clark was excited. "Video cassettes — that's a marvelous idea! I wish you the best of luck in developing them."

"Thank you," said Thom. "And how is our dear Miss Pamela Raven?"

"She seems to be doing very well. She's quite excited about the film."

"As she should be. I don't know if I admire her more as an actress or as a businesswoman. She was brilliant on the board of Cosmetique, or Cosmeco, as they are now called. I'll never understand why they retired her. On the other hand, her lovely voice has brought increased sales to Cosmeco since they began sponsoring our little quiz shows."

"Oh, that's good," said Clark.

"Yes, indeed, so much so that Mr. Kirkeby of Cosmeco is quite disturbed. I don't think he enjoys having Pamela Raven arrange deals without including him. He'll never admit that she can perform on the same level as her late husband, Lucien Irons!"

"Why should that be?" asked Clark.

"Well, the voiceover commercials were to be performed by

Mrs. Kirkeby, you see."

"Oh, dear," Clark chuckled. "Is there no hope for peace between Pamela Raven and Roger Kirkeby?"

"I'm afraid not," said Thom. "I believe she's in for a battle royal. The dynamics remind me of nothing so much as the time I tried to explain Americans to Winston Churchill…"

Thom gazed over his drink into the fond distance, and Clark hoped he wouldn't begin telling war stories. Clark had reasons to keep the subject closer to home.

"It was my impression that Pamela Raven is still on the board of Cosmeco," Clark commented.

"Of Cosmeco, no, but she's still on the board of Cosmetique, which has become a subsidiary, due to the visionary finances of our Mr. Kirkeby — though he must always live with the possibility of being introduced as 'the man with Pamela Raven's company.' It makes him quite livid," Thom responded.

"Yes, and Miss Raven has told me that each and every day, mail arrives at Mr. Kirkeby's headquarters addressed to 'Pamela Raven, President of Cosmetique'."

"Well, she is a fascinating woman," said Thom.

"That she is," said Clark.

"On the subject of fascinating women, I've been informed that one of my best employees, Miss Stowkowski, is a friend of yours. She certainly adds sparkle to her department."

"Oh, yes, Regina Stowkowski is a good friend. I've known her and her family for years." Clark had been wondering how to give the subject this particular turn, and Thom Pearson had done it for him. He wondered if there was anything that happened at CBS that Thom Pearson didn't know about.

"Yes, she is a sterling secretary and researcher — her superiors speak quite well of her work, as well as her charming personality. I chanced to wander through the research department myself, and I was quite taken with her — personality. Surely she has interests beyond the mundane secretarial duties?"

"Oh, she does. She is studying Journalism at Columbia, in fact. I believe she is only a few credits away from earning her degree."

"I'm glad to hear that. The profession could use more bright young people. What is her area of concentration?"

"Well, she has focused her training in newscasting as well as newswriting, and I know she wants to work in a television newsroom in some capacity," Clark ventured.

"Now, let me see... I believe George Myers at the Washington Bureau is interviewing for a new assistant. I'll arrange for him to see Miss Stowkowski immediately after the holidays."

"I'm sure Regina will benefit from the interviewing experience, whatever the outcome may be," said Clark.

"Yes, that's a good way to look at it," said Thom. "But please do me a small favor: don't mention this opportunity to Miss Stowkowski until I get the chance to call her into my office and tell her myself. It's one of the few pleasant types of conversation I get to have these days."

"I'll keep it under my hat. And thank you," said Clark.

"Think nothing of it. We're always looking for good people," said Thom. "You did say she was a friend..." One of Thom Pearson's eyebrows rose suggestively.

"Yes, she's a friend, an old friend of mine. Merry Christmas!" called Clark.

"Merry Christmas, Clark," Thom Pearson echoed.

Clark was elated as he wandered off to find Paul Hedges. Thom Pearson's innuendo, subtle as it was, had not been lost on Clark. It was well-known that Pearson and his wife, a beautiful society heiress, had an "open" relationship, and Thom Pearson was a rather handsome and distinguished older man, with a style not often seen any more. If he was interested in Reggie, Clark felt it could only help her career. And Thom Pearson was too much of a sportsman to renege on his offer to Reggie, even if she refused his advances. Clark hoped.

"I must leave," said Paul. "I've done my time."

"But it's so early," said Clark.

"I know, and that's why I must leave before Miss M. gets into her cups and decides I should be a permanent fixture."

"What's the matter?" asked Clark.

"Oh, do I look worried?" Paul nervously rubbed the furrow between his eyes with his fingers. He was so sure of its location that Clark guessed he must wear a taped mask while he slept to smooth it away.

"Oh, it's nothing — just a few more files I seem to have misplaced at the office. I'm sure Belle will find them when she returns from the holiday break."

"I wouldn't worry; I'm sure she will find them," said Clark, although they both knew the missing files were part of a larger scheme of mischief which they felt powerless to stop. "Let me walk you to the door."

"Thank you, Clark, but I don't need to draw any attention to my escape."

Paul looked as if he had something more to say, but he was unsure of whether to say it. Finally he broke his uncomfortable silence by speaking very rapidly: "I know this is out of the blue, but since you have changed your mind about going home for Christmas, would you like to come up to the children's home and have dinner with my son and me? I go every year and it's very nice — just a quiet dinner, but excellent cooking, and we'd both really enjoy your company!"

"I'll be glad to come," said Clark.

"Good! I'll pick you up tomorrow at two. We'll spend Christmas Eve in a French inn I know, a wonderful place, with a great bar and a very good restaurant — they specialize in fresh game — and on Friday, we'll drive over to the children's home in the afternoon. I hear the snow is perfect right now, and there are good ski slopes nearby, if you would care to go. You do ski, don't you?"

"I like skiing," said Clark. "Though my skis are in Maine. I'm sure I can rent some skis upstate. Let's make a weekend of it. I'll be glad to get away from the slush and the holiday crowds."

Clark was the last guest to leave, thanks to Adela. She pasted herself to his side, and by two o'clock in the morning, they were sitting alone in the debris, eating canned meatballs and drinking Almaden.

"I won't have a stove in this place," said Adela. "Fire hazard. But these meatballs are good cold, right?"

Clark noticed that Adela was always singing as she talked, much as Pamela Raven spoke in old-movie rapid-fire witticisms, when she wasn't lapsing into her salty southern drawl. Adela spoke with a constant vibrato and she waved her hands theatrically. Her voice was her best feature, and Clark wondered if she had ever been pretty. Her eyes were mere slits, glittery and very black in her fat face, and she had a mean little mouth, like the bow of a red shoelace. Her hair was just a ball of Brillo, dyed auburn.

No, Adela didn't have the sexual charm of Pamela Raven, but she had a good heart, and Clark felt a motherly warmth coming from Adela. And she did have a considerable talent, attested to by the numerous awards in the room. At one point during the party, someone had put an Adela Morgan record on the phonograph and several of the guests had begun dancing to it. Clark had seen Adela grow serious and almost shocked, silent for the first time during the evening, until the record ended. It was as if she considered her music too serious to dance to: one was supposed to sit and listen, with awe.

As Clark looked around her cozy, cluttered living room, at all of the photos and pillows embroidered by well-wishers, he saw that Adela had lived a full life, with four handsome husbands, and two nice-looking children. It was a shame that she had lost her daughter.

"I always went for the bad boys," Adela said through a meatball. "I see you're looking at my pickchas. If I hadn't made it to Broadway, I would have made a good moll, ya know? I can handle a gun. I'm a better shot than most men I know. I learned how to handle a pistol in one of my shows. You remember *Annie, Get Your Gun*, don't you? I'm too old for gangstas now, though I wouldn't mind havin' one more real man in my bed before my coitan call. Sure there's guys out there who would appreciate a gal like me?"

"Sure there are," said Clark.

"Not in my profession," said Adela. "Not in New York. They're all sissies. Maybe I'll have better luck in California."

The Decorator

CHAPTER 14

Traffic was light once Paul and Clark left New York City behind. Clark understood why Paul wanted to leave early in the morning: they had a four-hour drive ahead. As the suburbs of Westchester gave way to more wooded hills and open space, Clark wondered how he had stayed so long in the city without missing fresh country air. Paul was not as impressed with the landscape; he seemed tense, and grateful for Clark's company.

"This is usually a long drive for me," he said. "A long, boring drive. It's nice to have someone to talk to for a change. I hope you don't mind if we don't stop, except of course for rest stops. Chang made us a picnic basket for the journey — some roasted chicken sandwiches and vegetable crudités. I hope you like them."

Clark said that he did not mind driving straight through to Delaware County. He was eager to see the Catskill Mountains and the lake country while it was still daylight, and he appreciated Chang's cooking. Chang was Paul Hedges' butler-chef. Clark had eaten Chang's flavorful sandwiches at office parties, always with the crusts cut off. The basket was in the back seat, which was laden with ski equipment and packages for Richard Hedges. Clark was glad to be part of the important mission to brighten a child's Christmas. He didn't understand why Paul seemed so down, as Paul's frequent sighs and tense expression indicated.

"There's nothing to stop for, anyway," said Paul. "Nothing but fast food places, and I really don't like them. I don't understand how people can eat such low-quality food or how they can live so far from any culture, any life. Look at that ugly shopping center over there. Everything is so… ordinary. And there's a car with a deer carcass tied to the roof. We'll be seeing a few more of those, I'm afraid. How can people engage in a blood sport in this day and age? I could never live in a place like this. I do have to warn you that we will probably go to a McDonald's on this trip, godawful as they are. You see, my son, though he's eighteen, has Down's syndrome, as you know, and he functions on the mental and behavioral level of a seven-year-old. He likes McDonald's and Burger King, and he expects to go there, so we do. He's habituated to those chain restaurants and to the playgrounds outside."

Clark didn't see what was so bad about indulging Richard's eating habits. He had a secret liking for an occasional Big Mac himself. Paul seemed to object more to the commonness of the fast food scene than to the cuisine and Clark admitted to himself that he couldn't imagine the immaculate Paul Hedges being comfortable in a bright plastic booth surrounded by clown figures, or eating anything that required ketchup.

"Well, I guess Richard will be happy to see you and all these presents," said Clark. "What did you get him?"

"It's always so hard to shop for him," said Paul. "Because it's hard to know what level he's at. I've bought toys and games in the past that Richard wasn't ready for. I mean, he loves moving pieces and pressing buttons, but he doesn't connect to the games. Mrs. Robinson — she's the lady who operates the foster home where Richard lives — is always happy to give me guidance on buying presents for Richard, but still, you never know. Clothing is always useful, so I bought him a jacket and some other things. The large package contains a small stereo unit, and there's a headset unit too. Richard loves sounds — he smiles at the vibrations, and Mrs. Robinson says he can insert cassettes and use the Forward and Rewind buttons."

"What kind of music does he enjoy?" asked Clark, thinking of a possible last-minute gift for the boy.

"Oh, it's hard for me to say. I wouldn't want to get the wrong kind. Mrs. Robinson takes care of things like that when she takes the children on a shopping outing. I always send an extra hundred or two with Richard's monthly board to cover his expenses for movies and treats. Mrs. Robinson is quite competent and knowledgeable in training the children. She and her husband make their living providing child care, and I think they have six or seven children living with them now. Mrs. Robinson keeps a neat house and it's pleasantly decorated, though not what you or I would consider designer furnished. She's devoted to the children, and she keeps them on a tight schedule. The training of Down's syndrome children is based on repetition — you have to keep after them constantly to habituate them to care for themselves in the years to come.

They were driving through rolling, snow-covered hills and Clark admired the quaint farmhouses and roadside antique shops along the way. He saw skaters on a frozen pond, and he watched two redtail hawks fly out of the distant woods and make slow circles in the sky. There were quite a few yellow deer-crossing signs along the road, and he hoped Paul Hedges was wary and had good driving reflexes, as the road was icy and Clark knew deer could dash suddenly out of the woods and create a hazard. In fact, he was remembering one such incident involving his sister Vera in Maine, when an impact with a deer had totaled her car and sent it into a dangerous spin. The deer had walked away unharmed, but Vera had minor bruises and a bump on her forehead. Clark was thinking more about that memory than Paul's conversation.

"I suppose you're wondering why I don't take care of Richard myself and why he doesn't live with me," said Paul.

"Oh, no, I'm sure you have given a lot of thought to what's best for Richard," Clark said quickly, realizing Paul had taken his silence as a judgment of some kind. "Let me know if you get tired of driving and I'll take over."

"Thank you, but I like to drive," said Paul. "It relaxes me and it gives me something to do rather than think about where I'm going. Every time I make this trip, I can't help reliving the first time I drove up here, when Richard was only a week old. These visits have become a habit for me, but they always remind me of the trauma I felt when Richard was born. It was so sad for me to give my child up to someone else's care, and I always think about my wife and how she would be alive today if all this hadn't happened."

"It sounds like you still miss her," said Clark.

"Yes, I miss her," said Paul. "And I think I always will. She was the only family I had, except for Richard, of course, but we just couldn't keep him. You have no idea what goes into training a retarded child. Everything the child does requires constant repetition. You sometimes have to close their mouths for them because they forget to do that. And you have to watch their eating habits because they don't know when they've consumed enough. You very often see overweight people with Down's syndrome. Neither of us had the time, nor were we capable of that kind of training."

"When I was growing up in Maine, a couple up the road had a child with Down's syndrome, only we called her a Mongoloid back then," said Clark. "I'll always remember how tired the parents looked all the time. And I remember the sadness on their faces as they aged. They were very closed-in and not talkative to the other neighbors."

"They were probably ashamed, as we were, of having a 'Mongoloid' child," said Paul. "In those days, that was not where you wanted to be, the parent of a retarded child. Retarded people were hidden away in a closet. It makes me see how far we've come, though I personally still struggle with those cringing feelings when people stare at Richard. It's hard to have a child who doesn't look... normal. In fact, several of the children at the Robinson's have never seen their parents and they probably never will. They were just dropped off. The Robinsons are paid so that parents — if you can call them that — never have to deal with their own retarded children, or even admit that they were ever born."

Clark found a classical radio station and he broached other subjects, such as clients, for conversation. He wanted to distract Paul from the depression into which he was sinking, though he knew its cause was too deep and had been going on for so long that it might very well be at the root of the elemental sadness and loneliness of Paul Hedges. Clark hoped he would never experience a trauma like Paul's, though he supposed losing both his parents qualified as a trauma. Clark felt, somehow, that nothing could make him give up on himself as Paul had. He didn't see any reason why Paul Hedges couldn't remarry, or at least date women, and move on with his life. What was it Clark's mother used to say: "I never promised you a rose garden"? Wasn't that the truth!

At one p.m. they passed the Schoharie Reservoir, and shortly thereafter they checked into their rooms in the lodge at the Plattekill Mountains Ski Bowl. The air was invigorating to Clark. The slopes were breathtaking and sparkling with snow.

The Decorator

Clark was excited about the next day's skiing and he hoped there would be a ski bunny or two to chat up around the lodge fireplace. At the moment, though, they could only drop off their luggage and rush over to the Robinson's in order to pick up Richard in time for lunch and accommodate Mrs. Robinson's schedule. After a telephone conversation with Mrs. Robinson from the lobby of the lodge, Paul Hedges was indignant in regard to her schedule.

"What a woman!" he grumbled. "She wants us to take Richard tonight and only tonight so that I don't interfere with her Bingo game tomorrow! Remember, I'm paying a substantial amount of board. Bingo game! That's the kind of mentality we're dealing with, Clark — people who play Bingo. Can you imagine anything more asinine?"

"That is pretty stupid," said Clark.

Nevertheless, Paul Hedges was nothing but charming to Mrs. Robinson. He presented her with a Danish Christmas plate which promptly joined the others, also gifts from Paul, in her kitchen wall collection. Several children with the roly-poly physiques and characteristic faces of Down's syndrome — low, flattened skulls and slanting eyes — were sitting by the Christmas tree. One boy immediately jumped up and ran over to Paul Hedges.

"King Paul! King Paul!" Richard hugged his father and hung on his arms, all the while with an ecstatic grin splitting his face. When Paul introduced Clark, Richard greeted him with nearly equal enthusiasm.

"King Paul?" asked Clark.

"He calls me that ever since the time I placed a paper Burger King crown on his head," said Paul.

"Look, Dad! Look, Dad!" was Richard's refrain as he led his father around the house. Clark followed and examined the rough wooden objects Richard was evidently proud of.

"That's very nice, Richard. Did you make this by yourself?" asked Paul."

"Yep!" declared Richard. "Look, Dad! Look!"

"Richard goes to a BOCES school; it's a vocational school where they teach wood shop, auto mechanics, things like that. It's good training, and it's supposed to be public, but because I live out of the county, I have to pay as if it were a private school. I could send Richard to Princeton for what it costs.

They had followed Richard outside and into the back yard where he enthusiastically showed Paul the swing set Mr. Robinson had built the previous summer.

"But I suppose it's worth it because this is really a wonderful environment. Look at those rolling hills!" Paul waved his hand at the landscape. "I could never place Richard in a state or public facility. The children are sometimes badly treated in institutions. You see, Down's syndrome children won't cry, no matter how hard you pinch them. Isn't that interesting?"

"Richard Hedges!" Mrs. Robinson stood in the doorway with a dishcloth in her hand. "You know you have to wear your coat outside. Get in here this instant. Mr. Hedges, I don't see how you can allow Richard to get away with this!"

"Yes, Mother," Richard trotted into the house.

"And, Richard, you have all those nice presents from your father. It's time to open them." Mrs. Robinson gave Paul Hedges a no-nonsense look that indicated it was indeed time to move things along.

As Richard crowed with joy over his presents, Mrs. Robinson delivered a never-ending stream of instructions and corrections to her other foster children, her grown children and grandchildren who were visiting, and even to her husband. It was clear that she controlled a completely organized household and that everyone in it was programmed by her.

"No, you may not have ice cream and orange soda now, Richard. It is one forty-five, and you are going out to lunch with your father at two o'clock. I want you to go into the bathroom and what will you do?"

"Wash-my-hands-and-face," said Richard.

"And then I want you to go into your room and..."

"Change-inna-clean-shirt." Richard toddled off to follow her instructions.

Paul Hedges was growing distinctly edgy. Clark could tell he didn't want to sit with the Robinsons, though he was pleasant when Mrs. Robinson paused in her litany to offer anecdotes about Richard's progress, anecdotes which her husband echoed.

"Alfred, don't you have to pick up the groceries now? My word, look at the time!" exclaimed Mrs. Robinson as her hus-

The Decorator

band rose sheepishly to put on his coat. "Richard, what's wrong now?"

Richard stood frozen in the middle of the living room, staring and picking at a shirt in his hands. With a look of stubborn and perplexed concentration, he held the shirt up to Mrs. Robinson.

"Oh, there's a button missing. How did you do that?" asked Mrs. Robinson. "Well, never mind, it's not an important button, Richard. I'll sew a new one on later. No one will see that it's missing when you tuck your shirt in. Now put that shirt on."

Slowly, Richard shook his head. He refused to move.

"Come on, Rich," Paul coaxed. "Don't you want to go to McDonald's?"

"Yes, Dad." Richard looked from the missing button to his father's face with an expression approaching panic, but still he did not move.

"Richard Hedges —" began Mrs. Robinson.

"Come on, Richard," said Clark. He rose from his chair and offered his hand to the boy. "We'll find you another shirt. Let's go to your room, okay?"

"Okay!" Richard smiled and took Clark's hand.

"I don't like to go out without all my buttons either," said Clark. "We'll be right back."

Richard's hand felt very good in Clark's, soft and trusting. Clark had the instinct that Richard needed a friend amid all the Robinson house rules. He sensed a spark of independence in Richard, and he wondered if perhaps a less rigid environment would bring it out, or at least make the boy less uptight about a button.

That evening Clark fell into bed feeling pleasantly exhausted. The long drive and the cold, fresh air had contributed to his state, but he felt Richard Hedges had provided something more. The child was so affectionate and trusting and Clark felt quite protective and satisfied when Richard snuggled up to him in the car or laughed with delight at Clark's jokes. There had been a moment when Paul had gone into a drugstore for some aspirin and it was clear that he did not want Richard to follow him.

"Stay in the car with Clark," Paul said. "I'll be right out."

Clark wondered if it hadn't something to do with Paul's shame at being seen with Richard and his fear of people staring. Richard didn't seem to mind, and he was glad to have Clark's attention. I would bring him with me, Clark thought. So what if people stare? That's their problem. Clark also felt uncomfortable about the new side of Paul Hedges he was seeing. Paul had complained about the Robinsons' decor again during the ride to the lodge, especially the paper napkins and tablecloths Mrs. Robinson had purchased from Hallmark.

"Richard is living the way real people live," Paul had pointed out. "You know I don't live the way *real* people do because of the business I'm in. I don't go out and buy paper cloths for the Christmas party like normal people do. I may design paper cloths that Hallmark will sell to other people."

When Clark said goodnight to Paul, he was amused to see that Paul did wear a taped mask to smooth away his wrinkles while he slept. He also wore a black satin eyeshade to shut out any light. Clark recognized the eyeshades as those that were given to first-class passengers on airlines. Clark had a collection of shades that he had picked up on overnight trips to London and Paris. The shades came in handy, and he often shared his with Reggie. Clark used the shades to he could get some extra shuteye in the early morning. He thought Paul used the shades to hide under, hide away from his own concerns and fears: fears about being recognized as the father of a Down's syndrome child.

It vaguely disturbed Clark that Paul Hedges separated himself so distantly from "real" people. Did that mean Paul considered himself "abnormal?" And why was that a positive condition? Clark wasn't sure it was something to be proud of. The implied separation and loneliness worried him because he often felt the same way himself: he understood why it was déclassé for Paul to set foot in a house which did not contain linen tablecloths and placemats. Clark too had felt the depressing chill of cheap paint in jarring colors. He shuddered at the memory of sickly-sweet air freshener and overhead fluorescent lighting. But he also knew that not all "real" people succumbed to the lowest styles. The Stowkowskis, for instance, and some of Clark's own relatives, lived in warm, comfortable environments which did not cost much to create.

"There's a level of taste I'm talking about and a level of affordability," Paul had said. "I believe people who don't know rarefied air are much happier. When you live in rarefied air, as I do because of the nature of my business and the nature of my clients, you become dissatisfied with anything that isn't of that level. You don't want to go to Burger King. You don't want to live in a way that the real world lives. I would rather have zero than have something that isn't quality."

As Clark fell asleep, he considered, since rarefied air doesn't make people happy, is it healthy? In fact, if it meant sacrificing what is "real," he wondered if he wanted to continue breathing it exclusively.

CHAPTER 15

Reggie was ecstatic when she swung through Clark's doorway in her new red wool trapeze coat. Flakes of snow clung to her dark hair and eyelashes.

"Look," she cried. She dangled a ring of car keys in Clark's face. "Wanna go for a ride?"

"Do you have a car?" Clark asked incredulously, letting his New York *Mirror* fall to the floor. Clark had already read the paper, including Suzy's column, which had contained a note about Deirdre Dawn's newest decorating assignment — the Bel Vista in Los Angeles.

"I didn't know you could drive," he added.

"Come see it! It's beautiful!"

Clark grabbed his belted-back camel hair coat and followed Reggie downstairs. He supposed she must be on one of her exercise fads, or perhaps she was too impatient to wait for the elevator. He caught bits of her excited tale as she bounced down the stairs below him. Apparently Reggie's parents had given Reggie her brother's car because he had written from Vietnam and said she could have his Dodge Dart. The Stowkowskis had just purchased a used station wagon for Mama Stowkowski, so they no longer needed the Dart. Clark could never follow the changing story of which car belonged to which Stowkowski, as Papa Stowkowski was an automotive mechanical genius, and their driveway and the space in front of their Greenpoint building was always crowded with cars he was repairing or restoring for sale. Car repair was a men-only activity in Greenpoint, taking place on the weekends, usually all day, with loud radios and cases of beer on ice in clean garbage cans for the men's enjoyment. So far, Clark had never seen Reggie drive any of the sacred cars.

He recognized the silver Dodge Dart as soon as he saw it. He had admired the silver finish Papa Stowkowski had so carefully applied. Reggie's brother Charlie had jacked the monstrous-hooded shark of a car high up on special tires so that it resembled a gleaming spacecraft. A familiar blonde was taking photos of the car from every angle.

"How is Charlie doing?" asked Clark as he followed Reggie's racing figure toward the car. Seeing the car brought him a clear image of Charlie driving up in the Dart, wearing a white T-shirt, rolled to show off his new tattoo, with a bottle of Bud in his hand and a big, sunny grin on his face. Del Shannon's "Little Runaway" had been playing on the car radio, Clark remembered.

"Oh, he sounds okay," said Reggie. "He hates the war and the jungle and he's itching to come home. He got a piece of shrapnel in his thigh and he thought they'd discharge him, but they removed it in the base hospital in Saigon and it healed up nicely. They sent him back to his unit. He's not allowed to tell us where he's fighting."

"That's rough," said Clark. "I'm glad his injury was minor."

"Well, you know Charlie — he's such a tough guy — too tough, I'd say! He's still got that sense of humor though; you know what he wrote: 'Join the Army — See the World — meet new and interesting people — and kill them!' My Mom didn't think it was very funny, though."

"I bet not," said Clark.

Maria had jumped into the front passenger seat, so Reggie ceremoniously held the back door open for Clark. "Your car, sir," she announced with a little bow.

Clark hung back, pretending to be nervous. "I don't know about this... let me see your license."

"Shut up, you killjoy!" Reggie pushed him in and slammed the door.

Maria turned around in her seat to snap Clark's picture. She had one of those new Polaroid Swinger cameras. "Let's have a smile from our favorite boy!" she whispered. The camera flashed and Maria peeked out from behind it with her Cheshire cat-eyed smile.

"Hi, Movie Star!" Clark kissed her and submitted to her European-style double kiss, though it meant having to wipe sticky pink lip gloss off both his cheeks. "What are you doing in this heap? Where's your limo? Where's your lover, the movie mogul?"

"Hey!" objected Reggie, as she expertly eased out into traffic. A taxi driver leaned on his horn and she flipped him the bird, also expertly, Clark thought.

Maria was shushing him: "Shhh!" She looked around in mock paranoia. "I am on the lam from Alan Friedberg and his boring elocution lessons and the stupid Stork Club! I am so sick of cigar smoke, Dorothy Kilgallen, Cholly Knickerbocker, and the horrible Cub Room, I can't tell you!" She pointed her camera out the window at a blue-haired woman walking a blue-haired poodle down Fifth Avenue.

Clark was amazed at how Maria's English pronunciations had improved. All the lessons she had been taking were indeed showing.

"When do you leave for Hollywood?" Clark asked.

The flash popped. "Oh, I don't know. Whenever Allen says. I don't ask." Maria shrugged, dropping the camera in her lap and lit a cigarette. "Next week? Who knows? Who cares?"

"Come on, you should be excited," said Clark. "Once you start filming all this preparation will be over. And imagine — you might even meet Warren Beatty! Or maybe Elvis Presley!"

"This is true," Maria's eyes flashed interest. "But I will miss my *bella* Regina."

Reggie snapped her wrist at Maria and held out two fingers for Maria's cigarette.

"Forget Elvis. For Warren Beatty, I might come with you." She stuck the cigarette in the side of her mouth. "But I'd much rather meet Sean Connery. Ahhh." A bus cut her off and she blared her horn.

"Asshole," she said. For the first time, Clark could see Reggie's strong family resemblance to the Stowkowski men and it kind of turned him on.

"Do you mind telling me where we're going?" he demanded. "If it's to the tattoo parlor, I'm getting out of here."

"Cruisin'," Reggie smirked around her cigarette as she pulled into Central Park. Soon they were across town and streaking up the West Side Highway.

"Freedom!" she yelled out the window. "Maria, Mother of God, find us some tunes!"

Maria tuned in a rock station. "Ooh, it's *il Stones*!" she

The Decorator

exclaimed. "I saw them in a concert in Paris! They are hot-hot!"

"What is she talking about?" asked Clark.

"The Rolling Stones," said Reggie. "Gimme another cig, Maria."

"You don't smoke," said Clark, who hated the Rolling Stones. "Faggy bunch of screamers, the Stones. They're all drug addicts, and they sound like it, too."

"What!" Maria snapped her head around to gape at Clark, her mouth a pink 'O' of astonishment. "You are *loco*! Regina, Signor Clark is el square-o."

Reggie just laughed and sang along with Mick. They drove up to the Cloisters, through Inwood Park, and down into Harlem.

Clark promptly locked the doors. "You're nuts," he declared. "Does anyone remember the riots last summer? Or am I square to mention them too?"

"Oh, come on, chicken," said Reggie. "Let's get some soul food, some delicious ribs, for this New England boy. This place is great!" She pulled in front of a shabby bar with a faded sign in the window that said 'BBQ.' Two tall men in long coats and sunglasses came out, and rhythm and blues music poured out of the door before it swung shut.

"Don't you dare," said Clark, although he wasn't really afraid, and he was tempted to call Reggie on her bluff.

"Maria and I come here all the time, right, Maria?" said Reggie. "Where do you think I get my grass?"

"I'll bet you do." Clark didn't believe her. The two men just stood there, silent and unmoving. Though Clark couldn't see their eyes behind their dark glasses, he could feel the stares. It's another world up here, he thought, wondering if Allen Friedberg and his crowd would ever see it, except on the silver screen.

One of the men sauntered up to the car. He leaned over, until his face was in Reggie's window. "Nice ride," he said solemnly.

"Thanks," said Reggie. The man returned her sweet smile and walked back to join his partner by the bar door. "Now, are we going in or not?"

She read Clark's expression as a 'No.' "You're no fun. Where should we go?"

"El Morocco," said Maria.

"Home," said Clark.

"Maria, let's drop this wet noodle off at his little old apartment and go wild on the town!"

Maria winked at Reggie. "Yeah, let's have a crazy girls' night out."

"You do that," said Clark. "I have important things to *do*, unlike *some* people. What are you, a pair of lazy hippies? Lazy, dirty, banana-peel-smoking hippies, you should really take a bath!"

His imitation of Allen Friedberg made them laugh, and Reggie speedily drove him home.

The girls were back sooner than Clark expected. He had been examining the drawings he had done when he was stoned, and he decided they were terrible. He had come across a large stack of drawings, more drawings than he remembered doing, as he gave the apartment a deep cleaning, which it badly needed. Regina's superficial housekeeping skills had not improved in her new environment.

"No more grass," he said, as he threw the pages in the kitchen trash can. The drawings were no better than telephone doodles, he thought, and he disliked Op Art. "I didn't come this far to do high-school level art work," he decided. And maybe pot was to blame for the way he had allowed Reggie to lull him into their comfortable but unproductive routine. He didn't like the idea of stagnating at home with one person while life passed him by. And Reggie was becoming too dependent on him, expecting too much. He hoped she would be hired by the Washington news bureau and that she would take the job, otherwise he would have to break up with her; he feared that they would become another boring couple, especially if they kept getting stoned.

He really didn't mind giving up smoking marijuana. It had been a fun experiment, but he was tired of the red eyes and dry mouth it gave him, and he didn't like the way his waistline had expanded, due to the inevitable midnight 'munchies' that invariably seized them both after getting high and having sex. He thought Reggie was getting a little chubby too, though he would never say so.

It gave him pleasure to throw out all of the stray stems and seeds, along with the pipe ashes that filled his ashtrays. He would go back to cocktails, and gladly, for at least he could control his drinks and predict their effect. With the strength of pot being as variable as it was, one never knew if one would smoke a whole joint and feel nothing, or go into orbit from one toke. He was disposing of the incense too, for good measure, when he heard Reggie's key turn in the lock. The sound made his heart sink. What he wouldn't do for a private evening! Things will get back to normal when I return from L.A., he vowed.

But for now he endured the voluptuous double embrace of the two tipsy beauties, and he accepted the greasy bag of barbecue take-out that Maria thrust at him. They had returned to Harlem and were giggly and proudly secretive about their experience. Clark knew Reggie was playing a little game with him to make him jealous, and he noticed that Maria followed Reggie in everything, even repeating what Reggie said and copying her gestures. Maria followed Reggie around the house like a little kitten.

"Hey!" Reggie was digging in the trash. "You're throwing out these good drawings? Why?"

"Those are cool," Maria agreed, studying the drawings over Reggie's shoulder.

"You can have them if you want," Clark said.

"Yeah!" said Reggie. "I definitely want this one! You can have the others, Maria. I wish I had room for them in my place, but I don't."

"I'll take these," said Maria. "They are so cool. You are a real artist, Clark. I'll bring them with me to Los Angeles and they will remind me of you and of New York!" She carefully stacked the pages and slid them into her large suede shoulder bag.

They settled in the living room, and Reggie put a folk record on the phonograph.

"What on earth is this?" Clark had never heard such an obnoxious singer in his life.

Maria looked up from her *Mademoiselle* in shock. "He doesn't know."

Reggie leaned one hand on her hip and looked archly at

Clark over her shoulder. She looked very cute in her blue-striped sailor jersey and navy bell-bottoms, but her attitude was snotty. "It's Bob Dylan," she said, as if that explained everything.

"Sounds like a mosquito stuck in glue," said Clark.

"You're too uptight," said Maria. "Reggie, Clark needs to get involved! Maybe this will help you loosen up your mind so you can understand..." She showed Clark a square of tin foil, which she opened to reveal what looked like a miniature clod of dirt.

"What's that, horse dung? I can get involved with that in Central Park," said Clark.

"It's hash," said Reggie. "Hashish, from Morocco. Everyone in Europe smokes it."

"I've never heard of it," said Clark. "No, thanks."

"What are we going to do with you?" whined Maria.

"I've given up on him," said Reggie. "Honey, you're cute, but you'll never be *relevant*."

Maria rolled her eyes, and the girls giggled as they smoked the hash. It did smell very good, like Christmas spices, and Clark was tempted, but he remembered his vow. He was not going to risk everything that was important to him to waste his time with drugs. He continued his cleaning as the girls melted into the rug with blissful expressions.

When he was finished and the apartment looked the way it was supposed to, Clark poured himself a glass of wine. Maria looked like a goddess, reclining on the floor with her golden hair fanned out on the carpet. Her flat stomach was showing, and he wanted to put his tongue in her little belly button. Clark settled himself on the floor next to Maria, took her hand, and placed it on his thigh.

"So, what's the movie about?" he asked.

Reggie nudged Maria and shot a look at the hand.

Oh ho, Clark thought, something new. He should have known that playing house with Reggie would lead to jealousy.

Maria slid her hand away and shifted position, settling her head on Reggie's stomach. "What...?" she asked foggily.

"The movie. The one you're in, girl. Did you see your script yet?" Clark teased.

Maria smiled at the ceiling. When she spoke, her words

seemed to come from far away. "Yeees... It's like... how can I say it? It's like Tarzan, you know, and I am wearing a leopard-skin bikini on a planet of women, and the United States space ship of the future, you know, like crashes on our planet and it's really crazy... and an astronaut falls in love with me..."

"What happens next?" Clark wasn't sure he wanted to know.

Maria scrunched her face like a tired puppy. "I don't remember. I think we blow them up. Yeah, let's blow them up. I'm hungry."

That made Reggie laugh, for some reason, and Reggie's shaking stomach jiggled Maria's head, so she began laughing too, and then they were both giggling uncontrollably. Clark hoped he hadn't acted as silly as they did when he was stoned.

When the laughing stopped, Maria said: "Allen wants me to build my body, you know, with weights, for *Amazon Planet*. He got me a trainer in Hollywood. I hope he's cute."

"I'll bet he is," said Reggie. "Wow, you really are getting the star treatment!"

"I don't know — it sounds too hard," Maria pouted. "And I want Reggie to come with me... Reggie, will you marry me?"

Reggie was asleep, snoring lightly, which Maria found incredibly funny. Having had enough, Clark turned the lights out on both of them and went to bed.

It was New Year's Eve Day, and Clark had to assume from the growing collection of oversized throw pillows and gauzy garments strewn about his apartment that Maria Pucci had moved in, or was "crashing," as she put it, until her departure for the West Coast. She had joined Reggie in her cooking obsession, and as Maria was also partial to spicy and sweet foods, Clark doubted his waistline would return to normal any time soon. Maria's specialty was Italian pastry, and she was learning to cook Chinese food, particularly sweet and sour dishes, which was a strange combination, to say the least, especially as she had taken to dyeing her cannoli cream blue and green. It clashed oddly with the bright orange sauces she made, causing strange vibrations on Clark's plate. Clark could do nothing to influence Maria's cooking, but he did lay down one law: no one else was to move in or even sleep over, and for that he felt authoritative.

Maria was receiving an advance salary from Metropolis, by direct order of Allen Friedberg, who had flown out to California to go over the budgets and supervise pre-production on his next two films, *Amazon Planet* and *Tigress In The Dark*. Not a day passed when Maria and Reggie did not return to Clark's apartment overloaded with shopping bags and boxes from the best department stores on Fifth Avenue. All of Reggie's purchases, exquisite as they were, Clark had to admit, were gifts from Maria. At first she had tried to buy presents for Clark too, namely a Pierre Cardin suit, personal tailoring included, and an extravagant gold watch. He immediately, though kindly, made Maria return these purchases. He did not trust her sudden generosity and he watched with wary amusement as Maria assumed all of the payments for Reggie's auto insurance and filled the apartment with gladiolas, Reggie's favorite flower, enough for a funeral for a chief of state, as he teased.

"What's wrong with a friend buying me presents?" Reggie wanted to know.

"Well, you and I both know Maria is more than a friend, Reg," Clark explained. "And I have a feeling it's not only the gifts that are being bought."

"Oh, you're so proper," Reggie fumed. "Not everyone is from a sterile and stingy New England town, you know."

"We'll see," said Clark.

Sure enough, Reggie pulled Clark aside a few hours later.

"Can I talk to you?" she asked. She was swaying a bit, as they all were, from all the Dom Perignon champagne they had consumed as a pre-New Year's Eve lubricant. The champagne, of course, had been delivered to a Miss Maria Pucci, who was already indisposed on the couch.

"Sure you can talk to me — you already *are* talking to me," said Clark.

"I'm serious, Clark, Maria bought me a ring."

"Yeah?"

"Yeah. A diamond ring, from David Webb."

"Oh, dear, give it back. That's the Fifth-Seventh Street jewelry shop where Bambi Friedberg buys her baubles," Clark dismissed the whole affair with a wave of his hand. His glass was

The Decorator

empty, and surely that was a more urgent concern at the moment.

"I don't want to hurt her feelings, but I get the strong impression she thinks we're engaged now. She refuses to believe I'm not going to California with her, when we all know I'm going to Washington. What should I do?"

"Oh, just tell her you can't accept the ring — it's far to generous and all that. She'll probably forget all about it. And bring another bottle of champagne in here."

"I hope she does forget about it," said Reggie. But Reggie did not return the ring, nor did she plan to, despite what Clark might say or think.

Clark knew Reggie would get the position in Washington. It was a gut feeling he had, a certainty that Thom Pearson meant for her to be hired, and not a bit too soon. Clark didn't like the way Reggie's constant pot smoking had worsened her naturally lazy ways. That would never do in her profession. And he considered Maria to be a definite bad influence on Reggie. They were always whispering, and he was tired of the thick female camaraderie and secrecy in his own apartment. It seemed all the girls did was read *Mademoiselle* and talk about the criminal insensitivity of men. Except for Clark, of course, they were quick to add, as if he were somehow not quite 'a man.' It seemed to Clark that Reggie was reacting to the rape and that Maria possibly did not really like men at all, except for how she could use them.

He wondered if Maria Pucci and Pamela Raven were of the same mold, and if that was what it took for them to succeed. It certainly shattered the myth of the sex goddess movie queens that men dreamed about. How shocked most guys would be to discover that things were not quite as they seemed, especially in Hollywood. His own buddies from college and back home were mad with jealousy that Clark was living with two beautiful women, and that one of them was the sex bomb Maria Pucci, who had already appeared in several magazines as the new Metropolis starlet. Doreen Flower had even written about the decorator Clark Calloway, with all his girls about.

Clark's friends had called in droves to congratulate him on his "swinger" status and to demand details of the orgies they imagined took place in his bed. Clark did not set them straight, naturally, though the truth was far from that at this point. Clark kept both women at arm's length to avoid getting caught up in the drama he smelled brewing between them. Let people think what they want, was Clark's attitude — they will anyway.

But his relationship with Pamela Raven — that was his secret, and no amount of prodding could dislodge a clue from him. In fact, he had a New Year's Eve date with Pamela Raven at 21, with a special appearance by Allen Friedberg, who was hosting the party. It was an important night, but while Clark prepared himself for it, he did not forget to call Dannee Lou Baker in Washington. He was burning with curiosity about Pamela's rumored outrageous behavior at the State Dinner. He doubted Pamela Raven would give him much information, and he certainly didn't want to be influenced by someone like Doreen Flower or Suzy, Dorothy Kilgallen, or Cholly Knickerbocker, either.

16
CHAPTER

The airport atmosphere always gave Clark Calloway a charge. Airline employees were always so optimistic and outfitted in primary-colored Courreges uniforms. Security checks were very efficient now that airports needed to deter hijackers and mad bombers. The conveyor belts were fun and modern, and the loud-speaker address system was certainly commanding. Clark loved the bold airport graphics and colors, the space-age food service, the enormous hospital-type bathrooms — with the best vending machines — the panoramic views of planes arriving and taking off, the perfume shops, and especially the cherry Life Savers he always purchased in the airport newsstand. Besides, Clark was delighted that Deirdre Dawn & Company had just been awarded the contract to design the interiors of the new Conair 880 airplanes, as well as the interiors of the new Idlewild International Hotel.

Once his plane had taken off, and Clark was looking forward to his first Bloody Mary, mixed with a cute miniature bottle of Smirnoff vodka by a glamorous stewardess, he relaxed in the feeling peculiar to flying, that someone else was doing all of the thinking. The calm Midwestern accent of the pilot coming in over the plane's address system was capable and reassuring. Clark just didn't look down. That way he never had to think about how far away the ground was, or how many planes had crashed last year. If he didn't look down, he could read an in-flight magazine and forget that he was flying at all.

He still got a chuckle when he thought of Pamela Raven in 21 on New Year's Eve. She had been extremely angry that Allen Friedberg's chauffeur had the night off and that Allen drove the Rolls himself. She bitched until Allen put on his driver's cap, just as a joke. It made Pamela Raven feel so much better that she was being chauffeured — so to speak — that Allen decided to keep the cap on.

The party at 21 was a gala press event. Pamela Raven,

dressed in black, swept through the doors and into the bar, calling everyone by name. The staff was ready for her entrance, and had prepared her table, the first table to the left upon entering the room. That way Pamela could see everyone entering the room, and everyone could see her. The waiter knew to bring her an iced bottle of hundred-proof vodka, a glass, and a medium rare-cooked steak.

Reporters knew enough about Pamela Raven not to ask her any questions she hadn't reviewed in advance. They knew the movie star only gave coached and rehearsed responses. They surrounded her table anyway, trying to get her to comment on the early publicity photos for *Tigress in the Dark*, which featured Pamela Raven and Adela Morgan posing by a tombstone in a graveyard that was meant to be located somewhere in the Deep South.

Pamela refused to comment — she hated the idea, as she whispered to Clark, of "Two near-death actresses posing by gravestones!"

"Pamela!" a reporter shouted.

"Yes?"

"Pamela Raven, you have been described as regal and vulgar, cold and warm, highly sexed and puritanical, egotistical and modest, commanding and insecure, tender and tough, generous and selfish —"

Pamela yawned. "What do you expect: Metro never gave me any lessons in consistency."

At that point, Adela Morgan climbed up on top of a table at the other end of the restaurant, spread her legs wide apart, and bawled, "Everybody, down here! Down at the end of the bar!"

"That old slut," Pamela Raven commented, as the gang of reporters flocked away from her to interview her musical co-star in *Tigress in the Dark*. Clark actually liked what he overheard — and who could help but overhear! — Adela saying:

"I'll tell ya one thing I hope this picture does: I hope it brings back women's pictures! The men have had it to themselves too long. Forget all those pricks — it's time to think about us broads in films. All those war movies with killin' on the screen. But ya gotta admit, we women had it pretty good for fifteen years back then. And let's bring back the musical comedy pictures! We know what the people want! Here's to

The Decorator

the studios! They're finally returning to their senses. And here's to Allen Friedberg, the man who knows how to pick stars for his flicks..."

There was a general cheer, but during the uproar one female reporter, who was obviously infatuated by Pamela Raven and had stayed hovering by her side, was foolish enough to comment that Pamela Raven's big red picture hat was very flattering to the actress. "It give your face such an attractive radiance!" she gushed.

Pamela Raven responded: "Why the fuck do you *think* I wear it?"

That retort was still making Clark smile, even though he knew Pamela had said it because she was pretty near plastered with vodka, and she was not one to be outdone by Adela. In fact, Pamela had stirred iced vodka with her fingers at the table and told everyone how the Duchess of Windsor had ordered the inside of her vodka glasses sprayed with liquid amphetamine when Pamela Raven came to London. She capped off her performance by leaving, dramatically, before the midnight festivities because she had to be home by ten to see her favorite television show. She hated any change in routine. Pamela's attitude confirmed Dannee Lou's report of Raven's behavior in Washington, though that incident hadn't been nearly so amusing.

According to Dannee Lou, Pamela Raven had looked wonderful: "She always astonishes me! I forget every time how *much* Pamela Raven looks like a movie star is *supposed* to look! She made me, and everyone else, including President Johnson, just speechless!"

But Pamela Raven had also consumed a quart of liquid courage before the formal dinner and she had been so annoyed by the presence of the young wife of one of the Justices of the Supreme Court that everyone could see, and was embarrassed by, the older woman's obvious jealousy. True, the wife in question — her name was Debby — was only twenty-three and the judge was in his late sixties, which could have offended Pamela Raven's sense of propriety. And also true, Debby was monopolizing a handsome young assistant to the president and she did carry on for quite some time about her concern for "the environment," one of the subjects that young people these days just seemed to *use* to annoy their elders, as Dannee Lou conceded. But the young woman was blonde and beautiful, and she was actually presenting a good argument, so all attention at that end of the table was on her. Debby was so busy talking that she simply did not notice when the server brought the fingerbowls around and placed them in front of each guest. Dannee Lou said that she could feel Pamela Raven growing very tense next to her, and finally the movie star reached *across* the president's assistant to move the judge's wife's fingerbowl onto the doily where it was meant to be.

"That's how we do it!" Pamela Raven had snapped, much to the mortification of the young woman and the discomfort of everyone at the table. Not only the president's assistant, but the Interior Secretary and the Ambassador to the Organization of American States, came to Debby's defense, and they received a lecture from Pamela Raven on the shameful decline of manners in young people these days, which was awkward for everyone.

"Who am I?" Pamela asked rhetorically. "I am Pamela Raven, but once I was a waitress, and I've worked since I was age nine, learning everything I could. When I was first at Metropolis, I was happy when anyone corrected me. I learned and observed. Yes, observed anything. Everywhere. That's why I know, for Christ's sake, what to do with a fingerbowl when it arrives. What is wrong with the young people now? Nobody observes anything. And manners must be learned. I've tried to teach my niece, Holly, manners, too — and I'm still trying. Damn that Holly! Damn. Damn. Damn."

To make matters worse, Pamela Raven insisted on helping the White House waiters serve dessert to those on the dais, to demonstrate how she had worked her way through dancing school and to make the point that she, unlike certain well-known spoiled brats, was not afraid of a little work. It had been quite a scene, right out of a Pamela Raven film, much to, surprisingly, the president's delight.

As the plane flew over the Rockies, or so the pilot said — Clark would have to take his word for it — Clark thought about Pamela Raven's needs and accommodations at the Vista Hotel in Los Angeles. Roland Lee had frantically called for Clark's assistance, as he couldn't quite handle the pressures at

The Decorator

the hotel and Pamela Raven and Adela Morgan were due to arrive in Los Angeles in one week. Filming on *Tigress* had been delayed for over a month as Allen Friedberg had been fighting to drastically reduce the budget and the script had been rewritten several times to reflect the changes he ordered.

Meanwhile, pre-production for *Amazon Planet* was proceeding on schedule and Maria had been flown out for rehearsals on January 2nd. Clark had seen a publicity picture of Maria Pucci stepping off the plane in white marabou feathers, and she certainly looked the part.

The situation between Clark and Reggie had improved as soon as Maria had departed for the Coast and Reggie had gone back to work. Reggie had returned to reality, Clark thought, and he liked her much better that way. When he thought about Reggie's moving to Washington to begin her new job, he felt a tiny pang of loss that made him uncomfortable. Wasn't that what he wanted, for Reggie to succeed in her career? And hadn't he been feeling suffocated by the relationship a mere few weeks ago? He did and he had, but the idea of Reggie really going away and actually being *gone* when he returned made him lonely for her. He missed her already. He thought about how bored he had been with their homemaking routine and how he had even lost some of his sexual attraction for Reggie at times, and he wondered if maybe they were meant to be just good friends. If he was in love with her, why couldn't he make up his mind as to whether he could be without her or not be without her?

He had no easy solutions for this friendship-and-something-more. Clark had his own career ahead, and maybe it was too soon to think seriously about anyone. He was glad to be traveling to the West Coast to work for a while, because he wanted to get away from the fights and corporate intrigue between Deirdre Dawn and Paul Hedges. Paul had his suspicions that Deirdre was somehow orchestrating the chaos in the office with missing files and alienated clients, but he didn't know why. Clark knew something was going to blow up in that regard because Deirdre was behaving like a complete maniac and she had canceled her trip to Spain. He got a clear message that she had decided to stick around the New York office and become a problem to everyone around her with her distrustful accusations and ridiculous busywork orders for the staff. She even distrusted her domestic staff and accused them of wrongdoing of which they were totally innocent. Clark was extremely glad to fly away to California and leave the office behind him for a period of time. He knew Paul Hedges could handle Deirdre Dawn & Company, and he hoped Paul could handle the dowager duchess of decorating.

When the pilot announced the plane would be landing at LAX in a few minutes, Clark forgot his fear and looked down, hoping for a glimpse of the Pacific Ocean and the famous California beaches. As the aircraft circled at a sickening angle, he got an eyeful of the wide blue ocean with its deceptively calm and rippling waves, and he caught a glimpse of a thin, winding ribbon of beach along the coast, somewhat golden in color. The surrounding hills looked disappointingly barren and dry to Clark. In fact, the landscape was an ugly, wrinkled brown, and so was the thick smog for which Los Angeles was famous. The city itself was terrible looking, an absolutely endless stretch of low grey structures, like the maze of electrical devices inside a transistor radio. Clark got the claustrophobic feeling that the heartless mechanical city was drawing the plane into its magnetic bowels to swallow him forever.

He had no idea Los Angeles was so big; he had pictured a quaint desert town of palms and colorful movie sets, something like an amusement park, interspersed with sprawling, glamorous mansions like Disney castles. Instead, he saw one vast, uniform suburb. He did see the sapphire eyes of many swimming pools winking up at him through the smog; maybe it was nicer when you got down there — he hoped. They were close enough to see the looping arteries of freeways, crawling with unbroken streams of gleaming cars. The beach was no longer anywhere to be seen, and Clark looked forward to renting a car, once he had settled into his hotel, and driving away from the choking mess below as soon as possible. He had hoped the Bel Vista was near the ocean, though in fact it wasn't. He wanted to see the land of beauty and palm trees that lay beyond Los Angeles.

The taxi driver took Clark and his luggage to the Bel Vista Hotel in Beverly Hills, which he informed Clark was northeast of the airport, the opposite direction from the coast. Clark was

The Decorator

impressed by the very clean, wide streets of Beverly Hills, which were shaded by giant tropical trees and tall swaying palms. The spacious estates and pristine shopping establishments lining the road were constructed in a mind-boggling but entertaining variety of architectural styles. Clark decided he did like Beverly Hills after all.

The Bel Vista Hotel was a surprise; in contrast to the mostly pink or terra cotta and white fantasy-styled buildings nearby, it was tall, constructed of solid grey stone, and quite resembled the Ritz Plaza in New York. Even the swimming pool was under a glass dome, as if the hotel was built for a colder climate. Come to think of it, it wasn't as warm in California in February as Clark had imagined. The sky was cloudy, and he was glad to get out of the chilly breeze and into the warm Bel Vista lobby.

Roland Lee was a screaming nut. He couldn't do much more than push Clark Calloway in the direction of Pamela Raven's suite and squawk "DO SOMETHING!" before he was off on a hundred separate tirades directed at his staff.

The view of the shell-shaped, palm-shaded pool through the plexiglass greenhouse dome and the misty Hollywood Hills nestled in the distance was wonderful. Clark had no problem deciding how to personalize the suite for Pamela Raven. First, he ordered it totally repainted pale, light pink, known as Pamela's Pink, and he ordered new, matching pink linens to be delivered. The linens had to include three pink, king-size button-back French cases, two square pillow shams with French button backs, three regular-sized cases, and three pink neckrolls.

Then he hopped into his car, rented from the Hertz agency in the hotel and explored the blocks of furnishing and home design suppliers on Robertson until he found some inexpensive pink satin. With the help of a hired seamstress, he trimmed Pamela's bed in true movie-star style. There had to be a pink satin bedskirt, and of course, a pink satin valance, swags and jabots installed at the windows over the existing white sheers. Clark trimmed the dressing table with white eyelet over pink satin, and had the hotel electrician install Pamela Raven's necessary cold lighting. Clark also supervised the installation of the best showerhead in the bath and more towel bars in the dressing area, and the suite was ready for Miss Pamela Raven.

Unfortunately, Adela Morgan arrived first. She had flown on American, while Pamela Raven had taken the Twentieth Century Limited, as was her custom. Adela had a fit when she saw her co-star's suite — she went completely insane with rage and she trashed her room. She even threw a floor lamp through her window, shattering glass onto the landscaped lawn below.

When Roland Lee ran up to see what the disaster was, he got an earful: "You fucka! You think that Raven broad gets it all? What she gets, I get too! I've made my suite ready for you to do over completely, as you can see! Do it, or else!"

So, Clark Calloway had a little more instant-magic, last-minute decorating work to do. And Roland even ordered him to call someone to install unbreakable windows in the rooms, as well as in the hotel's public areas. Roland went so far as to decide that the windows should not open at all. He intended to control the hotel's climate with the heating, ventilation, and air conditioning systems, the same ones Doreen Flower used as her personal highway.

"I don't want anyone touching my windows, for any reason!" Roland raved. Clark guessed that this latest bad idea of Roland's was motivated partly by the negative publicity the New York Ritz Plaza had received when a guest had jumped to her death from the eleventh floor, just after Christmas. The Los Angeles window contractor Clark contacted agreed to begin the replacement work from the ground floor up.

Clark was measuring Adela's bed for a new mirror-frame headboard when the call came from Pamela Raven. There were smiles in her voice. "Clark, darling! I love what you did for me! Do come have lunch in my suite. I'm dying to see you."

When Clark knocked on Pamela's door and entered to her ringing voice calling, "Come in!", he was surprised to see that the actress was blindfolded and walking confidently about the room without running into any of the furniture. Pamela looked the actress-at-home part. She was dressed in a soft pink silk dressing robe, the cuffs of which were white marabou. Beneath the robe, which clung tightly to her body, she wore a white and pink long slip. And on her feet, white marabou open-back slippers could be seen as she stepped back and forward. Pamela could have been dressed for a shoot on the set of any one of her

The Decorator

films. She looked exactly like a "Tigress-in-the-dark," ready for action.

In fact, she turned her head toward Clark and spoke to him as if she could see him: "Have a chair, darling! I've ordered us some lunch. You do like calves liver and steamed vegetables. Good! Don't mind the blindfold — I'm just getting into character for my part — Tillie Macy is blind, after all. And this is not as difficult as it seems! The furniture is sending out vibrations, just as are you. I can *feel* them! Ouch! I broke my damn concentration.

Pamela rubbed her shin where she had banged it into the low, Oriental-style coffee table. "Maybe the vibrations are different in Los Angeles — it's harder than I thought. Will you please sit down so I can pick up the vibrations again!"

Clark wondered how Pamela knew he hadn't sat down yet, and he quickly scooted over to the white satin sofa he had just recovered and had accented with Siamese pink Thai silk throw cushions. He was completely charmed by Pamela's youthful energy and he was taken with the thought that perhaps because Pamela Raven had worked on her beauty all of her life, she was still working with her young self. Plus, Clark could watch the shapely Raven buns beneath her at-home peignoir, and she couldn't see him.

"Stop looking at my ass, Clark. I can feel you!" scolded Pamela. "They do say the blind are clairvoyant. Now, I'm just going to practice a few things."

She began to busy herself in a pantomime of dusting, sweeping, ironing, and dialing the telephone, all blindfolded.

"This is getting much easier!" she said. "Tillie does all of the things I do, after all! Riley and I read lines on the train all the way from New York and I know every one of my lines perfectly now. Riley and Mama are in the bedroom arranging my shoes... I only brought about a hundred pair this time. Wasn't that good of me?

"You know, I read three to four hundred scripts a year, and when I finally get something halfway decent, Allen keeps changing it — to save money! He's like a Jewish Nazi, and I love him, but if he orders another rewrite, he and I are going to have a serious talk. Of course *I* can adapt! I have a perfect memory, as everyone knows, but Adela's not too swift upstairs

— I'm surprised she can remember her lyrics. I believe she may be getting senile!"

Room service brought their trays, and Clark remembered to unfold the "serviette" for Pamela and place it in her lap the way she liked it. Pamela amazed Clark by eating her lunch and drinking her tea without taking off the blindfold or spilling a drop. When she had finished, she burped richly. Clark was surprised to hear another shorter burp behind him, and he turned around to see Miss Riley grinning naughtily.

"Come on, Riley, you can do better," exhorted Pamela. "Remember what I taught you: a good burp is at least three syllables long."

Pamela demonstrated, and Miss Riley broke out in peals of laughter. "No one can top you, PR! You're the best!"

"For sure. Be your best and teach others — that's my motto!" said Pamela. "Go finish my shoes."

"We're done, ma'am," said Miss Riley sarcastically.

"I'll be in to inspect your work, Miss Sassy!"

"Oooh!" cried Miss Riley in mock terror. She chuckled in a self-satisfied way, and disappeared again.

Clark had not seen either Pamela Raven or her assistant in such high sprits. The laid-back California air seemed to make them girlish and gay, though Clark was shocked by the burping and he changed the subject before Pamela could serenade him again.

"Did you practice eating blindfolded on the train too?" Clark asked.

"Oh, darling, I've had a *month* to do this, all alone in my apartment waiting to be called out here. Ever since I saw those terrible pictures they took of me at 21, I've stayed at home! If that's how I look, I see no reason to go out."

Clark wondered why Mama had always told him Miss Raven was unavailable when he called during the past month. Once he had gotten Pamela Raven herself, but she had pretended to be a Southern maid.

"Miz Rayvun isn't heah raht now. Who is callin'?" she had said. Clark didn't want to embarrass Pamela by letting on that he know it was she, so he had played along and left a message, but he had wondered what she was up to.

"Clark, you must never tell a soul what I am about to tell

you, but I had another reason not to leave my apartment. On New Year's Day I received the first of many threats on my life, over the telephone. I still don't know how the callers got my phone number. The callers were sometimes female and sometimes male, though I didn't recognize the voices.

"Needless to say, I've changed my phone number and I had extra locks added to my door. I won't allow the doormen to send anyone up, in case of a ploy. No one is to know this, but I've had FBI agents guarding me. Despite the change of numbers, the phone calls keep coming. The FBI tried to trace the calls, but the caller never stayed on the line long enough. The FBI finally decided it was a crank, but I'm not so sure. I'm frightened, and I'm not taking any chances. I've even got security guards outside this hotel suite. Did you see the gentleman outside my door? That's Harry. He's a security guard."

"Wow!" said Clark. "Why would anyone want to threaten you? How bizarre. I'm glad it turned out to be nothing. What did you do in your New York apartment all that time? Have you received any threatening calls since you've been in Los Angeles?"

"No, so far I haven't received any calls here — I've only been in Los Angeles for a few hours, though. As for the time alone in my apartment, I don't mind seclusion," said Pamela. "In fact, I'm famous for it. But I've been scared, and I decided to make a few changes. I did a lot of thinking. I've laid off the vodka and cigarettes, dropped ten pounds, and I'm exercising like a bandit! I think it's good for me."

"You look fabulous," said Clark.

"That's why I keep you around, angel — you always speak the truth! But seriously, you remind me so much of my dear, darling Jeff Williams — may he rest in peace. He was always there for me. He always said such sweet things, always the truth. And he was one of the few. Jeffrey was my first and maybe my last real friend in Hollywood. If he'd been straight, I would have married him in a second, and I'm sure it would have been the best and *only* marriage of my life. The studio did try to arrange our marriage — a Twilight Tandem, such marriages were called — to get Jeff out of the Lavender Swamp. But he had too much pride to live hypocritically, and I loved him too much to let him. It's too bad all the best ones are gay!

Though it's not too bad for you, I suppose!"

Clark had learned never to contradict Pamela. Instead, he told her about the state of Adela's room and how it got that way.

"Oh, she is such a child!" said Pamela. "She has no reason to be jealous of me. She has the better role, after all, and her name is first on all the promotions, due to the luck of the alphabet, or maybe the crookedness of her lawyer — he's like her fucking nanny, you know! I'm not fighting it because my publicist says we need to quell the rumors that Adela and I are feuding. She's worried, and I can see her point. But I just bet Weissman's the reason Adela got *her* director, Barney Higgins! Why Allen hired a director whose last hit was a musical *ten* years ago is beyond me! And you know Adela and Barney used to be A Thing, so I'm sure she'll get her way on every shot. Her part is so damn juicy already — Helen Macy is completely over the top! — and Adela's such a raging bitch that my only option is to underplay like mad. Imagine Pamela Raven playing for sympathy!"

It did seem unusual, as Raven had always played the *femmes fatales* and sexy psychopaths in the past.

Then Pamela Raven made Clark a wonderful offer. "I don't see how you can really enjoy Los Angeles properly when you're living in the Bel Vista cleaning Adela's cage and at the twenty-four-hour beck and call of that awful Roland Lee. Go and use my little house in Santa Monica. It's just a cottage, really, but it's five seconds from the beach, and there are no tenants living there right now. A young man needs his privacy, and I'd love it if you used my place! I'll have the keys brought to your room."

Clark was greatly flattered, and he gladly accepted Pamela Raven's offer.

CHAPTER 17

The air was clear in Santa Monica and fresh breezes blew in off the ocean. The sun shone brightly and Clark was happy to be free of the inland smog and atmospheric pressure. Clark enjoyed driving; he let his mind loose as he was behind the wheel. He thought about everything, everybody, and he solved his own problems on the open road. The rented car handled well and Clark appreciated the perspective from the driver's seat: he watched women applying mascara and combing their hair while making turns and changing lanes without mishap. It was true what they said about California Girls, Clark noted. There were a lot of tan, pretty blondes and they were not above a little flirting on the freeway. When Clark thought about the history of Hollywood's attraction for beautiful men and women who hoped to become stars, he realized that even though most of them did not become famous, they tended to marry and produce beautiful children, children who grew up to flirt with each other in Los Angeles traffic jams. California highways could not be compared to the LIE.

The road Clark followed to the address Pamela Raven had given him curved into the hills past small, high-gated houses. A FOR RENT sign was planted in the lawn of the rambling house he was looking for, a charming grey and white ranch-style cottage surrounded by lots of pink rosebushes. The house was neat and the white shutters gleamed in the sunshine. The house looked like many Clark had seen in Pamela Raven movies. He wanted to ask Pamela if this house had ever been used in a film. A pavilion-style garage sloped beneath the house, and as Clark drove into it he could see a dry swimming pool, its inside painted aquamarine, and a shuttered guest house in the tree-shaded back yard. A tall, thick, and prickly hedge sheltered the property from neighboring eyes.

The grounds were tended in perfect Pamela Raven style by

a local landscaper, and a maid came every other week to maintain the empty house. Pamela had warned Clark that a local realtor also had the keys to the house and might drop by unannounced to show the property to prospective tenants. With that in mind, Clark decided to keep his minimal belongings in their suitcase, and not to spread his things out in the house. Clark thought that Pamela was of two minds about renting the house, as she would be wiser to sell it. Perhaps this cottage, a love nest from her first marriage, held too many good memories for her to give it up. The house was furnished beautifully in white on white, and above the rounded, tufted-back sofa covered by white sheets was a magnificent portrait of Pamela in early days, dressed in a chartreuse gown and holding a yellow rose. Pamela's penetrating eyes in the portrait seemed to look everywhere.

Clark brought linens from the Bel Vista, courtesy of Roland Lee, as Pamela never liked guests to sleep on her monogrammed, Egyptian cotton sheets. To his surprise, the door to the master bedroom was locked. None of the keys Pamela had given him fit the keyhole in the doorknob. Clark settled his bags in the second bedroom, one furnished in 1940's California blonde. He placed his travel alarm clock on the end table, made the bed, and fell into it.

Clark was exhausted, but he did not feel he could fall asleep. The house was too quiet and the bed was too big and empty. It had been a while since Clark had shared his bed with Reggie, or anyone, and the loneliness was suddenly tangible, like a living, mocking presence.

He got up to use the bathroom and when he turned on the cold fluorescent lighting he noticed an odd thing. There were three bobby pins scattered on the sink, in the porcelain soap dish. When he poked one of them, he saw that a little puddle of rust was forming in a slight amount of water under the bobby pins. The rust will surely stain the porcelain, he thought, and he wondered what sort of careless maid would leave her bobby pins on a movie star's sink, especially Pamela Raven's sink. It was the sort of thing that would drive Pamela wild. As Clark threw the pins into the waste basket and wiped the orange water away with a tissue, he was relieved to find that they hadn't stained the sink, though that made him wonder.

The Decorator

Why were the pins wet? He thought Pamela had said the maid was due on Thursday of the current week, which was only two days away. Any water she had dripped nearly two weeks ago should have evaporated by now, and water which had dried on metal bobby pins would surely leave a rust stain. The water must be fresh and the pins recently placed. Clark decided Pamela must have been mistaken about the maid's schedule, unlikely as that possibility seemed.

The empty, silent house was beginning to give him the creeps. His footsteps echoed on the parquet floor in the dark green-painted living room. He found a telephone on an end table and sat on the edge of the sheet-covered sofa to ring Maria at the Bel Vista. After a few rings, the hotel operator picked up to tell him that Miss Pucci wasn't in, and no, she didn't know when Miss Pucci would return. It figured: Maria's film was still in post-production, but the new starlet already had a very busy social life, in the hippest L.A. spots with the fast young crowd, according to the tabloids. Clark felt slighted because Maria had not contacted him yet, nor had she invited him to meet any of the trendy folk, and it annoyed him that he cared.

"Bitch! Bitch!" he said, but he really didn't mean it. Maria deserved the attention she was receiving. After all, Clark wasn't exactly an old pal. He called Reggie in Washington, and when she answered he was so glad to hear her voice he decided to invite her to L.A.

"Hey, Reg! Pack your beach wrap, your sunglasses, and your espadrilles. I've got a house to myself near the beach and I need your company. I'll fly you out for the weekend, and I'll pay your tab, too!"

"Oh, Clark, that sounds good, but I really can't," said Reggie.

"What do you mean, you can't?" said Clark. "They don't have you working weekends, do they? Anyway, isn't there a holiday coming up — Presidents' Day weekend or something?"

Reggie laughed. "There are no holidays in the newsroom, Clark. I really am on the run all the time. It's terrific, I love it. Did I tell you I'm even co-writing news stories now? And this week I'm going to start traveling with the reporters and writing items right on the spot. George Myers says if an opening appears I can try reporting a local story myself! It all depends how I come across on camera. I'm so excited, Clark! I'll cover a dog show if he wants me to. Geez, I wish you were here to style me a bit, tell me how much eye shadow to wear. You always made me look my best."

"That's great, Reg," said Clark. "Congratulations — I knew you could do it. Maybe I'll fly out to see you when the Vista project is complete and you can show me around the capital. How is D.C.?"

"It's okay, though I don't have much time to explore. No one does. It's so weird here in that way. There's hardly any socializing and when there is, everyone talks shop, you know, politics. And most of the women are either secretaries or real housewives and hostesses. I haven't found any girl friends yet, and everyone asks me what my 'husband' thinks!"

"I'm sure you'll make friends once you settle in. Remember, you've only been in Washington for two months. And you don't sound lonely — in fact you sound great!"

"Well, I'm not lonely at all. In fact, I've got a great friend, and I want to tell you everything."

"What's that?" asked Clark, although something wary in her voice told him he already knew what that everything was.

"I wasn't going to say anything before I knew it was *anything*, you know, but I figure it's better if I tell you before you hear it from anybody else: I'm seeing someone seriously."

"You don't have to worry about that, Reg," said Clark. "We never had a problem with seeing other people. I expect you to enjoy yourself, make friends, meet a nice guy."

"Clark, maybe you never had a problem with it, but I did. And, anyway, this is different. I… I think I'm in love, really in love."

"Oh," said Clark. He didn't know what to make of that. He had known Reggie for a long time, and he wasn't sure if Reggie, like himself, was capable of really loving. When you're really in love, you have to give your soul to someone, and Clark was not about to give his soul to anyone. But was Reggie?

"I don't like telling you over the phone, because it seems so distant, but it's someone you know."

The Decorator

"Someone I know? Who?"

"John Downing, the reporter. Dannee Lou's brother?"

It all came back to Clark: the gallery, the night in the Polo Bar, Adela Morgan singing, and Reggie taking John Downing home. He had assumed Reggie's fling with John was just a passing fancy for both of them, and Clark had completely forgotten about it. He recalled now that Dannee Lou sounded a bit strained the last time he had spoken with her, and now he knew why: she didn't like keeping a secret from her friend.

"John's a good guy, Reggie. I've known his family for a long time, and they're really decent people. I'm happy for you, I really am. I'm happy for both of you."

Clark found that the words came easily to him — he really was happier for Reggie than he thought he would be. He had never been a jealous person, and in a way Reggie's involvement with John solved a problem. Friendship came much easier to him than commitment did, and now his soul was safe from Reggie.

"Wow, Clark, I'm glad you're taking it this way," said Reggie. "I thought I might upset you with my news."

"You haven't," said Clark, thinking she sounded a touch miffed that he wasn't jealous.

"Thanks, Clark. I love you, you know. I always will."

"If you decide you can make L.A. for a weekend, remember I'm here. And you'll love the surfing! Bye now. Good luck with everything. See you around!"

Clark had to hang up. He had a peculiar lump in his throat. As soon as he had hung up, the phone rang, giving him no time for introspection.

"Darling! Darling! Finally! I thought I'd never get through. The phone has been busy for hours!" It was Pamela, worked up and talking a mile a minute. She wasted no time on small talk, but invitingly told Clark to drive to the Vista as soon as possible so that she could take him to the studio. The director was about to shoot an important night scene, and Pamela wanted Clark to see her on the set and meet the people involved with the film, especially the idol Gabe Taylor. She explained that it was much easier for her driver to take them onto the lot than for Clark to attempt to convince the guards at the gate to let him pass.

"We have so many crazies trying to get onto the lot these days. Who would have ever thought we'd need to be protected from our own fans?"

Clark lost no time in driving to Beverly Hills. In the hotel's circular front drive, Pamela pulled him into her convertible limousine, complete with uniformed driver in the front and Miss Riley, Mama, and Princess Lotus Blossom in the back seat. Pamela looked ravishing in flowing pale peach silk with matching hat and back-swept veil. She wore dark sunglasses, so dark that Clark could not see her eyes, but he knew immediately that there was something emotionally wrong with her. She was tightly wired, speaking much too rapidly in her high, cheerful voice which Clark recognized as totally false. Miss Riley and Mama were quiet, very quiet and seemed shrunken into themselves. Miss Riley, who puffed on a cigarette, kept looking over her shoulder as if she feared a car was following them. Even Princess Lotus Blossom was whining.

"All right, what's going on?" asked Clark. "I love you, Pamela, but why are you squeezing my arm so hard? You're making handprints in my flesh, look. What's wrong with that dog? And why is Riley checking the road like that? Are we about to star in a car chase sequence?"

Miss Riley laughed nervously. "Pamela, I still say we should have taken a closed car."

"It's not funny," said Mama. "Poor Princess, it's going to be all right," she whispered, stroking the dog's long hair.

"Oh, dear," said Pamela. "I suppose Princess is picking up on our tension. Clark, the phone calls have started again, more threatening this time. I'm too terrified to sleep. But I just won't be intimidated into sneaking around in a closed limousine when I adore convertibles. This *is* Los Angeles, and I shall not give in to fear. This is my town — I helped make it famous.

"Clark, you mustn't be alarmed, but somehow those people have my direct phone number and are avoiding the hotel switchboard. I can't even begin to tell you the terrible things they're saying! And that Roland Lee is useless. Do you know what he said to me? He actually implied that my hundred-proof vodka was talking to me! How dare he? How dare he? Everyone knows I don't drink anymore."

"I don't like this at all," said Clark. "Have you told Allen?"

The Decorator

"Oh, he won't listen to me. He thinks I'm being melodramatic, just a demented, dried-up old actress. His brain migrated between his legs so long ago that he is no help to anyone, anyone who won't fuck him, that is."

"This worries me, Pamela," said Clark. "If you'd like, I'll stay in your suite until this nonsense stops. I'll answer your phone. I'd be only too happy to give the callers something to think about."

"You're a love, darling, but that won't be necessary. I ordered security guards to stand in the hall, twenty-four hours a day. As for answering the phone, Riley already tried that and they terrorize her too! They said the dirtiest things about her, about us! These people seem to know everything about me and the people around me — they know things about us that no one but we could possibly know, and it's driving Riley crazy!"

"I'll say." Miss Riley exhaled a puff of smoke. As far as Clark knew, she was a non-smoker. The threats must really be getting to her.

"And the suite! That's another thing. I've begged Roland Lee to move me to another suite, but the little piss-ant claims there are no other suites available. he keeps telling me how much it cost him to have mine custom decorated. But I'm not concerned about bed drapery now, but about my life, my very being!"

"What's wrong with the suite?" asked Clark.

"Well, it's not only the suite — it's the whole hotel. We're beginning to think the place is cursed."

"The Bad Vista," said Miss Riley.

"My shower water comes out brown, my underwear comes back from the laundry starched, and this morning I was served a raw egg for breakfast! Can you imagine lifting a cover and finding a raw egg on the plate waiting for you when you specifically ordered it hardboiled? I almost vomited."

"Roland Lee must immediately correct these things!" said Clark. "Things like that don't happen in a top hotel."

"He's hopeless," said Pamela. "The pathetic little hotel staff people claim to be innocent, of course. And since I'm the only guest who's having these problems, as our dear Mr. Lee was so kind as to inform me, it's my problem, I suppose. I think Allen and Lee are conspiring to paint me as a crazy… that's what I think. And I did not find Doreen's column about the "Perils of Pamela" in the *Hollywood Reporter* to be amusing. As a matter of fact, if I see her in the hall, she had better run before I pull her wig off and wring her scrawny, lifted neck! Why does she always have to live where I do? Why does she live at all? Why? Why?"

"I don't know," said Miss Riley. "But the item was called 'Pamela's Plague,' I believe, and as usual, Doreen exaggerates everything and makes us all sound cracked."

"Yes, if you believe what you read, you'd think I was ready for a rubber room somewhere, but I never, never believe the press. I don't even read what's written about me, though some kind soul never fails to inform me about it. Believing your own press, good or bad, is suicide for an actress. Look what happened to Jean Harlow. And Carol Landis. Why, she was so flaky, she once tried to get me to babysit her at a party. I did feel sorry for her: she could barely walk in that dress the studio made her wear. 'You're on your own, kid!' that's what I said. 'You can't be weak in this world, or the wolves'll get you!'"

Upset as she was, Clark couldn't help noticing that the new, un-vodka'd Pamela Raven was surprisingly tolerant of her recent discomforts. Or perhaps it was the joy of starring in a film again that made her less reactive to bad hotel service. The old Pamela Raven would have stormed out of the Bel Vista and checked into another hotel at the first sign of trouble. Which wasn't a bad idea, incidentally.

"Why don't you stay somewhere else?" asked Clark.

"I'd love to, Clark," Pamela said. "Don't you think I'd like to check into the Beverly Wilshire or the Beverly Hills Hotel — today, if that were possible? No, Allen has some smelly little boy's deal with Roland and I won't see a penny of my own until after the shooting is complete, due to some budgetary genius at Metro. Meanwhile, pretty little things like Maria Pucci are buying up the town. I suppose I'm lucky A.F. takes his cock out of Pucci's pucci long enough to pay my security guards."

"How about Cosmeco?" asked Clark.

"Ha!" shouted Pamela.

"Ha!" echoed Mama. Princess Lotus Blossom even yipped in imitation.

The Decorator

"See, even little Princess knows Cosmeco and Roger Kirkeby are history. Until further notice, we are stuck in the Vista," said Pamela. "It's enough to drive anyone to drink."

"What happened to Cosmeco?" Clark asked Miss Riley.

"Oh, I guess you didn't see Miss Raven's award from Cosmeco. They gave her a bronzed Cosmetique compact. She keeps it next to her Oscar. Cosmeco wanted to sponsor an episode of "This Is Your Life" for Miss Raven, but she wouldn't do it," said Miss Riley.

"Why wouldn't you?" asked Clark.

"Be serious!" snapped Pamela. "How could I go? After I worked my ass off for that company — I sacrificed my acting career for them too — I *was* Cosmetique and Cosmetique was me! And now they've washed me up! Screw 'em! And screw Kirkeby too! He was behind this! He did it because he didn't want to pay me any more. Now I have to pay for my driver, telelphone, secretary, and hairdresser out of my pension. I refuse to appear on some humiliating television show and pretend to be surprised by horrible little people from my ancient history. And I refuse to smile while Cosmeco stabs me in the back. Screw 'em!"

They turned into the imposing stone gateposts of Metropolis Pictures and the vast iron gates swung inward to admit Pamela Raven's convertible. It was a sight and a feeling Clark knew he would never forget: the ultimate glamour and prestige of rolling into the most famous movie studios in the world in a chauffeur-driven cream and beige leather Rolls Royce convertible with a beautiful movie star at his side. He knew why Pamela had asked him to come, and he was blissfully grateful that she had.

CHAPTER 18

Crowds of technicians and studio employees parted for the Raven chariot as it glided between the sets and sound stages of Metro's back lot. Pamela pointed out an uncertain-looking false-fronted structure as the "ante-bellum" mansion she lived in as Tillie Macy in *Tigress in the Dark*.

Crew members swarmed over the set with lights and electrical cables, transforming the evening into temporary, artificial daylight for an establishing shot. Saws roared and the sound of hammers rang sharply around the lot. A powerful scent of horses drifted from horse trailers around a barn and corral set, and Clark could hear the horses whinnying amid the shouts of their handlers. A crowd of staff people with clipboards followed director Barney Higgins around the lot, passing urgent communications to him along their chain of command. But a familiar figure in a bathrobe and jeans waddling by the director's side appeared to have his full attention.

"Look at Adela, the slouch," fumed Pamela. "There she is in those sloppy blue jeans and her old robe with makeup stains on the collar. And those slippers ought to be burned. How can she dare to be seen like that? I wonder what she's sucking up to Barney about this time."

The driver guided the car down a lane which resembled a carnival alley. Clark stared at the sets for movies he'd seen and the shells of famous houses from scenes he had almost forgotten.

"That's Dracula's Castle," Pamela pointed out. "And Frankenstein's, too — seen one spooky castle, you've seen 'em all. And Allen knows how to save money. That building over there?"

She tilted her hat in the direction of a long, low bungalow on the left. "Our dressing rooms were in there. That was my door, second from the right. As you can see, we had suites. One could actually live in those dressing rooms, and often I did.

Lucien didn't like that very much. He used to say, 'Your place is at home, with me.' I'm afraid we had quite an argument over that one and in the end, I let him win. In the end, what did it matter? I tried to make him happy and that's what counts. Lucien was my only husband who wasn't in pictures too, you see, and he didn't understand that Metro was my home for so long I didn't know how to live in a real home as other people do. If I had it to do over, I would have done more things Lucien's way. I would have been a better wife. You can't live your whole life thinking someone's going to die, can you? But maybe we should… maybe we'd appreciate each other more…"

Pamela stared dreamily into space, but she quickly snapped out of it. "Of course, those dressing rooms are all offices now. Accounting, I believe. We have to make do with trailers."

"Times have changed," said Mama.

"Well, the Golden Years ended long ago. The Big Picture died with Irving Thalberg and the War. Then all we got were stupid musicals and propaganda pictures. The 1940's — the trauma! With no good parts for women of a certain age. Oh, how I hated growing old! I never thought it would happen to me. On the outside, I was this woman with a plastic face that no one really wanted to see. Remember that song, 'Have I Stayed Too Long At The Fair'? It crushed me when I heard it. Because, you see, Metropolis promised me a rose garden, and they delivered, not just plot by plot, but acre by acre. And then they took it all away. The last time I drove through these gates, I was going the other way, alone, just like I arrived, with everything I owned in my car."

"But you came back to win your Oscar," said Clark.

"So I did! I'm not complaining. I was part of Hollywood when it was great, and I'm a part of it still. How many actresses can make that claim? One must be professional! It won't do to be a crybaby or throw a silly star tantrum, like some of these young so-called actresses do. Those spoiled brats even show up late on the set, which drives everyone crazy. Working with Marilyn Monroe just about wore Gabe out. Even Adela knows to be on time, always. Goodness, Riley — what time is it?"

"It's twenty to five, Miss Raven. You're two hours early."

"As it should be," said Pamela.

"Miss Raven is always early," whispered Mama. "Oh, I don't like those trailers. They're drafty, and I don't think that's good for Miss Raven. I'm worried about that cough."

"Nonsense. There is no cough." Pamela cleared her throat. "I just have a frog in my throat because I lay awake all night dreading those telephone calls. And I did break down and smoke a few cigarettes, damn it! I'll be just fine after I have a cup of tea."

The inside of Pamela Raven's trailer was like a greenhouse. She had received so many plants and flowers from fans and old friends that there was no more room for a single pot or vase. Flower arrangements covered the counters in the kitchenette and the small tables and bar in the sitting area. Potted plants sat on the carpet surrounding the loveseat and chairs. Clark thought the furniture looked awful and cheap, worse than in an old hotel. He would have to speak to Allen Friedberg about re-covering the upholstery. Pamela stopped to read a few tags on flowers in vases still swathed in tissue paper. "It's Gabe again. Dear old Gabe, I love the guy, but he never gets it that I don't appreciate plants in dirt or flowers that dry and fall off. Men! What can you do?"

Despite her complaints, Clark saw that Pamela's face flushed with pleasure when she read the florist's tags. Nor did he miss the sly looks Mama and Miss Riley exchanged behind Pamela's back.

While Mama bustled about laying down wee-wee pads for Princess Lotus Blossom, Pamela led Clark into the tiny bedroom, which was packed with racks of costumes. Hats and other accessories covered the single bed.

"People used to say you could confuse my dressing room with the wardrobe department, but those days are gone too," said Pamela. "*Tigress* is a simple picture. Production expects us to wrap up the shooting in thirty days, and Allen wants to bring it in under two million dollars. So far, we're within the budget. You know, Adela and I are taking a mere hundred and fifty thousand dollars and ten percent of the gross each, which is nothing. But we were advised not to ask for more because Allen won't pay it. I really don't mind, Clark — I believe in this picture. It's the best script to come along in years, and it may

The Decorator

be the last good one I'll get. Adela's lucky she got it at all. So, I don't mind roughing it a bit. I'm an old hand at it."

Mama brought an English rose china tea service into the sitting room. She carefully laid out the creamer, sugar, lemon wedges, and tiny silver spoons atop pink linen napkins on the silver tray. Miss Riley rustled from the racks in the bedroom to an ironing board in the sitting room, preparing Pamela's costumes for the night's shooting.

Mama set the tea tray down between the flower vases on the coffee table.

"I don't like it, Mr. Calloway," she said, with uncharacteristic boldness. "Someone has to have a talk with Mr. Friedberg. There will be no dressing rooms in the Mexico location this week. Miss Raven will have to change in… a car!"

She was almost too shocked to get the word out. "And after Miss Raven has been friends with Mr. Friedberg for so many years — he had his birthday party at her apartment one year, as a surprise, you know — and Miss Raven always remembers Mr. and Mrs. Friedberg's anniversary with a lovely gift. It's just not right to treat a lady so!"

"Mama worries about me too much. It's show biz, Mama! We have our ups and downs. A little adventure doesn't hurt my performance — in fact it may even help."

"Yes, it does," said Miss Riley. "Tell Clark about that British circus film — what was it called? — where you had to dance over the elephant droppings!"

She burst into laughter and Pamela joined her.

"*Sideshow*. I was leaping pretty high that day, wasn't I? And oh, for a nose plug! Though elephant shit smells better than some of the leading men I've had to kiss!"

"Oh, come on, it can't be that bad!" said Clark, laughing.

"Yes it can, my dear, yes it can! It was bad enough that some of the new boys were so intimidated by the great sex star, *moi*, that I had to jump 'em to get any action going. That's what the directors told me to do, 'Just jump 'em, Pam, or we'll never get that shot.' So it's not my fault some of those kisses continued off the set, is it? No, I'm talking about some of the older guys like poor Gabe, bless his heart, though he wasn't very old when the studio dentist pulled all of his teeth and gave him new choppers. Talk about denture breath, pew!"

"Well, you seemed to have gotten around that pretty well," said Clark, remembering the steamy Raven-Taylor screen clinches.

"That's because I started carrying a mint in my mouth, and I'd slip it to him along with my tongue. With Gabe it was worth it, but if the little girls out in movieland only knew what we actresses go through with smelly actors, they'd throw up on their popcorn. But seriously, I don't mind the challenges of making pictures. In London I got up at five every morning to make breakfast for the crew. They seemed to enjoy it, and I know I did."

Miss Riley held up a yellow scarf for Pamela's inspection.

"Can't you find the blue scarf, Riley? The one with the Swiss dots? I need something that will stand up to amber lights. They call it "love-scene pink," and I could be insulted that Barney insists on shooting me that way, but we need all the help we can get... some of us more than others..."

This last comment was directed toward the curtained window of Pamela's trailer, through which Adela could be heard yelling for coffee.

"It won't help," Pamela rang out.

"I heard that, bitch," hollered Adela. "I have things to do at night and people to do them with. When was the last time you got any action, you dried-up queen?"

The door to Adela's trailer slammed.

Pamela rolled her eyes. "Adela thinks she's hot now because she's screwing our director. Though he's no prize. I should know — Barney was my second husband — for three weeks!"

Miss Riley and Mama broke into peals of laughter and Clark joined in.

Pamela clapped her hands. "Let's go, kids! I've got to get into makeup."

Clark conducted Pamela Raven to the door of Makeup, where Pamela greeted an older makeup stylist with a cry of "I'm in your hands, Babe, help me now!" The makeup woman, whose name really was Babe, checked Clark out from head to toe when Pamela introduced him. Clark got the familiar feeling that Pamela liked to make people wonder if he was her young lover, and she certainly acted the giggling ingenue with him in public. He left them chattering away as Pamela asked about Babe's family members by name and inquired about their lives in detail. Pamela Raven certainly did have a stellar memory, much to the pleasure of those who worked with her.

Clark walked around the busy lot, following the directions Pamela had given him to Gabe Taylor's location. He tried to stay out of the way of the carpenters, caterers, and assorted frantic personnel, and he nearly tripped on thick electrical cables several times. The lot excited him, especially the pieces of interiors riding by on dollies and glimpsed through doorways. They made him think about interior design in a new, mobile way, especially as the furnishings and backdrops he saw were more complete and detailed than stage settings he had seen. The possibilities of designing sets for film were swirling in his head when he heard a familiar lusty laugh and an unmistakable voice calling him.

"Hey! Clark Calloway! C'mere!"

Adela Morgan was playing a rowdy game of poker with three technicians on a metal folding table by an equipment trailer. The pot in the middle of the table was sizable, and the men were smoking and pouring whiskey into their coffee. Adela slapped a burly red-headed guy on the back and shouted something in his ear which made him laugh and spit out his cigar.

"Hey, Kid Calloway!" Adela gave Clark a bear hug and a wet smooch on his lips. "These are my buddies, Mac and Joe, and this is Pete. Don't let 'em scare ya, they're rough tough cream puffs!"

The guys greeted Clark briefly without taking their attention from their hands.

"Clark's a big-shot New York decorator, out here to fancy up the Bel Vista Hotel. We're just playing a few hands to kill time until my scene. I'm behind, but it's a ploy. I'll take these maroons for everything they've got in the end. I used to play with Bugsy Malone."

"Sure ya did!" said Pete. "I've heard that one before. Quit stallin'. You in or not?"

"I'll raise ya one, what the hell. Take my chances. Where's the Widow Irons! Bet she's getting under two pounds of makeup right now. That old Hollywood glamour puss. The fairies do a better Pamela Raven than she does. More convincing. And more feminine."

"Yeah, you better watch your man around her," teased Joe. "I think I saw her going into his office wearin' nothin' but a smile and a raincoat."

"She better not try it. Barney's had that merchandise, and he spit it out because it tastes rotten. Everyone knows Raven fucked her way into pictures. She did porn flicks, too. They say chorus girls turn into call girls just to get off their feet, and Raven's no different. And that Holly's just like her aunt, trying to fuck her way in, only she doesn't have the sense to get her face redone and the fat cut away from her thighs. She already looks like an old broad from those drugs she takes. I heard she's been seen on the Sunset Strip these days, stopping cars."

"Holly's in Italy," said Clark. "She's working on a film."

"Film, schmilm," said Adela. "Holly's here, I tell you, giving blow jobs for five bucks, which is more than Pamela used to get."

The technicians broke into nasty laughter, and Clark bid them a quick good evening. As much as he disliked Holly Raven, he didn't like to hear Adela put her down when she wasn't around to defend herself. Pamela Raven, on the other hand, could match Adela barb for barb.

Her latest doozy, he recalled, was something about Adela being a cheap hoofer with the voice of a cow: "That Adela should keep mooing and drinking that Gallo wine. She's too old to give any good milk, and she's known to piss her pants in the best of bars."

Clark certainly didn't want to get between the warring actresses in their life-long battle. Though Pamela was feeling outnumbered now, Clark knew that at one point the tables had been turned: during Pamela's courtship and brief marriage to Barney Higgins, a man much older than she, Pamela and Adela had both appeared in *Blue Orchid*. Pamela's torture of Adela on the set was legendary — everyone knew how Pamela had made Adela change out of any dress which looked good on her and how Pamela made her shadow fall across Adela's face at every opportunity, rendering Adela nearly invisible in some of the footage. Pamela, too, had ordered studio guards to watch her dressing room — after she heard that Adela had looked at herself in Pamela's mirror. So Adela's current privilege was her revenge, and she was milking it for all it was worth.

In the corral, Gabe Taylor was having some trouble with his horse. Clark recognized him immediately — as he did on screen, in person the raw-boned actor looked taller than six foot one. Even at sixty, Taylor radiated an aura of all-American sexuality; as one publicist had said, he looked like Valentino in Jack Dempsey's body. Though Clark remembered seeing Gabe Taylor most often in black tie, the actor looked more natural in the Western-style sheriff's outfit he was wearing. Taylor was very tan and broad-shouldered, and his face still had the craggy features which had made him the biggest male star Hollywood has ever known, but he was overweight and moved stiffly, and he was having trouble with his horse.

Barney Higgins, looking withered, was sweating profusely under the lights. His bald head shone as he jumped up and down yelling "Cut!" He reminded Clark of a nervous Boston terrier as he ran around yelling "What's the problem?" The problem was, Gabe Taylor had not been on a horse in years and didn't particularly want to be on one, and the horse knew it.

"Gads, Barney, who ever heard of a sheriff on a horse in this century? Can't you get me a Model T or something?"

"Gabe, the script calls for a horse, and the public wants to see you on one, believe me. Somebody help Mr. Taylor dismount. Get me a different horse! Fifteen-minute break, everyone!"

Gabe Taylor ambled over to a canvas chair near Clark and lit a smoke. He exhaled a very tired sigh and watched the lights dim as the grooms led the horse away.

Clark moved a few seats closer to the actor. "Mr. Taylor? I apologize if I'm bothering you, but Pamela Raven asked me to introduce myself. I'm Clark Calloway."

He extended his hand, which Taylor grasped warmly and tightly.

"Oh, hello, Clark. Pam told me all about you, and any friend of hers is a friend of mine. What do you think of our little studio?"

"It's wonderful," said Clark. "It's amazing. It must be exciting to be a part of all this."

"Well, Clark, it's like a Christmas tree: when they turn the lights on, you know it's Christmas; the rest of the time you sit and watch the needles drop."

"What's going on with that horse?"

"He's stealing the scene from me, that's what's going on. You see, he's a horse and I'm not a horseman any more. I couldn't wait to get away from horses and cows, that's why I wanted to be an actor. Now, John Wayne, he was a football player, but he's a better horseman than I'll ever be. Or want to be."

Gabe spoke slowly and his gravelly Midwestern voice captivated Clark. This man, Taylor, had such power and he was doing nothing. His heavy-lidded eyes looked Spanish, as if he wore permanent, natural eyeliner. The hands were very large, and he smoked like a blue-collar laborer, sucking the life out of his cigarette. Even out of shape and in old age, Taylor looked poised on the edge of action, or violence. Clark could see why Pamela liked him.

"Do you like to hunt?" Taylor asked.

"No, not particularly," said Clark.

"Neither do I," said Taylor. "I still have the hunting lodge the studio gave me in the canyon. For my image, you know, the big outdoorsman. Ha, ha. But I do use it to fish, or just to get away from the city at times. If you like, I'd enjoy it if you came by tomorrow afternoon. We don't have to go fishing; we can just have a drink or two."

"Thank you, Mr. Taylor. I'd like to come," Clark felt honored, and as if he had just been invited to the boys' secret clubhouse. He wondered if Gabe Taylor had a sign on his door reading "No Girls Allowed."

"Call me Gabe. Criminy, here they come."

There was a pack of people rapidly advancing upon Gabe Taylor and the air was suddenly white with flash bulbs. Pamela Raven and Adela Morgan led the parade, smiling their brightest. Barney Higgins announced that it was time to shoot the publicity stills and that afterward he needed Adela and Pamela to read lines, as there had been script changes.

Pamela Raven, with her regal stride and fixed smile, appeared to be in her glory. Her lips and eyebrows were contoured lavishly, her skin looked buffed and waxed rather than simply made up, and her enormous eyes were glowing. Clark

The Decorator

saw that her hands were trembling; he knew how much she feared the press. She pulled Gabe Taylor into a private pow-wow, and Gabe hunched conspiratorially over his tiny co-star, looking like the Latin lover of bygone days. The energy between them was so charged Clark wondered whether Gabe was about to kiss Pamela or hit her. The cameras went wild and the reporters' questions about a rekindling of the old romance flew through the air.

Adela and Pamela fielded questions as they posed together with an air of sweet felicity. Adela, wrapped in some silken stuff like a fat couch, was bawdy and brash, with her head tilted back, her boobs thrown out, and her hand on Pamela's shoulder. Pamela gave Adela her indulgent, appraising glance, with her lips slightly parted and her eyebrows raised. It was totally phony, Clark knew, but convincing. Pamela with her chin lifted just so and her doe eyes on Adela gave the appearance of pure patience.

"Miss Raven, how do you feel about appearing with Mr. Taylor again, after all these years?"

"Are you kidding — it feels fantastic: Gabe Taylor is the King!"

"This King business is all b.s.," shrugged Gabe. "I was in the right place at the right time, that's all."

"What would you say is the secret of your success, Mr. Taylor?"

"He's got 'em, that's why," said Pamela.

"Yeah, but Pam swings more balls than I do, everybody knows that," said Gabe.

As Clark watched the two smiling professionals entertaining the press, he remembered a quote from an interview Gabe Taylor had given long ago. When the reporter asked Taylor what he thought would be his epitaph, Gabe Taylor had said, "He was lucky and he knew it."

In the parlor of the Macy Mansion, the two actresses read their lines. Adela Morgan paced the carpet, script in hand. Pamela Raven sat on a sofa and knitted. She had already committed the new lines to memory. Suddenly, Adela threw down her script.

"Are you going to stop knitting?"

"No," said Pamela coldly.

"I can't read lines with someone who won't look at me. It's creepy."

"I like to knit," said Pamela. "I believe the next line is yours."

"Barney! Make her stop knitting!"

"Just read the lines, Adela," said Barney Higgins. "We don't have time for this nonsense."

Adela picked up her script.

"Page forty-five," said the script girl.

Adela found her page, skimmed it, and looked at Pamela. "Do you knit when you fuck?"

Pamela smiled and kept knitting.

After the shoot, Gabe Taylor wanted to go out for dinner with Pamela and Clark. Pamela would go nowhere without a reservation.

"Oh, come on, Pam, it's late — we can get a table. Let's just stop into Romanoff's," said Gabe.

"I think not," said Pamela.

Despite the impropriety, she was tired from her hard day. She had worked a fourteen-hour day with only an hour break, and Clark could see the conditions hadn't been easy on her. She had been tense when Barney Higgins' assistant had repeatedly checked her water glass to make sure she was drinking water and not her hundred-proof. Every time Pamela found that her glass had been moved, her shoulders went up a little higher.

Adela had constantly criticized Pamela's performance. "Is *that* the way she's going to play it?" she had wanted to know, and unfortunately, Mr. Higgins had seen Adela's point each time. Clark, too, found Pamela's acting stiff and unnatural. She could not simply change expressions; her face underwent such contortions in moving from one emotion to another that the director would not film the process. He simply cut to Pamela when she had arrived at the appropriate expression.

Adela's work was not of the best quality either; her overacting made Clark cringe, and he felt she ruined her best lines. But Adela had been given better lines, and the director clearly favored her, so Pamela was powerless in the situation. Adela was already bragging that she would be nominated for an Oscar. Clark knew Pamela had a long history of bearing insults professionally, but she seemed to take her frustration out on Gabe by snapping at him off-camera. Gabe Taylor had no conflicts or arguments with Higgins, besides the horse problem, which was minor.

"Cool down," Clark had heard Gabe say. "It's only a movie." Pamela's reaction had not been favorable and Clark was not surprised she did not want to go out to dinner with Gabe.

Clark was thinking about these things as he drove back to Santa Monica. As he turned into Pamela's street, he nearly hit a motorcycle. Clark jammed on the brakes, and the motorcycle, with its two riders, zoomed past as if the driver didn't care that he had almost had a terrible accident. The female passenger gave Clark the finger as the bike sped away into the night.

"Great," said Clark as he parked the car. "Nothing like a near-death experience to get the blood flowing."

He opened the front door and settled his bag of takeout Mexican food and soda on the kitchen counter. When he switched on the lights, he was surprised to see two used glasses in the sink. He was certain he had not left them there, especially when he saw red lipstick on one of the glasses.

That realtor certainly is careless, he thought as he washed the glasses and put them away. He settled in front of the television to watch the news while he ate dinner. Robert McNamara and Bill Moyers were both resigning from the president's staff. In Vietnam, "Zippo squads" were torching peasant huts with cigarette lighters, and President Johnson had accused CBS and Thom Pearson of treason for televising that. It was too late on the East Coast to talk to Dannee Lou about the news, or about her brother's romance with Reggie, which was what Clark really wanted to discuss. He hoped when he did call Dannee Lou that she would tell him what he wanted to hear.

While Clark was brushing his teeth, he noticed that the bathroom waste basket was full of used tissues. Strange, he thought. The tissues were covered with a sticky tan cream. When he touched one, he found that it was grease paint. Someone had used this bathroom while he was gone, and that person had removed a lot of grease paint from his face. Or her face. That was not normal, and Clark could think of no reason for it. Feeling stupid, he ripped the shower curtain back and found no one there. But he did see something on the floor. It was a long, black hair. He picked it up and held it to the light. Was it the maid's? It was coarse and plasticky, not human hair. It was wig hair.

Well, who knows how long it could have been here? Clark thought. It could have been there for years. Maybe the maid or realtor wears a wig and tan face paint. Not likely, but what else could be going on?

Clark decided to find out. He fished a bobby pin out of the waste basket, one of those he had thrown away the day before. He took it to the master bedroom door and slid it into the keyhole in the doorknob. This works in the movies, he thought. But it didn't work in real life. The bobby pin merely bent and turned uselessly in the lock. Clark grabbed the doorknob to pull the pin out and the knob turned. The door was open, as it had been all along.

"Okay, I know this door was locked today," said Clark. He searched the room, having a feeling he would find nothing. He did find nothing, except for a few boxes of photographic paper in the closet. He wondered what it was doing there, but there was nothing sinister about it. He bent to look under the bed and saw a small, white rectangle lying on the carpet near the wall.

"Probably a mattress tag," Clark grunted as he reached beneath the bed to fish it out. "Ow!" Something had stabbed him. Clark picked up the tag and looked at his finger where a small puncture leaked blood. The tag was plastic and had a sharp pin on the back. He turned it over.

"*Carmelita,*" it read.

"What a stupid maid," said Clark. She probably has sex with her boyfriend in this bedroom because she thinks the house is empty, he thought. The grease-painted tissue papers still bothered him, but he forgot about them and went to bed.

In the middle of the night, the phone rang. Once, twice, three times. Clark groaned and squinted at the lighted dial of his alarm clock. Three-thirty. The phone rang again. Clark climbed out of bed and walked unsteadily on his bare feet through the dark house to the living room. He picked up the phone on the sixth ring.

"Hello?" he croaked.

There was no sound on the line. Clark became annoyed. "Hello! Who is this?" he demanded.

He heard breathing on the other end. He was about to hang up angrily when an eerie female voice whispered "Get out!"

"Hello? Who is this? How dare you —"

The voice again, louder: "Get out of the house! Get ouut!"

The caller wailed like a ghost and hung up.

"Shithead," said Clark. He hung up the phone and as he walked away it rang again. Clark picked up the receiver and slammed it down. He wanted to leave the phone off the hook, but he knew Gabe Taylor was going to ring him in a few hours to go fishing. Swearing, he poured himself a glass of water and went back to bed. Now he knew how Pamela Raven felt when she couldn't go back to sleep.

CHAPTER 19

*F*ishing started too early for Clark's taste. Apparently not too early for a drink, he thought, as he watched Gabe Taylor pour himself another shot of whisky from a large flask.

"Drinking and fishing go together," Gabe said. "Sure you don't want a nip? Keeps the chill off."

It was chilly under the trees on the stream bank where Clark fumbled with his lure. He was grateful that they were fly fishing. Touching a worm would have made him lose his breakfast, if he had eaten any. Gabe was a remarkable fisherman, or at least a great reel caster, as they hadn't caught anything yet. Maybe there is something to this, Clark thought, as he watched the graceful arc of Gabe's line into the still waters of a pool by the far bank. Clark's casting attempts were sloppy and his line kept drifting downstream, when it didn't lodge in the shrubs.

"There's a trick to it," Gabe coached. "Takes a lifetime to learn. Some say it's an art. Let me do that for you before you scare all the fish away."

Clark's rod dipped and snapped in Gabe's large hands, the line whirred out in a perfect arc. "There you go. Plenty of time to practice later, if you want to."

He handed Clark's rod back to him.

"Now what do we do?" asked Clark.

"What do we do?" Gabe laughed. "We *fish*. What do we do?" Gabe found Clark's question funny enough to bear repeating, and Clark was glad his own father had been a bookworm and uninclined to do "manly" things with his son. Gabe, on the other hand, looked the part of an outdoorsman in his khakis, waders, plaid shirt and fishing vest. He hit the whisky again and Clark sighed, thinking the libation might help Gabe find more humor at Clark's expense.

But after a few more chuckles Gabe fell silent. He squinted

at the water and contemplated it for many minutes. Several times, he slowly reeled his line in and cast it again. Clark remembered hearing something about being quiet while fishing, but he didn't know if you weren't supposed to talk. Gabe looked completely at ease, but Clark was already bored.

"Pamela Raven…" said Gabe at last. "She's some gal."

"Yes, she is," said Clark.

"Always was," said Gabe. He resumed staring silently at the water. When Clark was about to say something, Gabe took another drink and looked at him sideways. "I hear you know Holly Raven too."

"Yes. I did meet her and I spent a little time with her. I can't say I really know her."

"To hear Pam talk, you and Holly got to know each other pretty well."

"Oh, yeah, I…" Clark was embarrassed and he didn't know what to say. He didn't want to get himself in trouble with Pamela.

Gabe laughed. "That's all right. It's just like Pam to try to arrange everything in that kid's life, including her love life. You don't have to worry about saying anything to me. I know I wouldn't want to be caught between those two."

"How can you avoid it?" asked Clark.

"Well, I didn't exactly avoid it, if you remember the court case in 'fifty-five. What a mess that was. When Holly forced Pamela to choose between Holly or me, Pamela chose me, though she probably shouldn't have. It was too late for us, anyway. You have to understand, when I knew Holly and her sister Frieda, they were just little squirts. They were pretty shy, real sensitive girls; could be because they lost their Mom so young and their Dad was no good."

"It seems Holly and Pamela had quite a few problems getting along," said Clark.

"Oh, Holly told you that much, did she? I'm not surprised. Well, Pamela didn't know much about being a kid. She was just some poor little tyke who got kicked around half the cow towns in the Southwest. It was rough on her, and it made her tough. She didn't get any breaks. I know what that's like. As Pam used to say, 'There was not one goddamned moment on the Good Ship Lollipop!'

"Maybe she was hard on those girls, but what did she know about raising kids? Hell, Metropolis was the only family most of us had, and old Abie was like a father to Pam. Kind of a sick father, though. You see, except for Monroe, and that was much later, Pamela Raven was the only star completely created by the studio. Even her name was chosen in the studio's "Name That Star" contest."

"So Pamela Raven treated her adopted children the way Metropolis treated her," Clark mused.

Gabe landed a small trout, unhooked it, and tossed it back.

"You got it. Everything Pamela was given was on condition. Abie gave her love and money, and he controlled her with it. He bought her the Bel Air house, you know, her first house, so she could escape those mooching relatives of hers, but because of that Abie wouldn't hear Pamela complain when he started giving all the good parts to other dames." Gabe winced. "I tell you, it's scary when that happens."

"Did that ever happen to you?" Clark felt a tug on his line.

"Hey, you got a bite. Reel her in. Easy now… you got it… faster, come on. Yeah! Yeah, there you go. That one's a beauty." Gabe helped Clark unhook the six-inch trout. It was a pretty fish. Clark looked the other way when Gabe clubbed it.

"Did that ever happen to me? No, but Abe threatened to trade me a couple times. And there were plenty of times I lay awake wondering if I'd still have a career in the morning. We're all expendable, and when you're out of work in the picture business it's like walking on nothing. I tell you, I felt safer in the Air Force."

They reset their lines and went back to waiting. Gabe alternated swigs of whisky with drags on a non-filtered cigarette. The morning sun warmed the stream bank, and Clark admired the shrubs and wild flowers around him. The men's stillness encouraged birds to come closer and they filled the morning with their songs. Clark threw back a small fish and Gabe caught two good-sized ones.

Clark knew the older man had been a war hero, a gunner who made captain. The Germans had placed a big price on his head. Gabe Taylor had been in his thirties; he didn't have to enlist, but he was patriotic. That and the Flying Cross and the Air Medal he won made him an even bigger hero back home.

The Decorator

As they loaded their gear and the bucket of cleaned fish on ice into Gabe's jeep, Clark marveled at the man's life. He watched Gabe Taylor drive aggressively, cigarette clamped in his jaws, and Clark thought about how Taylor had always managed to catch the spirit of his times. He had represented new American glamour during the Thirties and had been a romantic war hero during the Forties. In the Fifties he had become a conservative Republican and he remained so. He had been a featured guest player in the grim national sport called "Hunt the Reds," and when Senator McCarthy had called, Taylor did not disappoint him.

People said that alcoholism got Gabe Taylor after the death of his wife. He had been charged with drunk driving on several occasions, and was a rumored regular customer of Hollywood prostitute delivery services. It was only natural, Clark thought. After all, Gabe had been known for his taste in messenger girls and diner waitresses, easy conquests and one-night stands. It was also rumored that he never tipped.

Back at Gabe's cabin, the actor made a pot of coffee and fried the fish in cornmeal with potatoes and onions. While Gabe was cooking, Clark explored the little cabin. It was exactly what Gabe Taylor's hunting lodge should look like: dark wood paneling, deer head trophies, gun cases, a large television, and a working fireplace. Gabe had turned the television on the moment he came in, a habit Clark knew Paul Hedges deplored among the "lower classes." The mildewed horse blanket on the torn sofa, the coffee table with its top covered with cigarette burns, and the stained lounge chairs would have driven Paul out of the room.

"Hey, Clark, time to eat!" Gabe called.

Clark enjoyed the fresh fish and strong coffee. He was ravenous, and it was an accomplishment to have caught his breakfast himself, with a little help from Gabe Taylor.

Gabe leaned back and lit a cigarette. "More coffee?"

"Yes, thanks," said Clark.

Gabe refilled the cups and added a healthy shot of Dewars to his own.

"Pam used to like to drink it this way with me. We used to sneak up here sometimes to get away from the prying eyes." He sipped his coffee. "How is Pamela, really?"

"She's fine, I guess, except for the crank callers."

"I don't mean that. Pam's always fine. I mean, does she seem lonely to you?"

"Yes, I think she misses her late husband a good deal."

"Ahh!" Gabe dismissed Lucien Irons with a wave of his huge paw and a snort of cigarette smoke. "He was never her type. And she's still paying his bills, isn't she? No, she's playing the grieving widow; don't let her fool you."

Gabe paused, uncomfortably, as if he wasn't accustomed to sharing his private thoughts with anyone, which Clark thought he probably wasn't. With that in mind, Clark poured a dash of whisky into his own coffee.

"There you go!" said Gabe. "You're a real man, after all! I was beginning to wonder. So, you know about women, don't you? Pam's not... seeing anyone, is she?"

Clark read between the lines. "No, she isn't," he said. "I'm certain of it. And I do know women. I have a girl friend in D.C." My goodness, he thought, I'm lying. Well, it's better than being seen as a competitor by Gabe Taylor. Not with all those guns in the house.

Gabe visibly relaxed. He took a drink right from the bottle and wiped his mouth on the back of his hand.

"I'm gonna do it," he said. "Pamela Raven is the only true, the only beautiful thing in my life, and I'm going to ask her to marry me. I'm gonna do it now, before I lose my nerve."

Clark waited in stunned silence while Gabe used the phone in the living room. Soon, much too soon, Gabe returned.

"Was she there?" Clark asked.

"She was there," said Gabe. He began clearing the table.

"What did she say?"

"She didn't say anything." Gabe leaned on the counter and tilted the whisky bottle to his lips. He took a long swallow before he put the bottle down. "I took that as a 'no'."

A young couple was riding horseback along Malibu Colony Beach as Clark drove along the Pacific Coast Highway. Pamela Raven had invited Gabe and Clark to Allen Friedberg's to see the *Tigress* dailies. Gabe was supposed to go, but he didn't want to. He said he had a few things to do, but all he was doing was smoking and staring at a football game on television when Clark left. Clark had accepted Allen Friedberg's second-hand invitation, though it meant he would have to rush to keep his tennis date with Roland Lee at the Bel Vista. Besides, he really wanted to see the Friedbergs' Malibu house.

The house was all glass, and it was stunning. It was perched on a cliff over the sea like a white diamond. Allen's Rolls was in the driveway and Allen Friedberg himself waved Clark up to a deck which wound around the house. Allen, his skin greasy from a recent facial, grumpily greeted Clark and led him along the deck to show off his house. The view was marvelous from every side. Clark especially liked the enormous glass swimming pool sunk into a lower deck which faced the ocean. And someone was in the pool. The lovely, seal-brown Anne Bates floated on a yellow raft in a white string bikini.

"Ain't she a peach?" said Allen. "She's a bitch. Speaking of bitches, we'd better drive down to the screening room before my wife wakes up."

"I thought Mrs. Friedberg was at the spa in Palm Springs."

"She was, she was, but she came back a day early. And wouldn't you know it, she walked right in on me with Maria in that pool. And we weren't doing the backstroke, if you catch my drift. Bambi hit the roof. Such screaming I've never heard. She wants a divorce, she wants the house, the whole nine yards. Annie, get the hell out of the pool!" Allen yelled, *sotto voice,* and the actress paddled her raft to the pool's edge.

"Lazy broad, Anne. I should fire her, but what an ass. Almost as cute as Angie Dickinson's buns. Almost. We can wait for the other bimbos downstairs. Hey, where the hell is Taylor? Wasn't he with you?"

"Gabe apologizes — he can't make it."

"No biggie," said Allen. "The two dragon ladies'll be here in a minute. I'll ring for some coffee."

They settled in the large projection room on the first floor. The jade-green suede theater seats were wide and well-padded, and the walls and plush carpeting were a matching green with an Art Deco motif in black. The wall sconces and chandeliers were of lovely Tiffany stained glass, and brass rails trimmed the aisle and bar. A thick green velveteen curtain covered a theater-sized screen and the projection booth in the rear of the theater was also full-sized and staffed by a projectionist.

"Those two are driving me insane," Allen complained. "Barney says they behave themselves on the set, but every night, like clockwork, the phone calls come. Last night it was Pamela first. She says Adela lied to a reporter, said they're both the same age when Adela's five years older if she's a day, and what am *I* going to do about it? I calm that one down and Adela calls me: now Pamela's making herself heavy on purpose and Adela hurt her back carrying her. See, there's a scene where Pamela's character faints and Adela has to carry her to the car. Well, Adela can't pick her up without straining her back, she says. How much can Raven weigh, ninety pounds? Ridiculous, isn't it? Every night they do this. Then Raven calls me again. She's out of her mind, says her dresses came back from the cleaners torn or something, and some crank caller is threatening her again. What the hell am I supposed to do, I'd like to know. 'Where's my security guard?' she bugs me. 'What security guard?' I say. And then I remember: I let him go yesterday. I can't afford to pamper these prima donnas any more. She's got hotel security. This harassment shit is all in her head anyway. She drinks, you know."

In light of his own experience with menacing phone calls in the night, Clark was about to word a tactful defense of Pamela Raven when her voice preceded her into the room.

"I hope I'm intelligent enough to be friendly with my ex-husband!"

Pamela entered the screening room, followed by Adela, who snapped, "Ex is ex for a reason! And ya don't have to throw yourself at him every time —"

"Ladies, please," said Anne Bates, who followed them in a baby-blue silk caftan. Her hair was wet.

"Stuff it," said Pamela. "I see nothing wrong with asking Barney for directions; is there anything wrong with that, Allen?"

"Oh, bullshit," said Adela, plumping herself down in a seat. "You should hear how she asks!"

She imitated Pamela panting and batting her eyes: "'Oh, Barney, I'm afraid I don't know how to do this scene...' What a load of crap!"

"Well, she doesn't," said Allen. "So knock it off before I

smack you."

Anne Bates curled up in a front-row seat next to Allen Friedberg. "Oooh, I can't wait to see my scene!" she gushed.

Pamela sat down next to Clark. "Allen! I beg your pardon?"

"You know what I mean, Pam. It's your silent film training, so what? She learned the ropes under the guys who directed the silent pictures. The directors used to tell the actors what to do while the cameras were rolling," Allen explained to Clark. "Even though Pamela is too young to have done silents, she's used to directors who treat her like a marionette. Some of you other broads could learn from her."

Adela glowered and Pamela snuggled into Clark's shoulder.

"Young, I like that! Let's stop all this talking and watch the rushes," Pamela said.

"They're called dailies now," Anne sniffed.

"Insufferable piglet," Pamela whispered to Clark as the house lights dimmed.

"Why don't you marry Gabe?" Clark whispered.

Pamela rolled her eyes. "I love Gabe. I would marry him, but it's not good for either of us," she whispered back. "What is a wife or husband? Someone to pick up after you and send your clothes to the cleaners and write down your messages on a little pad. Who needs that? Not Gabe and not me!"

"Shhhh!" hissed Anne.

"Shhhh, yourself," said Pamela.

The film was rolling. Clark gasped as Pamela's giant face appeared on the screen.

Pamela also drew in her breath sharply.

"It's *her!*" she sighed, transfixed by her own image. The light brought the screen Pamela to life, she glowed out of the darkness like a stone angel. Clark watched her walk across the screen, and as she walked, she drew the camera to her as if she contained an inner generator. This movie star existed in her own universe; she was completely different from any woman Clark had ever met, including the real woman seated next to him.

Adela too had a commanding screen presence, though not as hypnotic as Pamela's. She looked even heavier than she was and her voice seemed too loud and stagy for the screen. Pamela emoted like a smoldering volcano under the storm of Adela's performance. Clark thought Pamela's voice lacked variety; he preferred Anne's lighter, more spontaneous delivery, though he had to admit Anne had none of the power or charisma of Pamela Raven. Pretty as Anne was, Clark just couldn't pay any attention to her when Pamela Raven was on the same screen.

Compared to the tense atmosphere between the women, Gabe Taylor's performance was as simple as sunrise. Even though Gabe was not acting — there was no difference between Gabe Taylor on or offscreen, except for the hat he wore — he played himself consistently, and he was stubbornly all man. When Gabe grinned, Clark felt better, and he knew the audience would feel better too, as they always had.

When the series of short clips ended, Allen got on the bar telephone to Barney Higgins at the studio and harangued him about the lighting and the pacing. Overall, he felt the actors' line readings were good, but the production looked cheap and seedy. The color was grainy in places and he didn't understand why it wasn't consistent. Allen rudely waved Clark and the other actors out of the projection room while he was talking. A butler was waiting outside with Allen Friedberg's personal trainer, a muscle-bound hunk in a tank top and white sweat pants. The butler led Mr. Friedberg's guests to the door.

Pamela stifled a giggle. "Seedy!" she whispered to Adela.

"Hmmmph!" Adela agreed. "He pinches pennies so tight you can't see 'em, and now he says the production looks cheap. What a bastard he is."

"Allie?" a hoarse voice whined from upstairs. "Allie, is that you?"

"Lord help us," said Pamela. "It's Bambi."

"Let's scram before she sees us, especially you, Hot Pants," whispered Adela.

Anne did not need much convincing to scamper out the door and into her Porsche. Pamela and Adela giggled like school girls caught smoking in the bathroom as they ducked out the door.

"See ya on the set, Thunder Thighs," said Pamela.

"If you can make it, Liver Lips!" Adela grinned as she slammed the door of her sedan, and Clark was surprised to see

The Decorator

how much the two famous actresses enjoyed their age-old enmity.

The sunglasses went on before Pamela climbed into her limousine.

"Clark," she said, "where are you going now?"

"To the Vista. I have a lunch meeting with Roland Lee. We're playing tennis first, and then I'll have to go supervise the work in the nightclub."

"If you have a spare moment, would you be a love and stop into my suite?"

"Certainly I will," said Clark. "Is there a problem?"

"You could say there's a problem, though it has nothing to do with you. I would just like to show you how some dresses of mine came back from the hotel cleaners last night. They are in absolute shreds, as if someone hacked them apart, and Roland Lee won't return my calls."

"Do you think…" Clark began.

"Yes, I do," said Pamela. "I think someone is sending a message to me."

It was impossible to tell what feelings her eyes expressed behind the dark glasses, but the movie star looked very small and frail as she got into the back seat of her limousine.

CHAPTER 20

Tennis was Clark's game, but he had a hard time beating Roland Lee. It had been a few months since Clark had played, and though Lee was light, he was lightning fast and had the benefit of playing on his own court as well as weekly lessons from the hotel tennis pro. Because tennis is an integral part of doing business in Los Angeles, Lee had his reasons for improving his game. In the end, the younger man won, but just barely. Both men were sweating profusely in the California winter sun, and Clark was glad to hit the showers before lunch.

Lee was waiting for Clark in the Bel Vista's Cabana Café by the seventy-five-foot pool. As usual, the hotelier was sharply dressed, in a European-style white flannel suit with gold buttons, a neon yellow, wide-collared shirt, and flowing orange and yellow striped tie. His brown and white wingtips added show business flair to his outfit. Clark thought he appeared conservative by comparison in his navy blue serge suit with a shirt striped in subdued shades of watermelon, mint and navy. His wide tie was a simple navy blue linen, but he knew when he took his jacket off that he filled out his fitted shirt impressively, certainly in comparison to Roland Lee, whose skinny body swam in his loose suit. Clark was younger and better-looking than Roland, and his recent tennis victory had been gratifyingly witnessed by the flock of bathing beauties by the pool. Roland resentfully checked Clark out as he sat down at their white table under the yellow umbrella, and Clark smiled behind his new California sunglasses. Wait till I get a tan, Clark thought, I'll really drive the chicks crazy.

"Do you lift weights?" asked Roland.

"No," Clark smiled.

"I don't have time for that either," said Roland. "There's so much to do running this hotel, I can't make it to my own gym."

After they had ordered iced tea and deli plates, Roland's

secretary brought the day's mail to the table. As Roland nibbled on pickles and buttered rolls, he tossed most of the envelopes into a nearby waste basket unopened.

"Bills, bills, and more bills. Don't I ever get any good mail?" he asked. He sliced open an envelope from the Prudential Insurance Company.

"Excuse me a second, Clark, I gotta look at this one." Roland skimmed the letter and his red eyebrows furrowed in displeasure.

"They still don't get it! I don't want their management company handling my business — I'm taking care of it myself! I don't see why they don't understand that it's cheaper to pay me directly. Bureaucracies — those guys have no imagination."

Roland tossed the letter in the garbage. His eyes sharpened as they lit on an envelope with an official L.A. County Court seal.

"I don't even have to open this one to know I'm being subpoenaed again!" he said cheerfully. "Sorry, Clark, I'm being rude. I'll deal with this later."

"I'm sorry to hear you're having legal difficulties," said Clark. Or, rather, illegal difficulties, he thought, from the sound of it. The insurance idea definitely sounded like a scam.

"Oh, it's no difficulty. What these bozos don't understand is, I love to go to court. Trials are like Disneyland to me and there's nothing like winning over a jury to make my day. I mean, look who's suing me! A paperhanger, a measly contractor who did a shitty job. What makes him think he has the means or the brains to go up against me and my lawyers in court? He's crazy — he doesn't! He'll go broke without getting a dime from me. And I'll laugh in his face."

The waitress brought their lunch. She smiled nervously at Roland Lee as she set the plates down.

"Oh, I almost forgot. I have to take these with meals." Roland pulled a prescription bottle from his jacket pocket and set it on the table. Clark did not ask what the pills were for, but he could read RONALD LEVY typed on the label. He had heard that Roland Lee had changed his name, and he wondered why. Perhaps it had been to get around the anti-Semitism at the Hobe Sound enclave where Roland's ex-wife lived and played.

"Guess who was in this restaurant last Sunday? *My* restaurant?" asked Roland. He did not wait for Clark to guess. "Bobby Kennedy! And Ted Kennedy! They had breakfast at that table right over there. They were wearing tennis whites and I was hoping they'd play on my court, but they left. I heard they went over to the Beverly Hills Hotel to play. What does that hotel have that I don't have over here? Reputation, that's all, and I'll beat that some day. Do you know who was drinking in my bar last night? Dean Martin! With his lawyer."

"That's great," said Clark. He doubted the Bel Vista would ever win the celebrity crowd away from the Beverly Hills Hotel. Those tennis courts were said to be the finest in the world.

"You bet it's great. Hey, I heard you went fishing with Gabe Taylor this morning. How about inviting him over to the Vista for cocktails this weekend?"

Clark wondered how Roland Lee had heard about his morning so soon. He spied Doreen Flower sunbathing and pretending to read *Valley of the Dolls* on a nearby lounge chair and he lowered his voice.

"Gabe's a private kind of guy," said Clark. "Let's talk about the club, shall we? The Legendary Ladies Award Ceremony for Pamela Raven is coming upon us very soon."

"When you're right, you're right. And this is what I want: the club is a night spot, so I want the mood to be blue — a sort of deep midnight blue — and perhaps you can mix star lights into the blue decor.

Clark remembered a job he had once done where the backdrop curtain was a mix of twinkle lights woven into a blue lamé. He told Roland he might use the star curtains as a backdrop behind the disco floor and maybe for tenting above.

Roland insisted that the nightclub be leveled, in a Las Vegas way: "That way everyone can see."

Clark thought that idea a bit peculiar, because the nightclub should appear cozy and intimate, not like a bleachered movie house or stadium. Nor did he like Roland's preference for chromium-framed chairs; wood-framed chairs with slipcovered backs would be more appropriate. Roland Lee's continued list of wants included green-grey carpeting, though Clark tried to convince him midnight blue was a better choice. Lee wanted cream tablecloths. Clark told him pink tablecloths with pink

The Decorator

napkins would be more flattering to the ladies, and, too, Clark thought a red rose or two on every table would be the right finishing touch. Roland jabbered about sequin-covered walls and framed portraits of film actresses for the wall decor.

Wondering how he would ever meet all of Roland Lee's requests on time, Clark walked across the pool deck toward the hotel's main building. A row of hyacinths surrounded the cabanas, and Clark found Maria Pucci spreading her towel on a lounge chair protected by the shrubbery. She turned and smiled when she saw him, and before he knew what was happening, Maria flew into his arms.

Clark wrapped Maria in a big hug. "Hey, honey, you look super! Where have you been all this time? I've been calling your room every day!"

Maria took off her sunglasses to show Clark that her eyes were ringed and puffy.

"I have been partying too much," she said. "I'm taking the day off to rest."

She put the sunglasses back on and stretched out on the lounge chair. Something about the careless sprawl of her arms and legs reminded Clark of a young Pamela Raven, only Maria's wild printed bikini was the tiniest one he had ever seen.

"Come sit with me," said Maria. "And tell me what's going on. Is everything cool with you?"

Clark told Maria about the Santa Monica house and his visits to Metropolis Studios and the Friedberg house.

"Oh, shit, I was there too, last night," said Maria. "I just wanted to swim, but the old man wanted to fuck in the pool. He thinks he's Rock Hudson. I hate having sex in water even with someone I *like*, because you know water is wet, but it's not a good lubricant. he looked like a hairy old walrus and he's clumsy, too. He almost drowned me. I guess it might have been funny to watch, only his wife caught us and she did not think it was funny at all. It was very ugly, Clark. She made me feel like such a whore and he never even called me to make sure I was okay or if I made it home. Clark, I was so drunk I was seeing double on the highway. I don't know how I got home at all. Allen Friedberg is killing me."

"That's the Friedberg way," said Clark.

"Yeah, but I'm not going to put up with it. Now that the movie is done, I'll leave Metropolis and I'll go independent — I'll get a new agent, too. My astrologer says it's a good time for me to take risks and make changes, so I'm going to. I'm not taking this shit any more. I'm new in the business and my press has been fabulous. The columnists say that every producer in town is looking for the new face, and they say I'm it! Why shouldn't I play for the big time? I know how to do it... and I will!"

"Wow," said Clark.

"Yes, wow," said Maria.

"So what's this I hear about you and a certain rock star having a hot affair?"

Maria laughed. "That's a good one. If you can call Bobby throwing up on me and passing out in my bed an affair, it's pretty sad. He's a junkie, you know. No, forget it. Allen Friedberg doesn't give me enough time alone to see anyone. He thinks he owns me. But that's over now. You know, I'm sort of glad Bambi caught us. It gives me some time to myself and I'm going to get away from Allen Friedberg."

"That sounds like a good idea. But what in the world is a junkie? Is that some Italian expression?"

"It's a heroin addict, like from opium."

"I know what heroin is," said Clark. He told Maria about the threats and pranks directed at Pamela and about the strange phone call he had received at Pamela's Santa Monica house.

Maria sat up, suddenly very interested. "I get a lot of people calling me and hanging up, ever since I've been in L.A. And I received something disgusting in the mail yesterday."

She wrinkled her nose.

"What was it?" asked Clark.

"It was a picture of me from a magazine, a full-length publicity shot of me in costume from *Amazon Planet*. Some freak actually jacked off on it and mailed it to me. It was gross!"

"What did you do with it?" asked Clark.

"I threw it out, what do you think?"

"Man, there sure are some sickos out here," said Clark. "Do you think those things that happened to you have anything to do with what's going on with Pamela Raven?"

"I really doubt it," said Maria. She smirked. "A lot of peo-

The Decorator

ple have reasons to hate her, and perverts have always been into me, so what else is new? Hey! I almost forgot — there's a party tomorrow night at the Chateau Marmont, and I'm going. All kinds of groovy people will be there — Tuesday Weld, Dennis Hopper, maybe even the Beatles — all the cool people will be there. Want to come?"

"Why not," said Clark, though he had no idea who any of the people Maria mentioned were, except the Beatles, and he doubted they would actually be there. He had heard that the Chateau Marmont was a wild place, and he wanted to check it out.

"I have to get to work, okay? Watch out for that strange fan mail!"

"Yeah, I'll wear gloves when I open my mail next time. And if any more ghosts call you, call me! I'll come over and do an old-country exorcism!" Marie waved goodbye to Clark and called a waiter over to order a Fernet Branca for her hangover.

Clark went into the main hotel building of the Bel Vista through the annoying electronic doors, which never seemed to work correctly.

He went down to the nightclub work site in the basement, but the workers were away having lunch. Back in the lobby, he rang Pamela Raven's suite from the front desk and when he got no answer he tried Mama's room. The elderly maid informed him that Pamela was getting her massage from the hotel masseuse, but that she expected her to return any minute.

The desk clerk told Clark where he could probably find the contractor for the nightclub, and Clark did so. The foreman and his men were lounging in the grass by the hotel's rear parking lot with empty paper bags, and naturally there were beer cans lying about. They reluctantly returned to the job, and Clark discussed Roland Lee's orders with the foreman, much to the man's distress.

"Look, don't kill the messenger," said Clark. "I don't like it any more than you do. Just do the best you can. Let's get those measurements. I'll order the additional supplies this time."

Clark hoped he could find a reasonable price for milled cherrywood and white plaster torchéres on short notice. If he couldn't, well, Roland Lee would have to pay… if Roland ever paid.

As Clark was writing measurements on his clipboard, a hotel messenger appeared, with an urgent message for Clark from Pamela Raven.

The note read: CLARK, PLEASE COME TO MY SUITE ASAP! PR

"Oh, Clark, I want you to be here when the police come."

Pamela Raven was trembling and out of breath. "I was waiting for you to get here before I call Hotel Security, too. I don't want to deal with those lumberjacks by myself."

"What happened?" asked Clark. The suite seemed normal, except that Mama and Miss Riley were huddled on the couch in fear.

"This!" Pamela led him to her dressing room. "This happened yesterday, as I told you, but I want you to see it for yourself."

She showed him several dresses, or what was left of them, still in the hotel dry cleaner's plastic wrappers. The garments were shredded beyond repair, as if someone had attacked them with a razor.

"And now this!" She marched to her bed and ripped the sheeting and quilt away. The pink sheets were marked with a dozen black footprints.

"What is that?" asked Clark.

"Ink, I believe. Black ink. And those prints are from a woman's shoe, size nine at least. Oh, and that's not all." Pamela pointed to the window treatments where the tasseled sash cord had been fashioned into nooses, hangman's nooses. The nooses hung menacingly against the clear California sky.

"I can't take it any more! I swear, I'm losing my mind. Mama's health is too frail for these kinds of shocks. I must send her back to New York to take care of Princess Lotus Blossom. Princess has diarrhea from all this stress, poor baby. I can't risk anything happening to Princess, and these people are capable of anything. And Miss Riley's going home too. I don't need a secretary out here; she can handle my correspondence just as easily in New York. And Miss Riley doesn't need any more hate mail attacking her reputation. Riley, you may call Security now."

"Hate mail?" Clark asked.

Pamela showed him four envelopes addressed by typewriter to Miss Riley, care of Pamela Raven. One contained a newspaper photo of Miss Riley standing next to Pamela Raven at a Cosmetique convention. Someone had drawn a mustache on Miss Riley's face in Magic Marker. The word "DYKE" was scrawled across the photo. The other envelopes contained notes with typed obscenities indicating exactly what their author thought Misses Raven and Riley did together in bed. The envelopes were postmarked in Los Angeles.

"You should show these to the police," said Clark.

"I know, but what if they get to the press? They'll have a field day. Whether it's true or not, people will want to think so. There are a lot of sick people out there, Clark, and I have to think of Miss Riley's reputation. Mine is shot to hell and I don't care, but she still has a future ahead of her."

Miss Riley was about to pick up the phone and dial Bel Vista Hotel Security when the telephone rang. She jumped back as if the sound had burned her.

"I'll get it," said Clark. He strode forcefully to the ringing phone and picked up the receiver.

Before he could say hello, a woman's voice hissed, "How do you like your new sheets?"

"We like them a lot," Clark answered coldly. "We like them so much, I'm considering your design for the Deirdre Dawn fall bed linens line. Why don't you come over right now and demonstrate your design technique? Then I'll demonstrate mine on your face. And then I'll hang you from your own ropes. How'd that be?"

The caller hung up, leaving Clark with the disturbing feeling that he'd heard her voice before. It was crazy, but the caller sounded like a cruel imitation of Pamela Raven herself, in one of her villainess roles from long ago. No wonder Pamela was frightened.

"Oh, Clark, darling, that was so... manly!" cried Pamela. "You're my hero!"

She kissed him lingeringly on his cheek.

Miss Riley made her call, and the room was soon filled with brown-uniformed Bel Vista security guards as well as Beverly Hills police officers asking questions as a police detective gathered evidence. Roland Lee came up, and when he viewed the damage his response was to fire the hotel manager, Mrs. Hauser, and the laundry staff at once. He directed that most of the kitchen and housekeeping staff be fired also for good measure, and he set his personnel director to work to hire immediate replacements. In addition, he thoroughly insulted the captain of Hotel Security and ordered him to tighten his watch or Lee would be forced to retain the services of another firm to do the job.

Roland Lee clearly enjoyed firing people, and that day he was so charged up he started firing the policemen before he realized they didn't work for him.

A new suite on the other side of the hotel was prepared for Pamela Raven. Though it was smaller than the one she currently occupied, and not custom-decorated by Clark Calloway, Pamela was glad to move.

The move was to be a secret, but, as Fate would have it, Pamela's new rooms were next door to Adela Morgan's suite, and the Broadway star broadcast her sympathy to the rafters when she invited Pamela in for a meatball. Pamela had even accepted the offer. Pamela believed Adela understood her dilemma. Adela encouraged Pamela to hold on! She said she would even use her pistol — or a six-shooter, if necessary — should the bandidos show up in the hall outside their suites.

Adela assured Pamela that she had great hearing, and could even hear what went on beyond the walls. If Pamela was being attacked, a shout for help or a bang on the wall was all that was necessary, and Adela would come a-running, six-shooter and all. But Adela warned Pamela of one thing. Her room must not be filled with roses, the likes of which gave her grave allergies. The mere sight of roses sent Adela into shivers and hives.

Clark asked Pamela if she would like to ring Gabe Taylor to tell him the latest turn of events, thinking she could use the company, and that perhaps Gabe would have some ideas as to who could be behind all this, and how to protect Pamela.

"Oh, no, my dear," said Pamela. "He'd be over here with his guns making a roaring mess. And besides, he's in hiding from me for now, I'm sure. That's why he didn't show up at Allen's today. I *know* him. Clark, the man actually expressed his *feelings* to me yesterday. Whenever he makes the mistake of doing that, he scares himself and runs for the hills. I need to give him some

The Decorator

time. Believe me, I know him well. And I'll be fine now. So long as Adela shuts her trap. Why don't you go over there and keep her quiet while we unpack?"

Clark did drop in on Adela for a moment. Adela was relaxing on her bed wearing a red quilted bedjacket and slippers. Her hair was in curlers and she was watching TV and drinking Almaden white wine.

"Bad break for Raven, huh?" she commented. "I'm not crazy about her, as you know, but I don't want anything bad to happen to her, ya know? Get this — that scumbag Doreen followed me to my door today. She was hinting around that maybe I'm the one who's got it in for Pamela! I tried to smack Doreen with my pocketbook, but she beat it fast. She'd better not print nothing about me in that column of hers or I'll have her fingers broken. Want a glass of wine? Help yourself. I just love these 'Beverly Hillbillies,' don't you?"

Adela pointed at the television.

Clark politely declined the wine and excused himself, saying he had only dropped by and he had to get back to work.

"Oh, speaking of work, I have a job for you," said Adela. "Nobody knows this yet, so don't tell anyone, but Barney and I are gonna get married! Isn't that great? I'm thrilled, just thrilled. We're gonna do it in June, and I want you to design our wedding. Not that weak-link Paul Hedges or the snob society broad you work for, just you. Because I like you, kid!"

Adela had obviously had a quick change of heart, mused Clark. Clark congratulated Adela, and thanked her for the offer, but he explained that he would have to discuss it with Paul Hedges, due to the ethics of the situation, since Adela was Paul's client. Adela shrugged and howled with laughter at the comedy on her television. Clark had never seen her so happy, though he did wonder why she was not wearing an engagement ring.

Roland Lee's offices were in chaos. The fired manager and his staff were packing to move out and crowds of unhappy fired employees were complaining and screaming in the reception area, besides threatening a sit-in. The Personnel Director and his assistant were on the phones desperately arranging interviews, and it seemed that, generally, no one knew who was who and who worked where, who was fired, and who could be rehired. The fact that most of the employees and new candidates were illegal Mexican immigrants further complicated matters. All of the employees suddenly seemed to be related to one another in some way, and mysteriously could no longer speak English. What a mess.

Fidel Castro could walk in here right now and get a job at the front desk, and nobody would be the wiser, thought Clark. Roland Lee's office was locked, and the hotelier was nowhere to be found. Clearly, Clark would not find a quiet spot to call suppliers in the Bel Vista offices that day. The clock on the office wall read four-thirty, so Clark decided to call it a day, not that anyone in the office would notice or care that the designer was leaving the hotel.

The Santa Monica house reeked of cigarette smoke. Clark hated that smell, and he quickly opened the back door and the living room windows to air the place out. At least the prospective tenants or whoever had smoked in the house had possessed the courtesy to throw away their cigarette butts and clean the ashtrays. It smelled as if a convention of chain smokers had roamed around the house for hours.

Clark had eaten a mediocre dinner in a quaint Santa Monica bistro called Chez Jay. The place was popular with fashionable young film business wannabees, and Clark had enjoyed flirting with his waitress. She had slipped him her telephone number with his check and whispered "I get off at ten." His bill even had the waitress's juicy cherry-red lip prints smeared on it, and her name, Tammi, circled with a heart dotting the 'i.' Clark doubted he would call her, as she was too young and tacky, but he didn't throw her number away.

The bottle of California Chardonnay he had purchased at a local liquor store was perfectly chilled and the wine was crisp and aromatic. Clark poured himself a second glass and relaxed on the sofa listening to a classical radio station for a while before he called Paul Hedges.

As Paul reported, the weather was miserable in New York, grey and icy. To top it all off, Paul's cat had died. Clark had not known that Paul owned a cat. He expressed his sympathy and Paul replied that the cat, a white Persian named Babette, had been quite old and he supposed it was her time to go, but he was miserable about it. Paul sounded very down; in fact, he barely responded to Clark's tales of adventure in California Hotel- and Movieland.

When Clark told him about Adela Morgan's request, Paul sighed and said, "It doesn't matter to me if you take that job, but it probably won't happen. June is five months away, and the wedding might not happen. Even if it does, marriages just don't work out these days. I don't know why people bother."

Finally, Clark asked Paul if everything was all right. Paul poured forth the story of his complete frustration with Deirdre Dawn and the decorating company that bore her name. Deirdre had definitely been diagnosed with senility by her doctors, and her family in upstate New York thought it best that she not be burdened with business. Deirdre needed care and supervision, and the family would care for her. She had let her family's chauffeur collect her, under threat of a nursing home, and would live out her days in her ancestral home in Tuxedo Park, having imaginary tea parties with the Duchess of Windsor.

The task of sorting out the debris of the clients' affairs Deirdre had left in her wake seemed overwhelming to Paul Hedges. Unfortunately, many of the firm's oldest customers had canceled as Deirdre Dawn's prestigious personage was no longer associated with the company. Paul added that he might also consider giving up, and move to Florida to play golf.

The frustrations Paul had dealt with were definitely getting to him. The fact that Deirdre would no longer be in the office offered some consolation, however. And the fact that Salvatore Caneletto could no longer reach Deirdre was a consolation and another thorn off the rosebush.

Clark managed to encourage Paul, somewhat, with prospects of new business in Los Angeles, and a few ideas of his own for expanding the company. He reassured Paul that he would return to New York soon and help him straighten out the mess, but he refrained from telling Paul about the complicated machinations of Roland Lee.

"And, Paul, I know it seems like a hardship to lose clients, but just think about how peaceful it will be to work without Deirdre around to make things hell. Not to mention the clients she scares away. We'll do better without her, and we'll even have a good time, you'll see!"

Paul did not sound entirely convinced, but he was in a better mood by the end of the conversation than he had been at the beginning.

Dannee Lou Baker's Georgetown number was busy, so Clark finished the bottle of wine and wrote some notes about the Vista nightclub. When he tried Dannee Lou again, she answered.

"Oh, my, Clark Calloway, I'm so glad it's you, sugar! I have to best news to tell you!" Dannee Lou excitedly told Clark that her husband had come out of his coma and there didn't seem to be any damage to his memory or functioning. She was crying with delight and relief because her husband would finally be coming home that week, after the hospital ran a few more tests.

"I'm sorry I'm cryin' like this, but I guess I'm cryin' tears of joy. I never let myself cry when Steve was in the coma, because it would have seemed like I was mourning him and giving up on him. All that time, I thought I'd go out of my mind with worry, but I never gave up hope. I never did!"

Clark said that was terrific news. It was inappropriate to gossip about Reggie and John at a time like this, but Clark was pleased when, after Dannee Lou finished her story about the hospital, what the doctors had said, how Steve had looked at her when he first opened his eyes, what he had said, and their emotional reunion, she brought up the subject of John and Reggie's romance.

"I guess you've heard about Johnny and Regina being an item and all? Well, those two are inseparable. They've been seen together all over town, and it's a real fine romance from what I hear. Johnny doesn't usually talk about his girls, but the other day he called me and asked me what would be a good gift for Reggie. He said he's crazy about her, can't stop thinking about her! He's even planning to bring her home to Dallas at Easter to meet our Mama, if Regina wants to go. Now that's serious!"

"Tell him Reggie likes gold jewelry," said Clark.

"I did suggest jewelry, but Johnny was afraid it would seem premature to give Regina something extravagant at this time. He doesn't want to scare her off. He's already sent her flowers, and candy for Valentine's Day, so I suggested some perfume or a nice book. What do you think?"

"Reggie loves gifts, and she'd probably like those things, but jewelry will never scare her, believe me. In fact, if she has any doubts about the guy, a gold necklace or earrings would make her very happy. And remember, Reggie may be a simple-style girl, but she does know "Diamonds Are a Girl's Best Friend."

"Didn't you date Regina at one time? Oh, dear, I hope I'm not being inconsiderate of your feelings! I'm sorry if I am — I guess Steve's so much on my mind, I've forgotten my manners," said Dannee Lou.

Clark assured her that it was quite all right and that he wasn't offended. He explained that he and Reggie had been friends for some time before their relationship and that they had never been serious about one another. Meanwhile, he wondered why John Downing was so goddamned perfect. Didn't the guy have any faults? His sister would know, of course, but she wasn't telling.

"I'm a little concerned because Johnny is flying to Vietnam to cover the war. He's been to dangerous places before, but, as his sister, I worry about him. I heard Regina asked to go along and George Myers won't let her go."

"Well, he shouldn't" said Clark. "Reggie has no business going into a war zone. She doesn't have the experience, and it would be irresponsible of CBS to let her go. And furthermore, whyever would she want to do a crazy thing like that? She can't be so much in love with John that she would put herself in danger, can she? Or is it her career? Is she trying to impress the station with her bravery? I hope not."

"I don't think it's either of those things, Clark. Johnny tells me Regina has a younger brother, Charlie, fighting in Vietnam and his unit is supposed to be in Saigon for the USO show, which Johnny will be covering. He says Regina's family has not heard from her brother in some time and the Army thinks he may be missing in action, though they don't know for sure. Many American prisoners have been taken by the Viet Cong and until Private Stowkowski is found or reports for duty, no one can say if he's AWOL or worse. I hope he's all right. I can understand why Regina wants to find out for herself. It's frustrating to be at home and feel helpless because the Army can't tell you anything. So she *does* want to go out of love, but not for

Johnny. She wants to go because she loves her little brother. Johnny wouldn't let her go, even if CBS did. Not that there aren't plenty of American women in Vietnam already, nurses mostly. Didn't you know that?"

"Yeah, I guess I did. I just didn't think about it. I wish Reggie would think about it before she tries to do anything foolish."

"I'm sure Johnny will do his best to get a message to Charlie if he can find him. And don't worry, the network isn't progressive enough to send a female staff member to the front, so our Reggie is safe. Now tell me all about Hollywood!"

Clark did, and he was very tired by the time he hung up the phone. On his way to bed, out of curiosity, he checked the master bedroom door. It was locked.

"Damn it!" Clark yelled. "What the hell is going on here?"

Tomorrow, he vowed, he would find out.

The Decorator

CHAPTER 21

The sound of a vacuum cleaner woke Clark Calloway at nine-thirty a.m. Blaming the wine, but nevertheless angry that he had overslept, Clark threw the blanket aside and leaped out of bed. He quickly donned a bathrobe and grabbed the *"Carmelita"* nametag from his dresser, avoiding its pin this time. He dashed out of his room in his bare feet to confront the maid.

The heavyset, middle-aged maid with reddish hair pushing her vacuum down the hall was not what Clark expected. Undaunted, Clark pounced upon her, flourishing the nametag.

"Carmelita!" he accused. "I believe you left something here!"

The maid's pale blue eyes squinted at the name tag.

"I'm not Carmelita," she said placidly, and continued her vacuuming.

Clark switched off the vacuum. "Well, one of you maids is Carmelita! And she left *this* in that bedroom, along with a mess in the bathroom, and I want to know who she is!"

"Sir, we don't have nametags. And I'm the only maid who cleans this house, ever since Miss Raven put it up for rent, though it doesn't seem like she really wants to rent it, does she?"

"Never mind that," Clark snapped. "Someone has been coming in here and using the master bedroom for his or her own purposes. Someone who has a key! That door has been locked twice since I've been staying here, and I certainly didn't lock it."

"The master bedroom, sir?"

"That's what I said! Miss Raven would be very, very displeased if I should have to inform her about it. And there have been other problems: bobby pins in the bathroom sink! Used tissues in the waste basket! Used glasses in the kitchen sink! And yesterday, someone was *smoking* in this house — I smelled it when I came home."

The maid looked at Clark as if he had two heads.

"I don't know what you mean, sir. None of the doors are ever locked. I'm not sure I have the key to it," she fumbled with a yarn loop of keys in her apron pocket. "As for the other things you mentioned, I haven't been here since Thursday before last, as I was told to be. I'm always right on schedule," she said proudly.

The maid walked heavily to the master bedroom door and tried the knob. "That's strange. It *is* locked. Are you certain you don't have a key?"

"Of course I don't have a key," said Clark, more calmly this time. "Listen, I apologize for being short with you, but some of the things that have happened in this house lately have put me on edge. I'm Miss Raven's decorator, and as her house guest, I feel I'm responsible for these premises. And Miss Raven is quite particular about the way her property is maintained, as I'm sure you know. My name is Clark Calloway, of Deirdre Dawn & Company. I'll be staying here for the next few weeks. And *you* are?"

"Mildred, Mildred Craig."

"Well, Mildred, I'm pleased to make your acquaintance. I'm glad you're not Carmelita, whoever she is. I was about to give her what for. Now, if you wouldn't mind, let's try a few keys and see if you have the one to this door."

"All right, Mr. Calloway."

The fourth key Mildred tried turned in the lock and she pushed the door open. Both Mildred and Clark gasped and took an involuntary step back from the sight before them. The room was a mess. Someone, or a few someones, had definitely slept in the bed, and recently. Two opened army-issue sleeping bags were crunched on the bed, and rolls of clothing had been used for pillows. Clothing spilled from an open duffel bag on the floor, women's clothing, Clark noticed. A man's long leather coat hung in the open closet and men's and women's shoes tumbled from a knapsack on the closet floor. A woman's shampoo bottle and messy toiletries were scattered on the bedside table next to an overflowing ashtray and the remains of a candle which had burned down and spilled on the mahogany table. The room reeked of cigarette smoke, grease, and stale

The Decorator

beer, probably because the carpet was littered with empty Chinese take-out cartons and beer cans. Someone had read and discarded the L.A. *Times* as well, and left the end of a joint in the ashtray.

"Well, I never!" gasped Mildred.

"What in hell…" Clark was amazed.

"Mr. Calloway, are you absolutely sure there is no one else staying in this house?"

"Absolutely! No one but me! Miss Raven would have told me if she had another guest, and she didn't. It looks like there was a teenage party in here, a delinquent teenage party, and Miss Raven doesn't know anyone like that, nor would she let teenagers into her home." Clark pried the candle stub from the table and saw, to his dismay, that the hot wax had stained the precious wood.

"What a mess," said Clark.

"Let me clean that up," said Mildred. "I'll have to call my company and report this." She bustled out to get her cart of cleaning supplies.

Automatically, Clark unscrewed the cap of the shampoo bottle and smelled the shampoo. It had a pleasant lemon scent. The cosmetics were mostly by Max Factor, and the containers were old and scuffed, as if they had been carried around for some time. When Mildred returned, Clark helped her clean the room, scooping the strange clothing temporarily into the closet. The mostly black and Mod-patterned clothing had no designer or care labels and could only be described as "Beatnik" style, and from its aroma he could tell it hadn't been washed in a while. The woman's slacks were not exactly petite and her worn shoes were fairly large.

"Mildred," he asked, "are you sure you haven't seen or heard anyone odd in this house, or in the neighborhood? Have you ever run into the real estate agent or seen anyone unusual looking at the house?"

Mildred paused and gazed thoughtfully out the window into the backyard.

"Those blinds are supposed to the closed, and so is the window!" She shut the window, which was open a few inches. "I wonder if some kids broke in here for the night to have a party. The house is empty… come to think of it, I did see a motorbike coming out of the driveway when I arrived this morning. I thought some cyclists were just using the driveway as a turn-around. Do you think..."

"How many people were on the motorcycle?"

"Well, two. A man and a woman. The man was driving."

"Did you see their faces?" asked Clark.

"No, I didn't. They had their helmets on, you know, with those face shields, and I wasn't really paying attention to them."

"What time was this?"

"Oh, it was about five to eight. I always arrive on the dot of eight. Do you think we should call the police?"

"Not just yet," said Clark. "Let me handle this. I have to consider Miss Raven's best interests at the time, and negative publicity could be harmful to her right now. But let's do call your company, and I'll speak with the real estate agent to find out what she thinks of all this. Maybe she will want to change the locks, and it might be a good idea to secure that window."

"Yes, sir," said Mildred. "What shall I do with all this stuff?"

"Bag it and I'll save it. If Miss Raven does wish to involve the police, the detectives may find evidence in these things. You *are* wearing rubber gloves? Good, keep them on. Don't touch anything with your bare hands."

Clark had already decided not to alarm Pamela with the news of this intrusion. She had enough to worry about and there was no point in upsetting her further over an incident which he would do everything he possibly could to prevent recurring.

Being a man of the design and decorating trade, the first thing Clark did was call a local antique shop and arrange to have the mahogany bedside table refinished as soon as possible. Clark knew Pamela Raven would okay the expenditure, once she knew what had been going on at Santa Monica.

When he called the cleaning service and the realtor, he down-played his serious suspicions and emphasized that he would inform Miss Raven himself about the teenage prank, as he called it. Neither the cleaning company manager nor the real estate agent had seen or heard of any problems in the Raven house, and they were each quick to assure Clark that

The Decorator

their companies' representatives were above suspicion or blame.

The realtor, a Mrs. Morrissey, was also the president of her company, and she informed Clark that she had not shown the Raven house to anyone during the past week. Apparently the rent Pamela Raven was asking was far too high for most tenants to consider paying for the location or space. She was hoping only to hear from some prospective tenant who would pay the high rent for the *panache* of living in the home of one of Hollywood's most famous stars. Mrs. Morrissey was alarmed by the break-in, if that was what it was, and she agreed to send a locksmith over at once.

After Clark showered and dressed, and the maid finished her cleaning and left, he made coffee and toasted an English muffin. He went back to the master bedroom and dumped out the clothing the strangers had left behind. Clark thought he might discover something. Close examination of the items, however, revealed no clues as to their owners. There were no telephone numbers, matchbooks, or business cards in the pockets; there were no clothing labels. All Clark found were some gum wrappers, wads of tissue, and a few prophylactic rubbers. The last items Clark found were in a pocket in a man's black leather coat: a pair of black Ray-Ban Wayfarers' sunglasses. In a small black carrying case, Clark found some ladies' cosmetics, including the stub of a theatrical grease stick labeled "Indian Princess." The color of the stick was similar to that of the grease paint he had found on the tissues in the bathroom waste basket. Further investigation revealed that under the shoes in the knapsack was a black wig.

"Aha!" Clark announced. So the people in the bedroom were the same people who had been leaving annoying traces of themselves since Clark had arrived. He wondered if they were the motorcyclists, and if they had been the same bikers who had caused him to have a near-accident in his car two nights before. Clearly, whoever had left these clothes and the Ray-Bans behind intended to return. They must have left in a hurry. Perhaps they had arrived after Clark went to sleep. Could they have been bold enough to hide in the room while Clark was in the house sleeping? Clark decided to enlist Maria's help. Clark never traveled in Beatnik circles, but Maria might know people who did, and she might have heard something along the road or back road which could give him a lead about who was freaking out Pamela Raven as well as Pamela Raven's house.

Maria was in her room at the Bel Vista. "Hi, Clark. I was just going to call you! The strangest thing is happening."

"Well, you're not the only one dealing with strangeness. You go first, and then I'll tell you mine."

"My underwear is missing," said Maria. "All my underwear has been taken, my bras, garter belts, panties, everything."

"What do you mean, your underwear is missing?"

"Everything! Everything is gone. Nothing is in my dresser. Even the dirty underwear that was in my laundry bag is gone."

"Whew, that is bizarre. When did it happen? Is anything else missing?"

"I guess the underwear was taken yesterday or last night when I was out finishing some last retakes for good old Allen Friedberg. Nothing else is missing, but it's creeping me out to think someone was here in my room or maybe while I was sleeping and now he has my underwear! Nothing is sacred."

"Well, when I tell you what I found in one of the bedrooms this morning, you may want to come over here and look for your things, panties included!" said Clark.

"What?" asked Maria.

Clark told her about the Santa Monica mystery intruders, their leftovers and their smelly clothes. He tried to explain to Maria that he did not mean to joke about her underwear. He knew her grasp of English did not always include humor. Maria said she would drive to the house right away. Clark hoped she didn't really think her underwear was in Santa Monica.

"Maria, now is not the best time to come. I have some work to to this morning."

"Okay. How about this afternoon? And after I look at the leftovers — even if my panties are not among the stuff — do you want to go shopping with me on Rodeo? I want to buy a new dress for the party tonight. The *Hollywood Reporter* and *Photoplay* might do a cover story about me and my new picture. I want to look great at the party."

"That sounds okay, but I really want to take a break this

The Decorator

afternoon and get to the beach. I need some tanning up and it looks like a sunny, warm day — I haven't been to the beach since I've been here. Why don't you come over around four o'clock? We'll still have time for shopping, or dinner if you'd like. And you'll still have time to get into that party dress and make the scene."

Maria agreed, and Clark took care of his follow-through on the Bel Vista nightclub project by telephone. There wasn't time to explore a new source for fabric, so he simply called F. Schumacher to place an order for a thousand yards of diaphanous voile. After all, F. Schumacher had the fabric in stock and could ship immediately and on open account. Clark hated using the Deirdre Dawn charge for Roland Lee. He wondered if the firm would ever be reimbursed, knowing the Bel Vista's credit history. But time was of the utmost importance if the club was to open on schedule. He needed everything delivered to the Bel Vista immediately. He would inspect everything as it arrived. He spoke with the contractor at the Vista to hear how the work was progressing, and it sounded as if everything was going smoothly.

Clark hung up the phone and was about to put on his bathing trunks, a Speedo, when the phone rang again. Fearing it was Roland Lee with some petty plan to spoil his day, Clark was tempted to let the phone ring. But what if it was the evil caller? Or the intruders calling to make sure he wasn't home? What if they were one and the same? Clark leapt for the phone.

It was Adela Morgan, calling on behalf of Barney Higgins. They were beginning to worry about Pamela Raven. She hadn't shown up on the set for a ten a.m. call, and she wasn't in her room at the Vista. Anyway, Adela herself had seen Pamela get into her limo this morning at 8:30. Was she with Clark?

"No, Adela, she's not with me. Did you try Gabe Taylor?"

"The gatehouse guards called in to say that Gabe has driven onto the lot. He was alone. Friedberg will shit when he finds out we've lost a whole morning's shooting time! Do me a favor, sweetheart: tell Pamela to call Barney right away if you hear from her. And tell her she's in BIG TROUBLE! Okay? Bye, hon! Just tell Raven to get her ass on the set!"

A few minutes later a call came from Gabe Taylor asking Clark when he had last seen Pamela. Clark told Gabe about the events that had occurred at the Bel Vista the previous evening.

"That doesn't sound good. Even if Pam was very upset, she'd never miss a call. There's something bad about this," Gabe said.

"Did the limo driver check in with the hotel yet? Did you try Miss Riley or Mama?" asked Clark.

"The hotel desk clerk said the car is still out, according to the garage attendant. And Pam's assistants checked out this morning. Guess they went back to New York. This sounds crazy, I know, since it's completely out of character for Pamela Raven to miss a shoot, but I know a few places where Pammy goes when she's feeling down. I'm going to look for her. I have a feeling about where she might be. Do you think you can stick around in case she calls you?"

Clark said he would.

He didn't have long to wait. At noon a call came from Pamela Raven. She was out of breath and distraught. She gave Clark directions and told him to hurry, *please*. Then she hung up.

Alarmed and not knowing what to think, Clark jumped into his car and drove about sixty-five miles northeast towards the San Bernardino Mountains, as Pamela had instructed him. As he neared the mountains, the landscape became dry, hilly and deserted. When he came upon the ruins of the old Arrowhead Park Hotel, a hotel Deirdre Dawn had once decorated, Clark took a left on a side road and drove for about half a mile until he found a small gas station. Pamela Raven stood by the pay phone, nervously hopping from one stockinged foot to the other. She was hatless, her face was dirty, and her clothes were rumpled. When Clark stopped the car, she ran over and jumped into the passenger seat before he could get out.

"Drive. Drive. Drive as fast as you can," she said. "Just get me out of here. Take me back to the Vista."

"I have to get some gas, then we'll go. I didn't stop en route to refill," said Clark. "How in the world did you get all the way out here? And where are your shoes? Everyone's worried about you, including Adela and Barney, to say nothing about Gabe and Allen Friedberg."

"I'll tell you in a minute. Just fill that tank and get me out of here as fast as you can!"

During the drive, Pamela unwound and told Clark her tale — what had happened and how it all had happened. She had called for her limousine and it was waiting to take her to the studio as usual. Strangely, the driver was not her regular man; he was another Spanish-looking driver who told her that her usual Ben did not come to work today and he was the replacement.

"I did think it was odd, Clark, because the driver didn't sound Mexican, and he was unusually tall. You know, I've lived out here, and it's hard to conceal the Mexican look. I didn't like the appearance of him. His hair was too long and too greasy-looking, and when I asked him why he was taking me in a closed car instead of my usual convertible, he didn't even answer me or nod or indicate he had even heard me... but I knew he heard me!"

Pamela described how the driver at first took her toward Metropolis Studios, but when he got on the freeway, he drove past the usual exit.

"I banged on the glass partition between us, but he wouldn't open it. He just drove faster and faster, and I knew I was in trouble when he got off the freeway and started driving north. Then he was really speeding, and all of the drivers know I don't allow anyone to drive faster than 45 miler per hour. My heart was pounding so hard, I thought it would fly out of my chest! It would have been impossible for me to open the door and jump out. The car was speeding at 90 miles an hour, and who can jump out of a car at that speed without being killed on the highway?"

The driver had taken his captive out into the desert, where Pamela was certain he planned to kill her.

"I have never been robbed, or raped, thank God, or even had my pocketbook stolen, and I suppose he might have been trying to kidnap me, but my only thought was 'He's going to try to kill me.' I don't know why, but there it was. I was terrified, but then I started thinking and getting ready to plan a scheme to be released. I was going to be a heroine somehow — I just didn't know how — at that moment, in that speeding car. My mind grew very calm, and then I thought, 'I don't know what this bastard is going to pull, but I'll beat him at it. He's not smart enough to conquer me. I'm Pamela Raven, unconquerable queen of 148 major motion pictures, and I'm not finished yet!"

Pamela had tried the doors again and found them to be electronically locked. The driver had laughed when she tried pushing on the door handles... Pamela recalled that he had laughed in a sickening and menacing way. Eventually he pulled behind the abandoned hotel at Lake Arrowhead.

"It was so strange, so terribly strange how desolate that old hotel is now. The wind was blowing sand and dust about and the Arrowhead was just sinking into the ground, like it's collapsing from inside. There was absolutely no one about. It was like a ghost hotel. I could have screamed my head off and no one would have heard. But the strangest thing of all is that I know the Arrowhead Park Hotel like I know my own home. I was there when it was built, you know, and I was there for the opening night party in '39. And I was there over and over again with Gabe Taylor and with my husbands as well."

"Deirdre Dawn did that hotel," said Clark. His mind flashed on the photos of the Arrowhead Park Hotel he had seen at the office. "But tell me what happened next."

"Well, that hideous man let me out of the car, pulled and shoved me out, I'd say, but before he did that, I saw that he took some rope from the trunk, and he had a pistol stuck in the waistband of his pants. After he pulled me from the car, he pushed me ahead of him down the path toward the hotel's old kitchen entrance. I knew he was going to tie me up, so I had to do something quickly."

Like a perfect actress, Pamela had informed her captor that she had to answer an urgent call of nature and that, as a lady, she demanded privacy.

"He told me to make use of the dry old shrubs behind the hotel, full of nasty cactuses and probably snakes, too, and naturally I refused. I insisted on using one of the abandoned baths intended for hotel guests. And I absolutely refused to let the brute come into the bathroom with me. There's one good thing about growing old: when you yell at a man, no matter how rough he is, you remind him of his mother and he becomes embarrassed. Well, my trick worked. I simply escaped out the door which led from the bathroom into the suite, not into the hall where he waited for me."

The Decorator

"Then what happened? Did he follow you?"

"Of course he did, but as I said, I know that old hotel intimately, and he doesn't. I had to take my shoes off in order to run and I lost my hat along the way. I tore my stockings climbing into a dumbwaiter, too."

"You climbed into a dumbwaiter? How did you know it was safe?"

"I didn't, Clark, but in the old days things were built to last. I chanced that! That's one thing I can say for Deirdre Dawn. She always used products built so they would last. Why, her old green doors look as good today as they did in 1939! It was one of the dumbwaiters that lifted hot trays from the kitchen to the upstairs halls, where the room service people wheeled their trays into the rooms, and removed the dirty dishes. I operated the cables by hand: see how greasy my hands are? I must look frightful! I rode down to the first floor and waited. The dumbwaiter door was stuck on that side, or maybe there was a latch, I don't know. I could hear that terrible man looking for me in the kitchen, making a terrible racket, throwing pots and pans about and cursing in Spanish or Greek or something.

"After what seemed like hours, I heard a car drive away, so I rode the dumbwaiter up to the second floor. I hid behind the decaying draperies in the old ballroom, the same ballroom where the Marx Brothers performed and Judy Garland sang 'Come Love' on opening night... I danced with young Doug Fairbanks all night...

"Anyway, I hid among the drapery folds and I peeked out the window. Sure enough, that man was driving away in the hotel limousine. My, those draperies were dusty! And mildewed! They were chewed by mice, too. I'll never get the smell out of my hair."

"Did you leave the hotel then?"

"I waited for a while, about an hour or so, to make sure that man wasn't coming back. I didn't want to go down the main road he had taken, this one we're on now, because he might have been waiting for me to do that. Besides, I didn't see any signs of life along that road on the way out, and believe me, I was looking! I walked along that dusty little side road until I found this gas station. It was such a long walk, and I didn't have my shoes, and I never saw another car or truck. I thought

I'd never find civilization again. But now here you are! You've rescued me!"

"Yes, and we must go straight to the police."

"Oh, no, we can't. We mustn't. I'm a movie star. I'm not going anywhere looking like this. The police can wait until I resemble Pamela Raven!"

Clark drove Pamela back to the hotel and waited for Gabe Taylor to arrive while Pamela showered. When Gabe came in, he told Clark he would handle things from here. The actor had friends at the police department, and he knew who to call to make certain the matter was handled in the right way, the discreet way. Gabe also promised to have a few words with Roland Lee about the security and screening of his garage personnel. When Clark saw Gabe Taylor's face dark with anger, he was glad he was not Roland Lee.

If someone had stalked and stolen Pamela, the same person or persons could be after Maria, Clark thought. After all, the disappearance of all of a movie star's panties from her hotel room had to be masterminded by someone who knew the hotel and knew Maria's comings and goings. But what was the connection between Pamela and Maria? Why was no one stalking Adela or Anne Bates? Clark laughed out loud at the idea of anyone stalking Adela. That person would get a knuckle sandwich or a gallon bottle of Almaden cracked over his head in short order.

Maria was willing to go with Clark, but she wanted to take her car. Clark had admired the fire-engine red Fiat, and he agreed to drop off the rental if she would let him drive. On the way, he told Maria about Pamela's latest adventure.

Maria's eyes grew so wide she looked like an owl.

"*Santa Maria!* I didn't know Pamela was such a brave *bella donna.*" She continued in Italian in her astonishment.

Back at the Santa Monica house, Maria had an interpretation of the odd clothing: "These two are lovers, it is true, but he does not love her."

"What? How do you get that?"

Maria sighed impatiently.

"He does not leave his clothes here. See, these are his old shoes, Italian, very nice. Anyone who wears Italian shoes does not want to wear old ones. And besides, it's my intuition." She smiled.

"Do you 'intuit' anything else?"

"Yes."

Maria stared into the lenses of the black sunglasses in her hands as if they were crystal balls. "He is a Negro. My astrologer told me I will soon meet a Negro. I hope he's handsome…"

"Oh, give me a break, M.! Leave your astrologer out of this. What makes you think this guy is a Negro?"

"His sunglasses, of course. Only Black Panthers wear Wayfarers." Maria sniffed a blouse and wrinkled her nose.

"She's insecure, but cheap. She wants to be hip, but she isn't."

"How do you know that?"

"Silly *bambino*, these are last year's styles. And she did not buy these clothes, she sewed them, see?" Maria showed Clark a hand-stitched hem. "And her makeup is awful!"

"Why the greasepaint, do you suppose? And the wig?"

"I don't know, but unless she is trying to make herself look tan, I would say she disguises herself. What ugly shoes she wears! Let's get out of this room — this stuff is scaring me. What are you wearing to the party tonight?"

Clark had forgotten all about the party, and he had given no thought to his outfit.

Maria was unimpressed with the contents of his closet. "Ugh, look at all these boring brown shoes. So 1950s! Don't you have any boots? These shirts are all — blah! And your slacks are so square. Clark nobody at the party is going to trust you or even talk to you, if you wear these clothes. No, no! Put that tie back! Don't you dare wear a tie, *Signor*. I will take you shopping now. Please! Please let me take you. It will make me so happy."

Clark relented, though he made Maria promise: "No hiphuggers, no frilly shirts, and absolutely no medallions."

CHAPTER 22

The doorbell rang just when Clark and Maria were ready to leave to go shopping. It was the locksmith the real estate agent had sent over to change the locks.

"Go ahead and change the locks," Clark said. "But it won't do much good if they come in through the bedroom window."

"Isn't that a song?" asked Maria.

"What song?" asked Clark.

"She came in through the bedroom window…" Maria sang. "It's the Beatles."

"I think it was the bathroom window," said Clark. "Whichever window it is, we should have it locked, or they'll probably come back in."

The locksmith, a wheezing, white-haired Irishman, consulted a slip of paper from the pocket of his coveralls. A key & lock was embroidered over the pocket.

"I don't have any window locks with me," he said. "Mrs. Morrissey didn't say nothin' about that. I'd have to get them from my office, and I can't do that until tomorrow. Before I change this front door lock, I need the owner's signature."

He held the form out for Clark.

"I'm not the owner," said Clark, "but I am Pamela Raven's decorator and I'm authorized to sign for all services."

"Nope. No can do," said the locksmith.

"Clark, why don't you call Pamela at the Vista and tell her what's going on?" said Maria.

"You know, I've been thinking I should do that," said Clark. "I know she's had a terrible shock today, and I'd rather not disturb her further, but maybe it's time she knew about all the other monkey business that's happening around her. And I suppose I should have her permission before I change the locks on her front door."

He dialed the Bel Vista and the operator rang Pamela Raven's suite, but there was no answer. When Clark told the

The Decorator

operator who he was, she informed him that Miss Raven had left a message for him at the front desk. The desk clerk told him that Pamela Raven, Adela Morgan, Gabe Taylor, and Allen Friedberg had quickly gone on location in Mexico, just over the border in Tijuana; and that Miss Raven had authorized Clark Calloway, and no one else, to enter her suite. She had left her key for Clark in order that he check on her suite while she was gone, to make certain nothing "unusual" occurred. Pamela and company would return in three days, on Saturday, in time for the Legendary Ladies Gala and party, to be held at the Bel Vista's new disco.

Clark thanked the desk clerk and was about to hang up, when she told him he had still another message, from Roland Lee. The materials for the nightclub had arrived, had been approved by Mr. Lee, and Mr. Lee could not wait to see the blue-sequined fabric stretched across the walls. Lee thought the place would be dazzling, and so original. Construction was proceeding on schedule. Mr. Lee would, however, need Mr. Calloway to inspect the project on Friday, especially finishing touches such as candle holders and the bright red roses. Mr. Lee was unavailable for the rest of the day, Clark was told. The hotelier had appointments with theatrical and music agents, union representatives, technicians, and the hotel caterer to finalize plans for the tribute evening, and Mr. Lee would be in meetings until late that night.

The locksmith was awaiting Clark's word, but he had packed his bag and was evidently poised to depart. Judging from his red nose and the way the locksmith kept looking impatiently at his watch, Clark supposed the man was late for Happy Hour at some local tavern, maybe the Blarney Stone.

"Look," said Clark, "I know you need the form signed and I'm signing it now. Mrs. Morrissey instructed you to change the locks on this door and you are in her employ, are you not? I can telephone Mrs. Morrissey now and verify that for you. I'm sure you understand that we have an emergency situation here, involving the safety of Miss Pamela Raven and her property, and I suggest you do the job you were hired to do, or I'll have to speak with your supervisor."

The locksmith was unfazed.

"No, *you* look, buddy. I've never seen you before in my life and neither has Mrs. Morrissey. You look like a kid to me, and a smart-ass kid. How do I know you and the little blonde cha-cha-cha here are even supposed to be in here?" He nodded to Maria's tits. "Decorator? What the hell is that? Some fancy word for painter? You say you work for Miss Raven, but how do I know that? Until I hear from Miss Raven herself, I ain't changin' the locks. And by the way, I *am* the boss!" The locksmith, now red in the face and wheezing heavily, stood nose to nose with Clark, glaring at him.

"Well!" Clark took a step back. He was shocked and frustrated. He had dealt with tradesmen before, workmen who may have resented him for his youth and some who perhaps even disrespected his profession. This locksmith, however, who wore an American flag pin on his lapel, had probably served in World War II, and didn't like taking orders from younger guys, particularly those he looked upon as fancy decorators. He clearly believed that he was right and no one would convince him otherwise. Nor was he finished with Clark:

"And furthermore," he shook a thick, chubby finger in Clark's face, "I know Miss Raven and I know how fussy she is about her house. That woman hits the roof if anything goes wrong. I'm not doing a damn thing unless she says so, no matter what Mrs. Morrissey says. That old dame talks nothing but nonsense. Women! They got no business running a business. Talk, talk, talk, that's all they do! You look like one of them girls yourself, with your fancy suit and your nose in the air. Why don't you get a haircut? Decorator, hmmph! Like hell you say. You oughtta be over in Vietnam defending your country, not prancin' around here telling working men what to do. No, sir! If anyone catches hell from Pamela Raven, it ain't gonna be me."

Clark and Maria watched the locksmith get into his truck and drive away.

"Man, what a pig," said Maria. "He reminds me of my Uncle Nunzio."

"Never mind him," said clark. "There's nothing you can say to guys like that. I wonder how he stays in business. I'm calling another locksmith to come tomorrow. I'm tired of waiting around for these people. That guy did remind me of one

The Decorator

thing: I've got to drop that bedside table off to be refinished. Pamela would have a fit if she knew it was stained, and I can't say I'd blame her. There's a good antique shop on Main Street."

"Then can we go shopping?" asked Maria.

"Let's get a bite to eat first. I'm starved."

After Clark had dropped the table off at the restorer's shop in Santa Monica, they had lunch in one of the popular sidewalk cafés on Beverly Drive. While they were eating lunch, passersby and even people in cars slowed down to stare at Maria.

"What's wrong?" Maria asked. "Do I have some egg in my teeth or food on my face?"

"No," Clark said. "You're the new girl in town. Your picture is in the papers now, and you're going to be famous, remember?"

"Oh!" Maria laughed. "I forgot. I'm used to *men* staring at me, but now I'm thinking: what do all these people want?"

"Get used to it," Clark said.

The café was convenient to the shops on Rodeo Drive where Maria spent far too much money. Clark tried to pay for his own purchases, but Maria seemed to have an account at every shop, and she insisted that everything be charged to her. The salespeople in the shops were rude and standoffish to Clark until they recognized Maria. Usually someone whispered, and there were stares from the other customers, and then Maria was surrounded by fawning salespeople who couldn't do enough for her. Two teenage girls who were shopping for shoes asked Maria for her autograph, which she shyly gave them. Maria didn't look much older than they, and she was surprised and flustered by all the attention.

When Maria was satisfied that Clark would be dressed in the height of fashion for the party, she bought a delicately crocheted white minidress for herself, a pair of hot pink and yellow paisley stockings, and enormous candy-colored hoop earrings. She decided she needed a new pair of sunglasses and a white leather cropped jacket as well. When they were finished the tiny red Fiat was loaded with boxes and bags, and Maria was squealing with excitement as they drove away.

"Let's drop the stuff off in my room — we can change later — and let's have a cocktail or two at the Vista bar. And then we'll go to the PARTY!" she shouted.

"Good idea," said Clark.

It was very late when Maria drove Clark home from the party. She had smoked a great deal of pot and could not stop giggling, but she said it was safer if she drove, because she had not been drinking the champagne. She feared champagne would make her fat: too much sugar in the bubbles. Clark, on the other hand, had downed quite a few glasses of bubbly, as the loud music and strange people made him nervous at first. After several drinks, he didn't mind the blaring rock and roll or the bizarre guests as much. The party certainly was strange. The suite at the Chateau Marmont was decorated like a Chinese opium den. It was filled with smoke and scantily-clad men and women dancing and talking a mile a minute. Both sexes favored velvet and leather, and some of the men had such long hair, Clark at first thought they were women. Neglecting to bathe seemed to be in fashion, and body odor competed with the thick incense and scented candle smoke in the air, but somehow all of this worked at Chateau Marmont, with its interior so reminiscent of early Hollywood. Clark looked about at the Renaissance-style paneling, the high ceilings, the oak floors, the big paneled doors, and the wrought iron and bronze chandeliers. How he wished he could get his hands on the property. He could decorate it in the spirit of San Simeon — in the spirit of early Hollywood — when Theda Bara, Fay Wray, and Valentino reigned.

That spirit was needed at the present event; some of the women were so ugly and overdressed that Clark had asked Maria who they were, and she had told him they were men: "Drag queens," she said. Clark had never heard of such a thing, but he found them quite entertaining when he noticed they were impersonating old movie stars, and doing it quite well. There was even a Pamela Raven lookalike, who had obviously studied her old movies in detail. A huge queen in a Harlow-white satin gown and heels and a platinum wig offered Clark a snort of white powder from a compact mirror in her satin-gloved hand, but Clark declined. He didn't know what effect the white powder had, and he worried that it might be the fairy dust that made men want to impersonate ideal movie-star womanhood. In general, Clark distrusted the little

The Decorator

colored pills that some people popped like candy. Ups, downs, all-arounds — what did it matter? Some people took handfuls of pills to calm themselves down from the pills they had taken to pep themselves up. All that work to end up where you started, Clark thought. It's not worth it.

Two long-haired girls dressed like gypsies had floated over to snort the Harlow queen's powder. The blonde and the brunette both spoke speedily and simultaneously, and the drag queen had shouted, "I'm hitting my fifth day, and it's marvelous!"

Her fifth day without sleep, apparently. The three of them chimed in at once to inform Clark about their finances, talents, jealousies, preferences, prejudices, quirks, ideas, competitions, and diets, including what to eat before an audition (filet mignon, rare). The drag queen and the brunette got into an argument about what to eat for breakfast the day you sign a contract, and Clark began laughing. It was too ridiculous. The blonde joined in, and they were still arguing as they drifted away toward the bar.

The party was certainly entertaining. Most of the young people seemed to be related to or sleeping with someone famous, and Maria filled Clark in on all the details. Maria had introduced Clark to a young director, Eric Von Halst, who was eager to meet him. Von Halst insisted that Clark call him Eric, and he told Clark that he had wanted to meet him since he heard that the decorator from New York's Deirdre Dawn & Company was in town.

Eric was interested in bringing back the Thirties Baroque style of film noir for a modern detective series featuring a young detective who rides a motorcycle. Of course, everyone knew Deirdre Dawn was famous for Thirties style on a grand scale. After all, she had decorated Arrowhead Springs, and was famous for doing the Fairmount in Frisco, too! Would Clark be interested in designing sets for the films?

"It all depends if I can get the backing to make my movie," Eric explained. "But I know I'll get the money sooner or later. And until I do, it's more fun to be with people who are *doing* things, don't you think?"

Clark knew Eric Von Halst would have no trouble finding support for his project. He had that special something — you might call it energy — that appealed to young as well as old. And besides that energy, Eric Von Halst was the son of the legendary hostess and Hollywood columnist Edie Von Halst, and many in Tinseltown were terrified of her. As befitted his royal lineage, Eric Von Halst was interesting to look at, Clark thought. With his longish black hair and small silver hoop earring, Eric was attractive in almost a feminine way, although his deep voice and masculine movements made him seem straight. Or was he? Like many of the men at the party, Eric wore fashionably tight, hiphugging bellbottoms; his were striped in grey and navy. His matching navy satin shirt was open to the navel, showing his strong and hairless tanned chest.

Eric lit a joint and passed it to Clark, and as they smoked and talked, Eric's eyes grew larger and greener by the minute. There was something familiar about his long lashes and his wide mouth, and though Clark couldn't think of whom he was reminded, the familiarity made him feel comfortable and relaxed with Eric. Clark guessed that Eric was straight, as women had been climbing all over him, kissing him and dancing erotically with him before Maria had dragged him over to meet Clark. When Eric sat closer to talk to Clark, Clark did not mind. Maria, flushed and breathing hard from dancing, soon fell into the Marmont's brocade and tasseled silk pillows beside them and collapsed, leaning her head on Clark's shoulder.

"Don't you think she looks like a young Lana Turner?" Eric asked Clark. "Look at her color, such *clarity*, and she has that *starkness* of beauty, don't you think?"

"Yeah, yeah," Maria mocked. She draped herself across their legs, with her head on Eric's crotch, her blonde hair contrasting with the grey and navy of Eric's trousers.

"You know, it's funny. Everything becomes distorted when something you really want is sitting in your lap," Eric said.

"You bet it does," Maria said. She arched herself up until she was perched on Clark's knee. She began kissing his neck from collarbone to ear.

As if on signal, Eric's slender thigh slid over Clark's leg, and his arm draped around Clark's neck. It was surprising, but Clark didn't mind. His head was spinning, the music was throbbing, and he felt good. The two beauties pressing on either side leaned across him to kiss each other, and Clark closed his eyes, as two pairs of lips joined his.

"Clark Calloway!" a voice interrupted, an annoying, nasal voice. Clark looked up and Maria slipped off him and onto Eric's lap. Clark saw a short, young, but almost completely bald man with a large nose and thick glasses bearing down on him.

"Hey, Clark Calloway! It's you, isn't it?"

It was Steve Solinsky, Holly Raven's ex-husband. Clark recognized the face from a photo Holly had shown him last year, and he wondered if he was having a nightmare. He also recalled seeing several photos of Steve in Pamela Raven's family picture album, and of course Clark could never forget the face that Pamela had described in evil terms. Steve Solinsky was not the "son-in-law" Pamela Raven ever wanted.

Steve introduced himself and sat down next to Clark in the space Maria had quickly vacated. What an anti-aphrodisiac, Clark thought. As if in agreement, Maria and Eric got up and headed for the dance floor. Steve began to tell Clark his life story. He was the production manager for an adventure film being made by Metro, and he had run into Pamela Raven on the lot. She had instructed Steve to introduce himself to Clark, if he ever should encounter him, so wasn't this a spot of luck?

Clark disliked phony British accents and Steve Solinsky had one. Reluctantly, and only for the sake of Pamela Raven, and good manners, Clark followed Steve Solinsky to the bar. Clark somehow could not believe Pamela would want the two to meet, but he went along with Steve's story regardless. They had a drink or two and traded stories about the Ravens, auntie and niece, which was amusing for Clark, for about five minutes. Having once been married to Holly Raven (Pamela Raven's niece) was still Steve Solinsky's claim to fame, if not success in getting on to the lot at Metro. All of Steve's stories ended with the same conclusion: Holly was neurotic, a major neurotic; Holly was desperately crazed. Clark couldn't agree more, so he told Steve the censored version of his own initial encounter with Holly. Before leaving, Steve placed a business card on the bar in front of Clark and invited him for tennis, any time soon.

Not too soon, Clark thought. Not ever, if he had anything to say about it. He could tell after a few minutes with certain people that he didn't want to spend any more time with them, and Steve Solinsky was one of those people. Clark intentionally left Steve's business card on the bar.

It was time to go home. Even if Eric weren't interested, if Clark followed his impulses, he would probably return to fondling Eric in public and he might even go home with him one day. What a story that would make for the gossipers. Clark decided he had had enough of everything and if Maria wanted to stay at the Chateau and play games he would call a cab. It turned out Maria was also ready to leave and when she went to fetch her white leather jacket, Eric slipped his business card into Clark's hand.

Eric smiled crookedly and whispered in Clark's ear, "Call me! Keep the card as our first souvenir. The unlisted home phone number is on the back." Eric gently patted Clark's ass and turned to wink at him before he walked away.

Clark looked around and was relieved to see that everyone at the party was so involved in their own affairs that no one seemed to notice him. He slipped Eric Von Halst's card into a safe place — the inside pocked of his jacket — the pocket with the button.

"Do you think Eric looks a little like Reggie?" Clark asked Maria on the way home.

"Reggie? Not really." said Maria.

"He does, Maria. I've been trying to think who he reminds me of ever since you introduced us. Eric looks so much like Reggie, he could be her twin brother."

"Brother, sister, whatever you say," said Maria. "Do me a favor and give me a cigarette. They're in my purse."

She turned into Pamela Raven's block. "Hey, did you leave the house lights on?"

"No," said Clark.

Maria pulled into the driveway and they could see that Pamela Raven's windows were faintly lighted.

"Shit!" said Maria, braking just in time to avoid hitting a black motorcycle parked in the garage.

"Okay, this is it," said Clark. "Someone is in the house and

The Decorator

we're going to nail him. Wait in the car, or you can drive somewhere and call the police. I'm going in."

"I'm going in, too," said Maria. "Don't leave me here. Two is better than one. We'll go in together and surprise the creeps."

The front door was unlocked. The kitchen lights shone through the counter window used for serving the living room bar. Tall, lighted candles in brass holders sat on the coffee table, and two motorcycle helmets were on the bar. Faint music was playing in one of the back bedrooms. No one was in the kitchen, but dirty pans and plates indicated that spaghetti carbonara, garlic bread, and a sloppy Caesar salad had been prepared and eaten. An empty red wine bottle and an ashtray full of cigarette butts were also on the counter.

Clark investigated the bedroom and found no one, but the bags of clothing were gone. He switched off the lights and the radio that were on in the master bedroom.

"Psst, Clark! Come here!" Maria called.

He found her by the window at the end of the hall which led to the back of the house. The back yard was dark, but in the small window of the caretaker's cottage a light burned.

"They're in there," said Clark. "I'm gonna take a look. You go ahead and call the police."

"Don't go!" said Maria. "I'm scared." But he went, and she followed him.

Clark tiptoed through the back yard with Maria behind him, clutching the tail of his shirt. He knelt down beneath the window of the cottage and pulled Maria down to duck beside him. Slowly, he raised his head to look into the window. The cottage was furnished, and the light came from an altar candle under an open-topped hurricane globe. A woman with a familiar cap of synthetic-looking hair was stuffing clothing into bags on the single bed. Maria gasped, and the woman inside raised her head and showed her rectangular face.

Maria screamed as she was yanked away from Clark. Clark spun around to see Maria being dragged by a tall man who held one gloved hand around her neck and the other over her mouth.

"Luciano! Luciano!" Clark exclaimed.

The cottage door opened, and standing in the middle of the room with candlelight flickering on her face was — Holly Raven.

"Get back in the house," Holly demanded.

Clark jumped to his feet. "Wait a second, what's going on here? What the hell do you think you're doing? And what the hell are you doing here in L.A.?"

Holly laughed. "Get moving or you'll both see what we'll be doing here."

Luciano squeezed Maria's neck tightly as Maria's eyes grew wide and she moaned into his glove. Luciano was no longer the man she had met at the Village café. Nor was he the man she remembered having been her lover.

"Look at the big starlet now," said Luciano. "Look who's got you now, baby." He dragged Maria toward the house.

"Bring him inside!" he snarled at Holly.

"No one's *bringing* me anywhere," said Clark. He followed Luciano, who walked backward, struggling with a fighting Maria. Maria moved like a fighting cat as she kicked and kicked, but Luciano easily lifted her struggling body from the ground and carried her over his shoulder. Maria remembered Luciano's force and strength.

"Let her go! Let's be sane." Clark sprang at Luciano and took a swing at his head. Luciano ducked, and Clark felt something heavy and hard crash into the back of his skull. He spun around to see what hit him as Holly backed away, pointing a pistol at him with both hands.

"Stay away from him, Clark," she commanded. "I suggest you do what we say. Now!"

"Okay, but you two morons are going to regret this."

The back of his head throbbed. He turned to follow Luciano, and Holly shoved him rudely, but he did not stumble.

In the house, Luciano demanded that Clark and Maria sit on the sofa. Clark reluctantly accepted a cup of coffee from Holly — he couldn't understand her sudden graciousness — and Maria took a cigarette, which Luciano lit for her. Clark drank the strong black coffee quickly, hoping it would clear the remains of the party fuzziness from his head. Luciano paced angrily with the pistol in his hand. He looked thinner than usual and his black hair had grown over the collar of his jacket.

"These two assholes have seen everything, they'll ruin everything!" he kept repeating over and over, like a raving madman.

"What have we seen? What have we ruined?" Maria sobbingly asked.

"Shut the fuck up," Luciano snapped. "I didn't say you could talk."

There was something strange about Luciano's eyes — they looked empty, as if he weren't really seeing. Clark's mind was churning. He viewed Luciano with contempt and hatred. He had seen Luciano in action... his meanness to Maria, his brutality toward Reggie, causing her anguish over her abortion. Luciano had brainwashed Holly, probably by the force of his two heads... he knew what he was doing and had done to Pamela was cruel and vicious. Clark wished he could attack Luciano, and was contemplating a way to succeed, as his mind churned and churned. He was concerned that Luciano might actually murder Maria on the spot.

"He's crazy," whispered Maria. "Do you think he'll shoot us? He's like so many of the hoods back in Italy. He even reminds me of my first husband. Oh, how those Chicago days haunt me."

"Shut up!" Luciano screamed again, like a caged animal. He charged at Maria and she covered her face as if she feared he would hit her, but he only shoved her deeply into the sofa cushions.

"You're the ones who have been threatening Pamela Raven, aren't you?" said Clark. "You're the crazies who make the weird phone calls. You're the ones who are frightening Miss Riley and Mama. Why? Why? Why go to all this trouble and for what? I used to think you, Holly, were so bright and intelligent. What the hell is wrong with you? Have you and Luciano gone nuts?"

"I bet you stole my underwear, too," said Maria. "Perverts. Tell me, Holly, does he wear my panties before he fucks?"

"Go to hell, bitch!" Holly roughly slapped Maria across the face, and Maria jumped up to fight her. Clark quickly grabbed Holly's wrist and twisted it behind her back, attempting to control her, until Luciano clobbered him in the temple with the butt of his pistol.

"That's twice." Clark rubbed his head. "You two are really going to get it once the authorities know what you're up to."

"Shut the fuck up," said Luciano. "Don't think I won't shoot you, because I will if I have to." He lit another cigarette and began pacing the room, back and forth, back and forth, waving his pistol at Clark and Maria, obviously aware of their fright and his power.

"You don't know what's happening, man. You don't know what's going down, man!" Luciano's eyes shone more brightly than the speeded-up people's at the party. "There's a revolution, a big, wild revolution happening, and it's going to burn a lot of rich, white ass, white ass like yours. The Blacks are rising. The students and the Blacks are our side, man — the People are our side, and they're going to burn all you pigs' asses. There's a revolution happening, man! There's a revolution happening!"

Luciano's eyes rolled back and forth in his head and his pace back and forth across the room became quicker and more intense.

"What does that have to do with us, or Maria, or Pamela Raven? What are you trying to do, take over Los Angeles, take over the Bel Vista, take over the world?" Clark half-laughed at his own questioning.

Luciano spat on the floor.

"You think you're so fucking smart — you won't be laughing soon," said Holly. "We have our plan and our plan will work just as it's been working, just fine until you came in and interrupted the party."

"If it's as stupid as your first plan, you won't get too far," said Clark.

"What did we ever do to you?" asked Maria.

"Do? Shut the fuck up." Luciano knelt before Maria and rubbed the barrel of the gun along her thigh.

"What did you do?" He stroked her inner thigh lightly with the barrel, keeping his finger on the trigger as the gun moved up her leg. "You didn't do anything, that's the problem. People are starving in Italy, Maria, as well as here in the belly of the warmongering beast. If you're not for the revolution, you're against it. You're on the other side."

He pointed the gun at her crotch. "You've joined the Establishment, Maria. You're an Establishment whore. You, of all people, should know better."

He pulled the gun away and Maria let out her breath. There was blood on her lower lip where she had bitten it.

"I don't have time to talk about this now. You and I have

business to finish." Luciano grabbed Maria's hands and pulled her up. He pushed her ahead of him toward the door. "Holly! The helmets!"

"Luciano!" Holly whined. "Where are you —"

"Give me the helmets, you stupid broad," said Luciano. "And clean up this mess."

Holly brought him the helmets and he gave her the gun. "You know what to do," he said.

The door slammed behind Luciano and Maria, and in a moment the motorcycle fired the two Italians off to the highway.

"What are you going to do, Holly, kill me?" asked Clark. "Was our night together in New York that bad?"

"Ha, ha," said Holly. "Don't flatter yourself. You just wait."

She was watching him in a peculiar way. Her face didn't look quite right; it seemed to shift and blur. Clark blinked and squinted at her, but it was still happening.

"Why are you doing this? Do you hate Pamela that much?"

"Yes, I do," said Holly. "She made my life hell, and nothing's going to happen for me as long as she's alive. I don't give a damn about Luciano and his druggie revolution. I don't even know what he's talking about, and neither does he. I'm out to get *her,* and do you know why? The last time Aunt Pamela and I talked, or I should say fought, she told me she was cutting me out of her will. That old bitch has so much money she doesn't know what to do with it. And she's got bank deposit boxes filled with jewels from Harry Winston, Cartier, Van Cleef. She has enough jewels stored away to buy me a chateau in France, as well as a movie studio of my own.

"And she thinks she can just cut me off, after all I've put up with — lots of shit — from her! Not only is she not going to give me a cent, do you think she helps me get any work in films? Of course not — and it's not that she doesn't have the connections — she does! I happen to know she poisons producers' minds against me. She's done her best to get me blacklisted by every agent and casting director in town. Do you want to know why? Because she's jealous of me — jealous of me, jealous of my youth, my looks, my talent — that's why. It's my turn now and she won't let me have it because it makes her feel like the old has-been she really is. She's afraid I'll be more popular, more exciting than she ever was, because it's true, you know, I'm better — yes, you heard it — *better* than she is. I was trained, the legitimate theater, and I can *act*. Act — act! That's why she hates me." Holly was tearfully shaking and hysterical — hysterical with an inner rage.

Holly's really gone off the deep end, Clark thought. He supposed that Luciano's Italian film project for her had failed, if there had ever been one. So Holly hated Pamela enough to threaten her and frighten her, but what was Luciano's angle? He had a good, even glamorous, job and all the women he could handle. Why was he involved in Holly's petty, obsessive revenge scheme? And what was the point of it all? Clark decided to flatter Holly until she gave him more information.

"So, *Carmelita*, that was pretty clever, I must say. I suppose that's how you got into the Bel Vista. How did you ever think of that?"

"Oh, it was easy, really. You can do anything if you put your mind to it. I disguised myself as a Mexican and applied for a maid's job at the hotel. Luciano did the same thing and got hired as a hotel garage attendant. Once we were in, we took all the uniforms we wanted. The hotel is a crazy place the way Roland Lee runs it. Anyone can get in anywhere and do anything he wants."

Holly began washing the dishes, as she had been instructed by Luciano to do, but she kept a careful eye on Clark.

"And it was you who gave Pamela the raw egg and it was you who shredded her dresses, eh? I have to hand it to you, you really frightened her. And the footprints on the sheets were a nice touch. Was that your idea?"

"Yes!" Holly smiled proudly. "Most of it was my idea, though Luciano has a friend in the hotel kitchen who helped, a friend who hates Roland Lee. Most of the staff hates Lee, so no one cares what you do. I think my best idea was to have Luciano drive Auntie out into the desert, don't you? I was hoping she'd get fired from *Tigress*, or at least quit; but I heard she was really scared, and I guess that's enough for now. I wish I could have been there. I would love to have seen dear Auntie quivering, quivering out of fear for her life… the way I used to quiver in front of her. How miserable she made my childhood, and my Daddy's life, too!"

The Decorator

"And what, exactly, did Luciano plan to do with your aunt at Arrowhead Springs, if she hadn't escaped, I mean?" Clark had been inching toward the phone and when Holly's back was turned, he reached for it. At first, he thought Holly had thrown the wine bottle at him from the sound of it, but when he looked at the phone, it had exploded. A hole penetrated the wall a few inches from his head.

"The next shot will be closer to home," said Holly. "So I wouldn't try making any calls or anything else, if I were you."

"You're not going to shoot me, are you?"

"I don't have to," said Holly. She dried her hands on a dish towel and came into the living room.

"What do you mean?" Clark asked.

"You'll see," said Holly.

Clark wanted to ask Holly where Luciano had gone and why he had taken Maria, and if Luciano had been the one harassing Maria by phone and mail, but the questions kept slipping out of his mind. His eyes were drawn to the candle flame in front of him. It fascinated him. He tried to look away, but he was drawn back. He heard Holly's mean chuckle and he wondered if she saw what he saw. The flames on both candles appeared to be frozen, as if they were made out of wrought iron. In contrast, the patterns on the carpet were flickering and waving like flames.

"There you go," said Holly.

"Where?" asked Clark. The tiny veins in Holly's face were visible and pulsing grotesquely. "No, no…" he said. He had to look away.

"You're going on a little trip," said Holly. She laughed as she put on her coat.

Clark was still sitting on the sofa, but his mind was wandering amid the moving rug patterns. The patterns had assumed the shapes of people and animals in a metamorphosing landscape, and they seemed to be reenacting the history of the California Gold Rush. Clark could see the miners on the trails and the Indians hiding in the trees. He could see the flowing streams and the places where the gold was. It was fascinating. But it wasn't right. There shouldn't be people in the rug. Something was wrong with Clark's mind, and cold fear suddenly gripped his spine. His heart was pounding, and he could feel himself begin to sweat.

He tore his eyes away from the rug drama and confronted Holly: "What did you do to me? Did you poison me?"

"No," said Holly. "I wouldn't do that to you. I just put some top quality acid, LSD, in your coffee. You'll be taking a little trip for the next, oh... ten or twelve hours, maybe longer! Who knows when you'll come back? Some people never do, so just hang on and enjoy the ride. I wish I could stick around and watch you, but I've got to go to work at the Bel Vista. *Ciao!*"

Holly started to leave and Clark clutched her sleeve. "Wait! Don't go! You can't do this to me — what's going to happen? What if I go crazy? Please, you've got to get me to a hospital."

Holly laughed and pulled herself away.

"Believe me, Clark you don't want to be in a hospital when you start peaking on that acid. Think about all that death — then you really will go nuts. Just stay here and watch the nice rug and be a good boy until Mama comes back. Are these the keys to that Fiat? Cool!" Holly took Maria's car keys from the coffee table and left.

Holly was gone, and not only the rug, but the furniture and the very walls were alive and breathing. Clark could not feel his body any more; he had become one huge pair of eyes. Frozen in fearful wonder, he watched the pageantry unfold around him. The rug drew him most powerfully, perhaps because Holly had suggested it, but to Clark's mind, she knew something about it that he didn't: the rug had the answers. It split open before Clark into a maze of undersea crevasses full of square-headed, whispering creatures. They had a message for Clark, but he couldn't understand their language. He stared reverently into the waves of twisting designs and faces; he saw jewels vibrating with song and ancient hieroglyphics calling his name.

He knelt on the rug to look more closely and divine its meaning. He pondered the rug world on his hands and knees, and somewhere water dripped, probably in the kitchen sink. Holly, he thought, but he soon forgot her as the sound became a waterfall that splashed in the deep forest around him. Now it was a jungle; palms waved in the green walls and deep in the ground under the floor he could feel things growing. The candle crackled and he thought it was the sound of the roots of the

The Decorator

jungle plants growing around him. He was in paradise and he knew it for the first time: he had just entered the Garden of Eden.

Clark could not recognize his clothing. It felt tight and strange, like a skin he should shed. Meanwhile, all of the straight edges and square angles of the room and its furnishings distorted and bent into flowing curves and liquid pourings. Clark's own body wanted to be poured out of his clothes. He needed to dive into the curving world and swim in its flow. He slid out of his clothes and sat cross-legged by the candle nearest him. Its flame was still solid, like a stone, a stone altar. On and within the altar, something was forming. Clark stared into the frozen tiger's eye of the flame and he saw himself as a baby in its womb. The baby grew and emerged into the enchanted world. Clark sat still in the tropical night and watched his own birth.

23
CHAPTER

"Clark! Hey, Clark!"

Maria was shaking his shoulder. Clark opened his eyes. The candles had melted into pools of purple lava. Clark closed his eyes again. He saw on the inside of his eyelids a violet, electrical vein mask of his own face. When he opened his eyes, the mask was still there, hanging in front of him like a reflection in a mirror. He reached his hand out to touch the mask, and his hand went right through, leaving purple trails behind it. Clark moved his hand slowly through the air and watched the trails.

"Wow…"

When he looked at Maria, the mask of his own face superimposed itself over her own.

"There I am," he said.

"Oooh, brother, you're tripping," said Maria. "Your pupils are so big!"

Her eyes shone through the mask of his face like golden caverns.

"Maria… Beautiful…" said Clark.

Pink dawn tinged the clouds outside the window and Clark heard the sound of cloud wings, like angels in the sky. Maria helped him up and led him to bed. He was naked, he was weightless; he floated like the pink and violet clouds of morning. He lay on the bed and watched the inhabited sky through the window.

"There are angels on the roof," he said.

"I know," said Maria.

When he awoke, Maria fed him oranges in cold, juicy sections. She fed him with her fingers and the traces of LSD left in Clark's bloodstream told him she was a light-being feeding him the fruits of love. He felt the sweetness of the oranges blossoming in his blood and opening his heart like a flower.

"I love you," he whispered.

"Of course you do," said Maria. "You love everything and everything loves you, like you told me this morning. You were talking in your sleep and smiling the biggest grin I've ever seen. You definitely had a good trip, better than some I've heard about. You're lucky, boy. Acid scares me."

Clark's face did ache, and he wondered if it was from all the smiling. As he ate the oranges, the objects in the room ceased their faint vibrations and stabilized. He felt his body return to a solid and weighty state. Even the wallpaper pattern was still. Maria told him that the Vitamin C was bringing him down from his trip. It was the only thing that worked as far as she knew.

"Boy, are you lucky I got you off the floor this morning," she said. "That real estate lady came by this morning in her little beige wool suit with a nice little husband and wifey to see the house right after I got you into bed. If I hadn't come back here, she and a sweet old couple from Pasadena would have walked into Pamela Raven's house and seen Clark Calloway, the famous decorator, on the floor, naked, in a fetal position, whispering to the rug about love. How would that be for your career?"

Clark groaned and slapped his forehead with his hand.

"What about Roland Lee? I was supposed to be at the Vista this morning. He's going to have a nervous breakdown." Clark shot up in bed. "Pamela! We've got to warn her — Holly and Luciano are probably in the Vista right now, doing something terrible to her! We have to call the police — they've got to be stopped!"

"Whoa, steady there..." Maria pressed Clark back down. She reminded Clark that Pamela was still on location in Tijuana, working on *Tigress*. As for Roland Lee, he had called several times, and Maria had told him that Clark was indisposed after having eaten bad *tacos mariscos* and that he wouldn't be able to work that day.

"Lee reluctantly said okay, but he told me to tell you that the chromium-framed chairs came with the wrong color upholstery."

"Wait a minute! What about you? Where did Luciano take you and how did you get away?"

Maria said she would tell Clark the whole story over breakfast. She arranged Italian bread, croissants, cheeses and preserves, and made espresso while Clark got dressed. He was surprised to see that it was almost five o'clock in the afternoon. Maria set the table on the back deck, and Clark ate ravenously. Everything tasted ambrosial, and he wondered if it was the remainder of the LSD in his system that made the ordinary Italian breakfast taste so good.

While they ate, Maria told Clark that Luciano had taken her to a run-down summer cottage in Venice Beach where several people lived or crashed, she thought, judging from the mess and the decor. Several naked people slept on mattresses on the living room floor amid party debris. Leftist posters and books were everywhere. The walls were drawn on and painted with names, symbols, pornographic cartoons, and pseudo-poetic gibberish. She couldn't even begin to describe the mess in the kitchen.

Luciano took Maria to a private room upstairs and locked them in. He told her he knew she loved him and they were meant to be together. That was why he had sent her his messages. He said he would soon have a lot of money and they could live a life of luxury in Mexico or the Caribbean and have beautiful children. Luciano knew that was what Maria really wanted. She didn't want to prostitute herself for the capitalist tool that was the American movie industry, selling lies and fantasies to pacify the masses. She was waiting to be rescued by him, a true Italian.

Maria had asked him about Holly. Wasn't he with Holly? Was he in love with her? No, Luciano had said. He was only using Holly for the money she would get after they removed the likes of Pamela Raven from the world. He had quit his pilot job and was staying illegally in the U.S. to avoid serving in the Italian Army. In a digression, Maria asked Clark if he had noticed that Luciano was missing the little toe on his left foot. Clark said he hadn't noticed. Apparently Luciano had chopped off his own littlest toe the first time he was drafted, but this time the Army wanted him anyway. Pilots are always useful to their countries.

"Get back to Holly," said Clark.

Holly had opened a joint bank account for Luciano and herself in Geneva, and he already held the checkbook and her credit cards. Holly was a fool to think he could love her. His heart belonged to Maria.

"Boy, is he in for a surprise," said Clark. "Holly told me Pamela has written her out of her will. She's not getting a cent. Luciano is dumb... doing all this work for nothing. I almost pity him."

Maria said Luciano wasn't dumb. Holly was the beneficiary of Pamela's life insurance policy, and the amount was substantial, in the upper hundreds of thousands. Also, Luciano never believed Pamela would actually disinherit Holly. He knew the will had already been changed several times according to Pamela's whims, but he was counting on Pamela's familial affection. Maria's story confirmed that Holly knew nothing of the extent of Luciano's plan. Holly just wanted to punish her aunt, not kill her. She wanted to torment Pamela until Allen Friedberg, and all of Hollywood, would think Pamela Raven was a crazy old drunk. So far, her plan had worked.

The worst part of the ordeal, Maria said, was that she had to pretend she loved Luciano, that she cherished their romantic reunion. Her instincts told her that she had to go along with his fantasy if she were to survive. Luciano had stolen her underwear from her hotel room; he had made crank calls and sent obscene mail, and he had taken her to Venice against her will. He had even pointed a gun at her; she had no idea what he would do next. So Maria pretended to be charmed when Luciano demonstrated how he used her stolen panties to masturbate. He showed her a pair of handcuffs, a blindfold and gag, and a small whip he wanted to use on her, but she convinced him that those things were not necessary. She loved him and she was grateful to him for rescuing her. She wanted him alone and sex would be hot enough without his toys for now.

Maria had tried to seduce Luciano and he had responded with passionate moans, but he told her he needed to "get a fix" before he could go on, or he would get sick. She watched him cook a few bags of heroin and water in a spoon he held over a candle flame and inject it into a vein in his foot, and she realized he had become a professional junkie. No wonder he looked so unhealthy and had lost his reason. She wondered if Holly knew she was financing Luciano's habit. She doubted it, because Luciano was such a secretive person, which was why he chose to use veins in less visible places on his body. From what Luciano told Maria, she guessed that his addiction was costing Holly at least fifty dollars a day, sometimes more.

Once Luciano was high, he became amorous again, but he couldn't get hard. Maria allowed him to use a dildo on her, although the sight and touch of him disgusted her. She knew Luciano liked his toys, and if she could humor him enough she might be able to escape. Eventually he did nod off into a narcotic dream, and Maria had simply dressed herself and left.

When she was outside she had walked for a few blocks before she found a working pay phone in a seedy little restaurant on Abbott Kinney Street. She called the police, and they took so long to arrive that she thought they had not taken her call seriously. They may have thought she was some hippie girl impersonating Maria Pucci. When the squad car finally arrived, Maria gave the officers the address of the crash pad. She told them she had been abducted by Luciano Navarrone, who was an illegal alien, and then taken to a drug den. She also told them about Holly Raven and Luciano's plot against Pamela Raven. The police broke down the door, tore the contents of the little house apart, and arrested all of the inhabitants, but Luciano and his motorcycle were gone.

At the police station, Maria filed her complaint, but she felt the police did not take her allegations against Holly Raven seriously. They had asked Maria if she was on anything, and they had insinuated that she was really a girl friend of Luciano's who was out to get revenge. Maria wanted to press rape charges against Luciano, but the policemen eyed her skeptically and told her a judge would need evidence and since there was no sign she had been beaten or forced, she would have to go to a hospital for tests. One rookie cop even flirted with her and asked her if she was free on Saturday night.

Maria was not fond of policemen, and the situation disgusted her. The police did forward her description of Luciano to the Beverly Hills Police Department, where they would investigate the situation at the Bel Vista. Maria made a phone call to Clark from Venice, but she had gotten no answer, so she did not press the police to call the Santa Monica station. They had already had too much fun at the expense of her "domestic situation," and she had had her fill of police for the night. She

The Decorator

took a taxi to Santa Monica, where she found Clark naked on the living room floor.

"I'm glad they didn't send a squad car over here," she said. "Can you imagine the picture you would have made?"

"I can," Clark said. "I'd probably be in jail right now, and without my clothes. That wouldn't be very nice, now, would it? But we must tell the Santa Monica police the whole story, except for the naked part and the acid! I doubt the boys in blue want to hear my lysergic revelations, interesting as they are. We've got to put the police onto Holly and Luciano. They must be stopped and stopped fast. That Holly is a bad girl with a wicked imagination. I wonder where she is? And where is Luciano? I have a feeling we'd better get down to the Bel Vista as soon as we can."

The police arrived shortly and searched the house from top to bottom. They found no evidence that intruders had been there. All traces had been wiped away by Holly. Even the boxes of photographic paper were gone from the bedroom closet. Holly had been thorough; Clark remembered that she and Luciano had both worn leather gloves. The Santa Monica police were helpful, however. They listened to the story and after searching the house brought Clark and Maria back to the Bel Vista in a squad car, advising them to contact the police if they saw Holly or Luciano again.

When they got to the hotel, Maria immediately went to her room to shower and change, and Clark found Roland Lee in the nightclub, which Roland had appropriately named The Blue Grotto. The club looked wonderful, and Clark was glad to see that all of his decorating plans had been followed to the letter. Electricians were testing the lighting for the show and the dance floor, and the painters were finishing the marbelizing of the DJ booth. Roland Lee was in the middle of it all, shouting orders, stepping in wet paint, and making a nuisance of himself. When he saw Clark he frantically waved him over to the front row of the royal blue velveteen-covered chairs.

"I hope you're feeling better, but I have to say it's been murder setting up this event all by myself and I hope I've not forgotten anything. It seems to me the fabric on these seats is a bit impractical and the carpeting in the aisle seems a bit off-color. Can you see that the blue doesn't match the chairs? So

I'm not paying for it, would you? No, you wouldn't. And there's not time to have it all redone, is there now. I hope no one notices. Do you think anyone will? And I want you to know you and your Deirdre Dawn staff had better be more careful with your matching of colors. The manager of the Ritz Plaza tells me that your Paul Hedges has screwed up the colors in the model suites. You know I've given Deirdre Dawn & Company that job; the Kahane office is furious and so are all the other decorators who competed for the job... but you're with me, here in L.A., dealing with these Hollywood broads, so I owe you something. But tell that Paul Hedges to watch the color matches — and you watch the color matches, too! And I must say I hate the tablecloths those Awards Association ladies chose for the dinner. They are far too peachy with the pink napkins, but the ladies, especially Mrs. Friedberg, won't listen to reason. They have my caterer going crazy too, because they think the dinner rolls are too big and they sent out for *packaged* ones and now they are saying the potatoes should be *au gratin*, rather than boiled and parsleyed. Can you believe that?"

Clark listened to Roland Lee's roster of complaints for as long as he could stand it and until he could interrupt with more urgent news that there were saboteur impostors on Roland's hotel staff who planned on murdering Pamela Raven right on the hotel premises. Clark skipped the details of his encounter with the unidentified culprits, knowing as he did that the press would be sensational enough without Roland Lee's premature contributions, but Clark insisted that Lee direct his security force to search the hotel for the intruders and that Lee tighten hotel security as much as possible until the two were caught.

"What nonsense," snapped Lee. "I've had police here all day, crawling all over the place, getting in the way and alarming the guests, and they found no one. It looks very bad for the hotel. The publicity is not good. I don't like it. And Pamela Raven isn't even here — she's at Cedars Sinai Hospital, where's she's perfectly safe!"

"Cedars Sinai! What do you mean? I thought she was in Mexico. What happened to her?"

"Oh, nothing has happened to Pamela. Don't you read the papers, for Chrissake? Gabe Taylor had a slight stroke in Baja last night and everyone from Metro flew back here. The press really made a mess of my lobby today. And they think they're getting their own press room here tomorrow night to cover the Gala! They can forget about that. What a pain in the ass! Anyway, they're all over at Cedars Sinai, waiting for Taylor to regain consciousness. Pamela Raven hasn't been away from his bedside all day, and she won't talk to anyone. Jesus, how could you miss that? It's all over the radio, too. You must have been very ill. I wonder what you ate? It couldn't have been anything from my restaurant — none of the guests have complained. Did you eat here last night?" Roland peered worriedly at Clark.

Clark reassured him that the culprit was probably some off shrimp from the late-night taco stand on Hyperion. He excused himself to talk to the florist and supervise the swagging of jabots and tails along the bandshell. When he was satisfied, he collected Pamela's key from the front desk and checked on her suite. Nothing was out of place and nothing was disturbed. He was phenomenally tired. When he went into the bathroom and turned on the lights, his heart skipped a beat. Someone had written DIE, BITCH across the sink mirror in Pamela's trademark ruby lipstick. New razor blades were scattered on the sink.

He got over his surprise quickly and he yawned as he wiped the mirror clean and threw the blades away. The pranks weren't scary any more, now that he knew who was behind them. Poor, sick Holly, he thought. And that drug addict, Luciano. They're certain to be caught, and won't they be pathetic then? He decided to sleep in Pamela's bed to thwart any other attempts to intimidate her. He told himself he wasn't afraid, but he propped a heavy side chair under the doorknob so that no one could open the door, and he checked the closets and even under the bed. He threw the bedcovers back to make sure there were no nasty surprises beneath them before he crawled between the sheets.

CHAPTER 24

Pamela Raven was not thrilled about the ceremony to come. Clark watched her throw open her closets and tear gowns out, only to reject them one by one.

"I want to wear something simple," she said. "But what in my wardrobe could possibly be considered simple? Simple is just not the Raven look."

She finally chose a peasant skirt of black crushed velvet and a red gypsy-style silk blouse as her topper. She complemented the ensemble with a choker of twelve-millimeter black pearls and her ruby earrings.

"How do you like my Spanish Gypsy get-up?"

She spun in a circle and twirled her skirt for Clark, showing off her shapely thighs in her sheer black hose.

"It's lovely, but I think it would look even better with that red and black paisley shawl of yours," Clark suggested.

Pamela found the shawl and Clark draped it over her shoulder just so.

"Oh, thank you, Clark. I like this scarf so much. I only wish I hadn't left my paisley shoes in New York. I suppose black patent leather will just have to do. I'm not looking forward to this party, but isn't it great that we don't have to leave the hotel to go to it? The weather is so chilly, and I will give Roland Lee this: building a discothéque in the hotel is so convenient."

Despite Pamela's bright chatter, she had made it clear to Clark that she dreaded the gala. Gabe had woken up at last, and the doctors were doing what they could for him, but it was possible that his speech would remain slightly impaired and that he might require a wheelchair for a short time. His scenes in *Tigress in the Dark* had been shot, so the film would survive.

"Gabe is a true gentleman," Pamela said. "Like a real trouper, he waited until his last scene was shot before he had a stroke. I would rather be with him tonight than attending this horror show. Right now I wish I had a vodka, hundred-proof,

The Decorator

straight up, but I made a promise to myself that I won't drink any more. God, it's easy to pour something into you that provides a momentary flash or courage or makes the hours pass or the pain disappear. Oh, my dear old friend vodka, how it did relax me. It chased away the butterflies and put a certain safe distance between me and everybody else. It was my protection. But you know, after Lucien died, the vodka controlled me. I wanted it dulled... I just don't want to turn into a blowsy old relic."

Pamela did not touch her spinach salad. She drank tea and talked about Gabe. She told Clark the details of Gabe's condition and her worries about him.

"I love that man, I really do. I don't want to lose him."

"Why don't you marry him, Pamela?" Clark asked. "He loves you."

"I know, and it's hard to explain, but I just can't. There are too many ghosts in my mind, you see. I guess I'm haunted by younger versions of Gabe — ghosts. His bounce and grin when he was 25, his sad eyes when he was 45... And I liked my elastic body and fast mind. I don't dig the geriatric scene."

She stared out into space over her teacup. "Life deals from the bottom sometimes, don't it?" she said softly.

Clark weighed the pros and cons of telling Pamela about Holly and Luciano, and he decided she had to know. He spoke awkwardly at first, but he got the story out and over with. Pamela listened with wide eyes, but she pulled herself up tall in her chair, and when Clark was finished she regarded him coldly. She didn't believe it for a minute. She said that Holly was foolish and she might be swayed by bad companions from time to time, but she would never ever-ever break the law. Pamela had an amazing ability to deny unpleasant facts when they were staring her in the face, particularly facts about herself, her relations with her staff, and her ties with her family.

"But, Pamela, I'm sorry — I just thought you should know —"

"Never mind, Clark. It's an undiscussable," Pamela snapped, as she busied herself with final maintenance to her coiffure. Just as suddenly, she changed her mind.

"Oh, Clark, it's not that I don't believe Holly holds anger for me. I know she's entitled to some anger. She didn't have an easy upbringing. I didn't believe in heredity; I believed in environment, but I can be wrong. She and her sister ended up just like my late brother Bill. He was their father, you know. And their mother was a woman of no substance at all — completely irresponsible!

"And when the girls were little, I was having such a god-awful time learning my part in life that I never had time to project myself into other people's positions, to find out what they were feeling. For most of my life I'd get a *simpatico* rating of zero. I've enjoyed my life, but I've worked too hard, and I expect everyone else to work as hard as I did. Thinking about what happened to Gabe, though, makes me wonder if it's all so damned important."

Pamela sighed, reapplied her red lipstick, and blotted her lips with a tissue. "At the time we can only do what we were capable of doing. And the show must go on. ON with the show!"

She flung her suite door open and gave Clark her most dazzling smile.

The theater and the tables on the dining platform were packed, and the room buzzed with conversation.

"Clark, stay backstage with me," said Pamela. "I'm petrified."

She jumped back nervously from the place where she had been peeking out through a tiny gap in the curtains.

"My God, look at all those people out there! Why do they come to see me? What the hell have I got to say that's interesting? I'm scared stiff. I'm a person made to be seen on film, not in person."

As if he could hear her, Bert Parks, the affable emcee for the evening, announced that they would begin showing a still montage from Pamela Raven's best-loved films, and the house lights dimmed.

As the theme song from *Surrender* played, Pamela leaned over to Clark and whispered, "But seriously, who am I really? And why bother?"

Clark shrugged and grinned. "Break a leg," he whispered.

Sure enough, when the curtain opened, Pamela Raven walked to center stage with her shoulders back, her breasts held high, and that Raven stride. The crowd cheered and showered her with red roses from the centerpieces. She

The Decorator

picked them up one by one and the audience gave her a standing ovation.

Her eyes were misty as she gripped the microphone and said in a husky voice, "I never knew there was so much love."

When her speech ended and several of her old comrades and rivals, including Barney Higgins and Adela Morgan, had come on stage to trade jokes and memories, Pamela asked everyone in the audience to pray for Gabe Taylor while he was in the hospital, and she made her exit.

One surprise absentee of the evening was Allen Friedberg; he had planned to make a short speech. Allen was nowhere to be seen at the party, a fact that no one could quite understand, including darling Bambi, who was very much in attendance, dressed from head to toe in white maribou and sparkling aquamarines with amethysts on her neck, ears, wrists and fingers.

Off balance, Pamela bumped into Clark backstage. "Ooops, let's go. I've had enough. That was one of the greatest evenings of my life. And I'll never go through it again!"

"But what about the party?" asked Clark.

"Forget it," said Pamela. "I'll make my appearance and kiss-kiss on the way out the door. Gabe needs me."

Pamela and Clark worked their way through the crowd. Congratulations, compliments, hugs and kisses delayed Pamela for nearly an hour.

"We made it. I wonder where Allen is?" Pamela scanned the room. "Oh, there's that cheap Maria Pucci. I think she sees you. Let's get out of here before she comes over. I see Bambi, but no Allen. Hmmm. Where in Christ's name was that Allen tonight?"

The room was hot and the crowd was so thick by the stairs that led to the round landing above the dance floor that Clark and Pamela had to push their way through. Just as they got to the stairs, someone nearby commented that he smelled smoke. In a moment everyone was talking about the smoke and trying to go up the stairs. Black, acrid smoke began to pour into the newly completed nightclub, and Clark and Pamela were crushed against the wall of the staircase. The lights suddenly went out and the screaming began. Panic had set in.

"Come, let's go the other way," said Clark.

"I can't see a thing," Pamela complained. "Why can't we go

upstairs? Where are you? Where are you, Clark? I'm losing you."

"I'm right here. I'm right here, Pamela. Hold my hand. Hold on tightly. We've got to get out of here. I heard someone say the electrical doors won't open upstairs. Maybe they're working on the other side."

Clark's eyes were tearing from the smoke, and it was hot as an oven in the panicked crowd. In total darkness, he led Pamela through the crush of people into smoke and air which grew hotter.

"We can't go this way," he gasped. "It's too hot."

"We must be near the exit that leads out to the pool," said Pamela. "I found the wall — here, feel your way along it. Aren't we supposed to crawl or something?"

Clark, holding Pamela's thin hand, led her along the wall, feeling his way like a blind man, until he reached the automatic glass door. It wouldn't open.

"Get down low," he said. "I've heard there's less smoke near the ground." He could see a line of small flames running along the wall by the stage, and with a roar they sprang up the curtains. The club was suddenly illuminated with an orange glow and the crowd of screaming people with smoke-blackened faces could be seen.

"Maria!" Clark shouted, thinking he saw her, but the fire smoldered down to a red glow after it consumed the curtains, and the room was plunged into darkness again.

Pamela pulled Clark down to the floor where she sat with her head buried in the folds of her long skirt.

"Here, cover your face with my skirt. It helps."

Clark's face was burning hot and the skirt did block the heat and smoke somewhat, but he and Pamela were coughing and he knew it was only a matter of time before the fire consumed all of the oxygen in the room. If they didn't get out soon, they would die.

"The Hertz agency!" he yelled. Its plate glass wall was behind the curtain in the dining room. He only hoped he could break the glass when he got there. He stood up and the unbearable heat threatened to rip the skin from his face. His ears, nose and eyelids particularly hurt. He covered his face with his sleeve and, thankfully, heard sirens blaring outside the hotel.

The Decorator

He hoped the firemen would get them out in time. Pamela had fainted next to him, and as he carried her dead weight toward the Hertz agency, he stumbled over other people who had also fainted from the heat and lack of air.

The blue velvet curtain over the plate glass and the blue-sequined wall covering had caught fire, and the light of the flames guided Clark to the wall. Clark set Pamela down and tore the burning curtain away, heedless of the fire on his arms and face. Grey moonlight flooded the dining area from the car rental office, and Clark could smell his own singed hair and clothing. He found a dining room chair and began beating it against the glass with all his might. Others soon joined in to help. The glass cracked, webbed, and then burst, and people were able to stream out of the burning club. Firemen broke into the agency with their axes and they carried unconscious people out into the courtyard. Pamela Raven was one of the first to be whisked away in an ambulance.

The scene was terrible. Everywhere Clark looked, he saw limp bodies, smoke-blackened faces, women crying, and people moaning in pain. They looked like the Vietnamese villagers he had seen on television. Ambulances were taking people away, but there didn't seem to be enough of them, and the fire had spread to the upper stories of the hotel.

Clark cursed Roland Lee: "Damn Roland Lee, and his electrical doors and unbreakable windows!" If Roland had replaced all of the glass in the hotel as he had wanted to, Clark realized that he and Pamela would be frying like bacon at the moment. They had been lucky, and he hoped the guests upstairs in the rooms would be just as lucky. An ambulance attendant wanted Clark to get into an ambulance.

"There's nothing wrong with me," Clark said. "Take the other people. I have to find Maria. Where is she? Did you see Maria Pucci? And Adela Morgan — where is Adela?"

"I think you should come with me, sir. Your body has been burned," said the ambulance attendant.

Clark's burns were not serious. He was treated for minor burns and smoke inhalation and given a bed at Cedars Sinai. He could not rest; his mind was racing, reliving the horrible ordeal at the Blue Grotto. He had to know — where were Pamela and Maria and Adela? Were they all right? He insisted on knowing to which rooms Pamela, Adela, and Maria had been sent. He knew they were alive and out of danger, thanks to the information given to him by the head nurse on the floor.

Adela had actually made an early exit from the event, and she had been near the top of the staircase when the lights went out and the room filled with smoke. Thus Adela was asphyxiated only for a brief moment or two before the fire brigade arrived and brought her into the air. Adela credited her aversion to roses as her savior. You know Adela just couldn't stand the roses on the tables at the Blue Grotto: those roses that Roland Lee had placed on the tables for Pamela's award party. When Adela saw those roses and got a whiff of them, she did her thing, said hello to some folk, and made her way to the exit — just in the nick of time... for Adela's sake!

Clark went to visit Maria. Maria wanted to watch the fire on the TV news. Clark, in his hospital gown and slippers, sat by her bed, and they watched clip after clip of the Bel Vista in flames, the rescues, the celebrities caught in the fire, and the speculations as to the cause of the fire. The only thing anyone knew for sure was that the fire had started in a basement storage area below the nightclub, hundreds of guests, celebrants, and hotel workers had been taken to area hospitals, and the death toll was four; the names of the victims were yet to be released.

One of the reporters sent from the East Coast to cover the fire was John Downing, Dannee Lou's brother, and Maria was happy to see him on the screen.

"Oooh, he's so handsome, isn't he? Maybe he'll come here and interview us! He could do a piece on the survivors and our feelings. And maybe Reggie is here with him. Do you think she might be?"

Clark would enjoy seeing John again and speaking with him about Reggie's life in Washington. Clark didn't think John Downing was as good looking as Maria did, but then... there was a bit of jealousy there. And Clark was quick to recognize his own feelings. He wanted Reggie to enjoy her life. He had told her that, and he knew John Downing was a good bet for her and a happy future.

By morning, the most serious news was that Allen Friedberg, president of Metropolis Pictures, was in critical con-

The Decorator

dition, with burns over eighty percent of his body. He had been trapped in the tenth-floor bedroom of noted gossip columnist Doreen Flower. The windows in her suite did not open, and Miss Flower had survived the flames by immersing herself in a bathtub of water in the totally tiled bathroom which the flames could not penetrate. She had escaped serious injury, but was slightly parboiled. Both Flower and Friedberg were found naked, but speculation on that score was tempered by concern for Allen Friedberg's condition. The doctors at Cedars Sinai were besieged by reporters every time they crossed the hospital parking lot. Clark now understood why Allen Friedberg had never attended the awards ceremony.

The next day, Clark received a telephone call from Reggie in Washington. She was concerned, and relieved that Clark was well and would soon be as good as new.

"Hey there, guy!" she said. "I've sent you a big bouquet of mixed flowers. I'd kiss you if I could do it over the phone. Isn't this a switch, though? The last time we were involved in a hospital, I was the one in the bed! Are you okay? I hear you were the big hero."

Reggie sounded great. She told Clark she had been dieting, she was wearing her hair longer, and she wore a diamond engagement ring on her finger.

"Nice ring?" Clark asked.

"Oh, yeah," Reggie described her shimmering diamond. "John and I are engaged. I'm sending him over to see you guys. But I want to hear about your adventures! I've called Maria too, and she told me you guys had a run-in with Holly and Luciano. Do you think they set the fire?"

"That depends on whether you're asking me as a friend or as a reporter," Clark replied.

"Both!" said Reggie, and Clark told her the whole story. An orderly brought Clark's lunch in, but he let it sit until he finished the conversation with Reggie. Clark asked her if she had heard anything from her brother Charlie.

"Not yet," Reggie said. "We're all worried. Do you know that more guys have already died in this war than died in Korea? Ten thousand soldiers have been killed already, along with fifty thousand civilians, and who knows how many guys are in POW camps. That's a lot of people! 'And the Old Fool

Says Push On.' But they haven't found Charlie's body, so there's still hope."

"Yes, Charlie's a tough guy," said Clark. "He's a Stowkowski, remember? Whatever happens, I'm sure he'll get through it... So, when's the wedding?"

Reggie told Clark she and John were getting married in June, in Dallas, and of course she wanted Clark to come. She was excited about meeting John's family, the wedding plans, and the honeymoon they planned to take in Bali, but she had another surprise for Clark.

"Guess what? Here's my big news: Thom Pearson wants to sign me on as a news correspondent in New York in six months when Ed Bradley retires. That means I'll be in New York and John will be in D.C., so we'll be one of those commuting couples. We can make it. Dannee Lou says Washington couples do it all the time."

Clark was very happy for Reggie, and he gave her his heartiest congratulations, even though his face smarted from the burns. When she hung up, he rang the nurse for a painkiller, and he was just drifting off to sleep when his bedside phone rang again. It was someone named Eric. Eric who? At first Clark couldn't remember meeting any Erics, but when the caller asked him how he was feeling and said he was worried about him, Clark remembered Eric Von Halst and the party at the Chateau Marmont. Eric told him he had raised the money to make his film and he had a great script. Casting would begin the following week, and Eric thought he could go for a big-name actor or two. He told Clark Metro smelled a hit, and they were after him to let the studio produce the film, but he wanted to stay independent. Then he offered Clark the set design job.

"Let me think about that, Eric," Clark said, even though he was excited enough to say yes right away. "Thank you for thinking of me, but you know I'm half-owner of Deirdre Dawn & Company now, and I need to consult with my partner before I make a big California commitment."

"Is it the money, Clark?" asked Eric. "If it is, don't worry about that. I'll take care of you, babe. Just ask."

Clark thanked Eric and said he would get back to him. He hung up and lay back on his pillows. The narcotic painkiller

The Decorator

surged through his body in little waves of pleasure, and he thought about living in California. He was tempted. He would like it, he decided. And designing for the movies was a far cry from feathering the nests of the Bambi Friedbergs of the world. He would have to see what Paul Hedges had lined up for the company next season in New York, but he wasn't looking forward to it. He liked the idea of starting over in a new, glamorous business. And he liked Eric, definitely. Eric's tone had been businesslike, L.A.-style, during their conversation, and Clark liked that. He had a feeling they would work well together. He didn't think he was ready to involve himself romantically with a man, or a woman for that matter. He couldn't see himself as that walking cliché, a gay decorator — but he very much liked the idea of being friends with Eric Von Halst.

Allen Friedberg died that night. Clark heard the news from Pamela on the hospital phone. Most of the people who had been in the hotel fire, except for Doreen Flower and a few others with severe burns, were ready to be released. Because people had died, including someone as famous as Allen Friedberg, the police investigators were eager to find suspects in the case. Arson had been determined to be the probable cause of the fire, but the arsonist and his method were still unknown. All of the hotel guests and employees, including those who had attended the gala, had been questioned by police. Clark had told them all he knew, especially about Holly and Luciano, but the suspects had disappeared. Of course, Roland Lee had no record of their employment at the Bel Vista, as they had used aliases. Roland Lee had his own problems; he was under suspicion of insurance fraud and he had been charged with several fire code violations which had caused the fire to spread and had made it difficult for the firemen to rescue people from the building. Clark wondered if Roland Lee would enjoy prison as much as he did trials. He would probably tie up the courts with legal maneuvering for some time, but the general consensus was that he deserved a prison sentence and a hefty fine.

Allen Friedberg's funeral was well attended. All of the major entertainment executives, friends and enemies alike, were at the Gates Kingsley Gates funeral home. Clark sat with

Adela and Barney Higgins. Maria and other younger actors and actresses were in the pew behind him, and in the front row sat Bambi, her children and grandchildren, and other family members. Metropolis Pictures had provided bales of lilies, arranged in towering cascades of yellow and white. The rabbi was very good, Clark thought, and the memorial testimony read by Thom Pearson was moving, though it was apparent that Pearson, along with Allen Friedberg's other associates, were impressed more by the man's power and drive than by his values and personal qualities. There were more grey suits from Manhattan than tennis tans from Malibu in attendance, which made the front two rows look more like a business meeting than a Hollywood funeral.

Bambi Friedberg cried inconsolably in the arms of her son. She didn't look like a woman who stood to inherit the entire fortune of a husband who had neglected and tormented her. Despite their problems, Bambi really was mourning Allen. Clark knew how she could turn on the tears, but they seemed genuine this time. He also knew Deirdre Dawn & Company would never see the money owed them by the Friedbergs.

Allen Friedberg had been immediately buried, so there was no open coffin, to Clark's relief. He always wanted to remember people as they had been, not how they looked in their coffins. He still regretted paying his last respects to his parents after the embalmer had done his work. Every time he remembered them, he had to push the waxen images away, as they were still strongest in his mind. When he remembered Allen Friedberg, he thought of the garrulous, cigar-waving mogul on his balcony overlooking Central Park at night, but he also thought of unpaid bills and nasty telegrams — his feelings were decidedly mixed.

Adela cried a bit and Barney tried to comfort her. Maria did not shed a tear, though she said she was grateful to the old geezer for the influence which would no doubt eventually give Maria Pucci her own star on Hollywood Boulevard. Toward the end of the ceremony, Pamela wheeled Gabe Taylor in to pay his respects. Gabe looked much better than he had in the hospital; he had lost a little weight.

Before Clark left, he stood in line to offer his condolences to Bambi Friedberg.

The Decorator

"Oh, Clark," she sobbed. "I don't know what I'll do without my Allen. I don't know what I'll do in that big apartment all by myself. Who am I going to take care of now? Who am I going to talk to? You will come over and visit me, won't you?"

"Of course I will," said Clark.

The photographers were thick around Gates Kingsley Gates as the mourners emerged. The flash bulbs were white-hot as Clark came down the steps with Maria. Press surrounded them and peppered the mourners with questions as well as flash bulbs, as they escaped into their limousines.

As Clark's driver sped him away from the funeral home, he thought of something he hadn't told the police. He took the detective's card from his suit pocket and he asked the driver to take him to the Beverly Hills police station.

The story was in all the morning newspapers. The cause of the fire had been discovered to be photographic paper and a match, which spread to dusting rags and cans of cleaning solvent in a storage room in the basement of the Bel Vista Hotel. A box of fuses and circuit breakers on the wall of the room had been destroyed by the flames, rendering the Vista's electronic doors inoperable. Because photographic paper leaves little residue when burned, the investigators had been unable to find the evidence until an anonymous source had informed them of it.

The big news was that one of the alleged arsonists was none other than television comedy player Holly Raven, whose famous aunt Pamela Raven was a guest in the hotel at the time of the fire. Tests of materials found at the site of the fire and in Holly Raven's hideaway in Pamela Raven's Santa Monica house, as well as a house in Venice Beach used by suspected arsonist Luciano Navarrone, were being conducted, and the search for the two suspects continued.

Holly Raven was apprehended the following week. It was the first Monday in March, 1966, when policemen accompanied Miss Raven down the steps of a town house in San Francisco's Haight-Ashbury district. Another tenant had turned her in. Navarrone was not there, and Holly claimed to have no knowledge of his whereabouts. For two weeks, her face was front-page material, and headlines screamed about the abduction of the movie star's niece by an Italian

Communist terrorist group. According to Holly Raven, she was held hostage by Luciano Navarrone, a former pilot for Monte Napolitano Airlines, and his armed cohorts in Rome, where Holly was starring in an art film. She had been taken by force back to the United States, where the kidnappers hoped to receive a large ransom from Pamela Raven. Holly had been drugged and made to commit crimes and acts of terrorism in the name of Liberation of the Masses. She portrayed herself as a helpless victim who had no choice but to cooperate with her captors who, in the process, has brainwashed her. And she named Luciano Navarrone as the arsonist at the Bel Vista Hotel.

The odd thing was, Pamela Raven believed her. Or maybe it wasn't so odd. Anyway, it was "undiscussable," as Pamela said when Clark helped her pack her belongings to return to New York. Most of her clothing had been smoke-damaged, so there wasn't much to pack. They kept the television on so they could listen to the non-stop coverage of the Pan American hijacking as they packed. One of Holly Raven's credit cards had been used in a downtown Los Angeles department store, and the purchases were delivered to an address in East L.A. It turned out that one elderly lady, a Mrs. Guerrera, had been given the card by her granddaughter. The girl, Rosa Guerrera, was seventeen, and her parents were migrant farm workers. Rosa's handsome Italian lover had only stayed with Rosa and her grandmother for a week. He had left the credit cards and other belongings behind. The day he disappeared, Luciano Navarrone had hijacked a Pan Am 707 at LAX. He had been clever. He had worn his pilot's uniform and had flashed his old ID for airfield clearance. He waited until the plane had been cleaned and refueled and until a pilot and stewardess boarded to inspect the aircraft. He then forced the pilot to take off by taking hold of the stewardess and by holding a gun to her head. The pilot flew to Miami and refueled there, where according to news reports, the kidnapper released both the pilot and the stewardess. While heckling the air traffic controllers on his radio, Luciano had chosen a runway and taken off.

The news report Pamela and Clark listened to confirmed that Luciano Navarrone had piloted the aircraft to Havana, Cuba, where the plane remained.

"What an insane person Luciano Navarrone must be,"

commented Pamela. "Holly would never have been involved with a man of Luciano's insanity. It's impossible for me to believe she was involved with him."

The newscaster went on to report that Holly Raven was currently being evaluated for treatment at a top Beverly Hills private psychiatric facility, courtesy of her aunt, Pamela Raven. Clark knew that, although Pamela had not had the time to visit her niece, she had sent Holly a care package of flannel nighties, chocolates and magazines, and Holly's favorite butter cookies in the blue tin. Pamela had no reason to stay in Los Angeles. *Tigress in the Dark* had been cancelled, as only two-thirds of the film had been shot before Allen's death and no one else at the studio wanted to take it on. There was some talk that Friedberg's daughter Julie might ascend to a position of authority at Metropolis, but that possibility was only in the discussion phase. If *Tigress* were to be rescheduled and put back on target… Pamela would consider the opportunity then — and no doubt Adela would reconsider then, too.

Pamela accepted the situation.

"It's fine, really. I don't need to do any more movies. I'm looking forward to moving back to my little apartment in Manhattan and catching up on my TV shows," she told Clark. "Are you really going to stay here?"

"Yes, I think so," said Clark. "I'd like to try living in Los Angeles for a while. Maria is staying, you know. *Amazon Planet* is already such a hit that they're going to do a sequel, and she's up for another part, in a romantic comedy with Warren Beatty. I've accepted the job on the Von Halst picture. I really want to design for films. I just haven't told Paul Hedges yet."

Clark never got the chance to tell Paul. The telegram from Paul Hedges came the morning. Clark returned to Santa Monica after seeing Pamela off at the airport. In the telegram, Paul expressed his concern for Clark's well-being after the fire, and he hoped the fire at the Bel Vista had not upset Clark greatly; perhaps the insurance payments would arrive more quickly than Roland Lee's payments to Deirdre Dawn & Company ever would. Finally, the telegram informed Clark that Paul Hedges was retiring from the company. He would discuss the details with Clark in New York, but basically he wanted Clark to take over the business, as Paul was tired of it all and his doctor had recommended he retire. Paul wished to move to San Diego with his son Richard as soon as possible.

Clark called the office in New York. Belle told him that Mr. Hedges was upstate helping the Robinsons prepare Richard for the move. Belle was tearful about Paul's decision.

"Why does Paul have to retire? He's still young. I think he'll miss us and he'll miss the company, won't he? What is he going to do in San Diego? It's so far away, Clark, and he doesn't know anyone there. I wish you would come home soon. We heard about the fire, of course, and we were all so worried. I'm very relieved that you're all right. I just can't get used to all these changes — you've been away such a long time and then Mrs. Dawn retired and now Paul is leaving. I know for sure that Paul will never miss the back and forths with all those clients, particularly the group over at the Ritz Plaza. And Roland Lee has instructed his manager to advise Paul and our New York office to put a hold on all the redecoration at the Ritz Plaza: the fall-out at the Vista is having its effect on the New York office, too. Paul is delighted he doesn't have to deal with Lee's people any more. But it's just not the same in the office without you."

"I've missed you, too, Belle. Just hang on till I get there. I'll be in on the next plane." Clark made a reservation, packed, and went for a long walk on the beach. He walked by the ocean, thinking.

Maybe he'd take up painting again, and do a show with Winterspoon. Maybe he'd call on Reggie and see what she might be up to... a call to wish her well, to reminisce about what life might have been for the two of them together. Or maybe he'd go back to Deirdre Dawn & Company and light some fire under a new staff. He knew he'd never hire that culprit Canaletto, even though, according to Belle, he'd been looking for his job back. Canaletto had told Paul Hedges that Deirdre herself was the villain, and had requested that he cause problems for Paul and Clark. Clark could understand now why Deirdre had been so tough and difficult. Her mind had been fading and she just didn't want to give up. The young grow old... some sooner than others.

He watched the sun shine on the water as the waves rolled in and out, and he decided what to do.

CHAPTER 25

The game was three-handed gin. Gabe took a card and threw out the jack of spades.

"There's a nice jack for you," he said.

"I don't want it," said Pamela. She scowled at her hand. "Who dealt me these cards?"

"You did," said Clark. "And I could have used that jack last hand."

"That's what they all say." Pamela discarded the queen of diamonds, and Gabe groaned.

"How can you give that to him?" Gabe asked. "Didn't you see he's making diamonds?"

Clark went down.

"He's got a diamond necklace there, Pam, thanks to you. And I can't play on it," Gabe grumbled.

Pamela played her cards on Clark's, and Gabe was able to get rid of a few of his own.

"What's that, forty points for you, Gabe? You still owe me seven dollars." She tallied their scores on a note pad. "Mama, these ashtrays need to be emptied! And bring Mr. Taylor another drink."

"No you don't," said Gabe. "Bring me a Coke, Mama! Clark, do you see this woman? She's trying to get me drunk. Let's use *my* deck next hand. Raven's cards are marked."

"How can you say such a thing?" asked Pamela. "I'm an honest woman."

"That'll be the day," said Gabe. "Deal the cards, boy."

It was an early evening in late August in Pamela Raven's apartment. The windows were open and a Frank Sinatra album, courtesy of Gabe, played in the background. Gabe had pulled his wheelchair up to the table. He and Pamela were both smoking and drinking Cokes. Clark had a ginger ale, and he was enjoying the snacks Mama brought in from the kitchen.

"I hear Holly's writing a book," said Clark.

"Yes," said Pamela. "It's about her experience as a hostage of those terrorists."

"That'll be a work of fiction," said Gabe.

"Mama, what do I do?" asked Pamela. Mama looked at Pamela's hand over her shoulder. "See that one? I don't know if I should keep it, but I don't really want to give it up. Do you know what I mean?"

"Yes," said Mama. "It's a hard decision."

"Wonder if they'll market Holly's book as a fairy tale?" said Gabe.

"What the hell, I'm going to get rid of that three. And I'll hold onto this one."

"That's what I would do," said Mama.

"Pam, I know you can go down, but you're holding out on us. Why would you want to do that?" asked Gabe.

"I can't go down, Gabe. How is that Hedges boy, Clark?"

"Oh, he's doing great," said Clark. "He's living on an avocado ranch in Escondido, California with his dad, and both dad and son are doing well — real well."

"And Clark is doing so well with Calloway and Company. What is it Allen Friedberg used to quote: 'If I am not for myself, who will be? And if I am only for myself —'"

"— who am I?" Gabe finished.

"Gin," said Clark.

"Well, I'll be darned," said Gabe. "You gave him another card."

"I did not," said Pamela. "He would have ginned anyway. Look at that hand of his. Isn't that right, Princess?"

The black and white dog in Pamela's lap looked up at Clark and waved her tail.